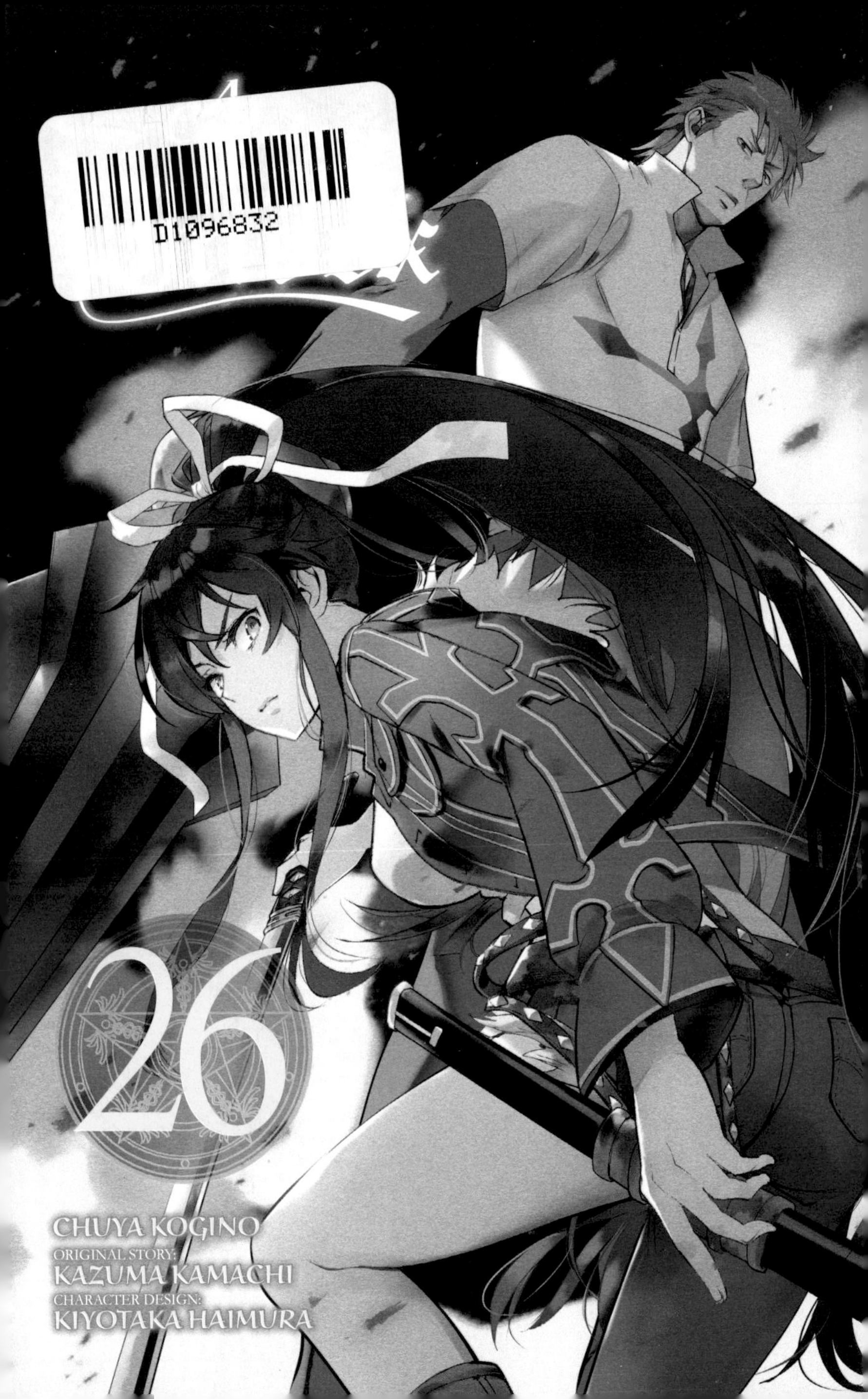
26
CHUYA KOGINO
ORIGINAL STORY:
KAZUMA KAMACHI
CHARACTER DESIGN:
KIYOTAKA HAIMURA

A CERTAIN MAGICAL INDEX 26 TABLE OF CONTENTS

Index Librorum Prohibitorum

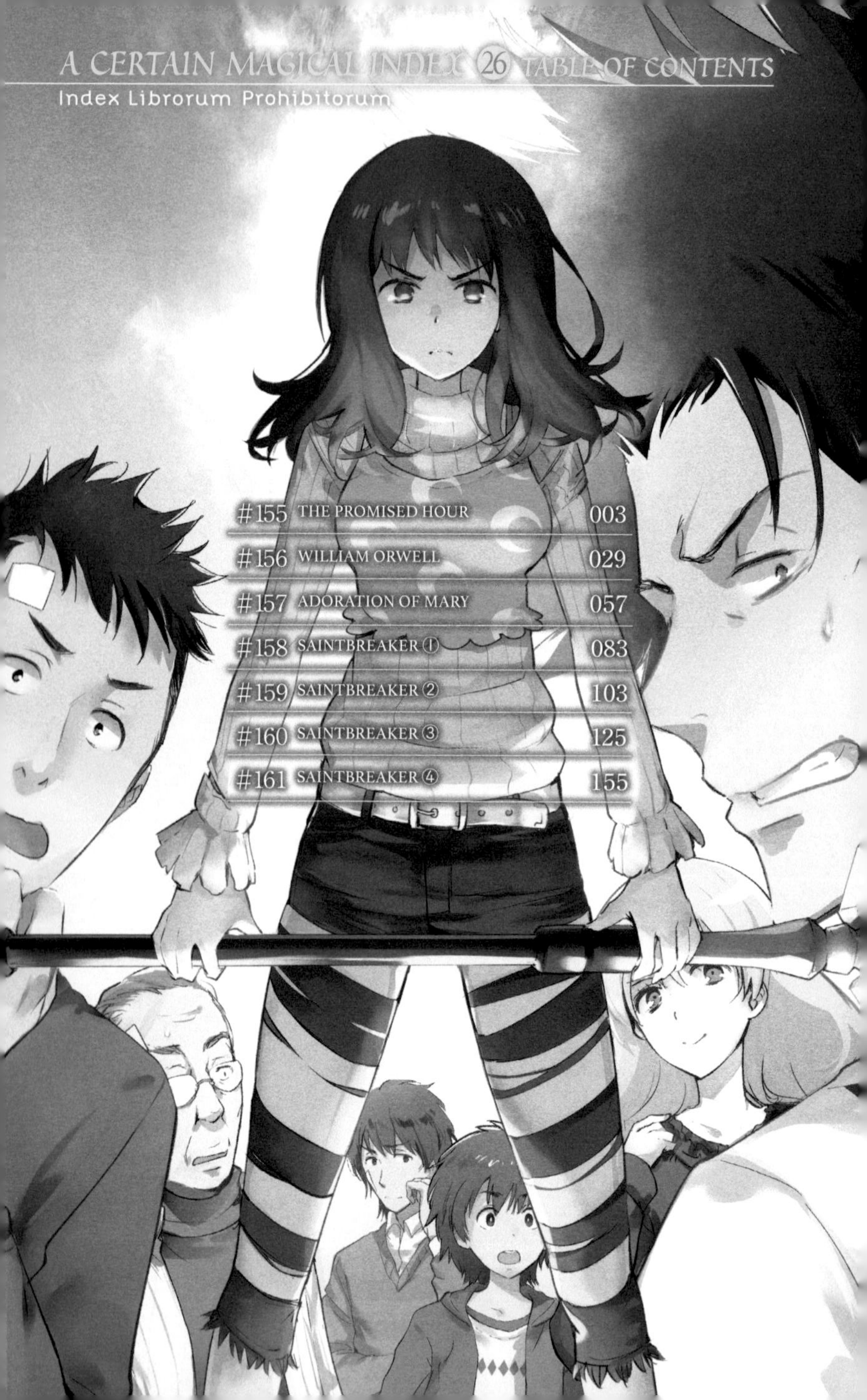

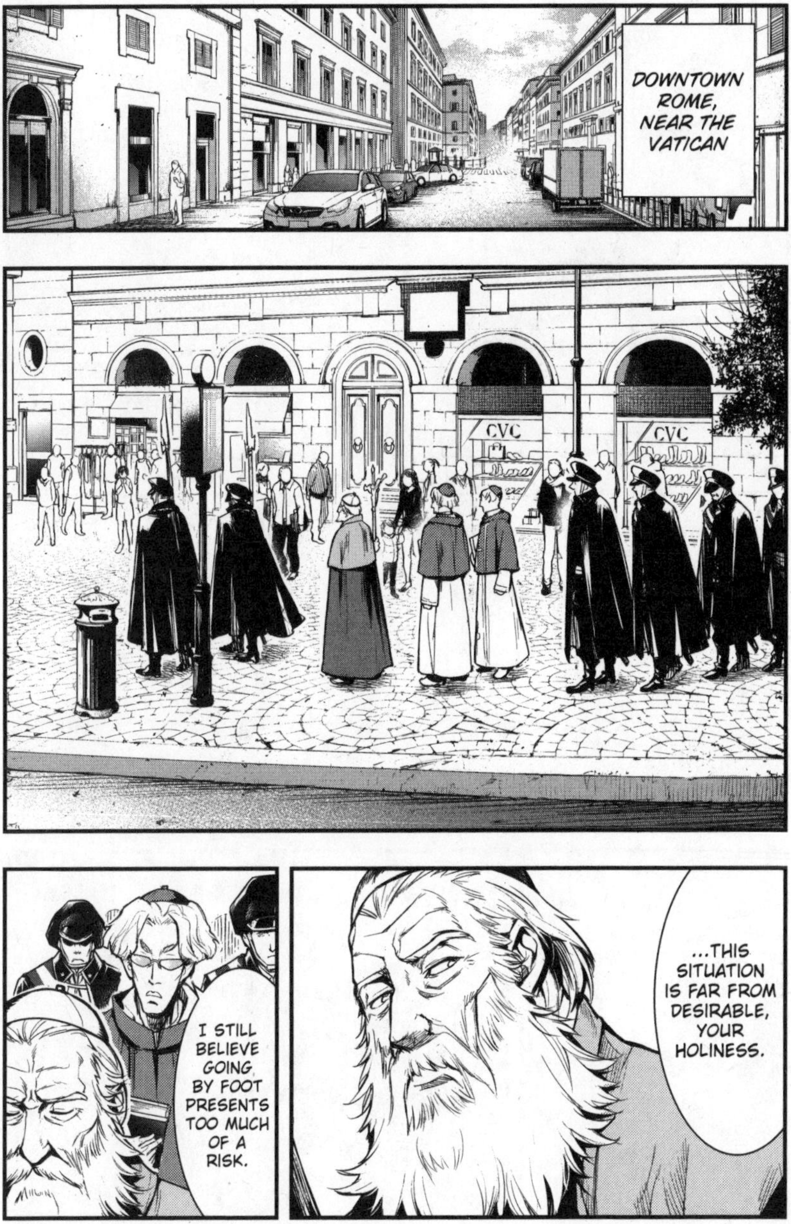
DOWNTOWN ROME, NEAR THE VATICAN
CVC
CVC
...THIS SITUATION IS FAR FROM DESIRABLE, YOUR HOLINESS.
I STILL BELIEVE GOING BY FOOT PRESENTS TOO MUCH OF A RISK.

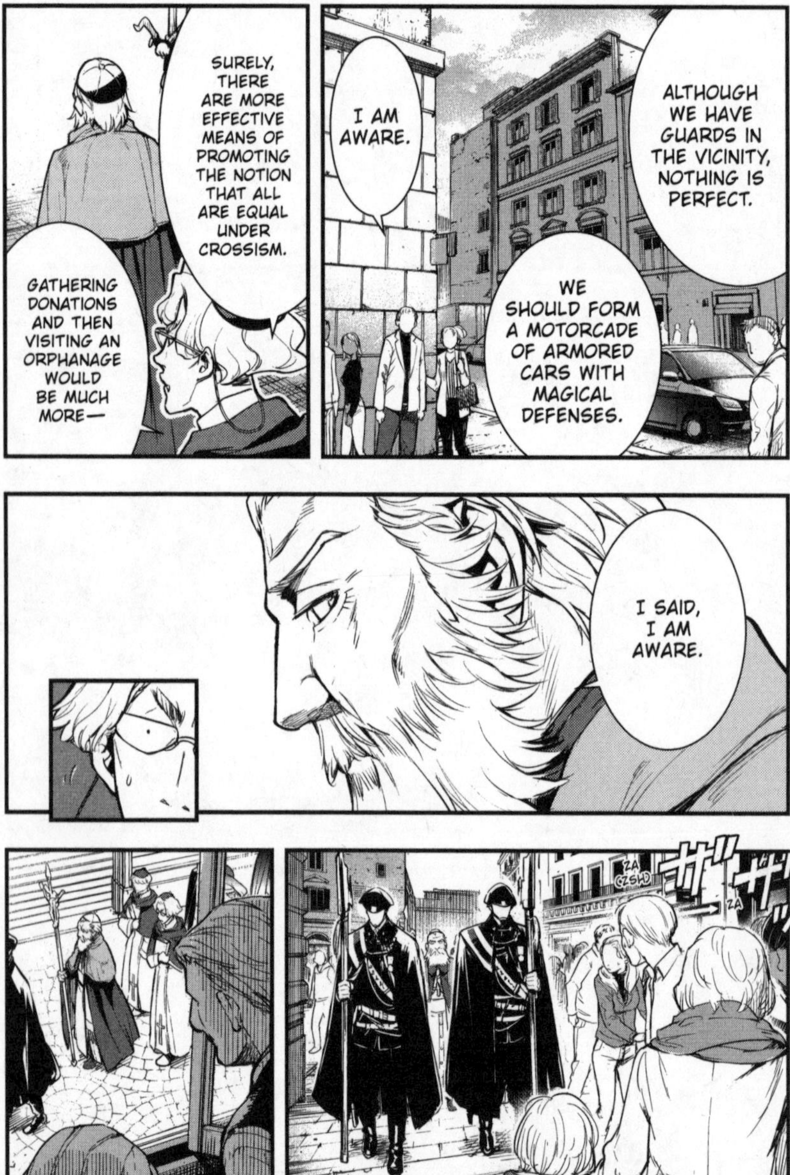

ALTHOUGH WE HAVE GUARDS IN THE VICINITY, NOTHING IS PERFECT.
WE SHOULD FORM A MOTORCADE OF ARMORED CARS WITH MAGICAL DEFENSES.
I AM AWARE.
SURELY, THERE ARE MORE EFFECTIVE MEANS OF PROMOTING THE NOTION THAT ALL ARE EQUAL UNDER CROSSISM.
GATHERING DONATIONS AND THEN VISITING AN ORPHANAGE WOULD BE MUCH MORE—
I SAID, I AM AWARE.
ザッ
ZA CZSHD
ザッ
ZA

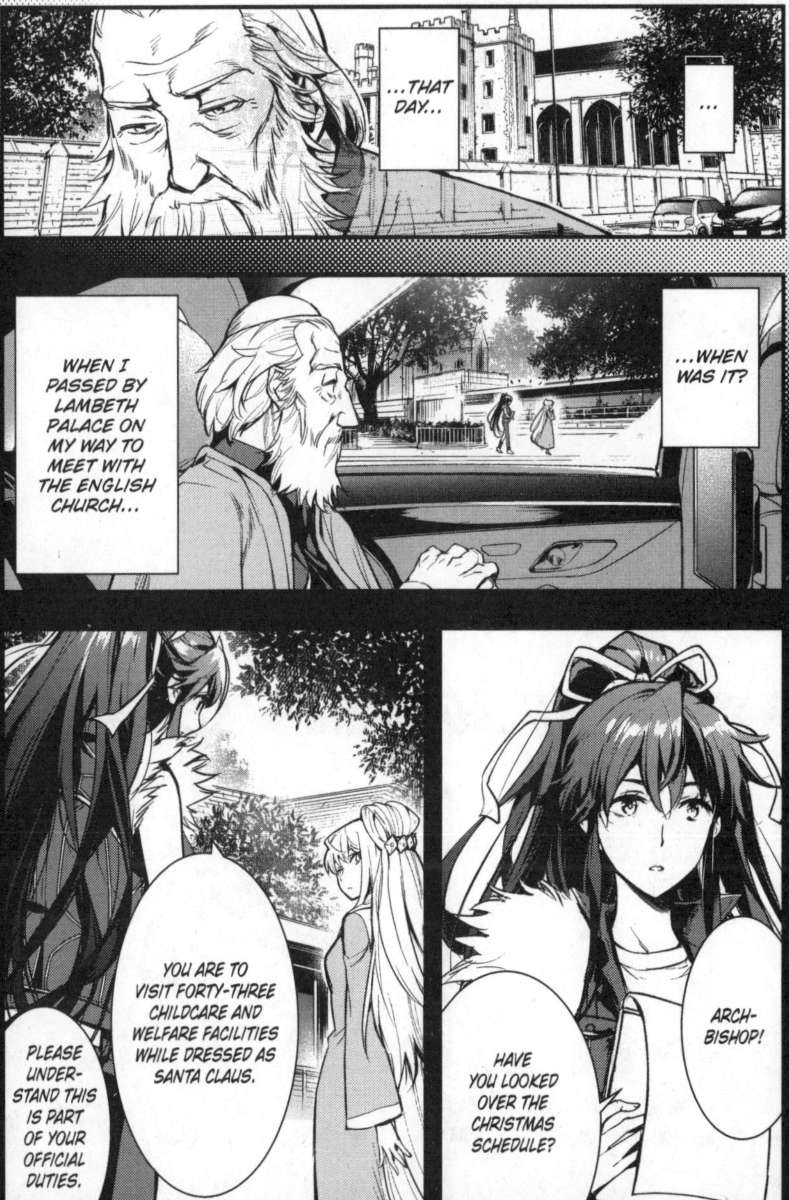
...
...THAT DAY...
...WHEN WAS IT?
WHEN I PASSED BY LAMBETH PALACE ON MY WAY TO MEET WITH THE ENGLISH CHURCH...
ARCH-BISHOP!
HAVE YOU LOOKED OVER THE CHRISTMAS SCHEDULE?
YOU ARE TO VISIT FORTY-THREE CHILDCARE AND WELFARE FACILITIES WHILE DRESSED AS SANTA CLAUS.
PLEASE UNDER-STAND THIS IS PART OF YOUR OFFICIAL DUTIES.

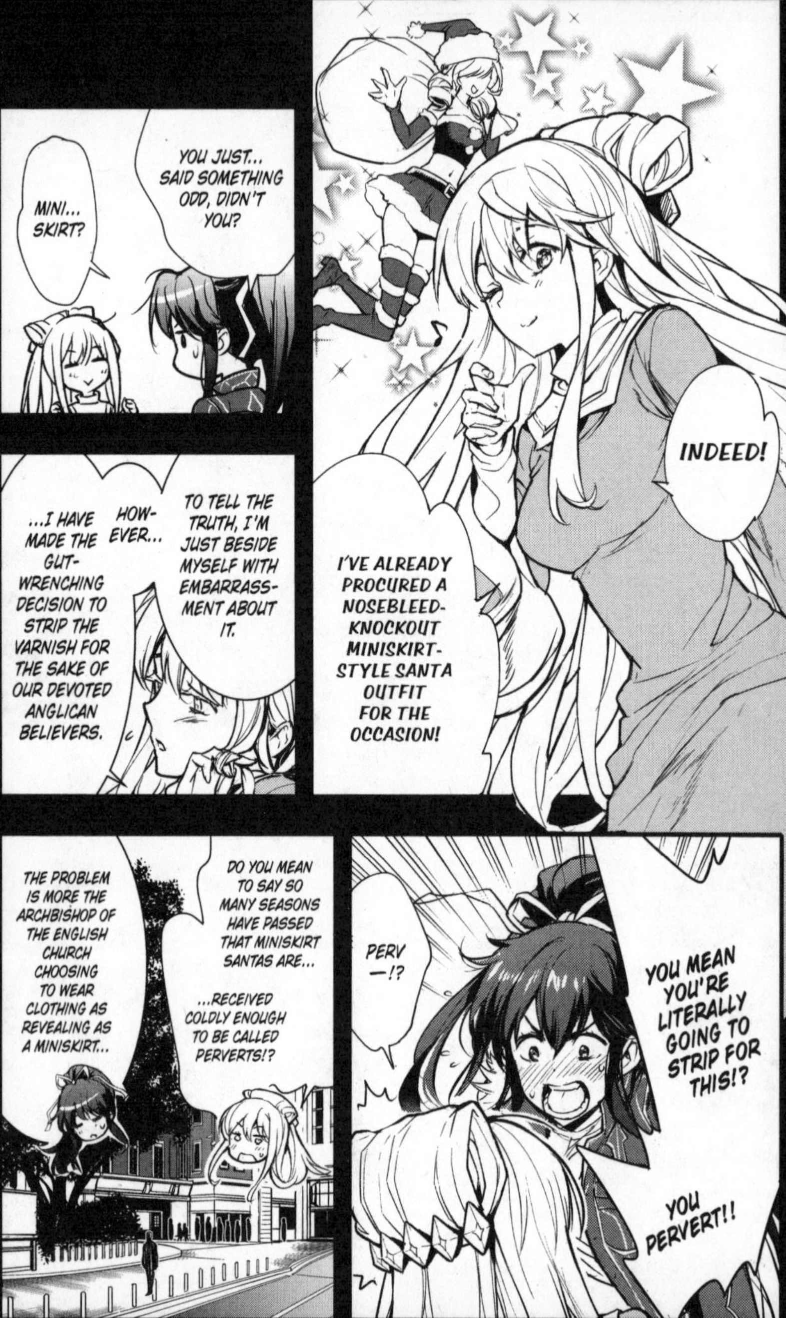
INDEED!
I'VE ALREADY PROCURED A NOSEBLEED-KNOCKOUT MINISKIRT-STYLE SANTA OUTFIT FOR THE OCCASION!
YOU JUST... SAID SOMETHING ODD, DIDN'T YOU?
MINI... SKIRT?
TO TELL THE TRUTH, I'M JUST BESIDE MYSELF WITH EMBARRASS-MENT ABOUT IT.
HOW-EVER...
...I HAVE MADE THE GUT-WRENCHING DECISION TO STRIP THE VARNISH FOR THE SAKE OF OUR DEVOTED ANGLICAN BELIEVERS.
YOU MEAN YOU'RE LITERALLY GOING TO STRIP FOR THIS!?
PERV—!?
YOU PERVERT!!
DO YOU MEAN TO SAY SO MANY SEASONS HAVE PASSED THAT MINISKIRT SANTAS ARE...
...RECEIVED COLDLY ENOUGH TO BE CALLED PERVERTS!?
THE PROBLEM IS MORE THE ARCHBISHOP OF THE ENGLISH CHURCH CHOOSING TO WEAR CLOTHING AS REVEALING AS A MINISKIRT...

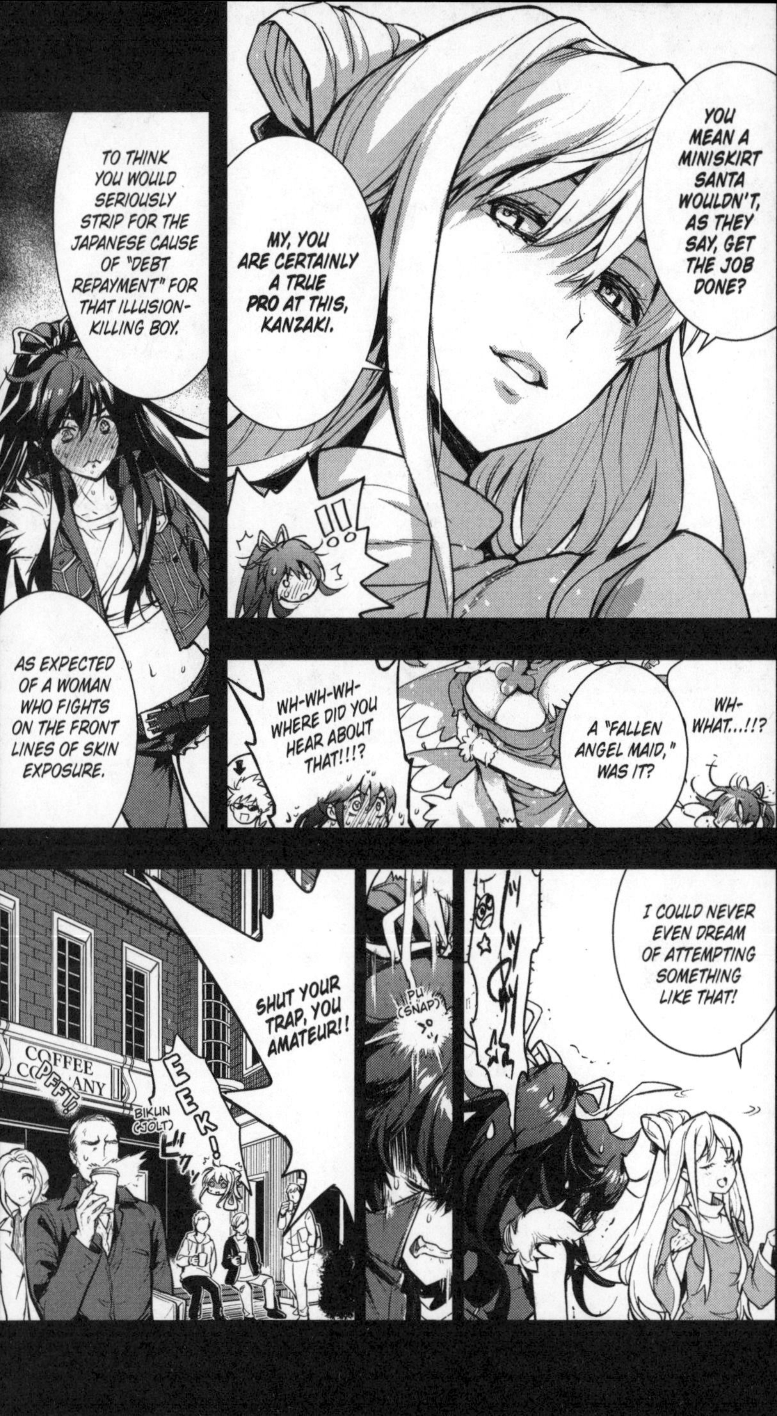
YOU MEAN A MINISKIRT SANTA WOULDN'T, AS THEY SAY, GET THE JOB DONE?
MY, YOU ARE CERTAINLY A TRUE PRO AT THIS, KANZAKI.
WH- WHAT...!!?
A "FALLEN ANGEL MAID," WAS IT?
WH-WH-WH-WHERE DID YOU HEAR ABOUT THAT!!!?
TO THINK YOU WOULD SERIOUSLY STRIP FOR THE JAPANESE CAUSE OF "DEBT REPAYMENT" FOR THAT ILLUSION-KILLING BOY.
AS EXPECTED OF A WOMAN WHO FIGHTS ON THE FRONT LINES OF SKIN EXPOSURE.
I COULD NEVER EVEN DREAM OF ATTEMPTING SOMETHING LIKE THAT!
PU (SNAP)
SHUT YOUR TRAP, YOU AMATEUR!!
EEEK!
BIKUN (JOLT)
PFFT!!
COFFEE

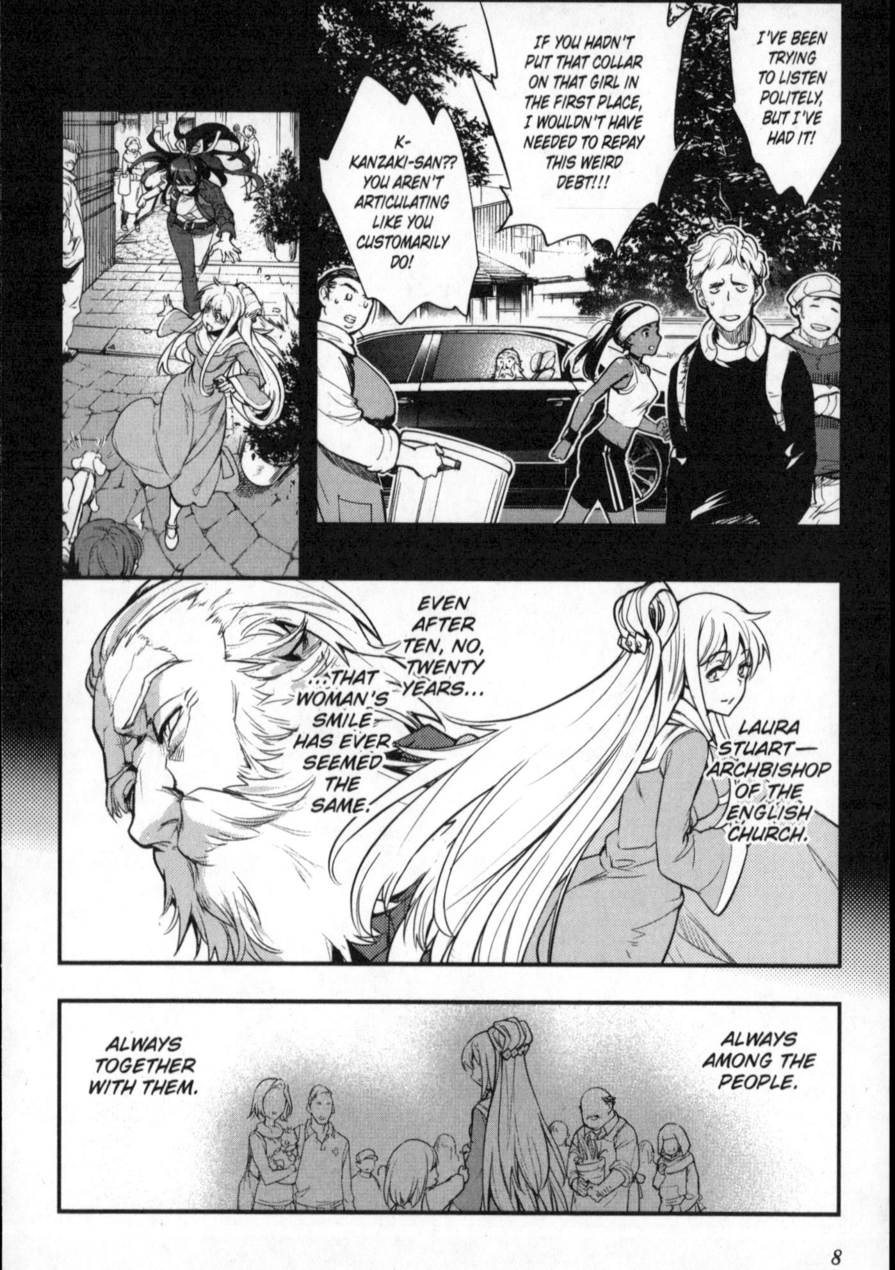
I'VE BEEN TRYING TO LISTEN POLITELY, BUT I'VE HAD IT!
IF YOU HADN'T PUT THAT COLLAR ON THAT GIRL IN THE FIRST PLACE, I WOULDN'T HAVE NEEDED TO REPAY THIS WEIRD DEBT!!!
K-KANZAKI-SAN?? YOU AREN'T ARTICULATING LIKE YOU CUSTOMARILY DO!
LAURA STUART—ARCHBISHOP OF THE ENGLISH CHURCH.
EVEN AFTER TEN, NO, TWENTY YEARS...
...THAT WOMAN'S SMILE HAS EVER SEEMED THE SAME.
ALWAYS AMONG THE PEOPLE.
ALWAYS TOGETHER WITH THEM.

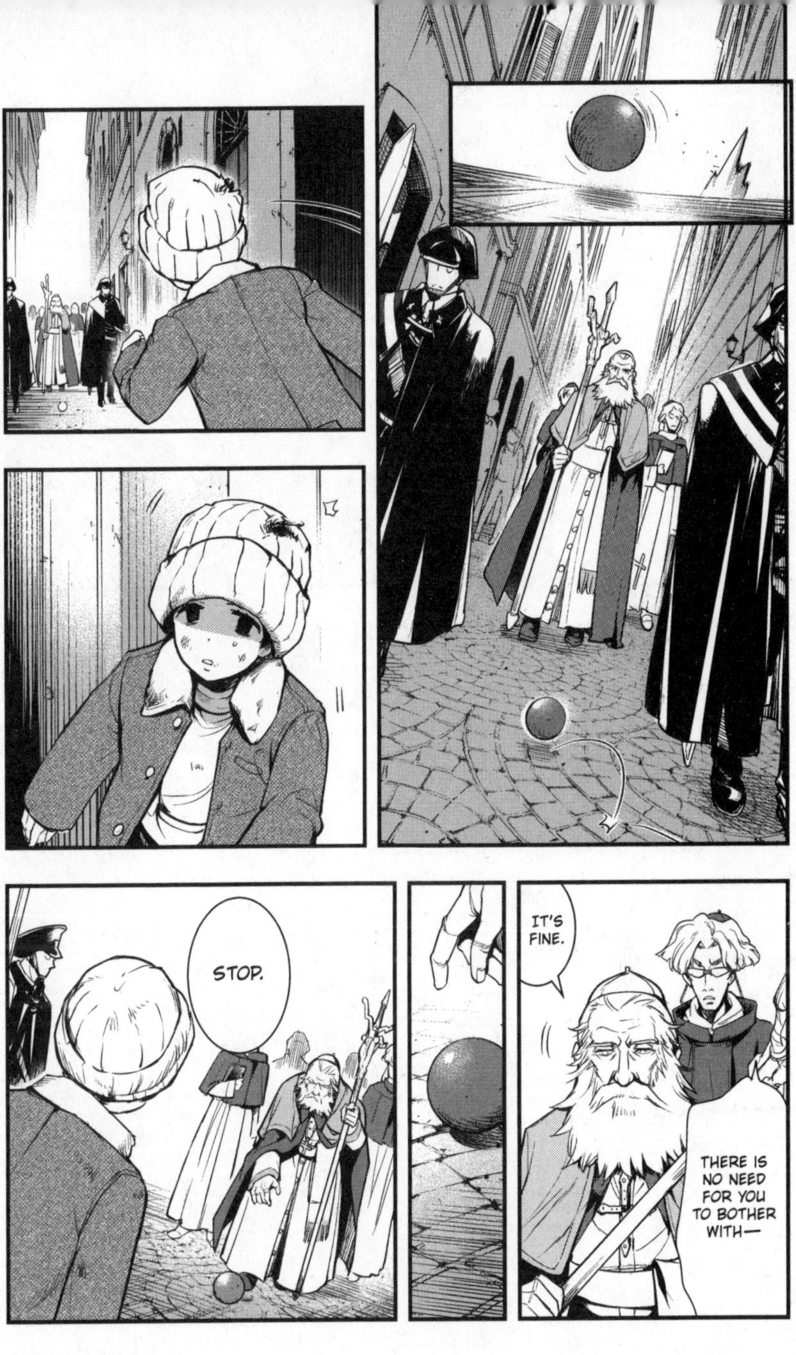
IT'S FINE.
THERE IS NO NEED FOR YOU TO BOTHER WITH—
STOP.

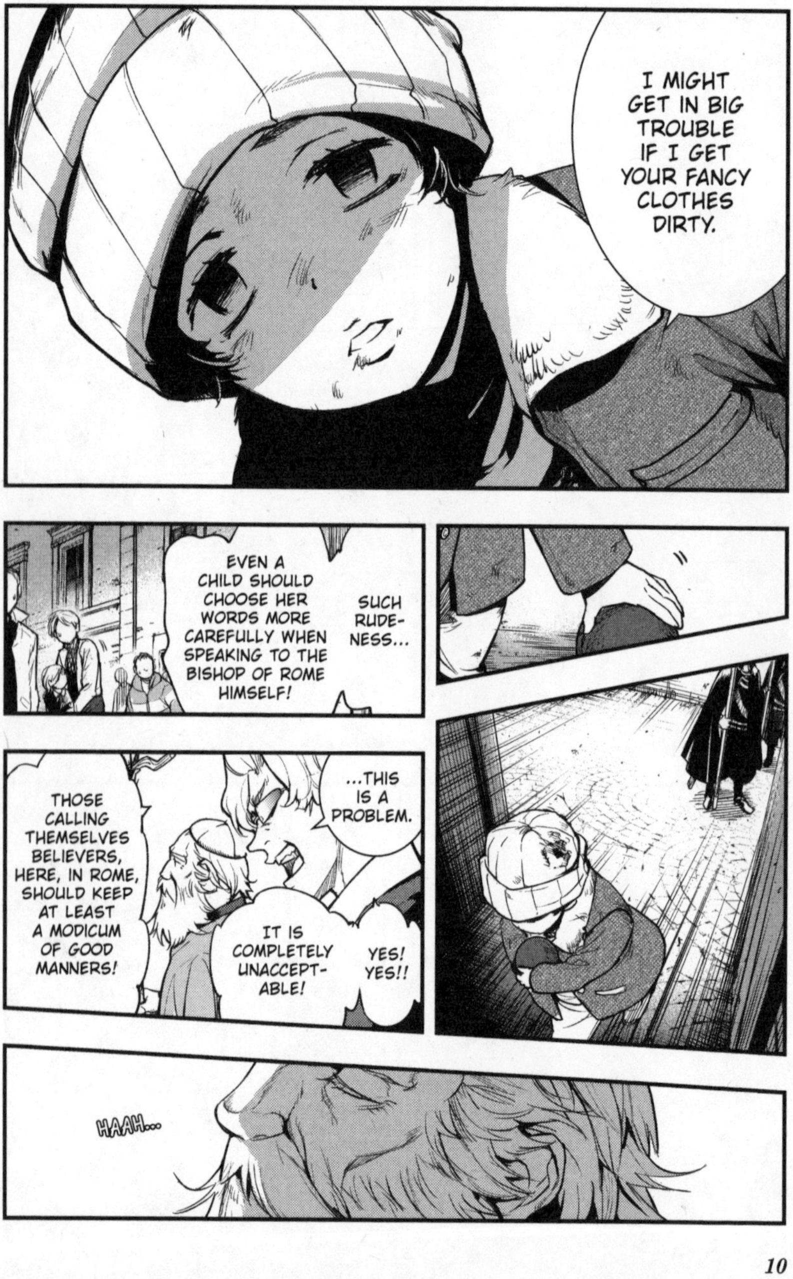

I MIGHT GET IN BIG TROUBLE IF I GET YOUR FANCY CLOTHES DIRTY.
SUCH RUDENESS...
EVEN A CHILD SHOULD CHOOSE HER WORDS MORE CAREFULLY WHEN SPEAKING TO THE BISHOP OF ROME HIMSELF!
...THIS IS A PROBLEM.
THOSE CALLING THEMSELVES BELIEVERS, HERE, IN ROME, SHOULD KEEP AT LEAST A MODICUM OF GOOD MANNERS!
YES! YES!!
IT IS COMPLETELY UNACCEPTABLE!
HAAAH...

#155 THE PROMISED HOUR

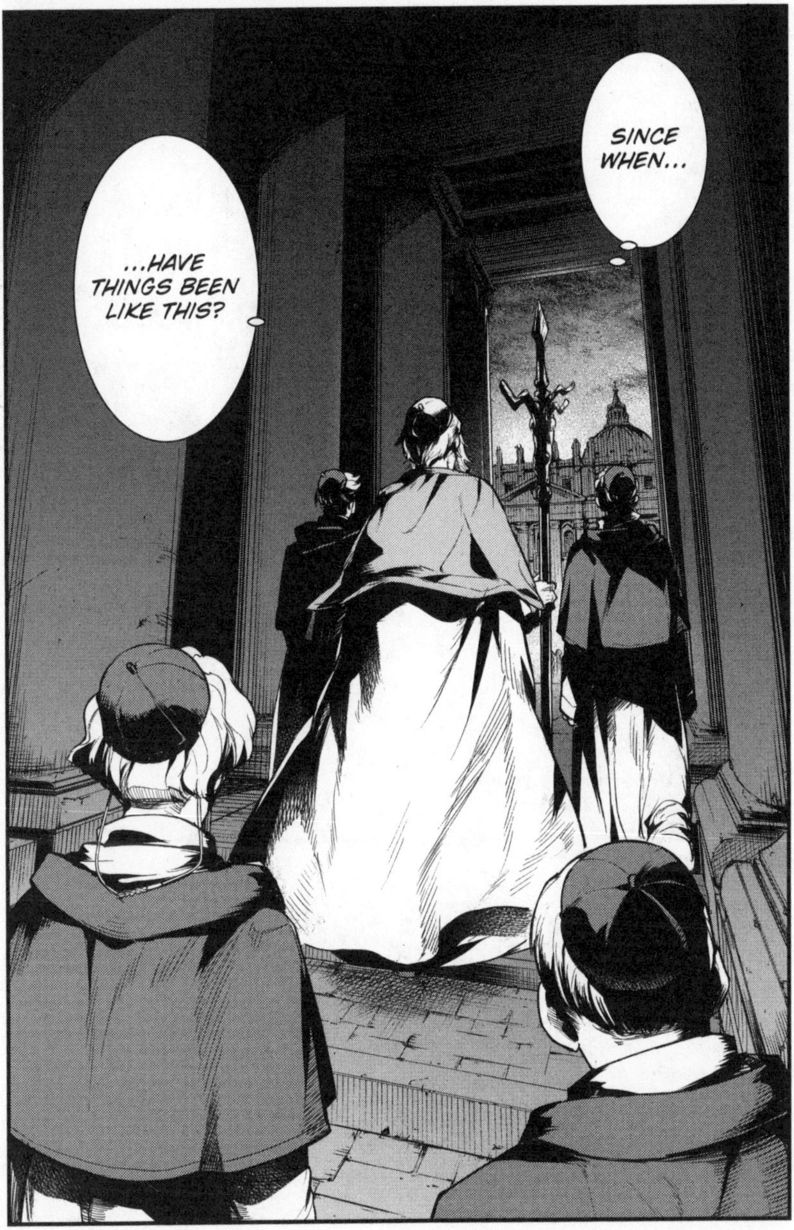
SINCE WHEN...
...HAVE THINGS BEEN LIKE THIS?

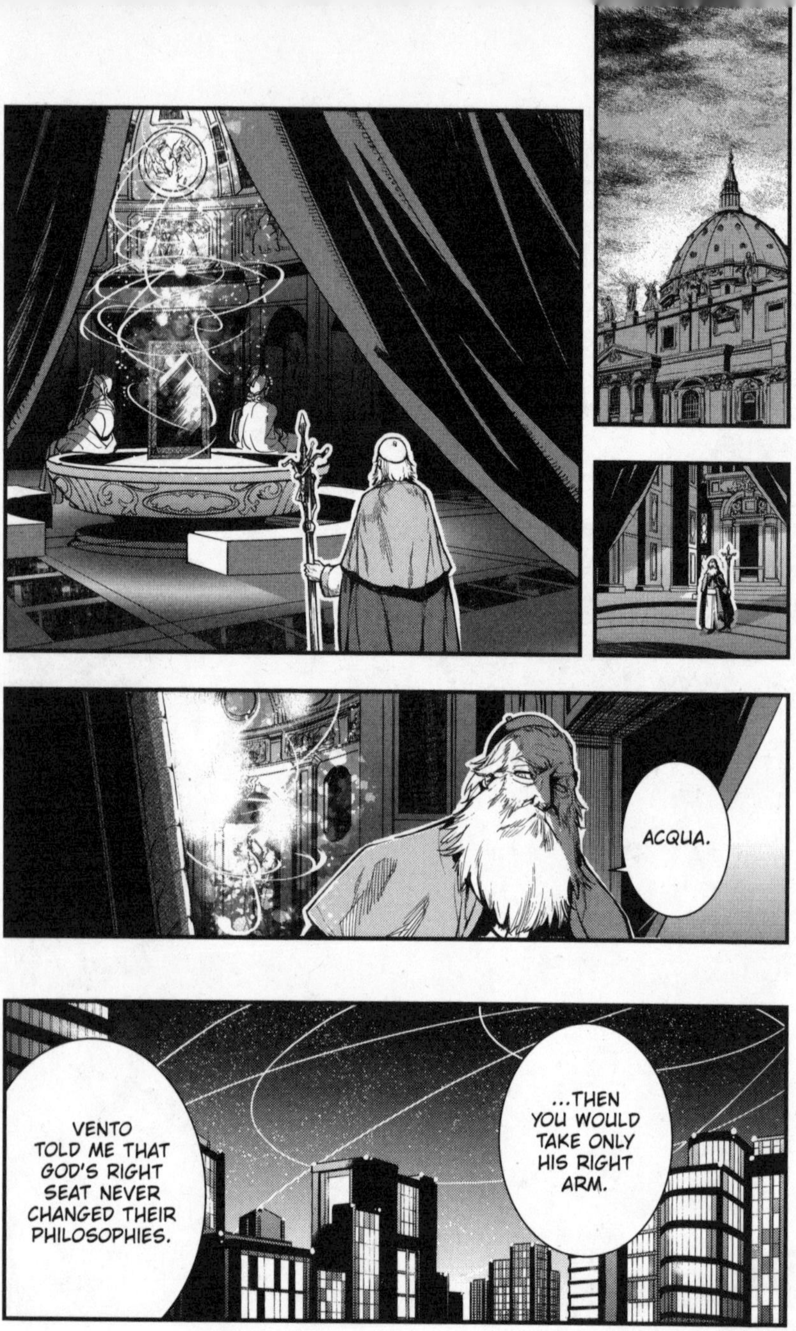
ACQUA.
...THEN YOU WOULD TAKE ONLY HIS RIGHT ARM.
VENTO TOLD ME THAT GOD'S RIGHT SEAT NEVER CHANGED THEIR PHILOSOPHIES.

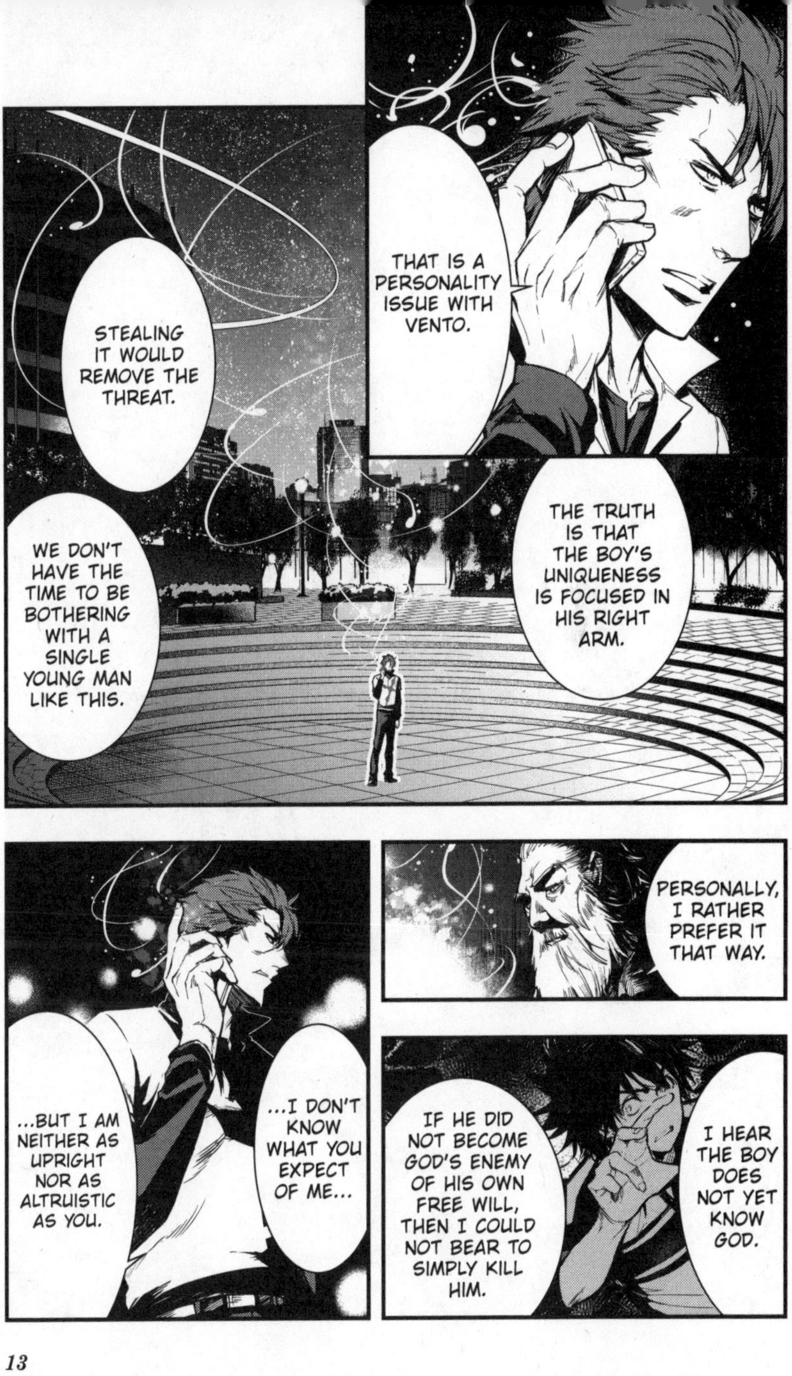
THAT IS A PERSONALITY ISSUE WITH VENTO.
THE TRUTH IS THAT THE BOY'S UNIQUENESS IS FOCUSED IN HIS RIGHT ARM.
STEALING IT WOULD REMOVE THE THREAT.
WE DON'T HAVE THE TIME TO BE BOTHERING WITH A SINGLE YOUNG MAN LIKE THIS.
PERSONALLY, I RATHER PREFER IT THAT WAY.
I HEAR THE BOY DOES NOT YET KNOW GOD.
IF HE DID NOT BECOME GOD'S ENEMY OF HIS OWN FREE WILL, THEN I COULD NOT BEAR TO SIMPLY KILL HIM.
...I DON'T KNOW WHAT YOU EXPECT OF ME...
...BUT I AM NEITHER AS UPRIGHT NOR AS ALTRUISTIC AS YOU.

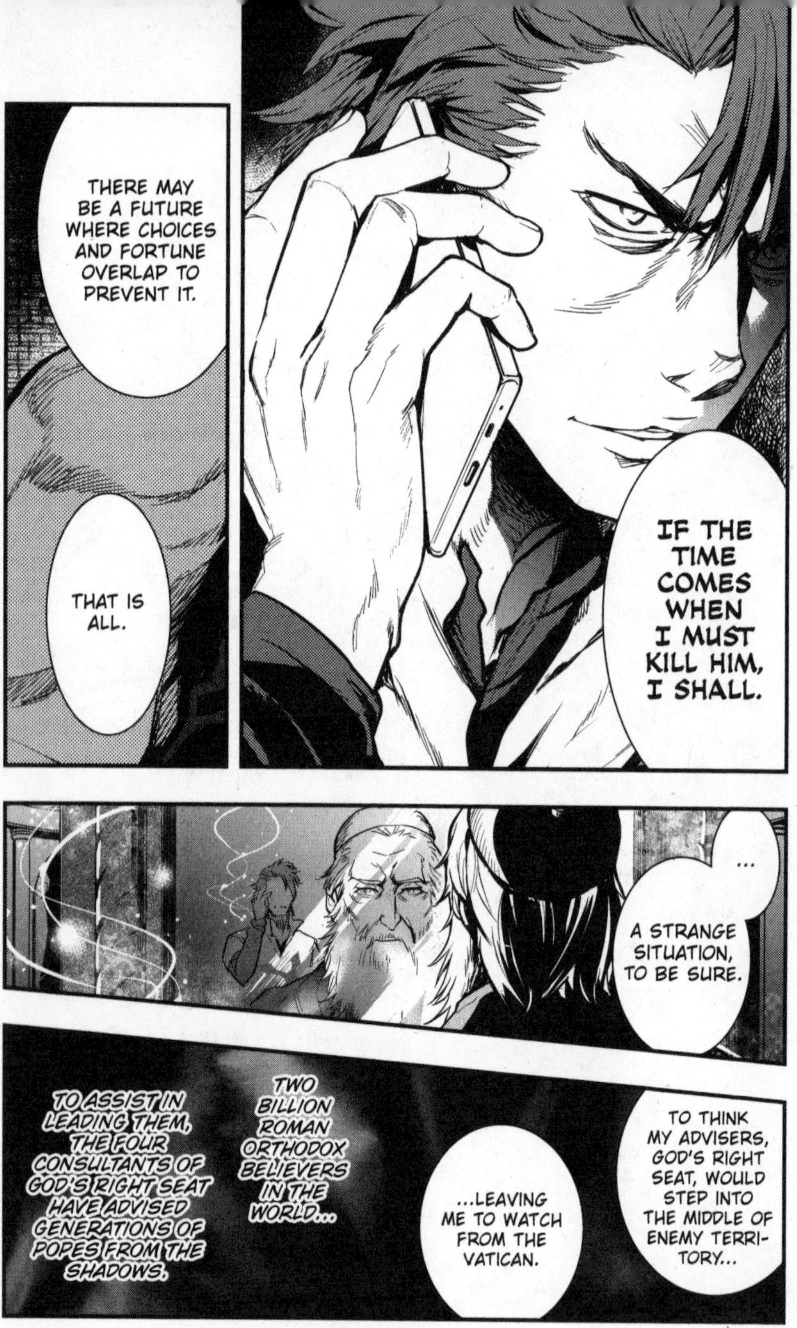
IF THE TIME COMES WHEN I MUST KILL HIM, I SHALL.
THERE MAY BE A FUTURE WHERE CHOICES AND FORTUNE OVERLAP TO PREVENT IT.
THAT IS ALL.
...
A STRANGE SITUATION, TO BE SURE.
TO THINK MY ADVISERS, GOD'S RIGHT SEAT, WOULD STEP INTO THE MIDDLE OF ENEMY TERRI-TORY...
...LEAVING ME TO WATCH FROM THE VATICAN.
TWO BILLION ROMAN ORTHODOX BELIEVERS IN THE WORLD...
TO ASSIST IN LEADING THEM, THE FOUR CONSULTANTS OF GOD'S RIGHT SEAT HAVE ADVISED GENERATIONS OF POPES FROM THE SHADOWS.

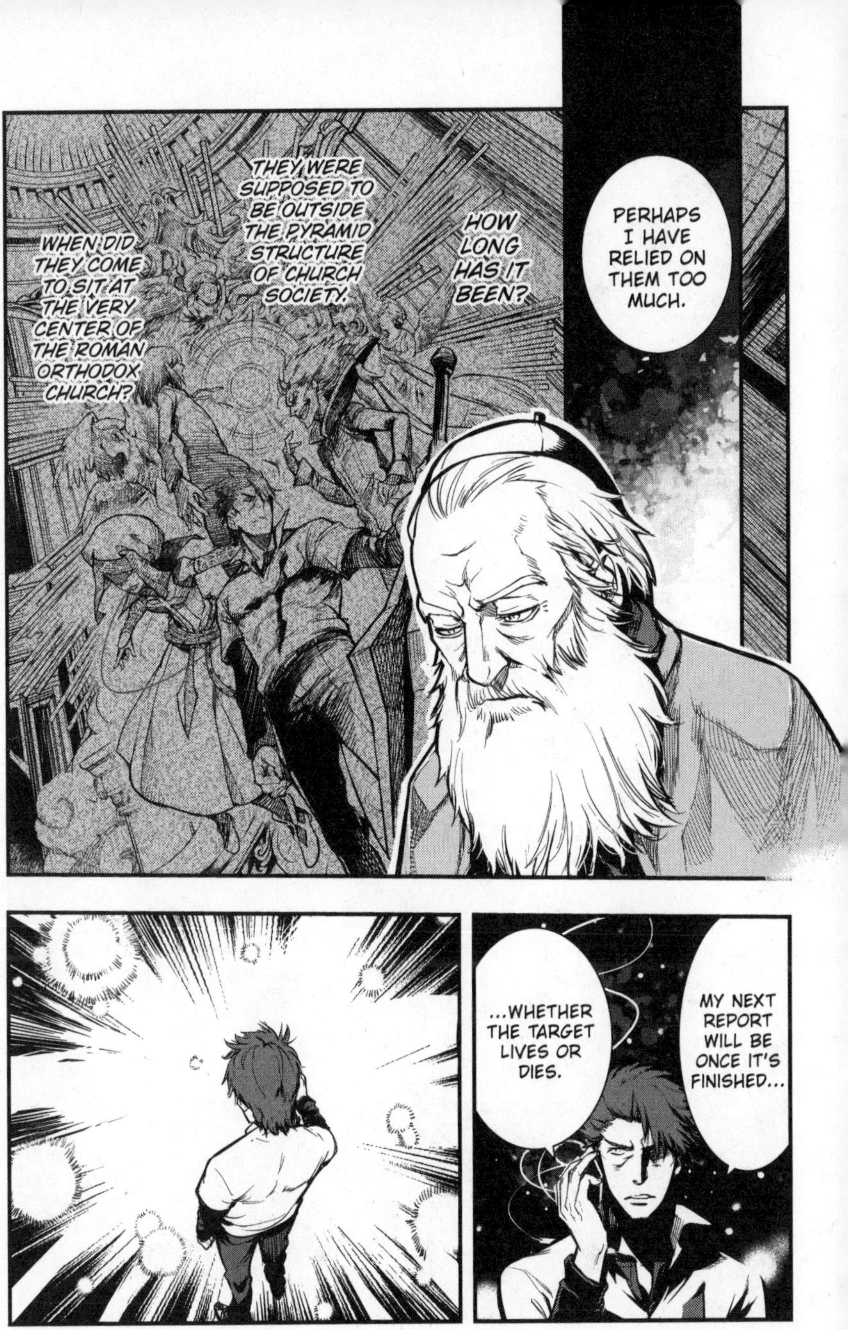
PERHAPS I HAVE RELIED ON THEM TOO MUCH.
HOW LONG HAS IT BEEN?
THEY WERE SUPPOSED TO BE OUTSIDE THE PYRAMID STRUCTURE OF CHURCH SOCIETY.
WHEN DID THEY COME TO SIT AT THE VERY CENTER OF THE ROMAN ORTHODOX CHURCH?
MY NEXT REPORT WILL BE ONCE IT'S FINISHED...
...WHETHER THE TARGET LIVES OR DIES.

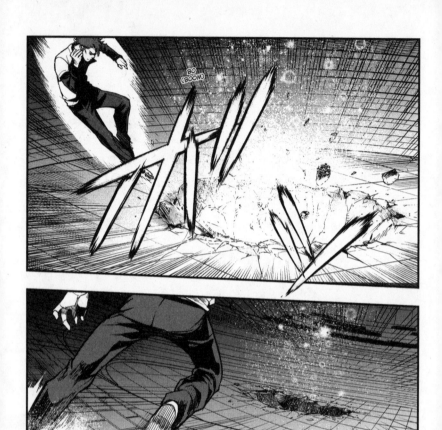

BO
(BOOM)

BIIIIII
(SKREEEEEE)

WRRN

THEY SPREAD SOME SORT OF PARTICLES IN THE AIR THAT DISMANTLE MATTER.

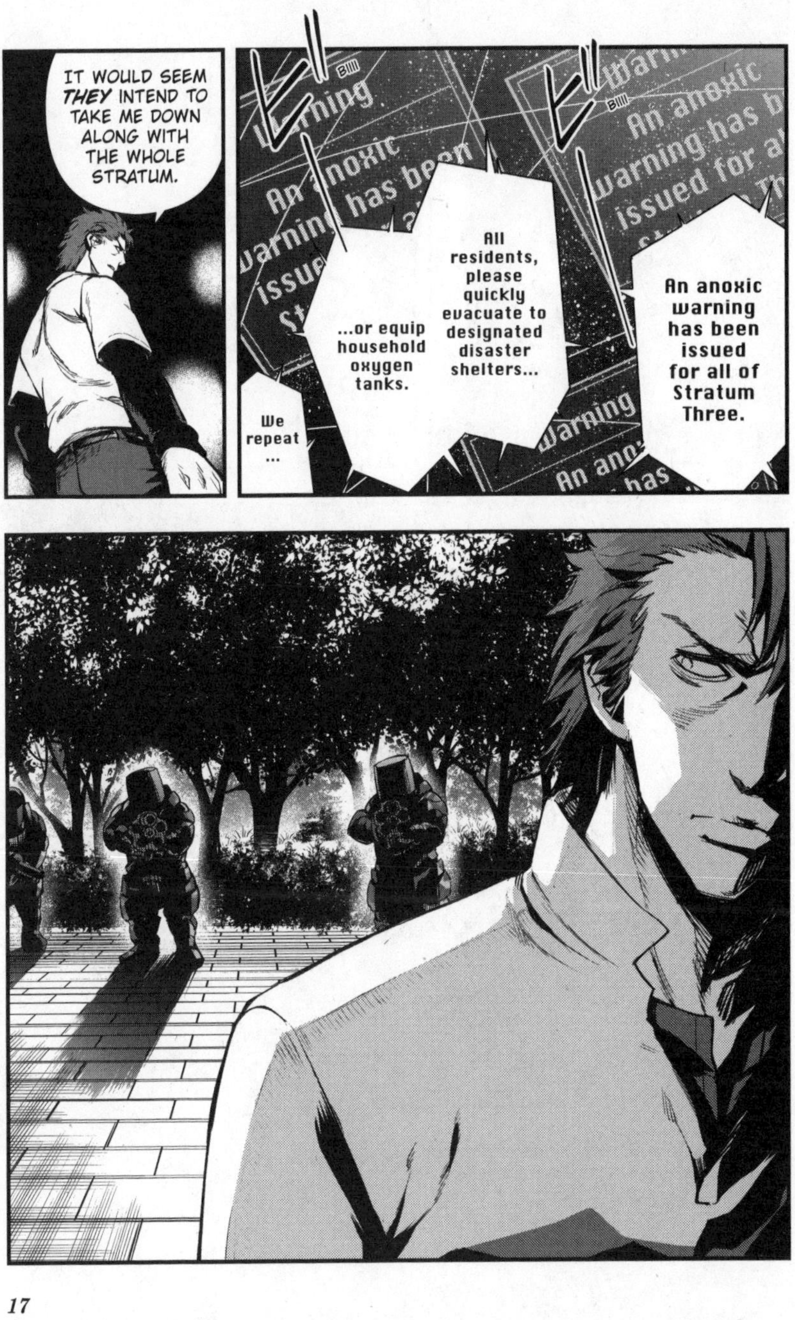
BIIII
BIIII
An anoxic warning has been issued for all of Stratum Three.
All residents, please quickly evacuate to designated disaster shelters...
...or equip household oxygen tanks.
We repeat ...
IT WOULD SEEM *THEY* INTEND TO TAKE ME DOWN ALONG WITH THE WHOLE STRATUM.

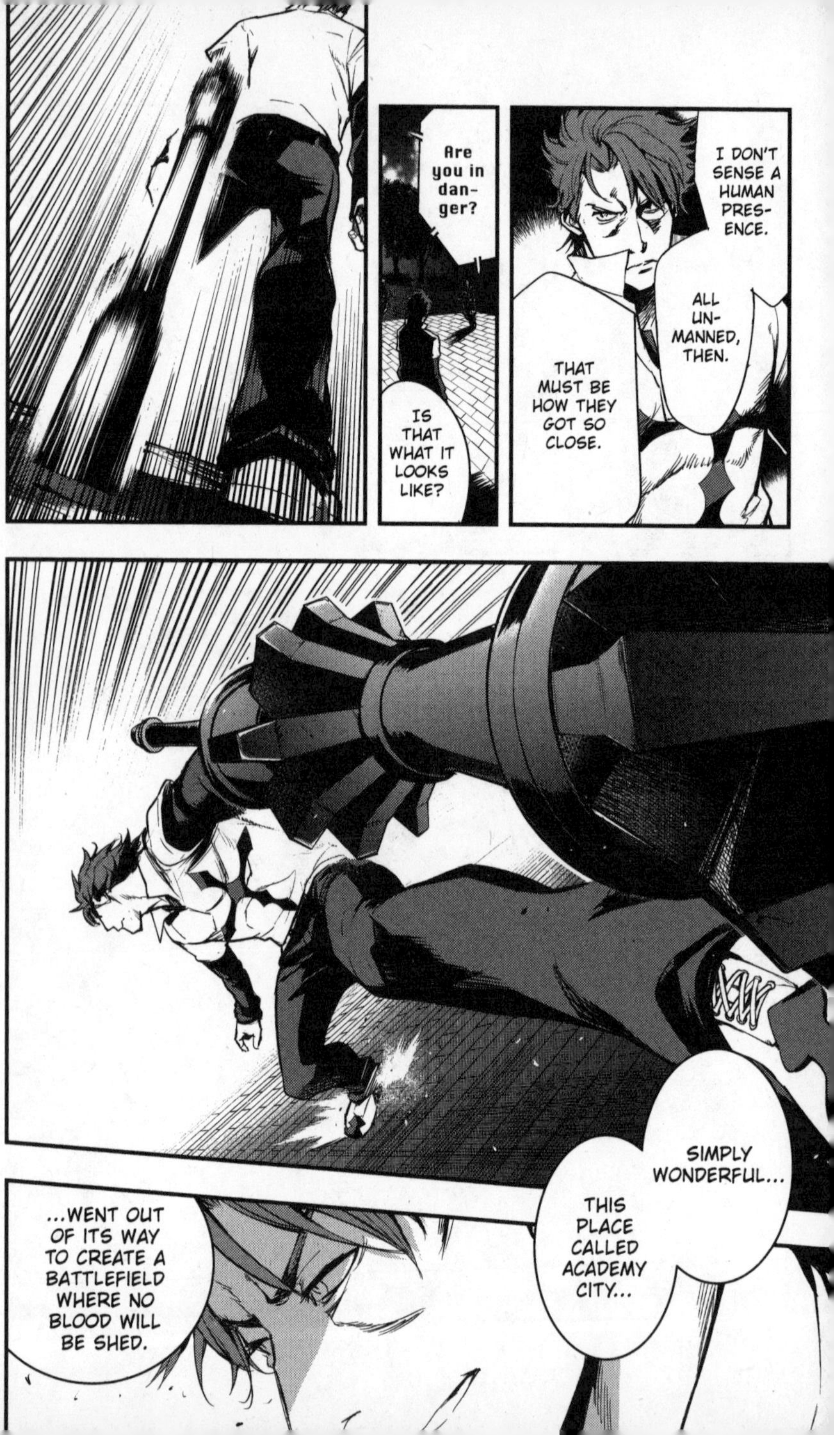
I DON'T SENSE A HUMAN PRESENCE.
ALL UN-MANNED, THEN.
THAT MUST BE HOW THEY GOT SO CLOSE.
Are you in danger?
IS THAT WHAT IT LOOKS LIKE?
SIMPLY WONDERFUL...
THIS PLACE CALLED ACADEMY CITY...
...WENT OUT OF ITS WAY TO CREATE A BATTLEFIELD WHERE NO BLOOD WILL BE SHED.

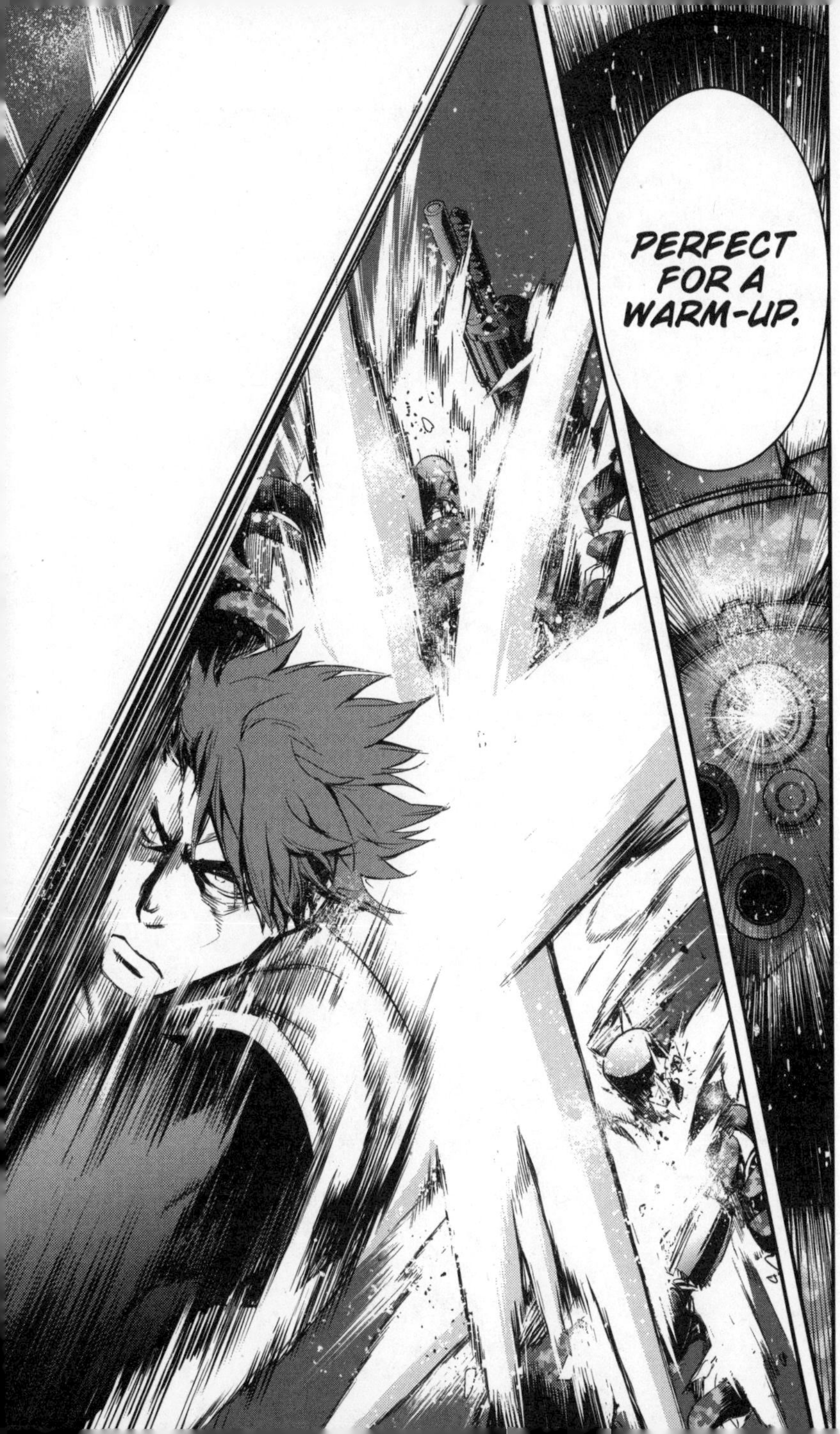
PERFECT FOR A WARM-UP.

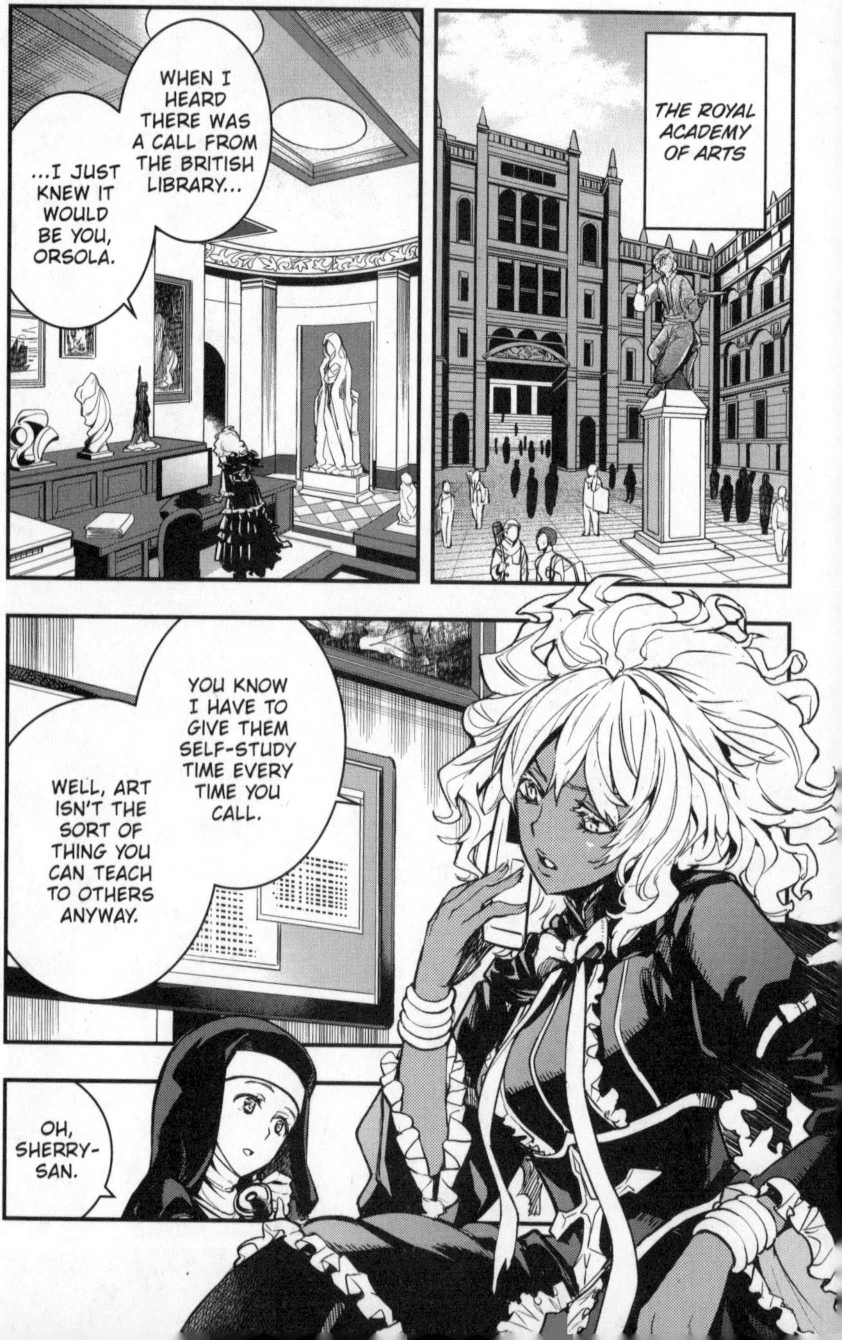
THE ROYAL ACADEMY OF ARTS
WHEN I HEARD THERE WAS A CALL FROM THE BRITISH LIBRARY...
...I JUST KNEW IT WOULD BE YOU, ORSOLA.
YOU KNOW I HAVE TO GIVE THEM SELF-STUDY TIME EVERY TIME YOU CALL.
WELL, ART ISN'T THE SORT OF THING YOU CAN TEACH TO OTHERS ANYWAY.
OH, SHERRY-SAN.

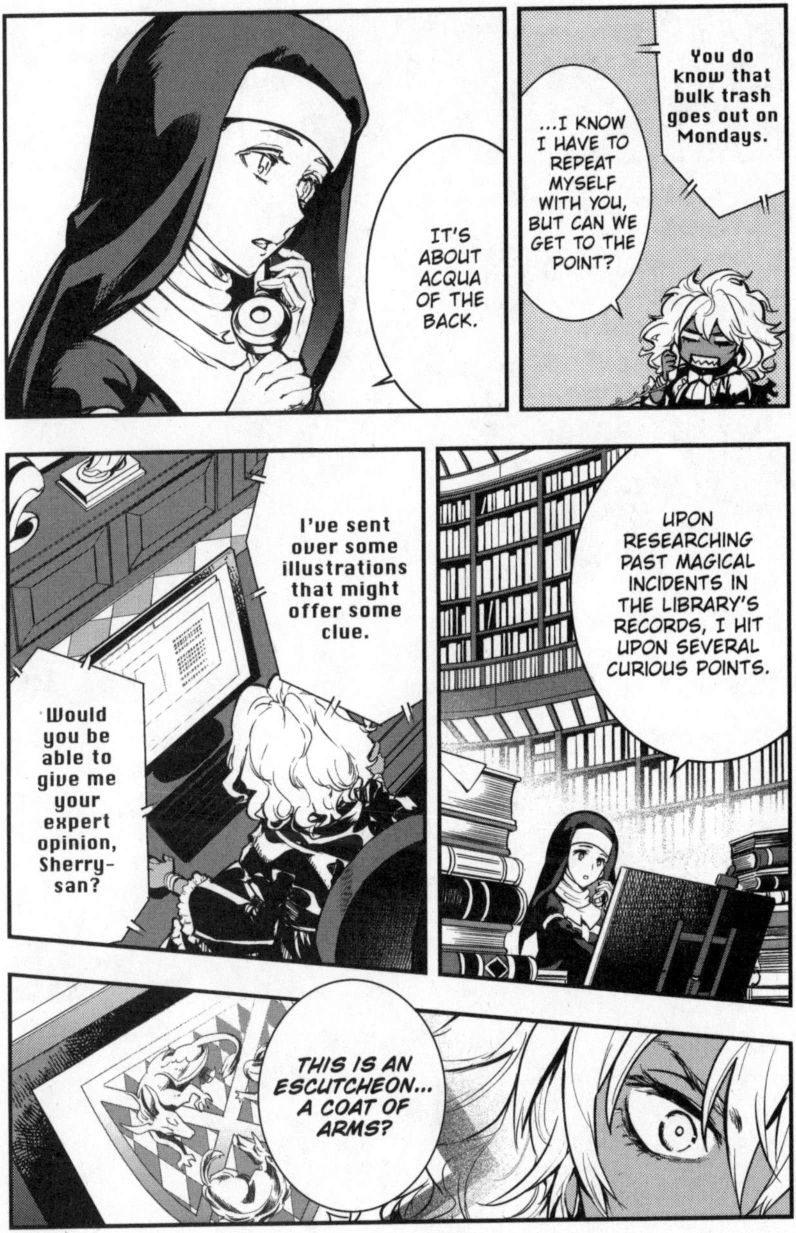
You do know that bulk trash goes out on Mondays.
...I KNOW I HAVE TO REPEAT MYSELF WITH YOU, BUT CAN WE GET TO THE POINT?
IT'S ABOUT ACQUA OF THE BACK.
UPON RESEARCHING PAST MAGICAL INCIDENTS IN THE LIBRARY'S RECORDS, I HIT UPON SEVERAL CURIOUS POINTS.
I've sent over some illustrations that might offer some clue.
Would you be able to give me your expert opinion, Sherry-san?
THIS IS AN ESCUTCHEON... A COAT OF ARMS?

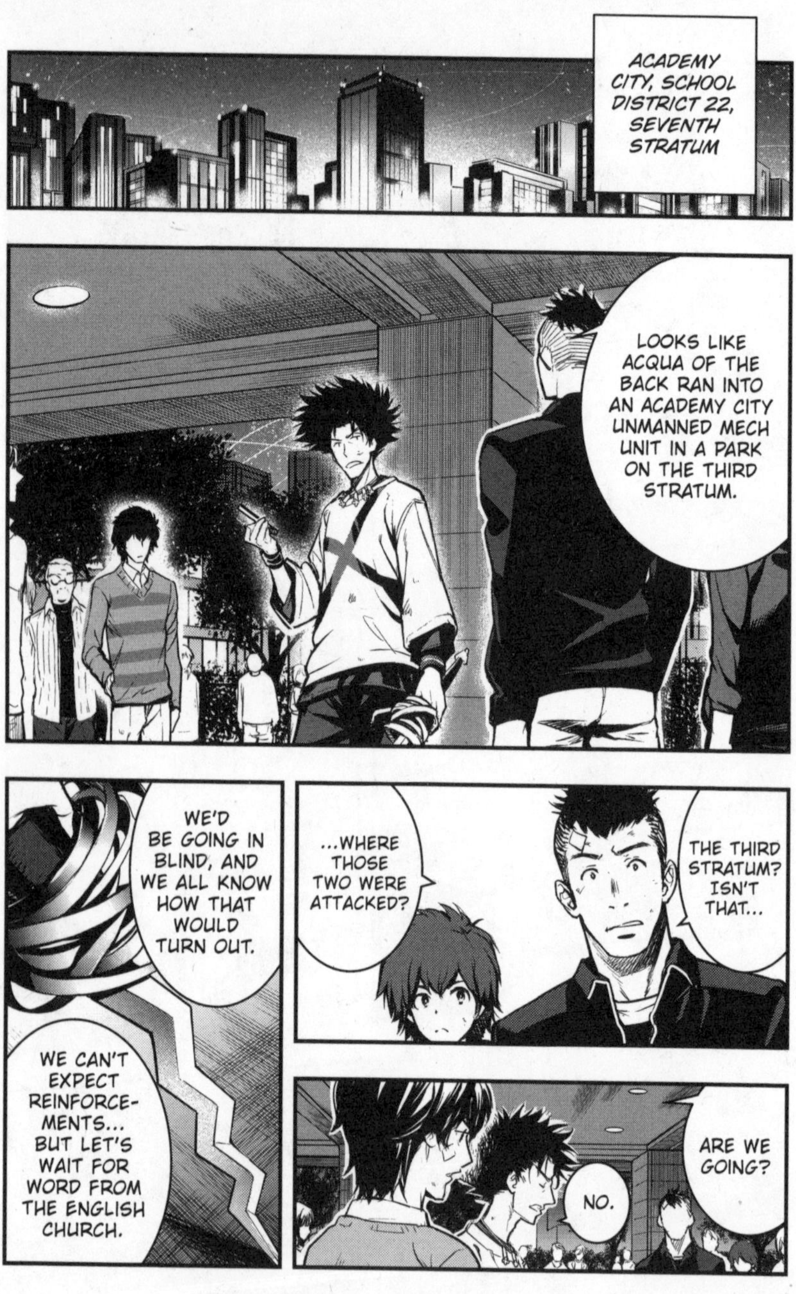
ACADEMY CITY, SCHOOL DISTRICT 22, SEVENTH STRATUM
LOOKS LIKE ACQUA OF THE BACK RAN INTO AN ACADEMY CITY UNMANNED MECH UNIT IN A PARK ON THE THIRD STRATUM.
THE THIRD STRATUM? ISN'T THAT...
...WHERE THOSE TWO WERE ATTACKED?
ARE WE GOING?
NO.
WE'D BE GOING IN BLIND, AND WE ALL KNOW HOW THAT WOULD TURN OUT.
WE CAN'T EXPECT REINFORCEMENTS... BUT LET'S WAIT FOR WORD FROM THE ENGLISH CHURCH.

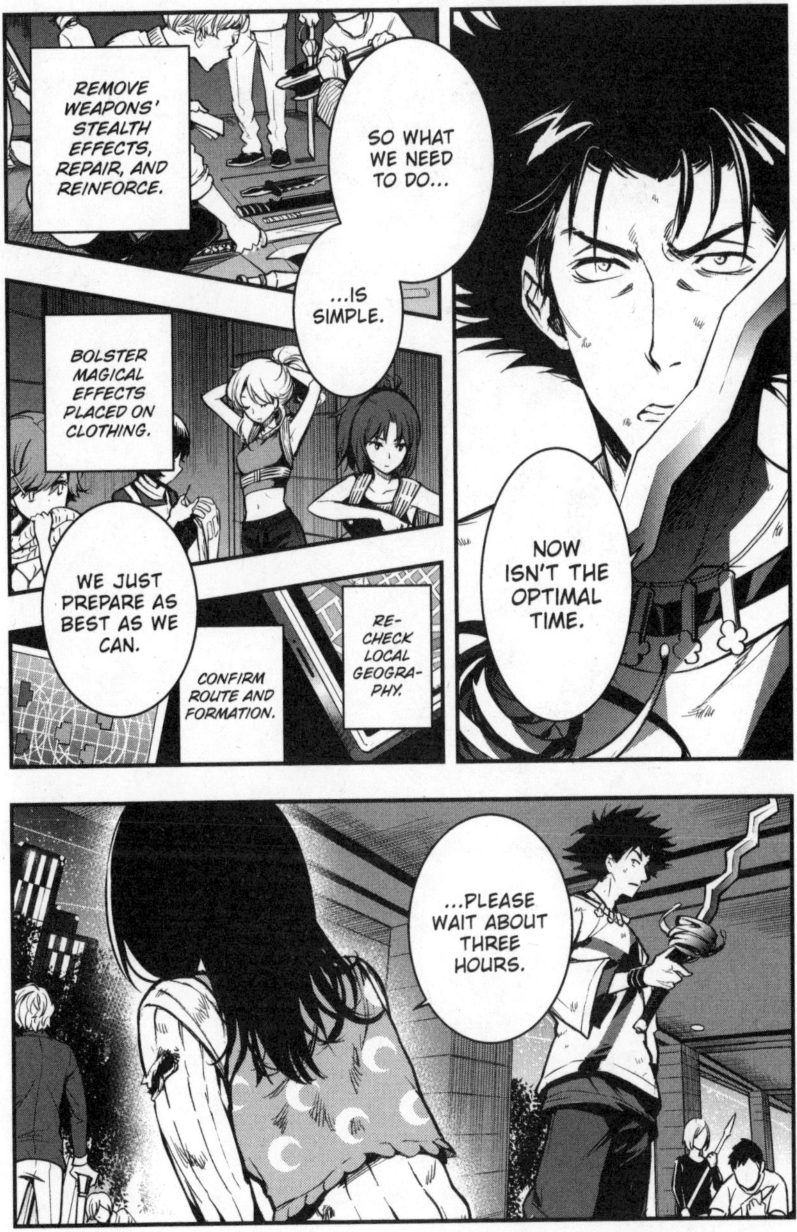
NOW ISN'T THE OPTIMAL TIME.
SO WHAT WE NEED TO DO...
REMOVE WEAPONS' STEALTH EFFECTS, REPAIR, AND REINFORCE.
...IS SIMPLE.
BOLSTER MAGICAL EFFECTS PLACED ON CLOTHING.
WE JUST PREPARE AS BEST AS WE CAN.
RE-CHECK LOCAL GEOGRA-PHY.
CONFIRM ROUTE AND FORMATION.
...PLEASE WAIT ABOUT THREE HOURS.

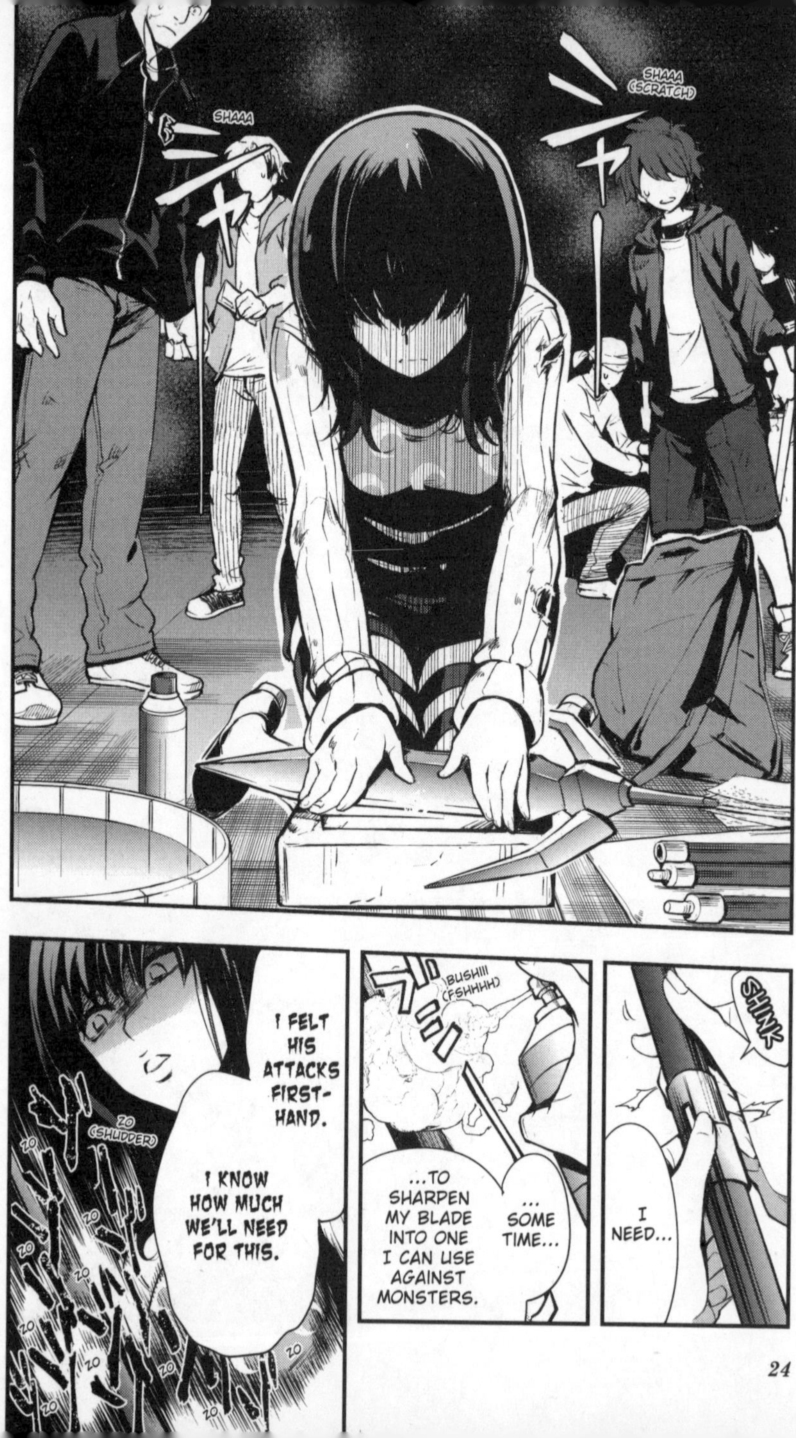
SHAAA (SCRATCH)
SHAAA
SHINK
I NEED...
BUSHIII (FSHHHH)
...SOME TIME...
...TO SHARPEN MY BLADE INTO ONE I CAN USE AGAINST MONSTERS.
I FELT HIS ATTACKS FIRST-HAND.
I KNOW HOW MUCH WE'LL NEED FOR THIS.
ZO (SHUDDER)

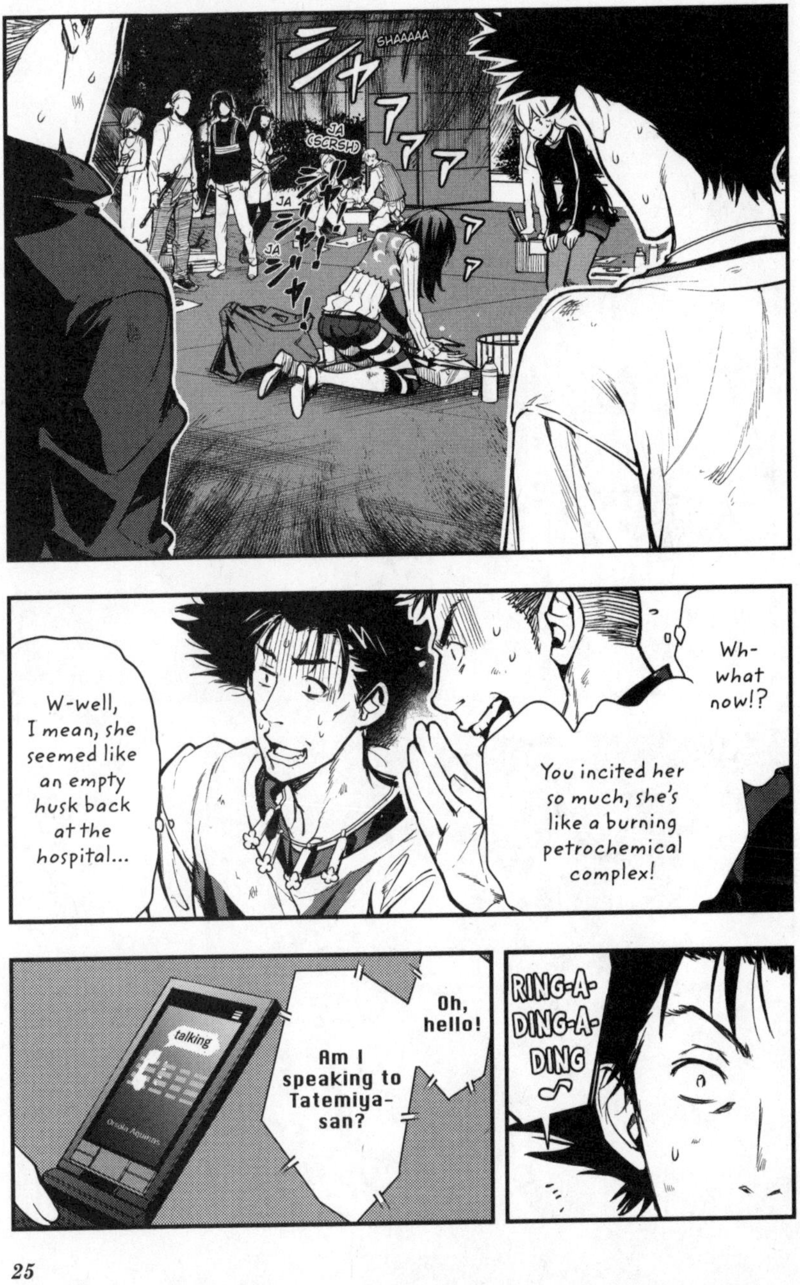
シャアアアアア
SHAAAAA
ジャ!ジャ!ジャ!
JA (SCRSH)
JA
JA
Wh- what now!?
You incited her so much, she's like a burning petrochemical complex!
W-well, I mean, she seemed like an empty husk back at the hospital...
RING-A-DING-A-DING ♪
Oh, hello!
Am I speaking to Tatemiya-san?
talking

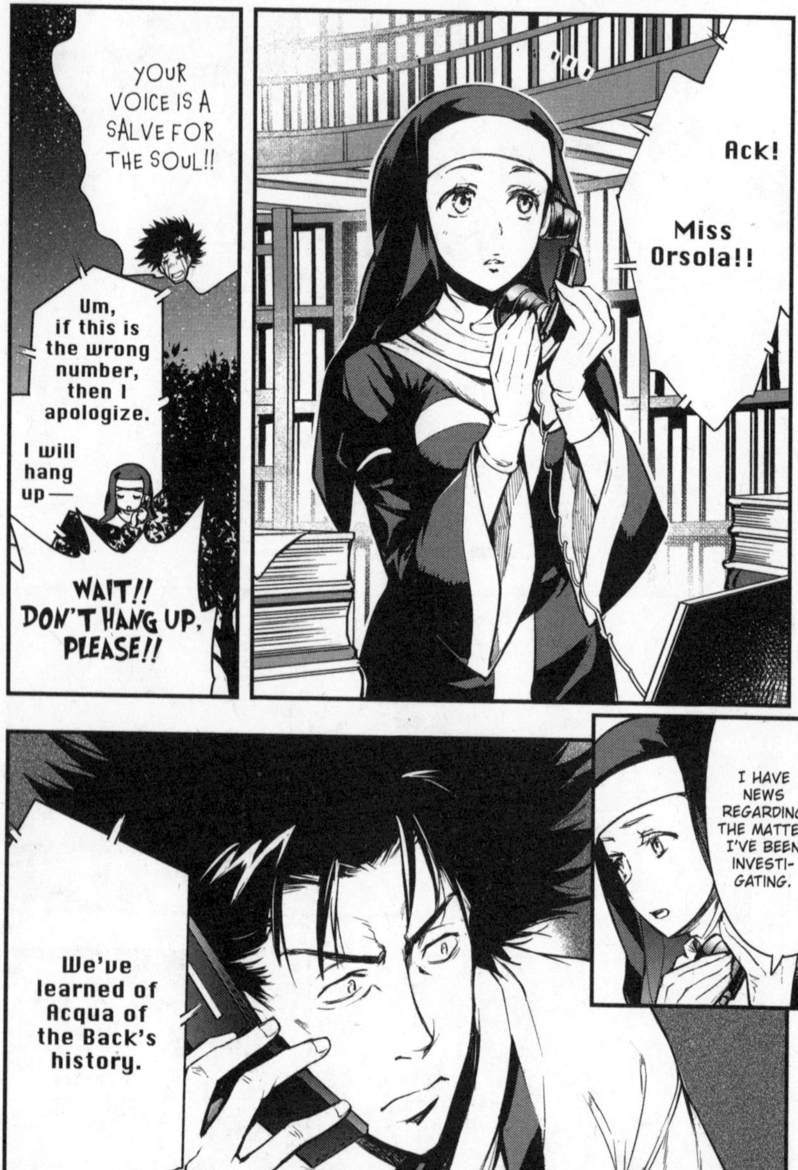
Ack!
Miss Orsola!!
YOUR VOICE IS A SALVE FOR THE SOUL!!
Um, if this is the wrong number, then I apologize.
I will hang up—
WAIT!! DON'T HANG UP, PLEASE!!
I HAVE NEWS REGARDING THE MATTER I'VE BEEN INVESTI-GATING.
We've learned of Acqua of the Back's history.

A Certain Magical Index

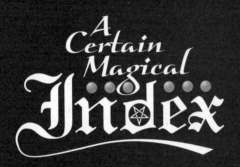

A Certain Magical Index

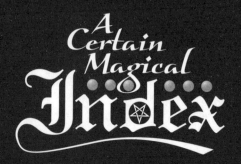

#156 WILLIAM ORWELL

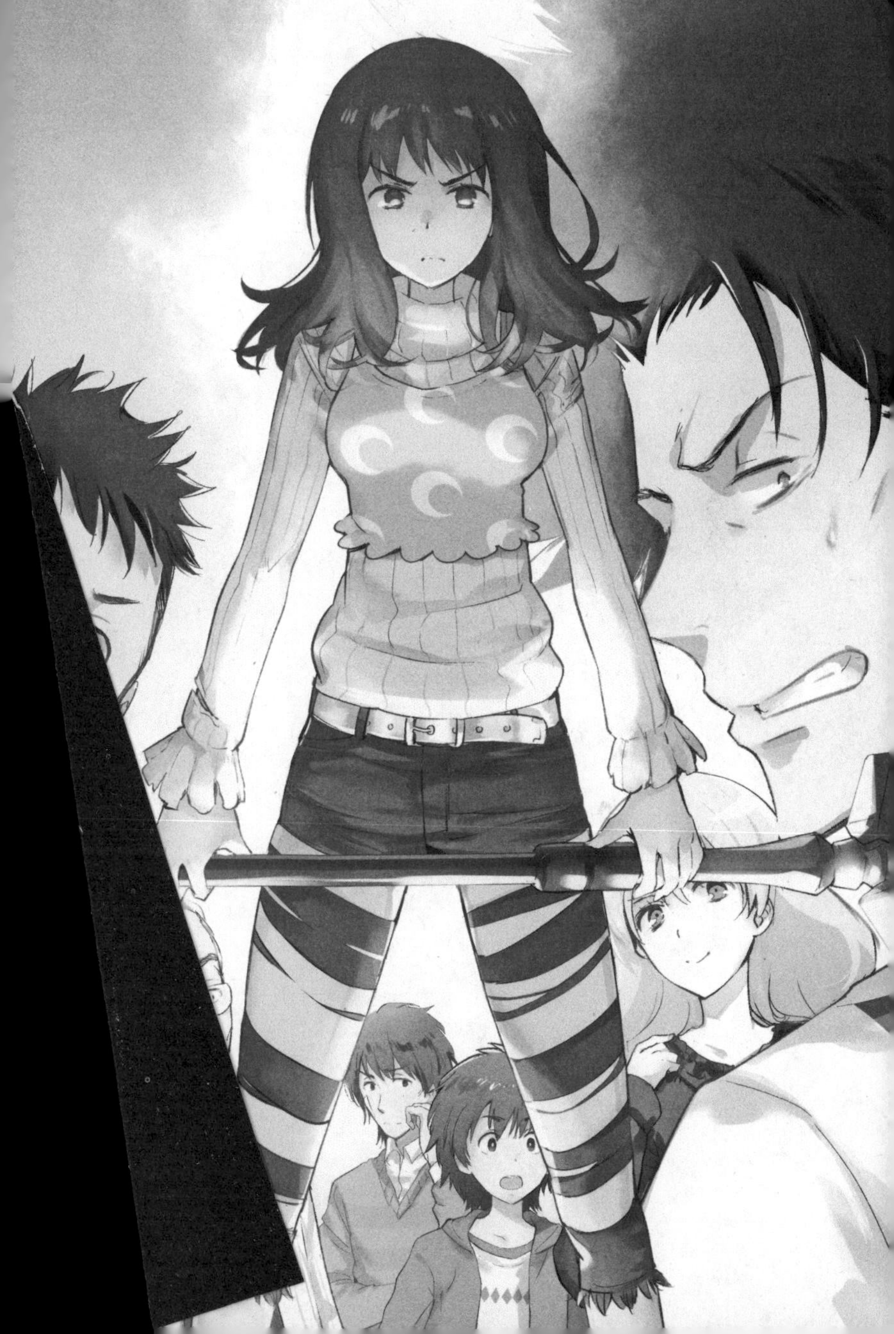

A Certain Magical Index

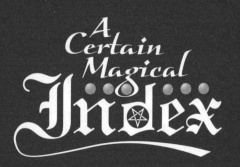

MAN, YOU'RE A HUGE HELP, MISS ORSOLA!

If we know Acqua's origin, we might find a clue to beating him!

...Apparently, Acqua of the Back was once a Knight of England.

WELL...

...OF ENGLAND?

A KNIGHT...

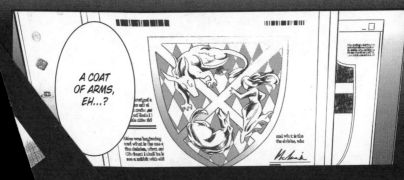

A COAT OF ARMS, EH...?

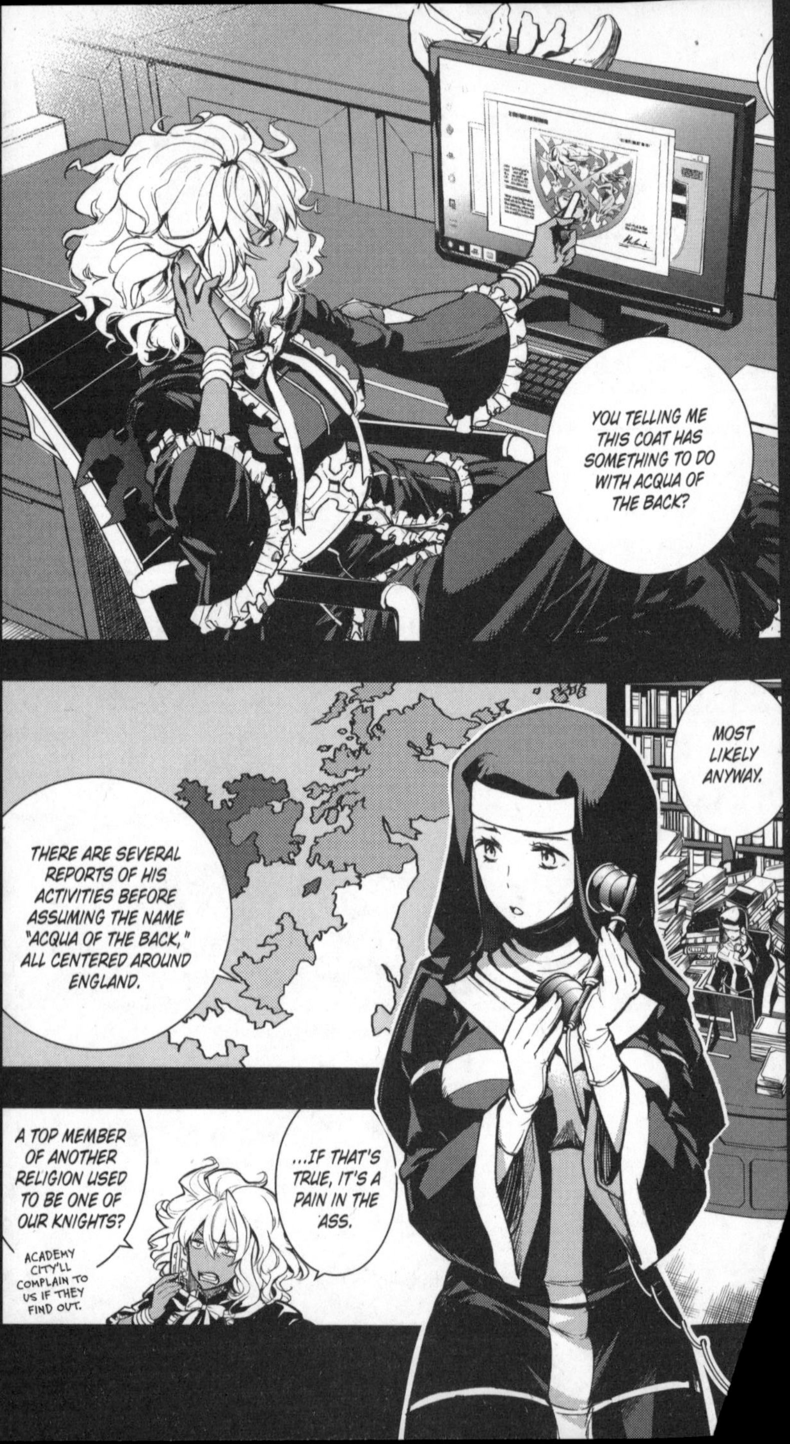
YOU TELLING ME THIS COAT HAS SOMETHING TO DO WITH ACQUA OF THE BACK?
MOST LIKELY ANYWAY.
THERE ARE SEVERAL REPORTS OF HIS ACTIVITIES BEFORE ASSUMING THE NAME "ACQUA OF THE BACK," ALL CENTERED AROUND ENGLAND.
...IF THAT'S TRUE, IT'S A PAIN IN THE ASS.
A TOP MEMBER OF ANOTHER RELIGION USED TO BE ONE OF OUR KNIGHTS?
ACADEMY CITY'LL COMPLAIN TO US IF THEY FIND OUT.

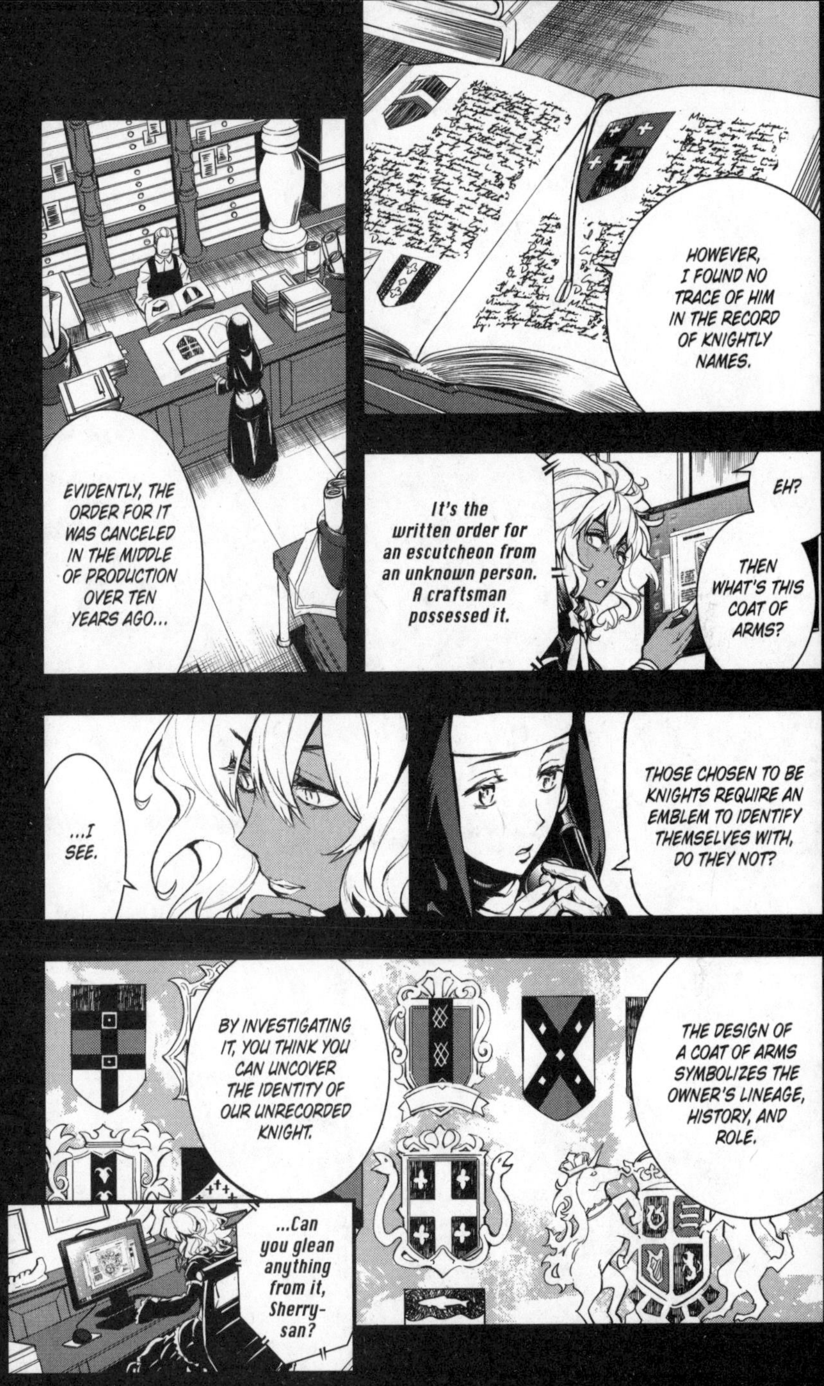
HOWEVER, I FOUND NO TRACE OF HIM IN THE RECORD OF KNIGHTLY NAMES.
EH?
THEN WHAT'S THIS COAT OF ARMS?
It's the written order for an escutcheon from an unknown person. A craftsman possessed it.
EVIDENTLY, THE ORDER FOR IT WAS CANCELED IN THE MIDDLE OF PRODUCTION OVER TEN YEARS AGO...
THOSE CHOSEN TO BE KNIGHTS REQUIRE AN EMBLEM TO IDENTIFY THEMSELVES WITH, DO THEY NOT?
...I SEE.
THE DESIGN OF A COAT OF ARMS SYMBOLIZES THE OWNER'S LINEAGE, HISTORY, AND ROLE.
BY INVESTIGATING IT, YOU THINK YOU CAN UNCOVER THE IDENTITY OF OUR UNRECORDED KNIGHT.
...Can you glean anything from it, Sherry-san?

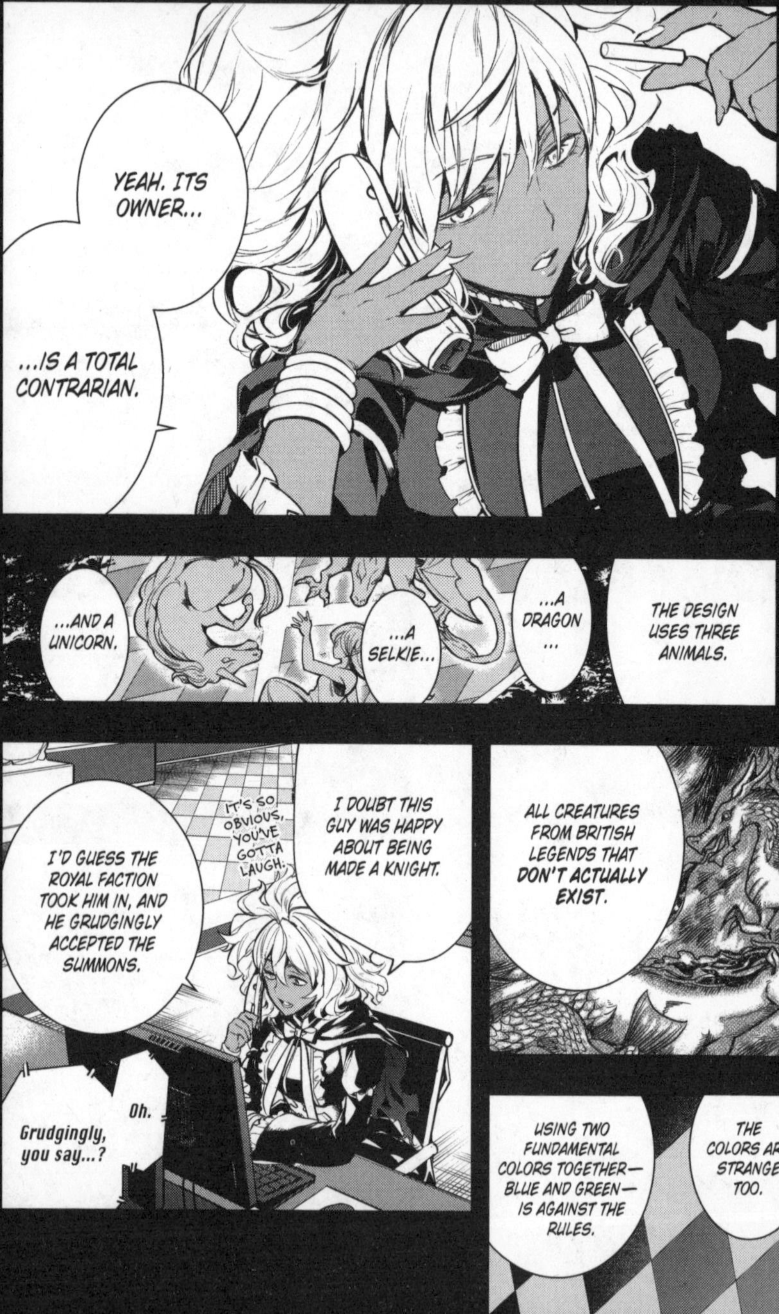
YEAH. ITS OWNER...
...IS A TOTAL CONTRARIAN.
THE DESIGN USES THREE ANIMALS.
...A DRAGON ...
...A SELKIE...
...AND A UNICORN.
ALL CREATURES FROM BRITISH LEGENDS THAT **DON'T ACTUALLY EXIST**.
THE COLORS ARE STRANGE TOO.
USING TWO FUNDAMENTAL COLORS TOGETHER—BLUE AND GREEN—IS AGAINST THE RULES.
I DOUBT THIS GUY WAS HAPPY ABOUT BEING MADE A KNIGHT.
IT'S SO OBVIOUS, YOU'VE GOTTA LAUGH.
I'D GUESS THE ROYAL FACTION TOOK HIM IN, AND HE GRUDGINGLY ACCEPTED THE SUMMONS.
Oh.
Grudgingly, you say...?

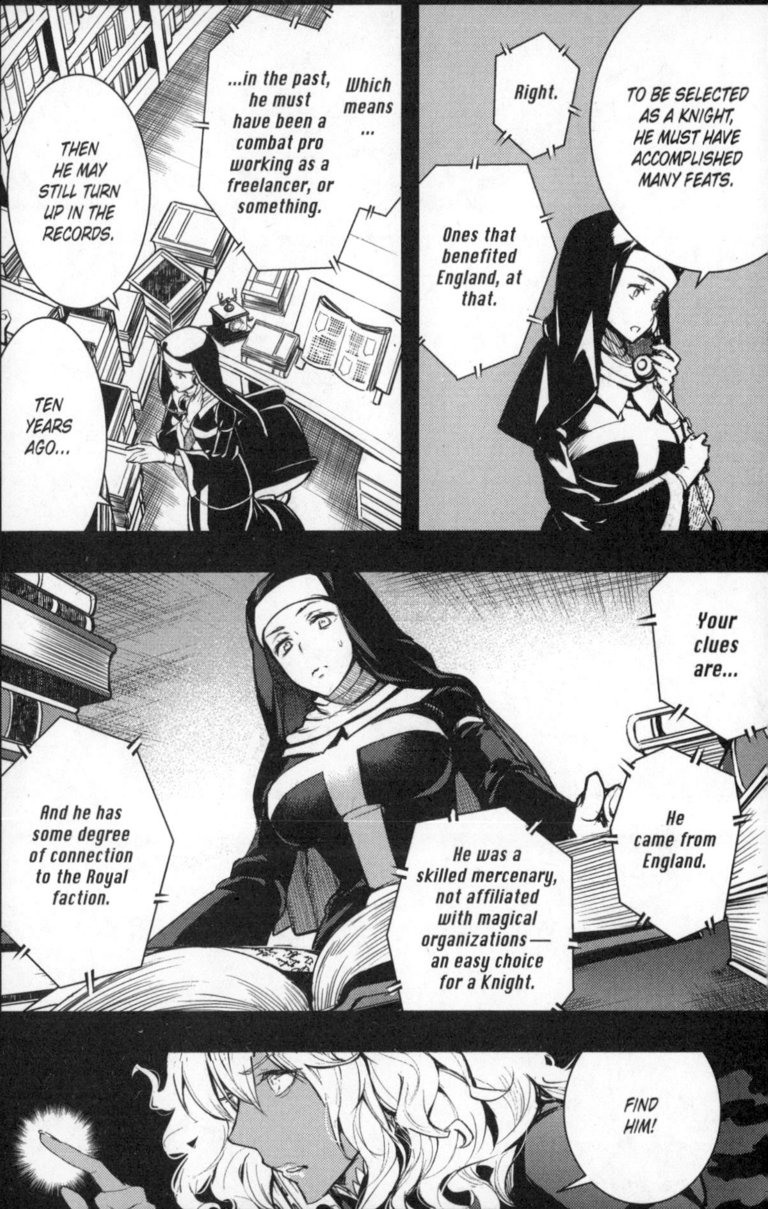
TO BE SELECTED AS A KNIGHT, HE MUST HAVE ACCOMPLISHED MANY FEATS.
Right.
Ones that benefited England, at that.
Which means ...
...in the past, he must have been a combat pro working as a freelancer, or something.
THEN HE MAY STILL TURN UP IN THE RECORDS.
TEN YEARS AGO...
Your clues are...
He came from England.
He was a skilled mercenary, not affiliated with magical organizations—an easy choice for a Knight.
And he has some degree of connection to the Royal faction.
FIND HIM!

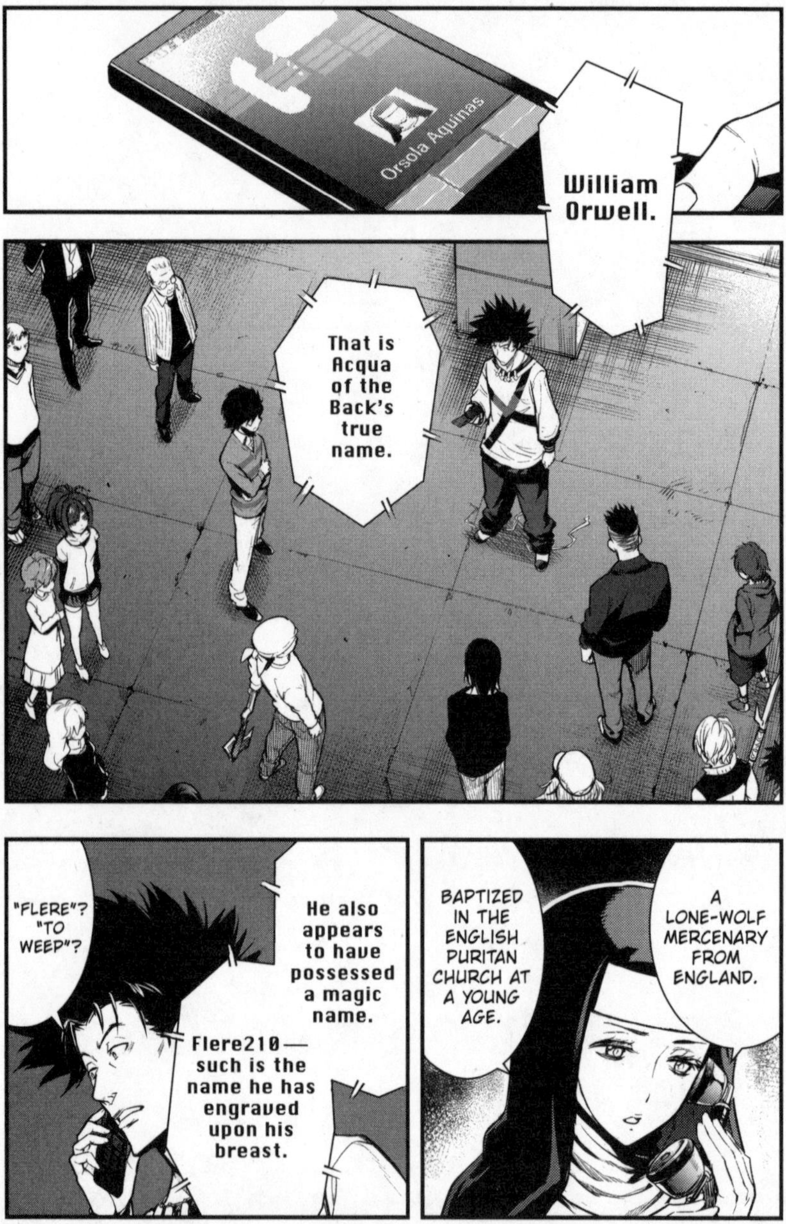
Orsola Aquinas
William Orwell.
That is Acqua of the Back's true name.
A LONE-WOLF MERCENARY FROM ENGLAND.
BAPTIZED IN THE ENGLISH PURITAN CHURCH AT A YOUNG AGE.
He also appears to have possessed a magic name.
Flere210— such is the name he has engraved upon his breast.
"FLERE"? "TO WEEP"?

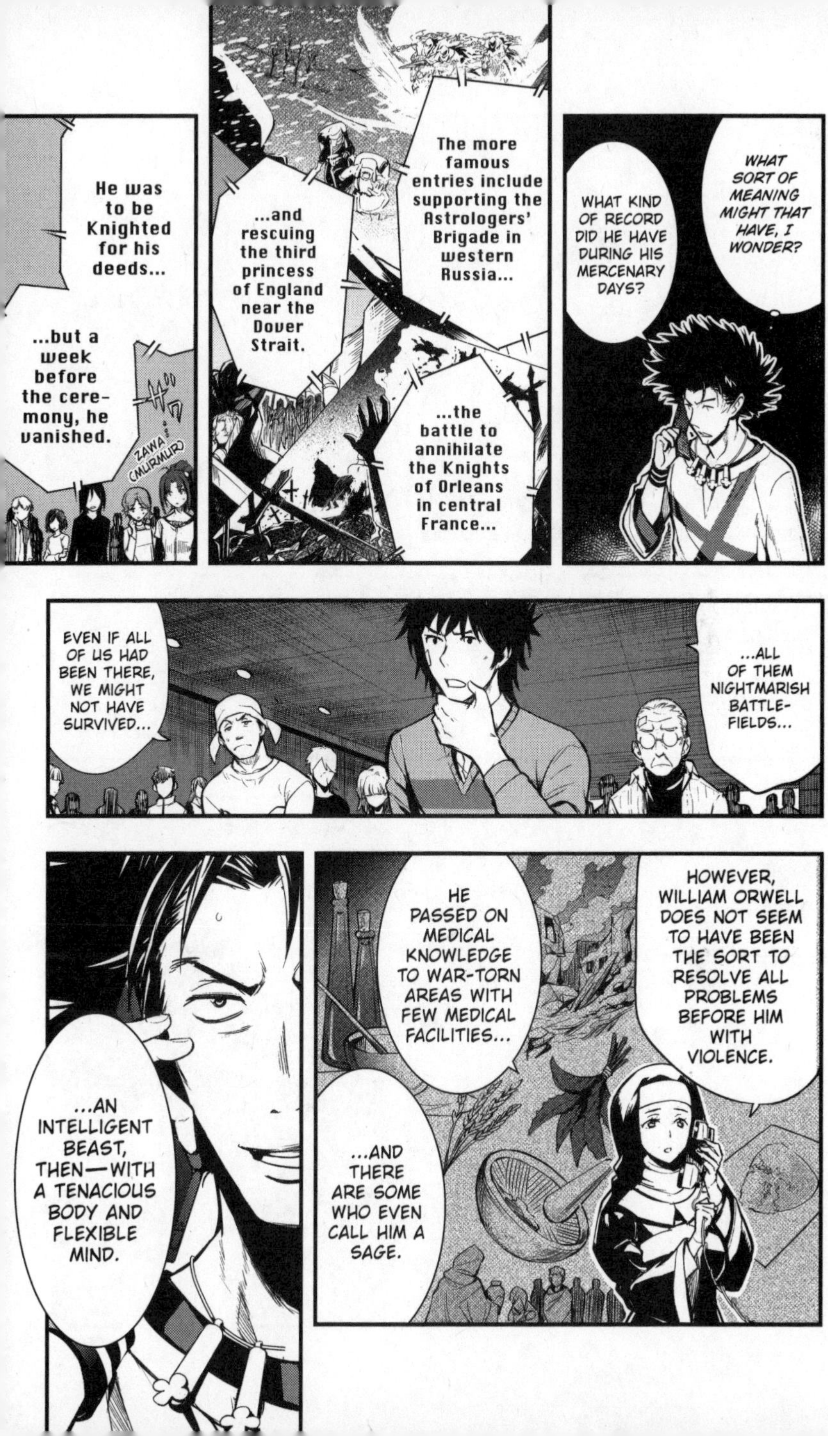
WHAT SORT OF MEANING MIGHT THAT HAVE, I WONDER?
WHAT KIND OF RECORD DID HE HAVE DURING HIS MERCENARY DAYS?
The more famous entries include supporting the Astrologers' Brigade in western Russia...
...and rescuing the third princess of England near the Dover Strait.
...the battle to annihilate the Knights of Orleans in central France...
He was to be Knighted for his deeds...
...but a week before the ceremony, he vanished.
ZAWA (MURMUR)
...ALL OF THEM NIGHTMARISH BATTLE-FIELDS...
EVEN IF ALL OF US HAD BEEN THERE, WE MIGHT NOT HAVE SURVIVED...
HOWEVER, WILLIAM ORWELL DOES NOT SEEM TO HAVE BEEN THE SORT TO RESOLVE ALL PROBLEMS BEFORE HIM WITH VIOLENCE.
HE PASSED ON MEDICAL KNOWLEDGE TO WAR-TORN AREAS WITH FEW MEDICAL FACILITIES...
...AND THERE ARE SOME WHO EVEN CALL HIM A SAGE.
...AN INTELLIGENT BEAST, THEN—WITH A TENACIOUS BODY AND FLEXIBLE MIND.

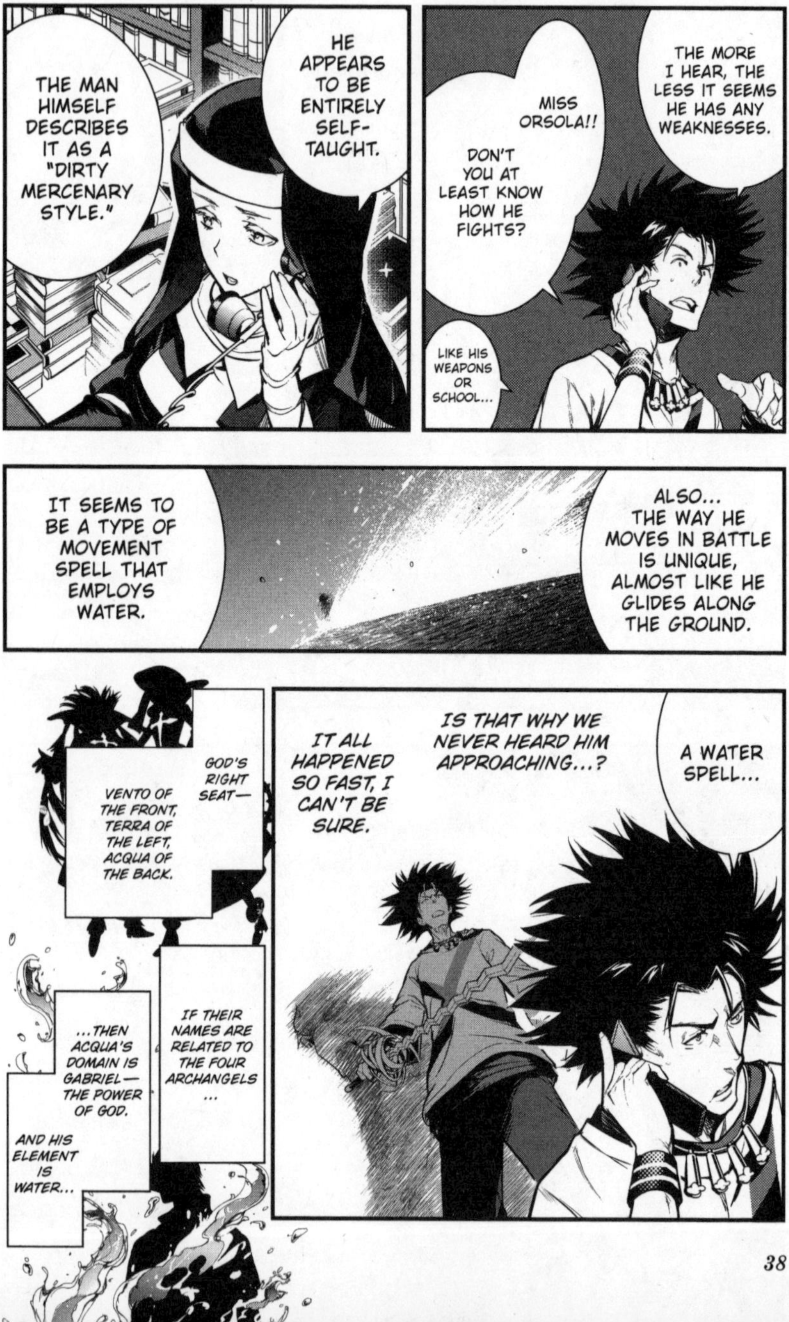
THE MORE I HEAR, THE LESS IT SEEMS HE HAS ANY WEAKNESSES.
MISS ORSOLA!!
DON'T YOU AT LEAST KNOW HOW HE FIGHTS?
LIKE HIS WEAPONS OR SCHOOL...
HE APPEARS TO BE ENTIRELY SELF-TAUGHT.
THE MAN HIMSELF DESCRIBES IT AS A "DIRTY MERCENARY STYLE."
ALSO... THE WAY HE MOVES IN BATTLE IS UNIQUE, ALMOST LIKE HE GLIDES ALONG THE GROUND.
IT SEEMS TO BE A TYPE OF MOVEMENT SPELL THAT EMPLOYS WATER.
A WATER SPELL...
IS THAT WHY WE NEVER HEARD HIM APPROACHING...?
IT ALL HAPPENED SO FAST, I CAN'T BE SURE.
GOD'S RIGHT SEAT—
VENTO OF THE FRONT, TERRA OF THE LEFT, ACQUA OF THE BACK.
IF THEIR NAMES ARE RELATED TO THE FOUR ARCHANGELS...
...THEN ACQUA'S DOMAIN IS GABRIEL—THE POWER OF GOD.
AND HIS ELEMENT IS WATER...

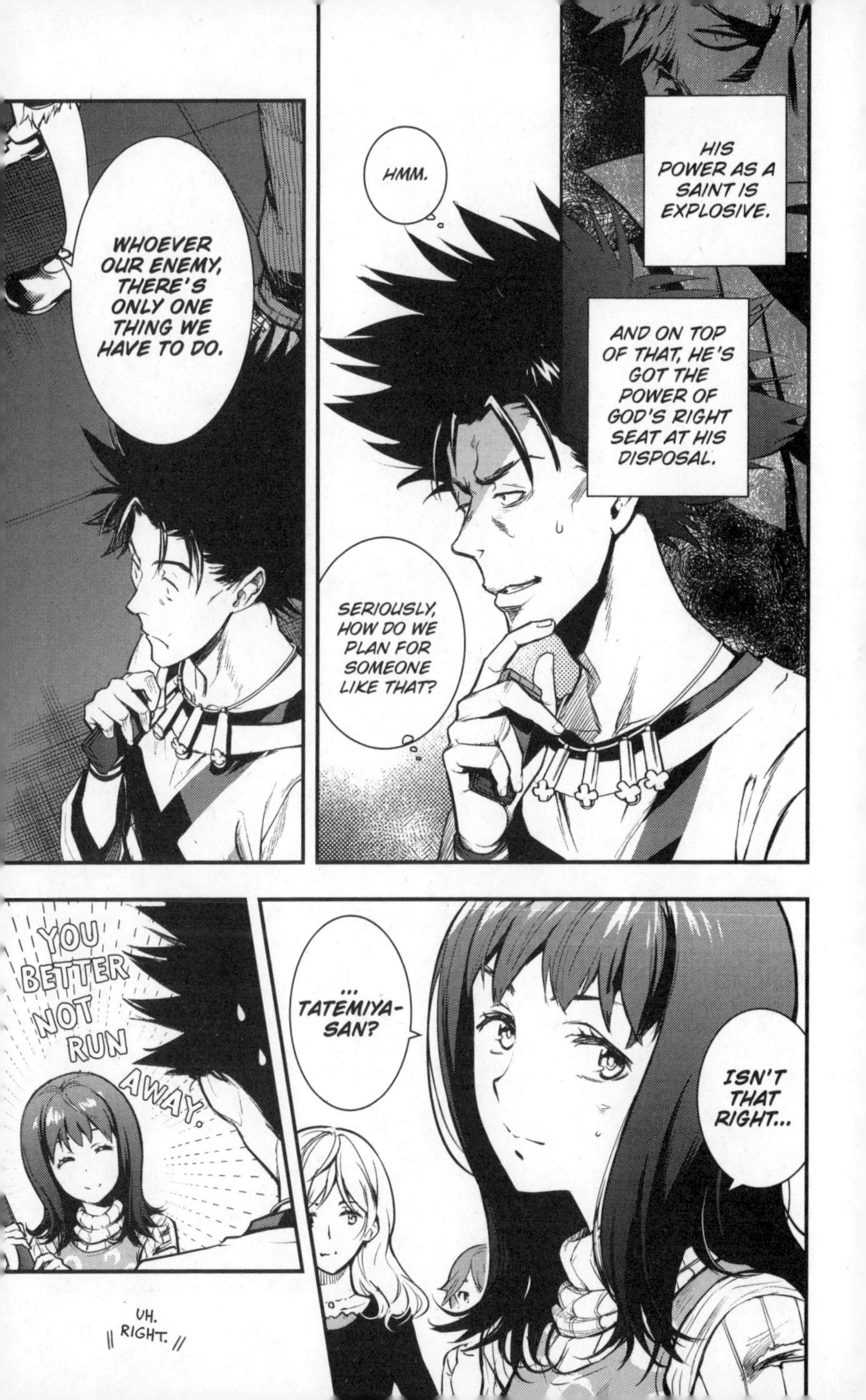
HIS POWER AS A SAINT IS EXPLOSIVE.
AND ON TOP OF THAT, HE'S GOT THE POWER OF GOD'S RIGHT SEAT AT HIS DISPOSAL.
HMM.
SERIOUSLY, HOW DO WE PLAN FOR SOMEONE LIKE THAT?
WHOEVER OUR ENEMY, THERE'S ONLY ONE THING WE HAVE TO DO.
ISN'T THAT RIGHT...
...TATEMIYA-SAN?
YOU BETTER NOT RUN AWAY.
UH. RIGHT.

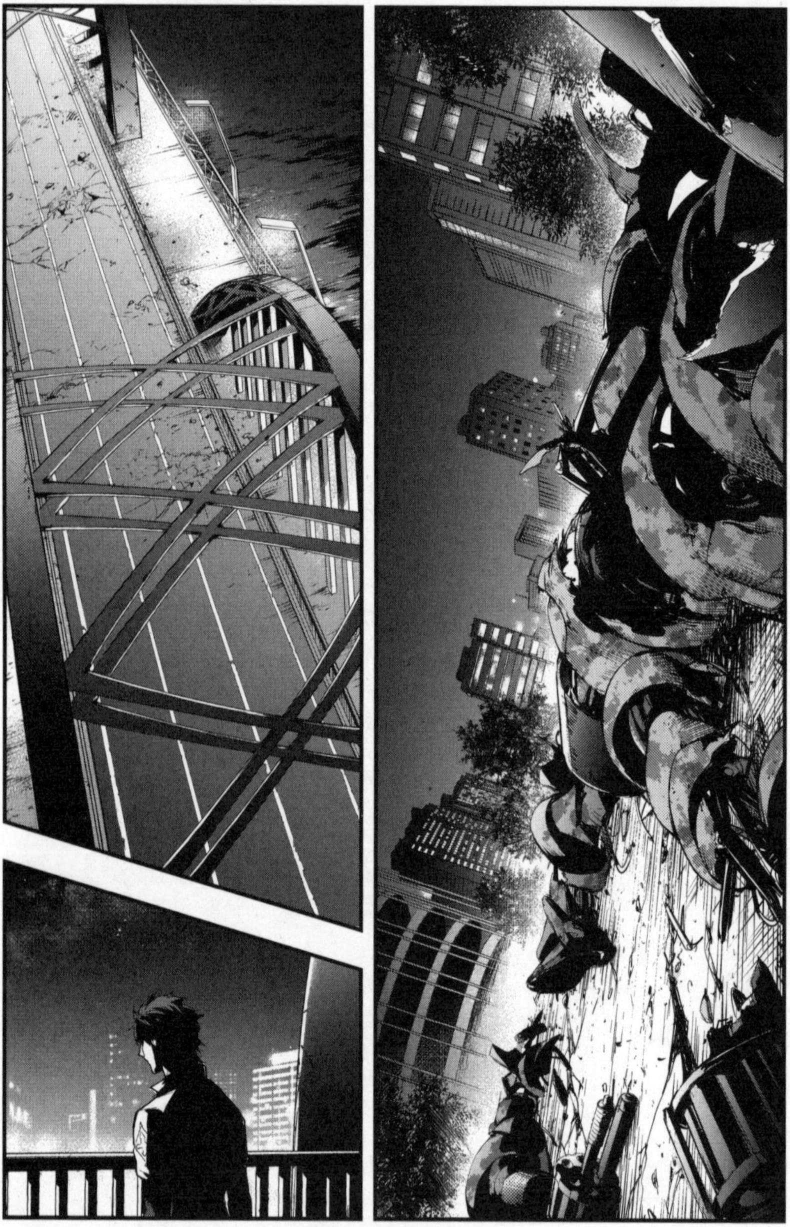

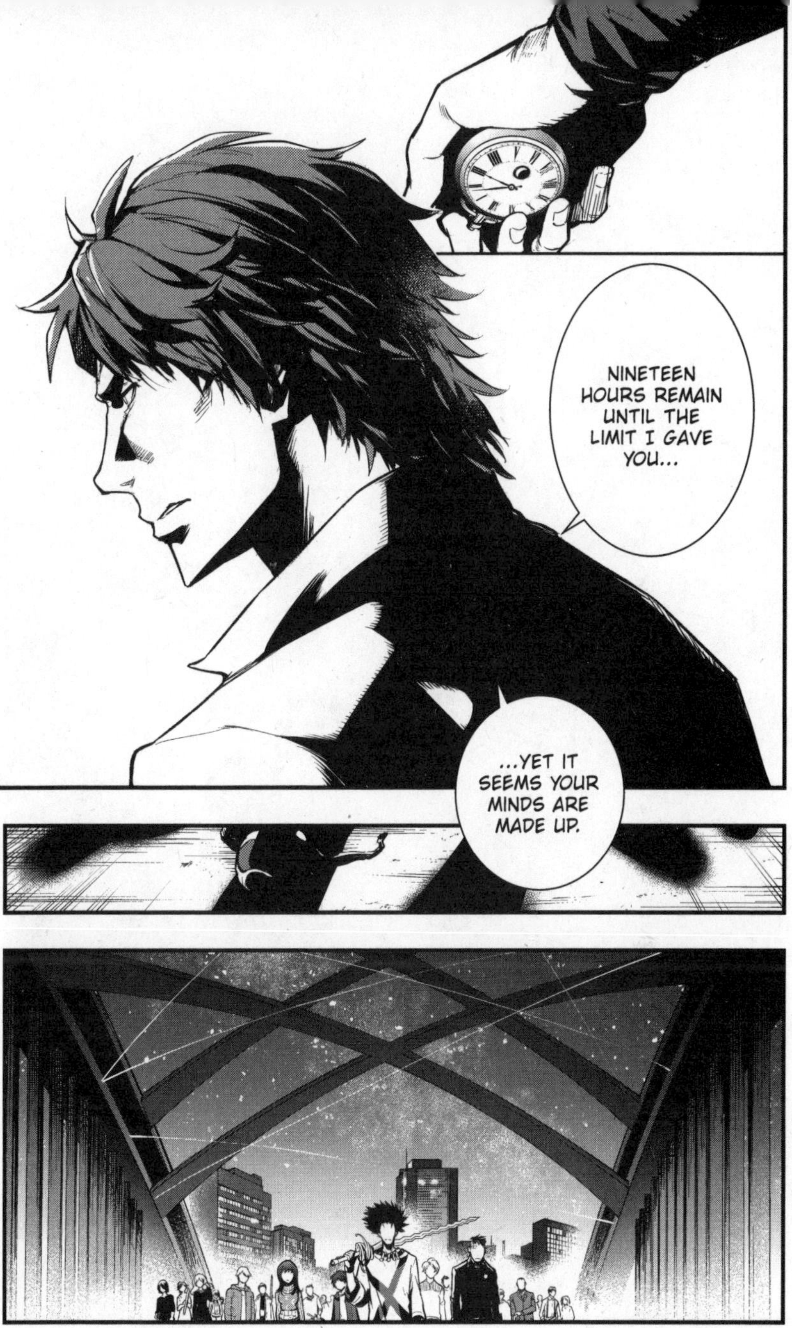
NINETEEN HOURS REMAIN UNTIL THE LIMIT I GAVE YOU...
...YET IT SEEMS YOUR MINDS ARE MADE UP.

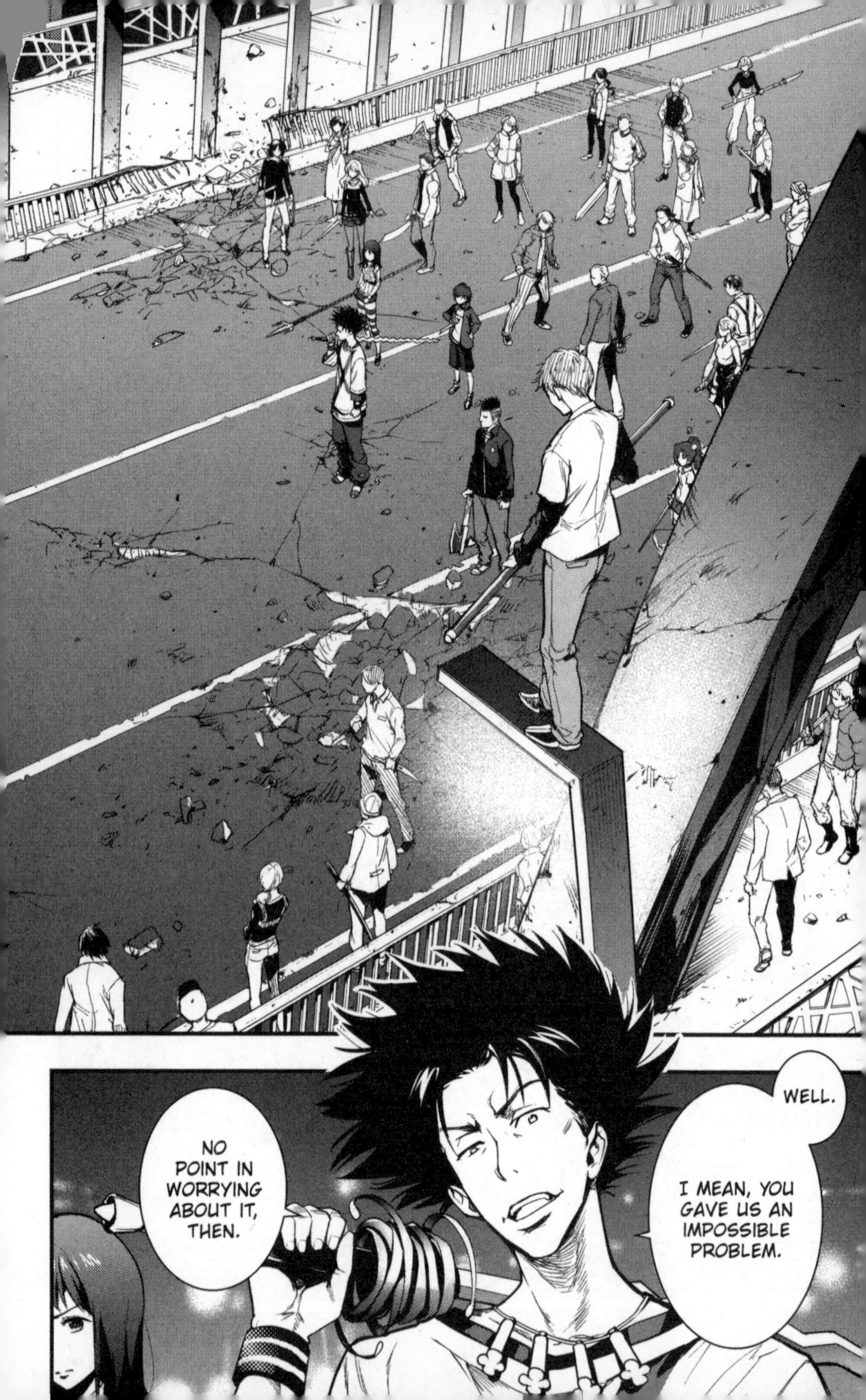
WELL.
I MEAN, YOU GAVE US AN IMPOSSIBLE PROBLEM.
NO POINT IN WORRYING ABOUT IT, THEN.

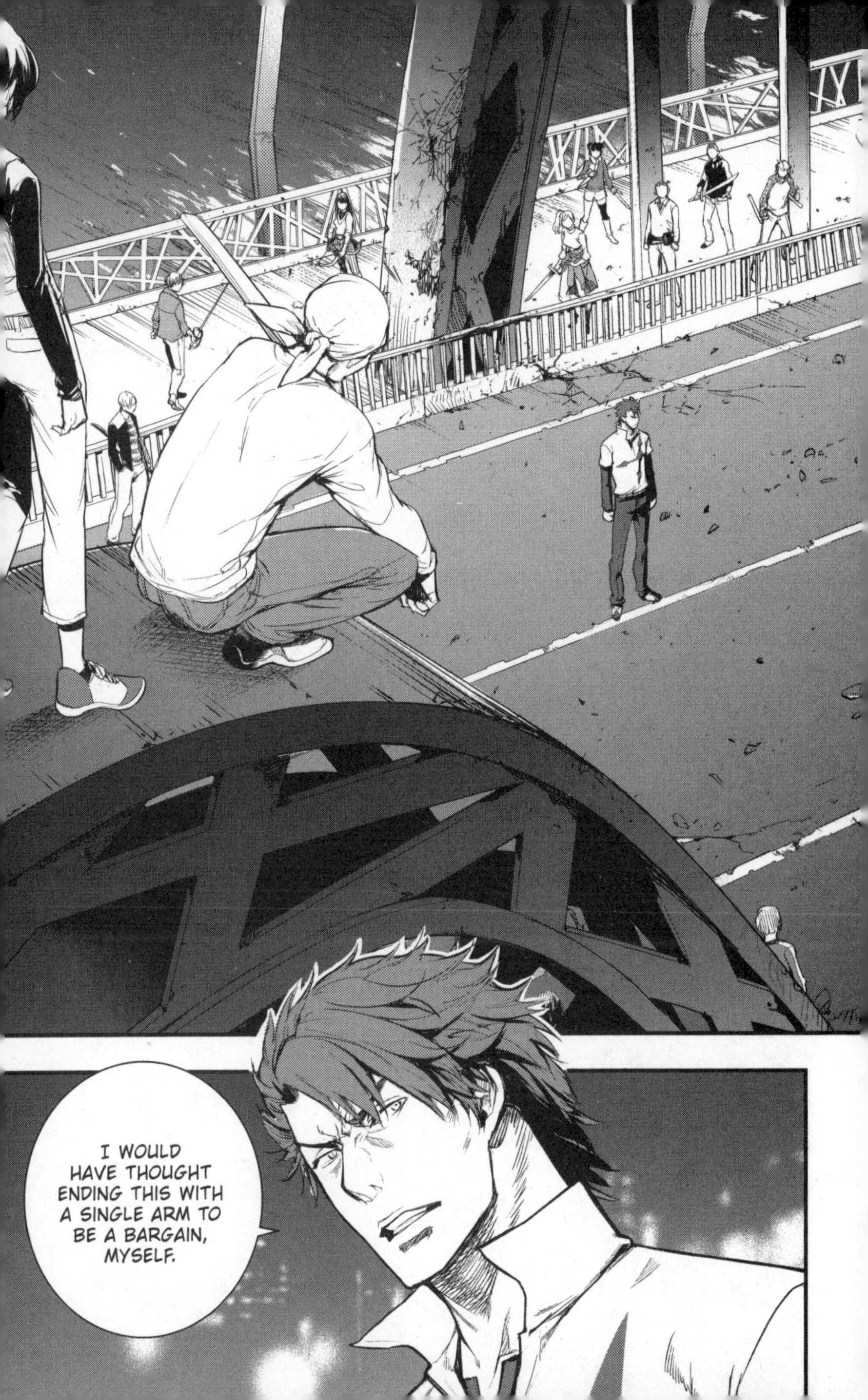
I WOULD HAVE THOUGHT ENDING THIS WITH A SINGLE ARM TO BE A BARGAIN, MYSELF.

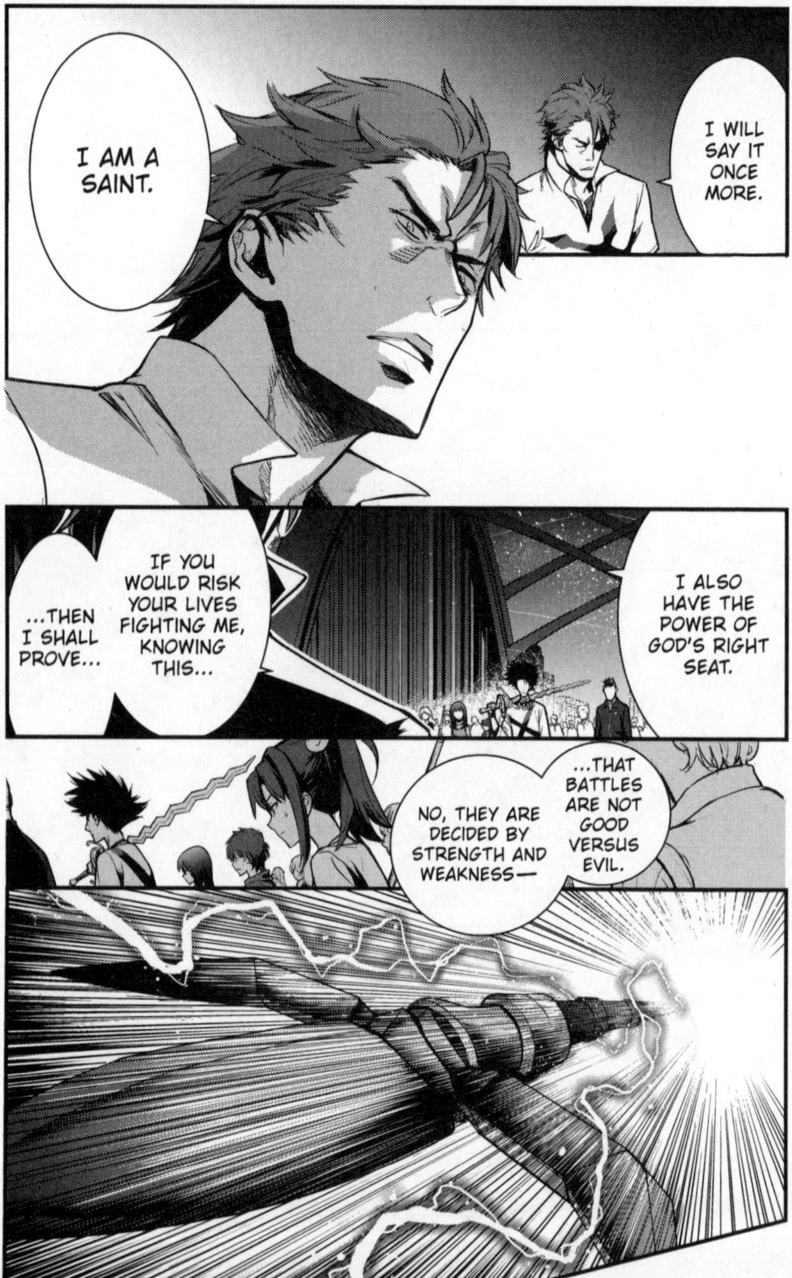
I WILL SAY IT ONCE MORE.
I AM A SAINT.
I ALSO HAVE THE POWER OF GOD'S RIGHT SEAT.
IF YOU WOULD RISK YOUR LIVES FIGHTING ME, KNOWING THIS...
...THEN I SHALL PROVE...
...THAT BATTLES ARE NOT GOOD VERSUS EVIL.
NO, THEY ARE DECIDED BY STRENGTH AND WEAKNESS—

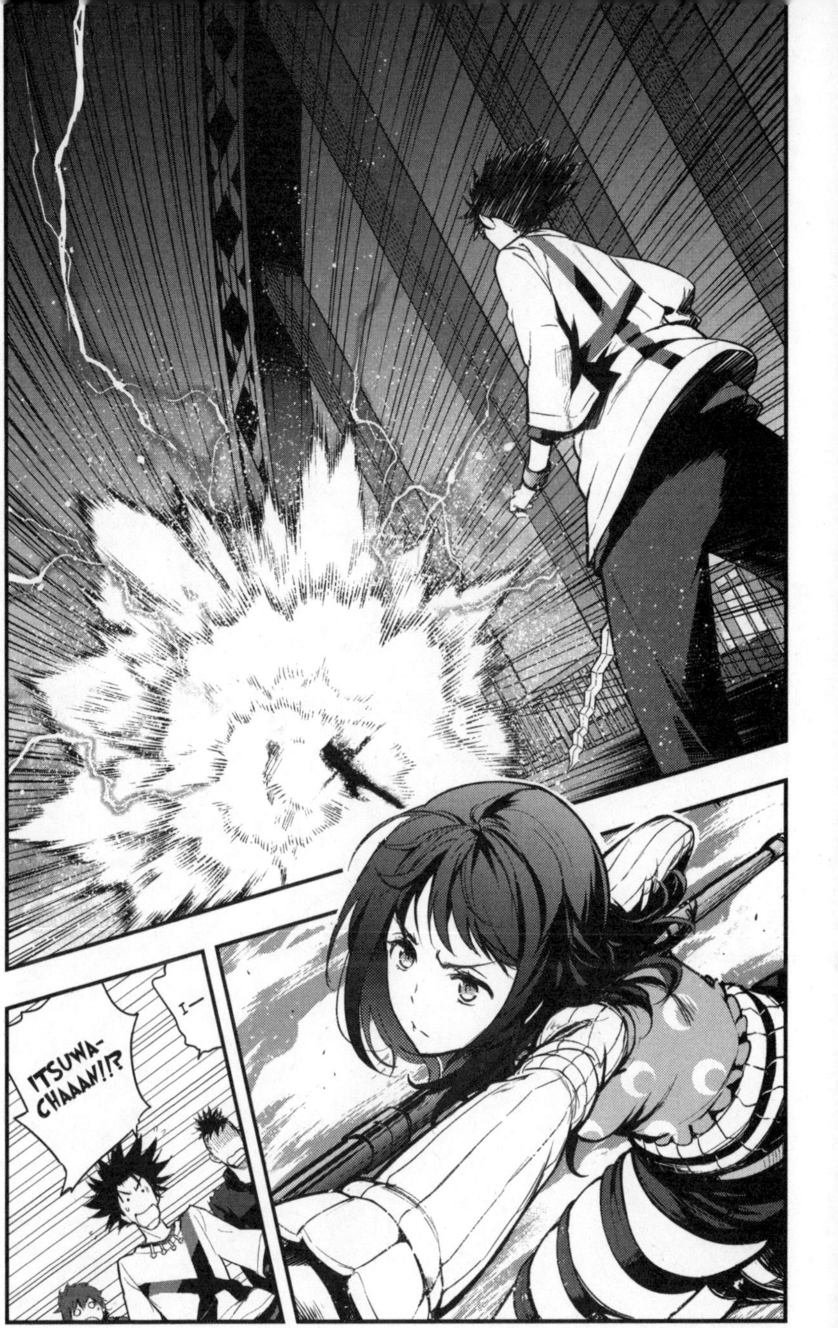
I—
ITSUWA-CHAAAN!!?

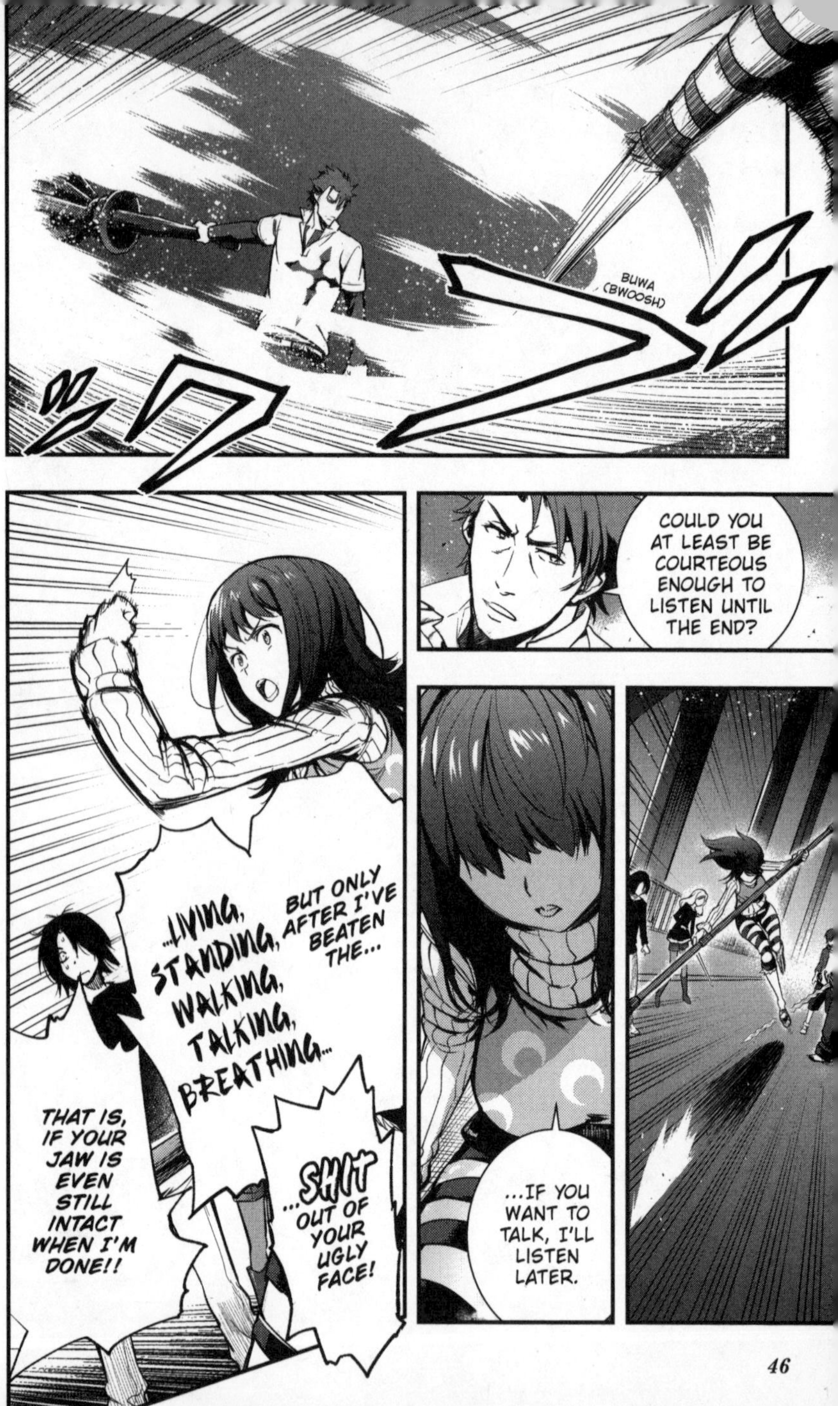
BUWA
(BWOOSH)
COULD YOU AT LEAST BE COURTEOUS ENOUGH TO LISTEN UNTIL THE END?
...IF YOU WANT TO TALK, I'LL LISTEN LATER.
BUT ONLY AFTER I'VE BEATEN THE...
...LIVING, STANDING, WALKING, TALKING, BREATHING...
...SHIT OUT OF YOUR UGLY FACE!
THAT IS, IF YOUR JAW IS EVEN STILL INTACT WHEN I'M DONE!!

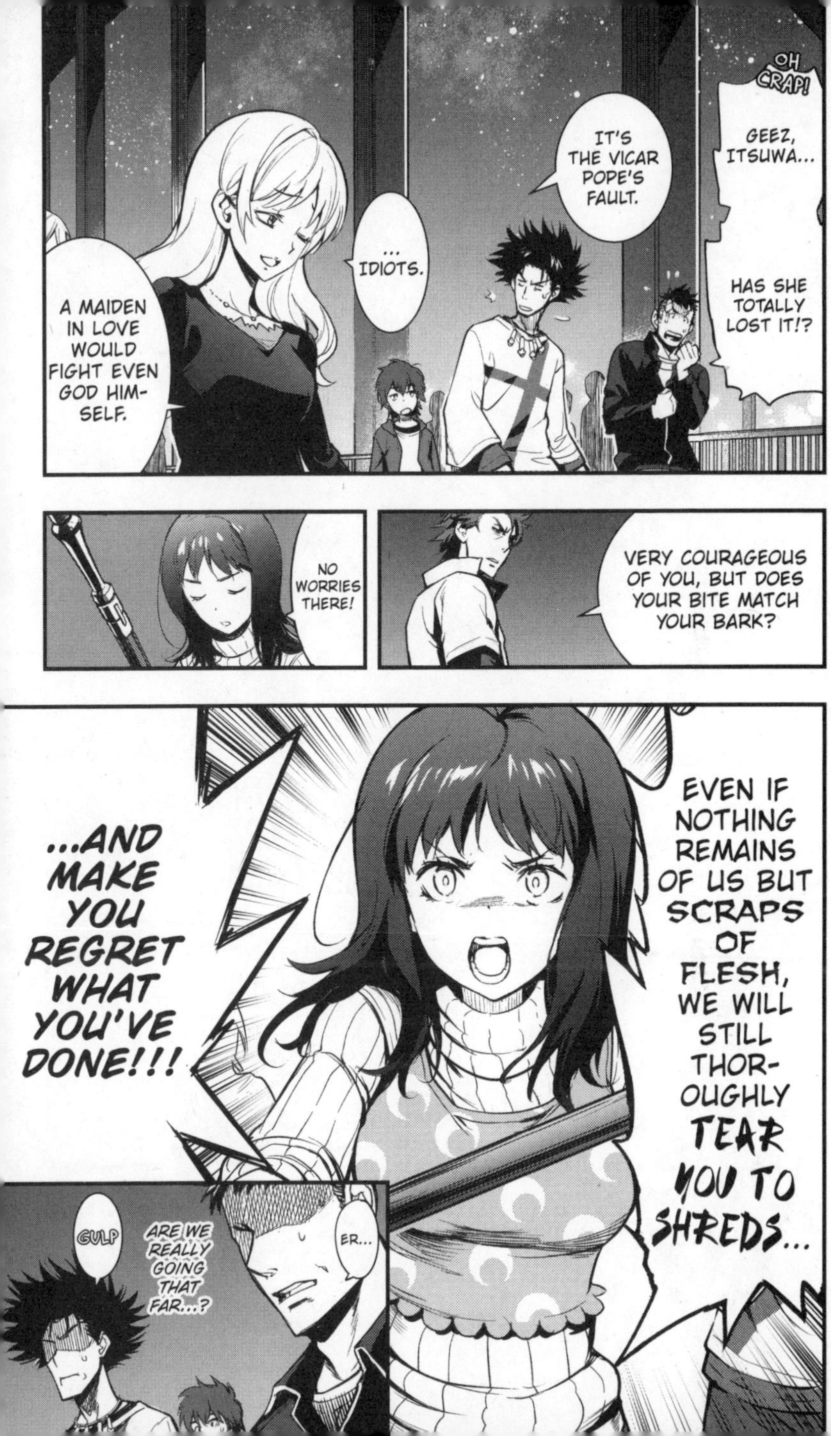
OH CRAP!
GEEZ, ITSUWA...
HAS SHE TOTALLY LOST IT!?
IT'S THE VICAR POPE'S FAULT.
... IDIOTS.
A MAIDEN IN LOVE WOULD FIGHT EVEN GOD HIMSELF.
VERY COURAGEOUS OF YOU, BUT DOES YOUR BITE MATCH YOUR BARK?
NO WORRIES THERE!
EVEN IF NOTHING REMAINS OF US BUT SCRAPS OF FLESH, WE WILL STILL THOROUGHLY TEAR YOU TO SHREDS...
...AND MAKE YOU REGRET WHAT YOU'VE DONE!!!
ER...
ARE WE REALLY GOING THAT FAR...?
GULP

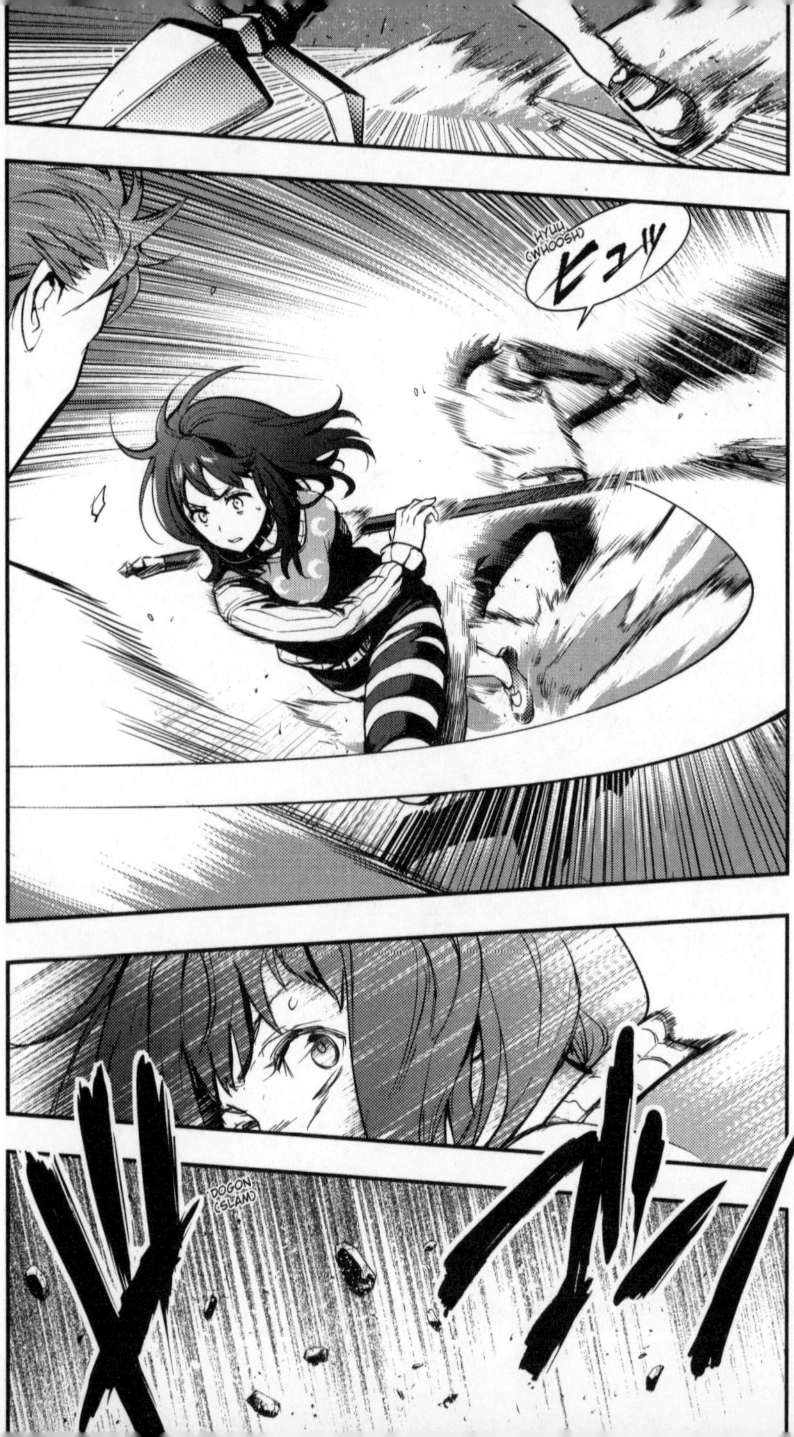
ヒュッ
HYUU (WHOOSH)
ドゴッ
DOGON (SLAM)

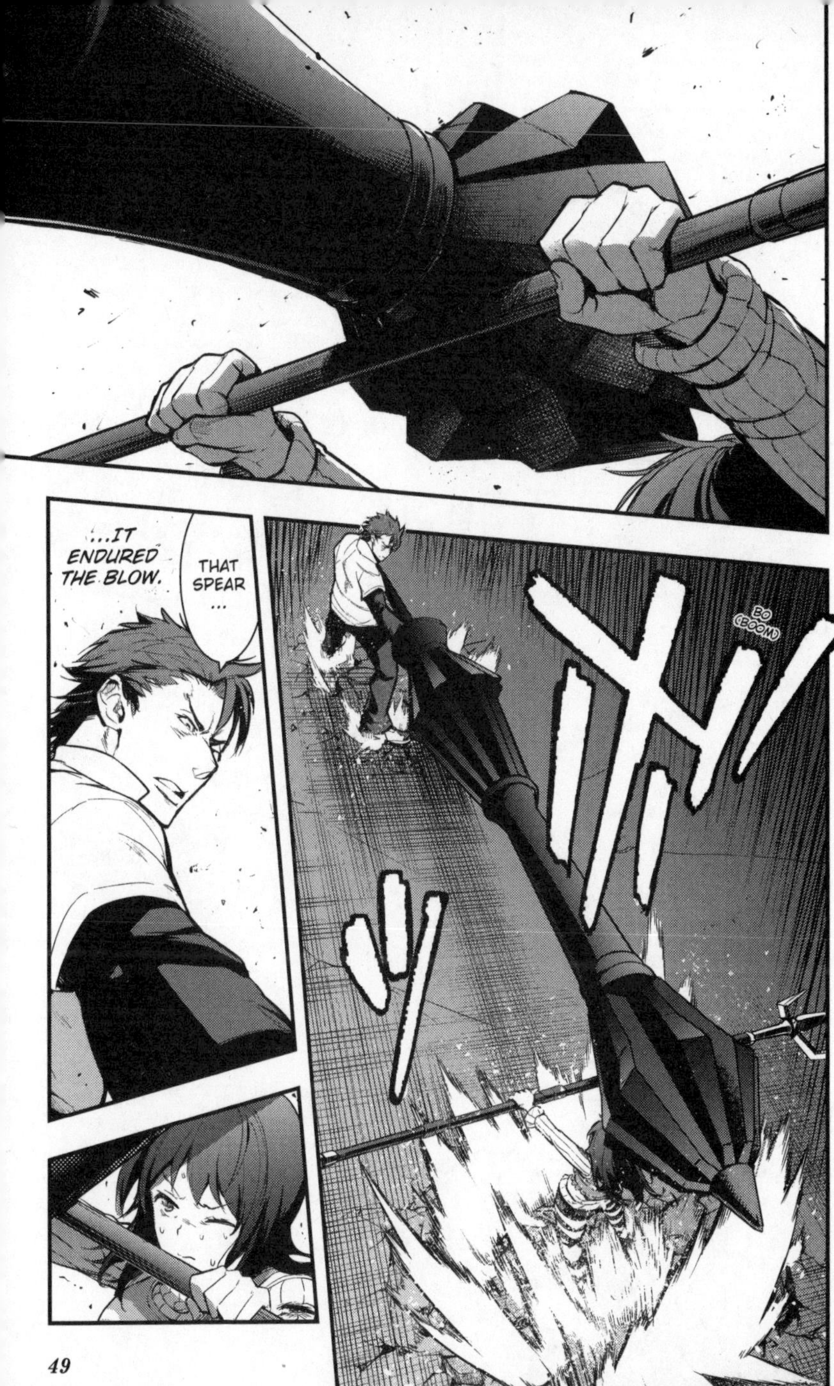
BO (BOOM)
THAT SPEAR ...
...IT ENDURED THE BLOW.

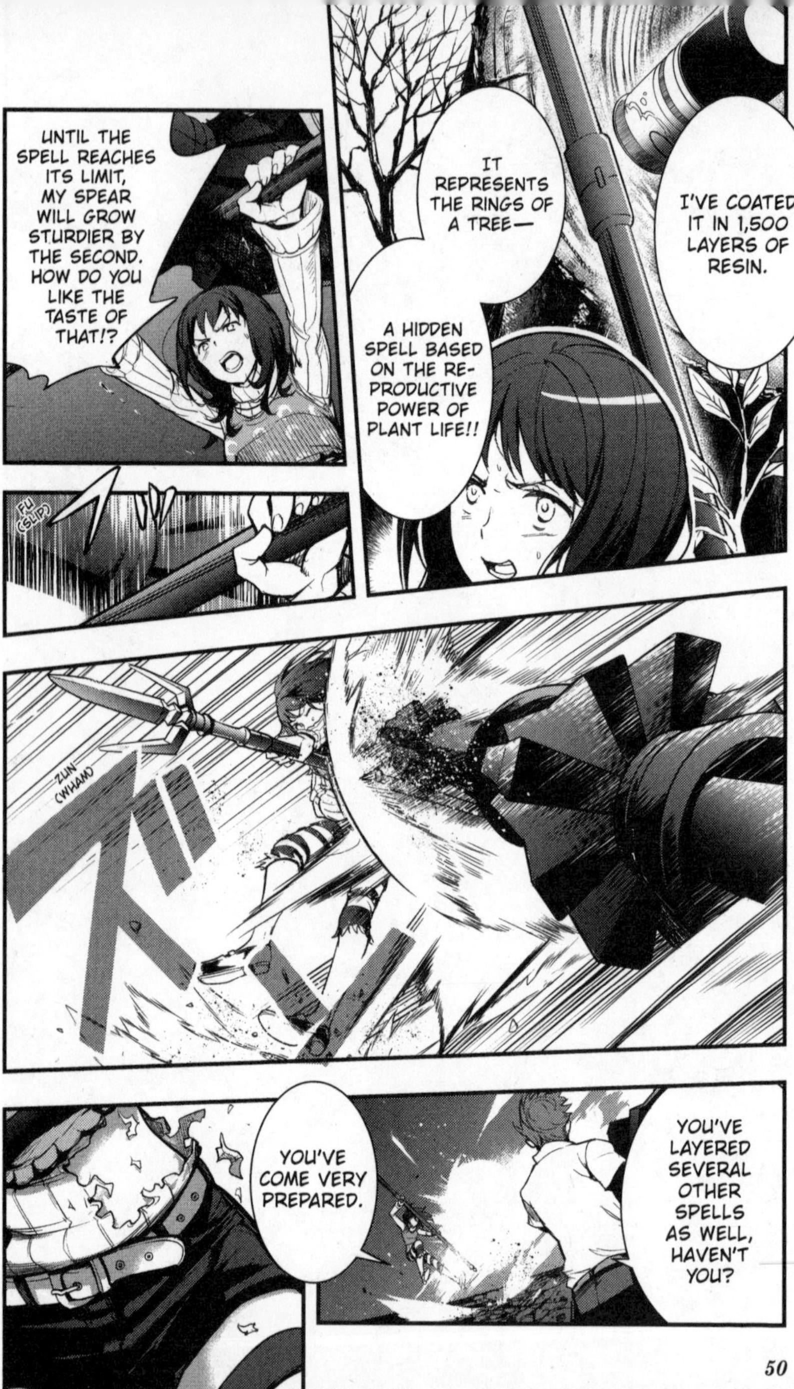
I'VE COATED IT IN 1,500 LAYERS OF RESIN.
IT REPRESENTS THE RINGS OF A TREE—
A HIDDEN SPELL BASED ON THE RE-PRODUCTIVE POWER OF PLANT LIFE!!
UNTIL THE SPELL REACHES ITS LIMIT, MY SPEAR WILL GROW STURDIER BY THE SECOND. HOW DO YOU LIKE THE TASTE OF THAT!?
FU (SLIP)
ZUN (WHAM)
YOU'VE LAYERED SEVERAL OTHER SPELLS AS WELL, HAVEN'T YOU?
YOU'VE COME VERY PREPARED.

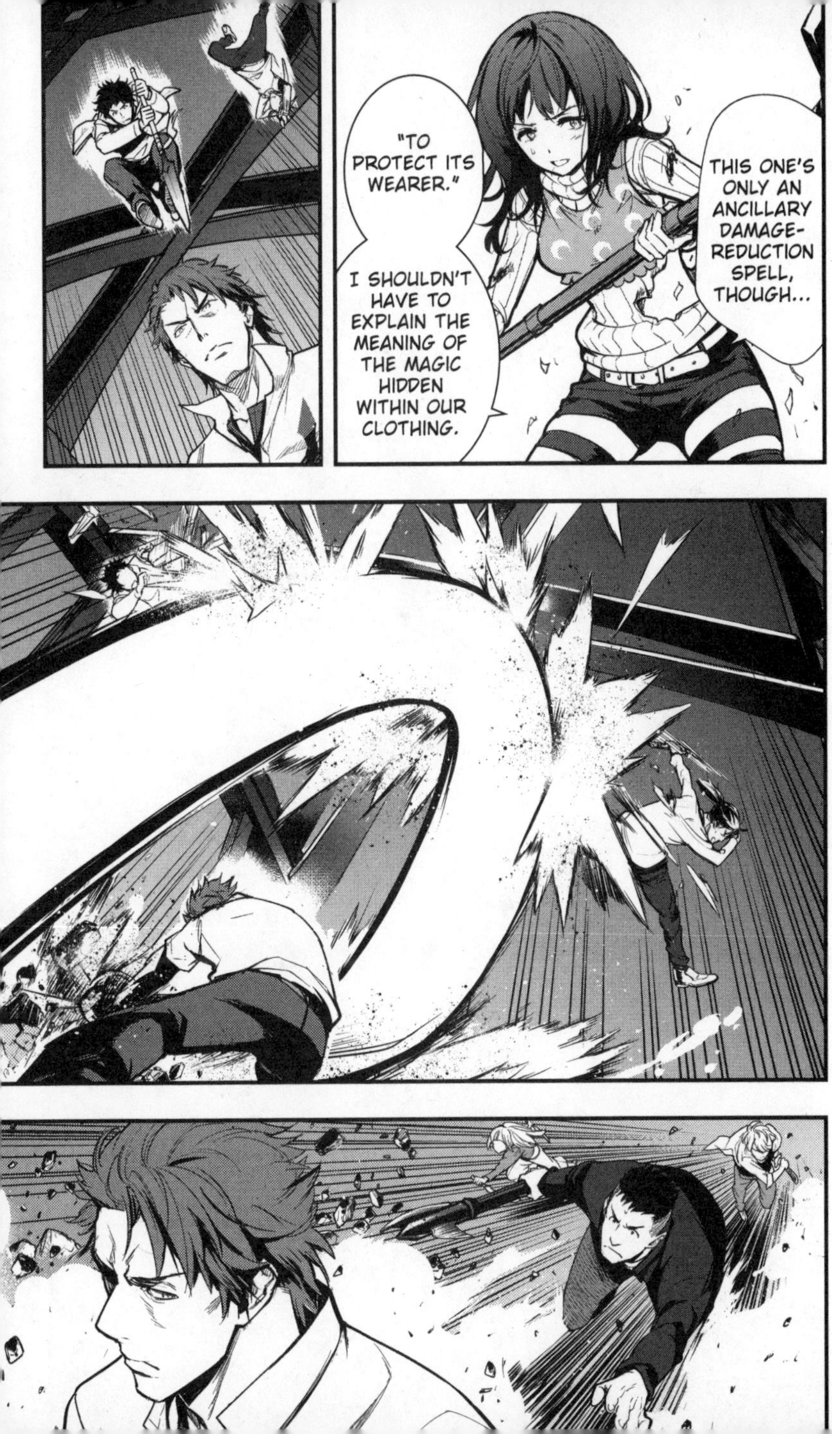
THIS ONE'S ONLY AN ANCILLARY DAMAGE-REDUCTION SPELL, THOUGH...
"TO PROTECT ITS WEARER."
I SHOULDN'T HAVE TO EXPLAIN THE MEANING OF THE MAGIC HIDDEN WITHIN OUR CLOTHING.

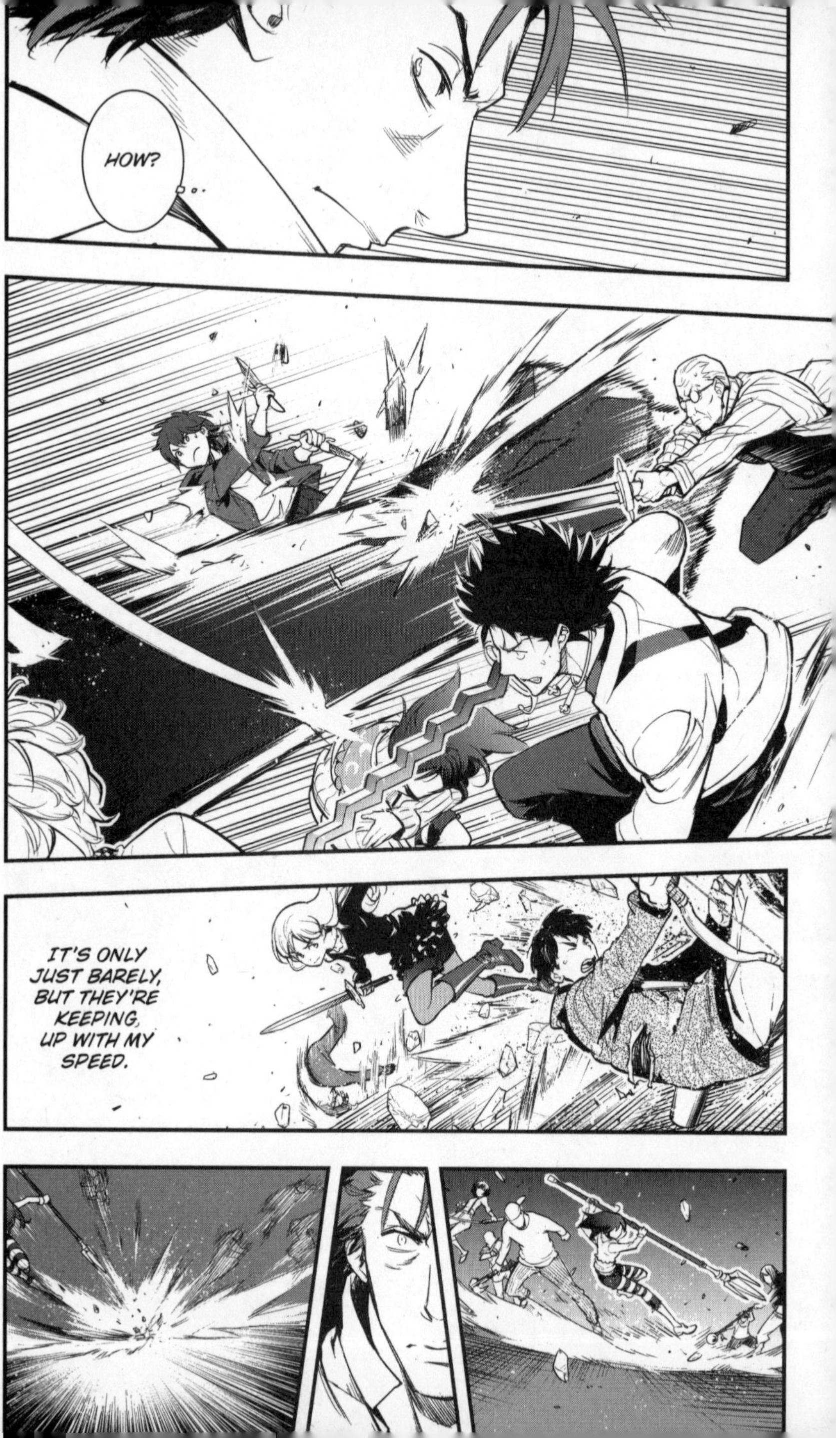
HOW?
IT'S ONLY JUST BARELY, BUT THEY'RE KEEPING UP WITH MY SPEED.

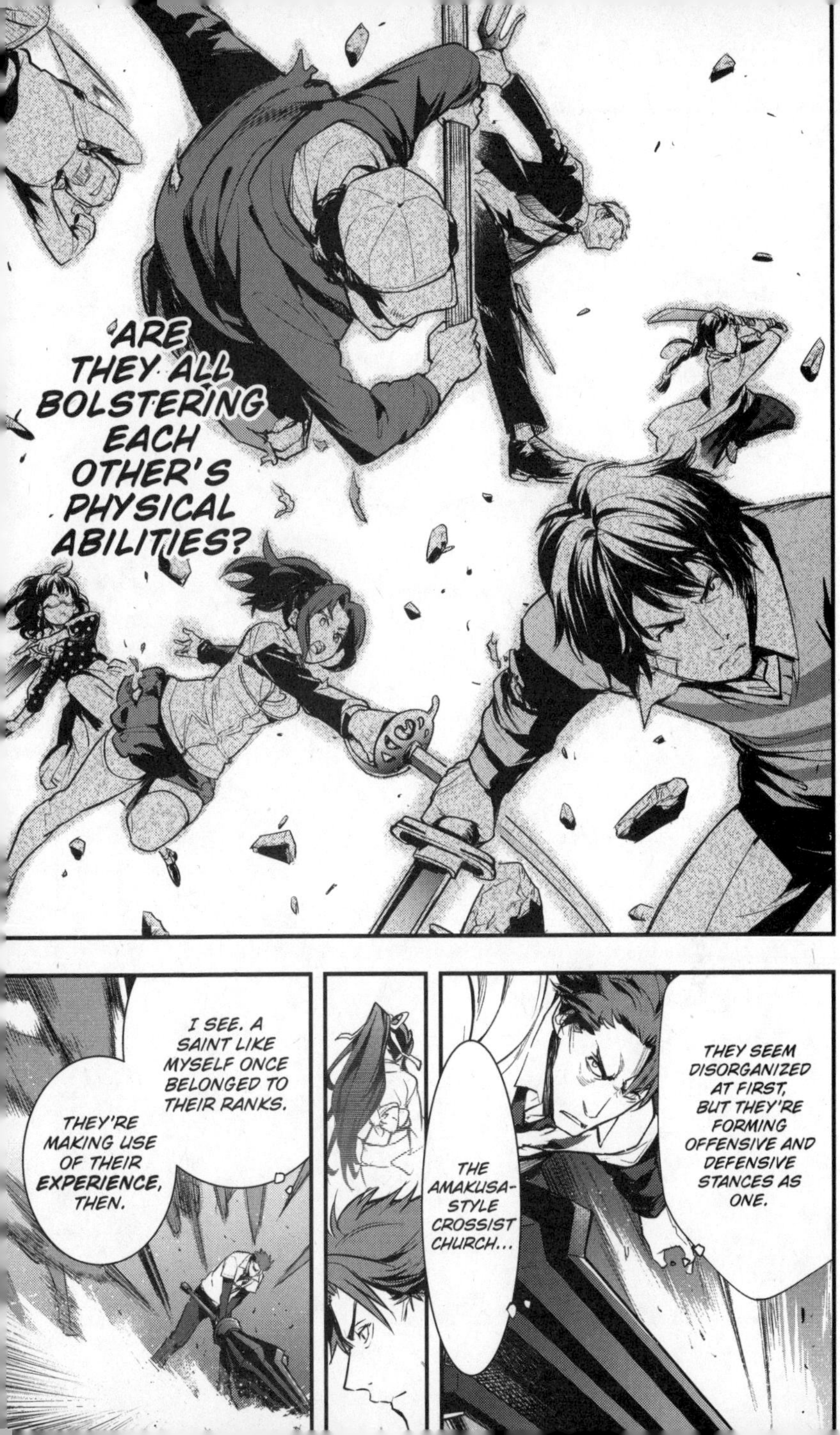
ARE THEY ALL BOLSTERING EACH OTHER'S PHYSICAL ABILITIES?
THEY SEEM DISORGANIZED AT FIRST, BUT THEY'RE FORMING OFFENSIVE AND DEFENSIVE STANCES AS ONE.
THE AMAKUSA-STYLE CROSSIST CHURCH...
I SEE. A SAINT LIKE MYSELF ONCE BELONGED TO THEIR RANKS.
THEY'RE MAKING USE OF THEIR EXPERIENCE, THEN.

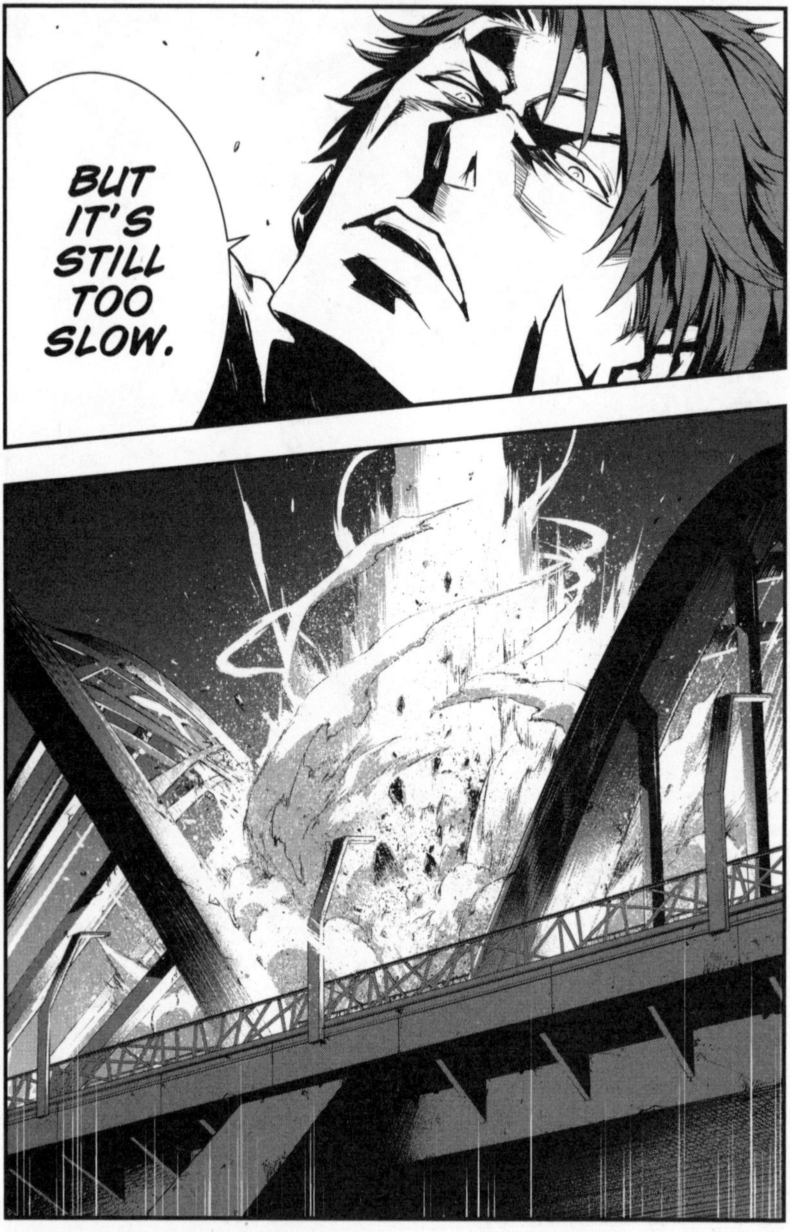
BUT IT'S STILL TOO SLOW.

A Certain Magical Index

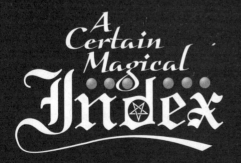

A Certain Magical Index

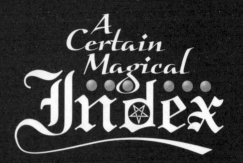

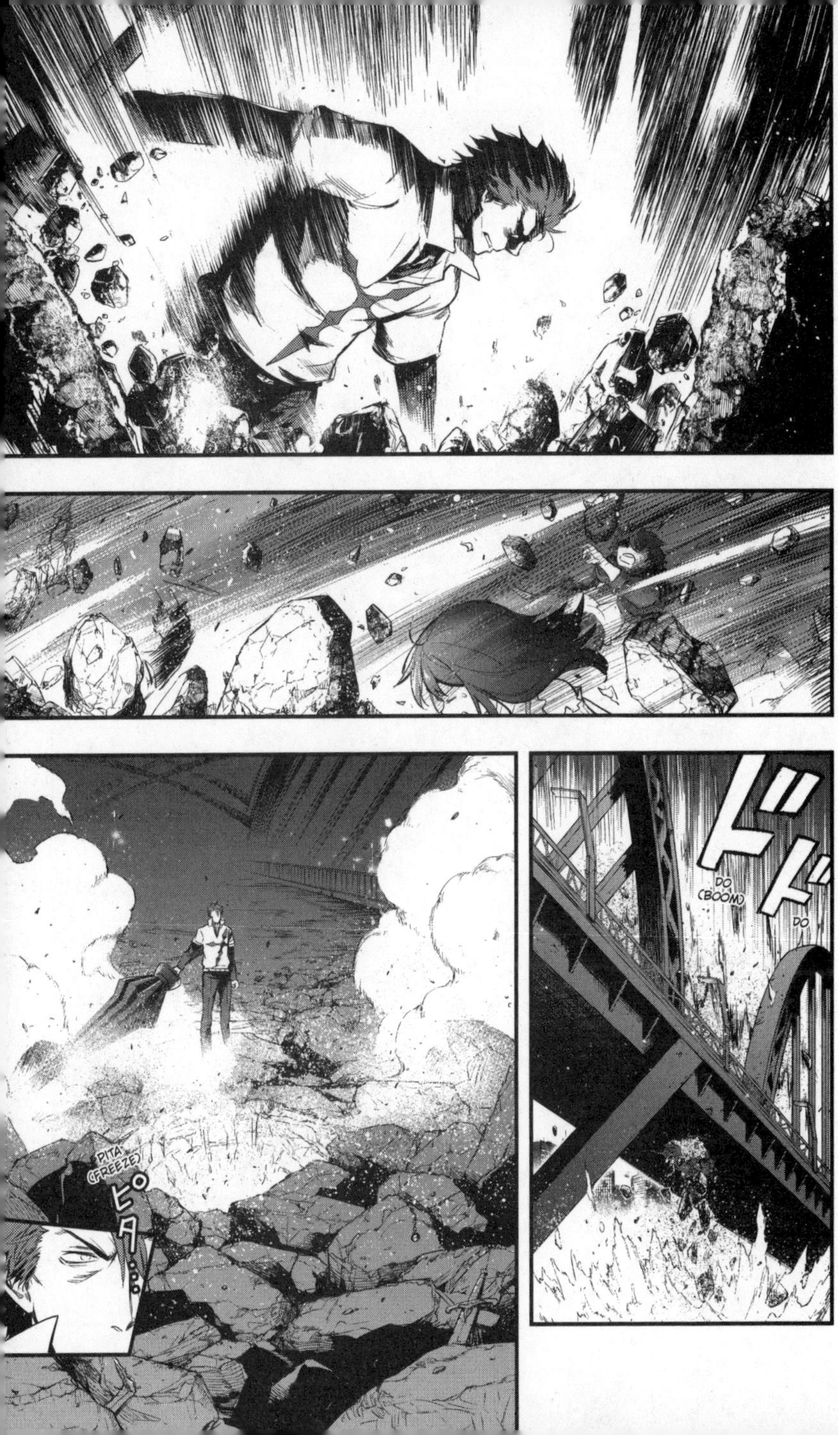
ドド
DO (BOOM)
DO
ピタ
PITA (FREEZE)

#157 ADORATION OF MARY

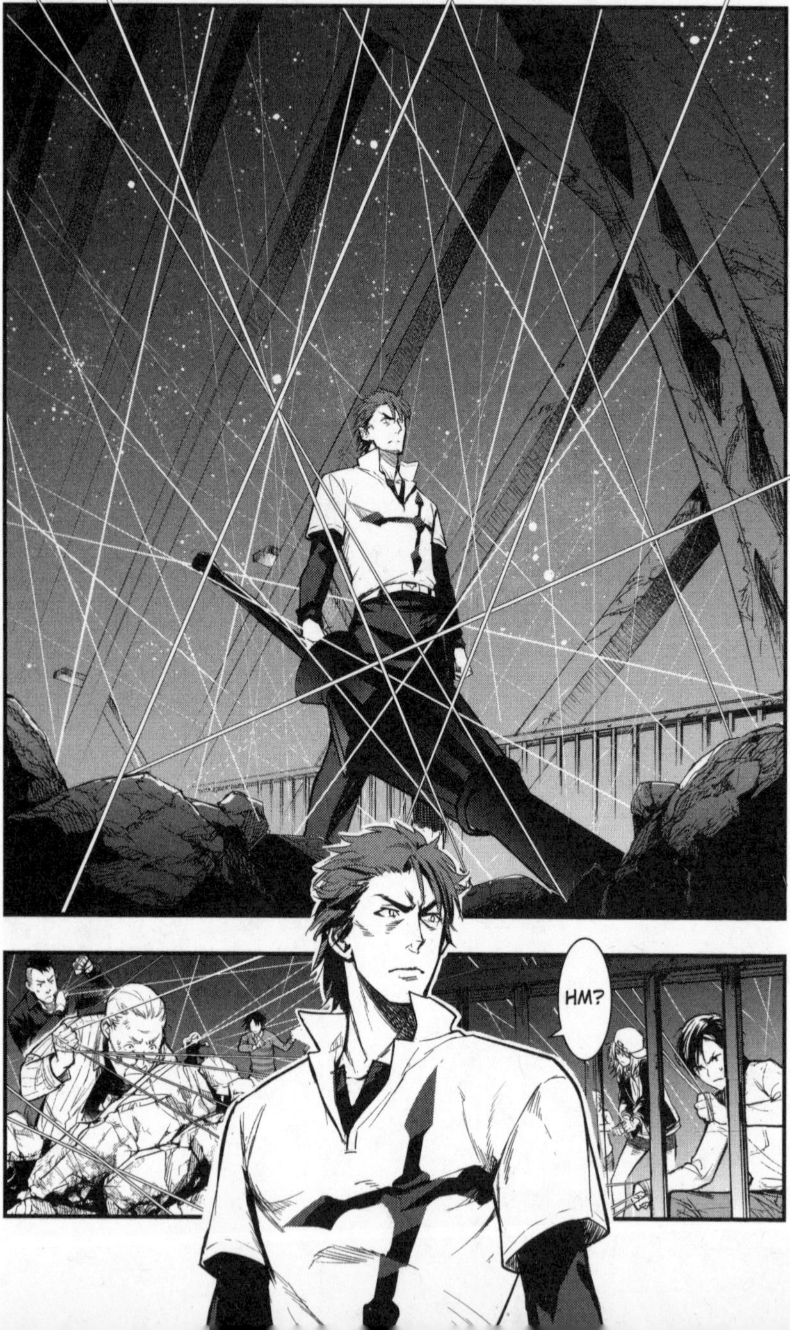
HM?

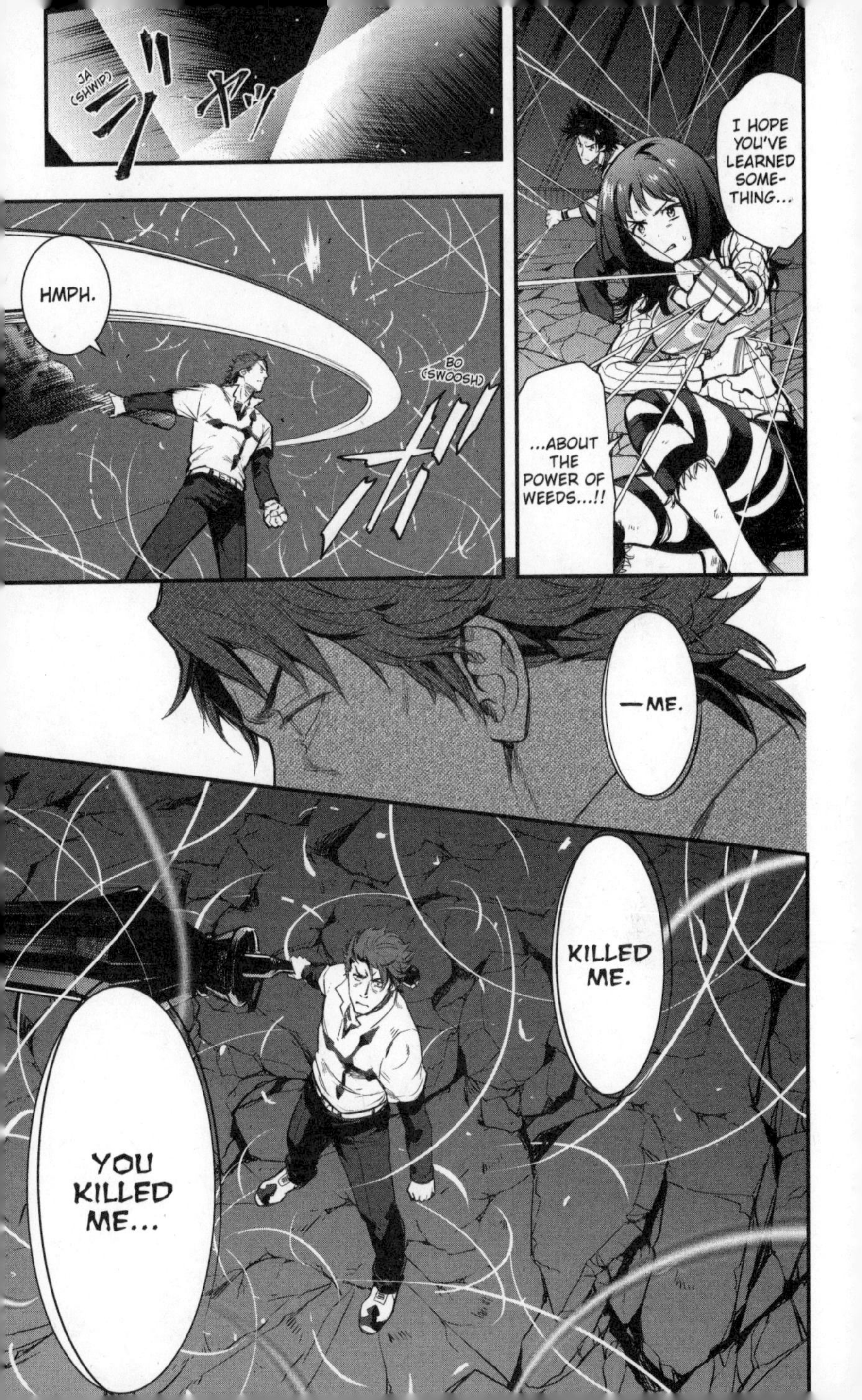
I HOPE YOU'VE LEARNED SOME-THING...
...ABOUT THE POWER OF WEEDS...!!
ジャッ
JA (SHWIP)
HMPH.
ボッ
BO (SWOOSH)
—ME.
KILLED ME.
YOU KILLED ME...

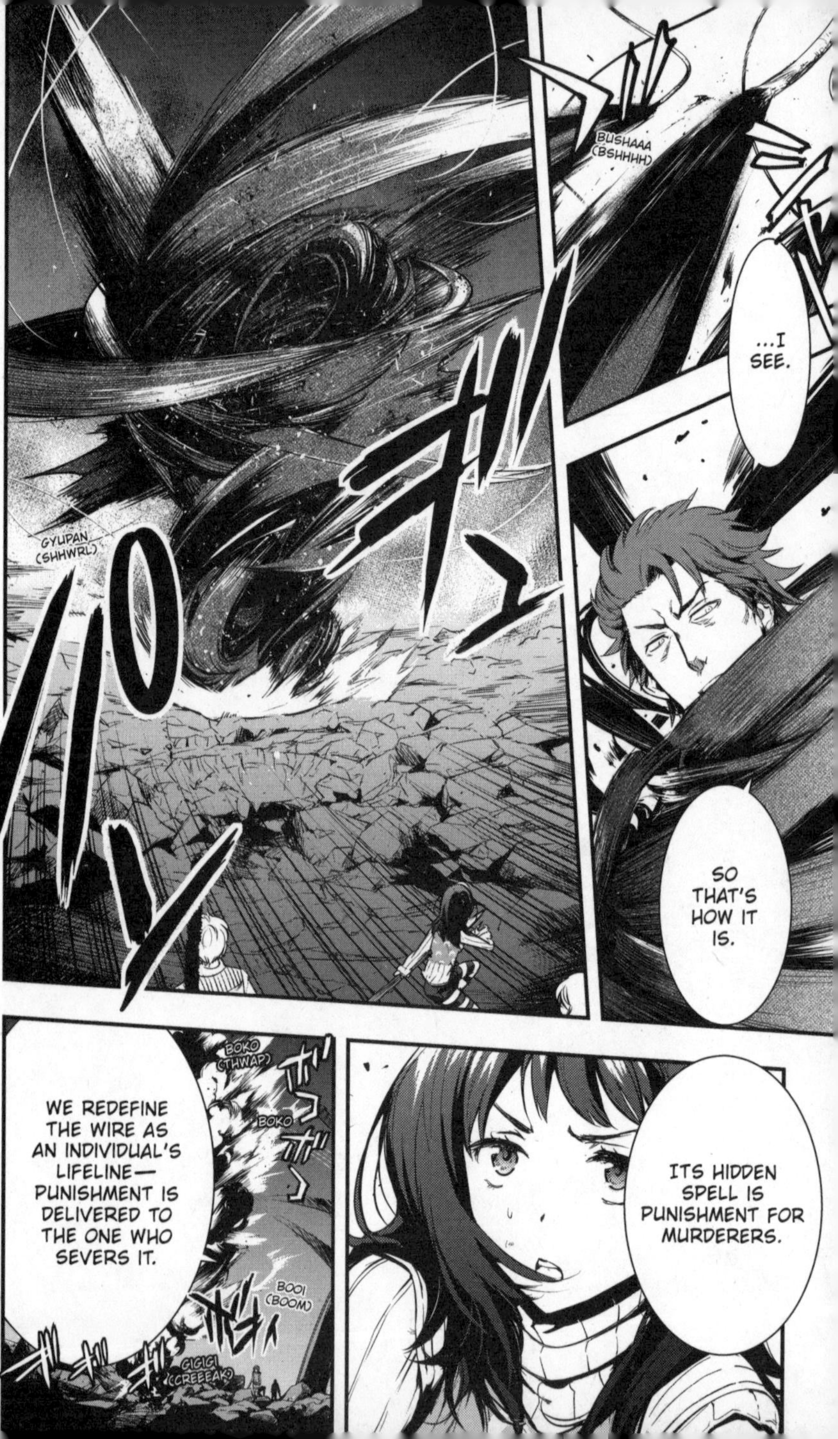
BUSHAAA (BSHHHH)
...I SEE.
SO THAT'S HOW IT IS.
GYUPAN (SHHWRL)
ITS HIDDEN SPELL IS PUNISHMENT FOR MURDERERS.
WE REDEFINE THE WIRE AS AN INDIVIDUAL'S LIFELINE—PUNISHMENT IS DELIVERED TO THE ONE WHO SEVERS IT.
BOKO (THWAP)
BOKO
BOOI (BOOM)
GIGIGI (CREEEAK)

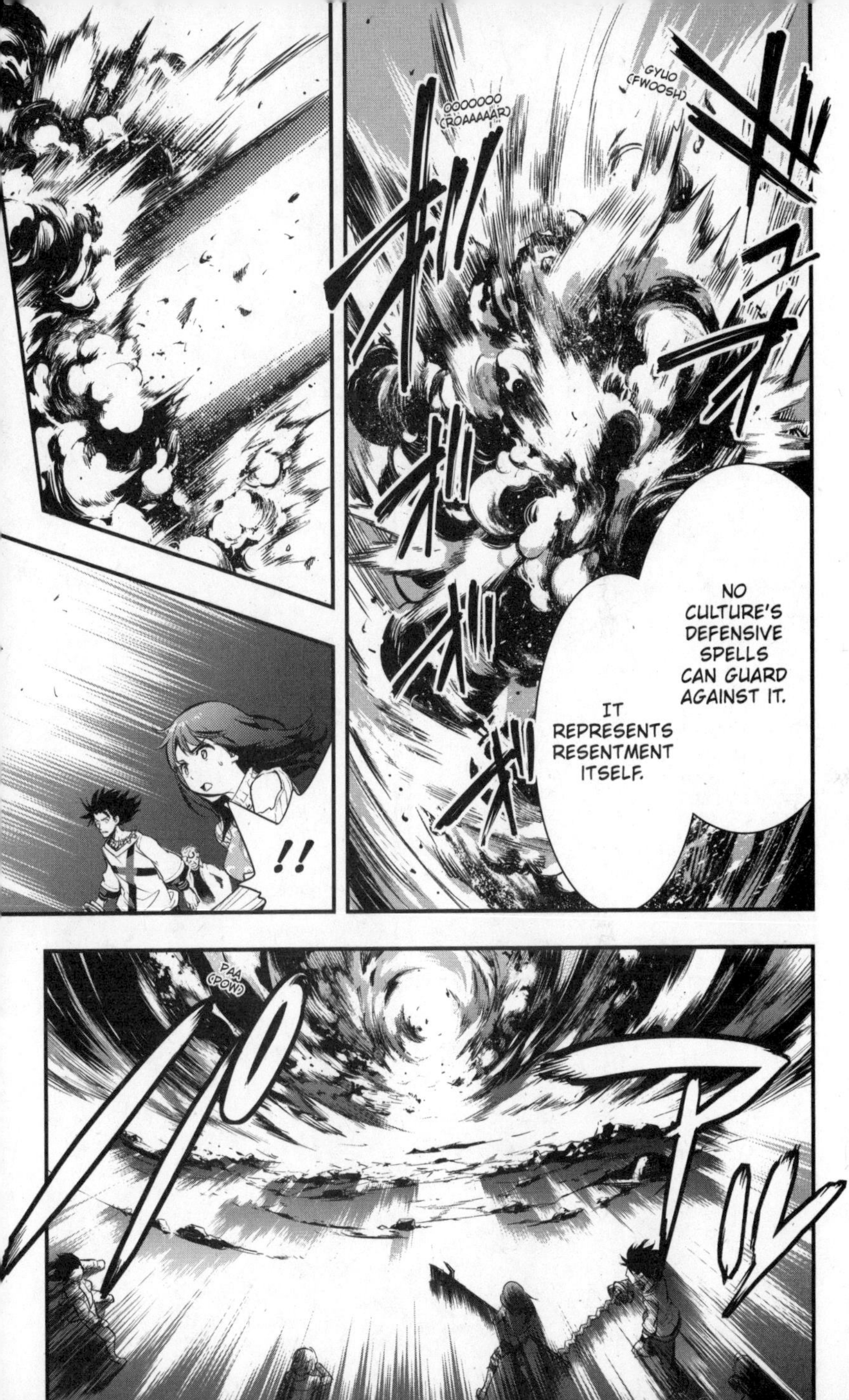
GYUO (FWOOSH)
OOOOOOO (ROAAAAAR)
NO CULTURE'S DEFENSIVE SPELLS CAN GUARD AGAINST IT.
IT REPRESENTS RESENTMENT ITSELF.
!!
PAA (POW)

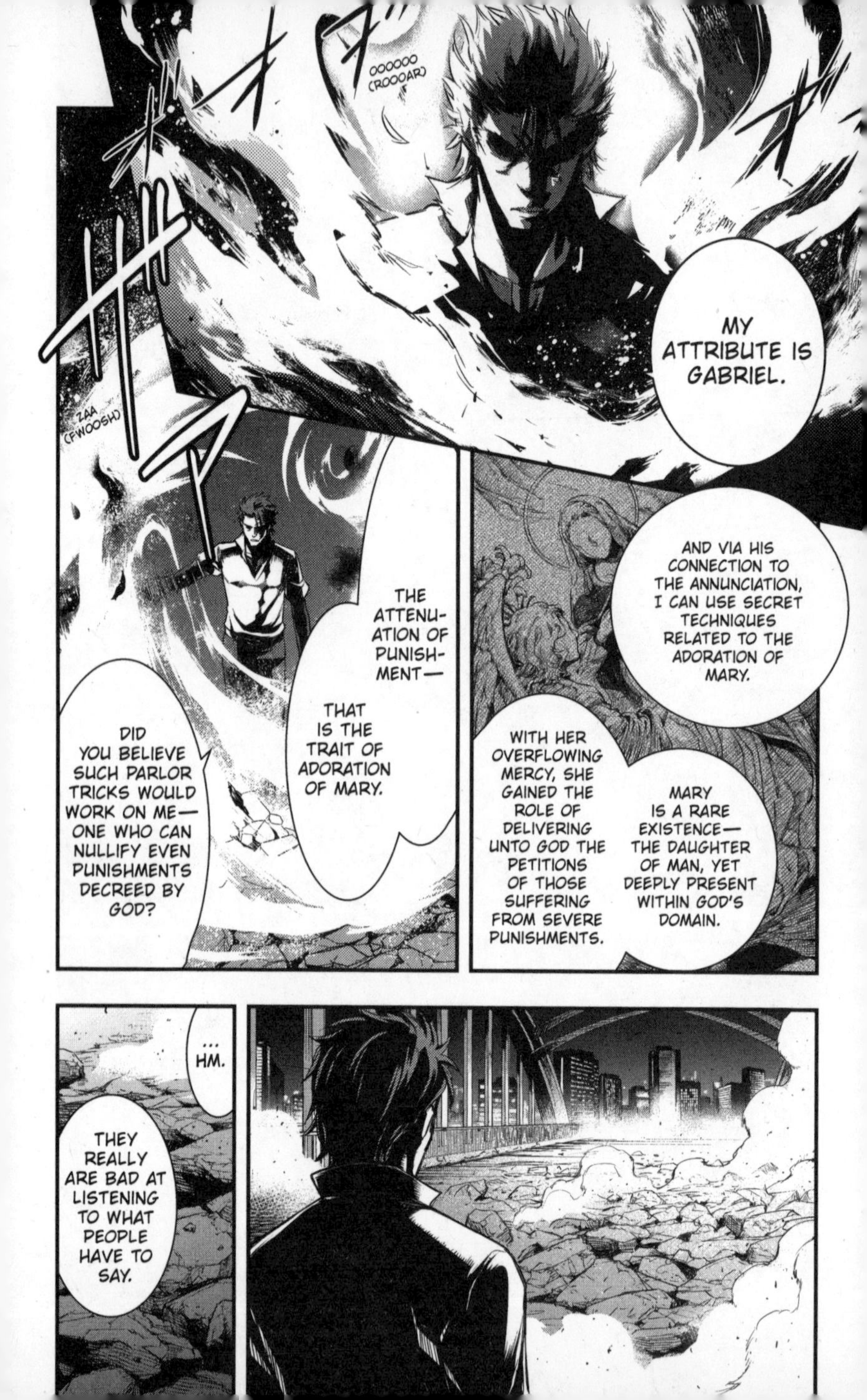
OOOOOO (ROOOAR)
MY ATTRIBUTE IS GABRIEL.
ZAA (FWOOSH)
AND VIA HIS CONNECTION TO THE ANNUNCIATION, I CAN USE SECRET TECHNIQUES RELATED TO THE ADORATION OF MARY.
MARY IS A RARE EXISTENCE— THE DAUGHTER OF MAN, YET DEEPLY PRESENT WITHIN GOD'S DOMAIN.
WITH HER OVERFLOWING MERCY, SHE GAINED THE ROLE OF DELIVERING UNTO GOD THE PETITIONS OF THOSE SUFFERING FROM SEVERE PUNISHMENTS.
THE ATTENUATION OF PUNISHMENT—
THAT IS THE TRAIT OF ADORATION OF MARY.
DID YOU BELIEVE SUCH PARLOR TRICKS WOULD WORK ON ME— ONE WHO CAN NULLIFY EVEN PUNISHMENTS DECREED BY GOD?
... HM.
THEY REALLY ARE BAD AT LISTENING TO WHAT PEOPLE HAVE TO SAY.

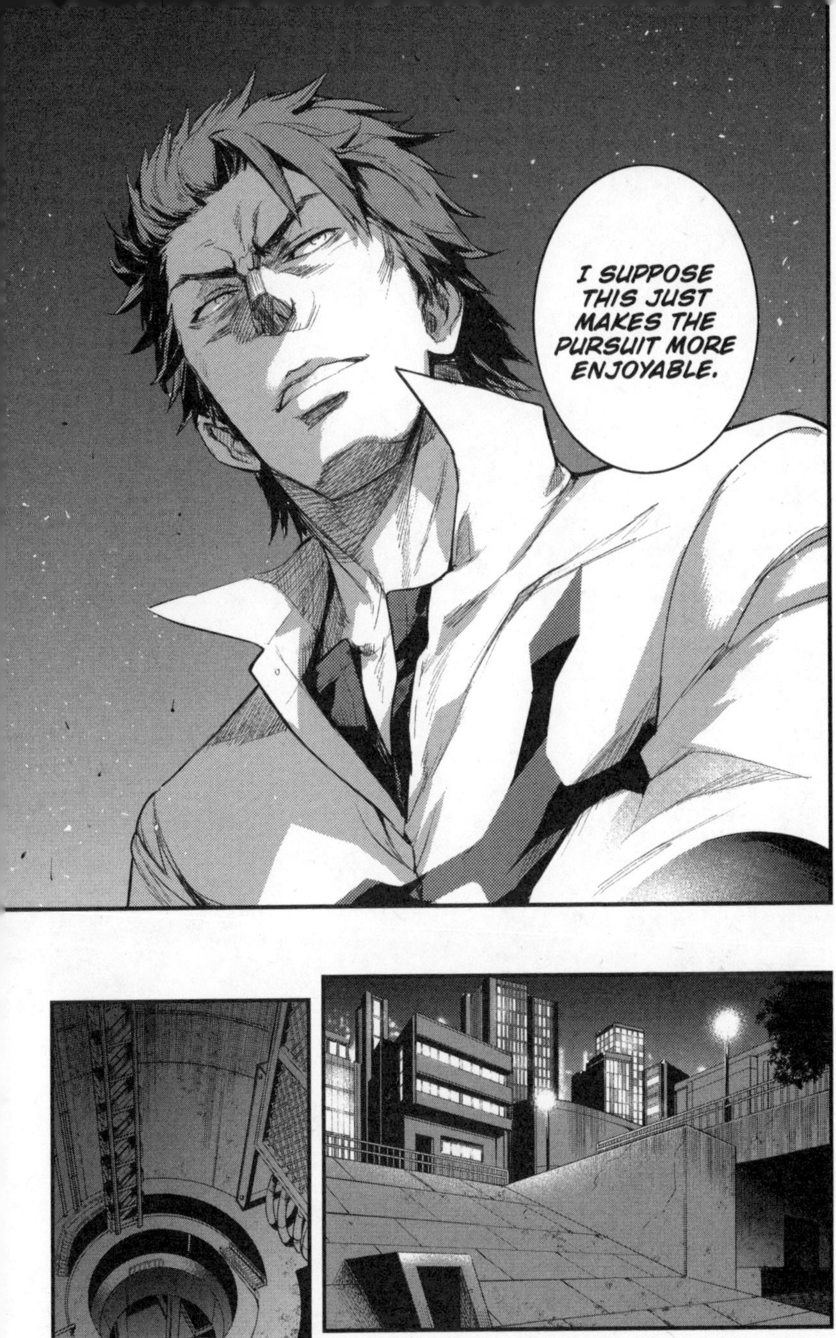
I SUPPOSE THIS JUST MAKES THE PURSUIT MORE ENJOYABLE.

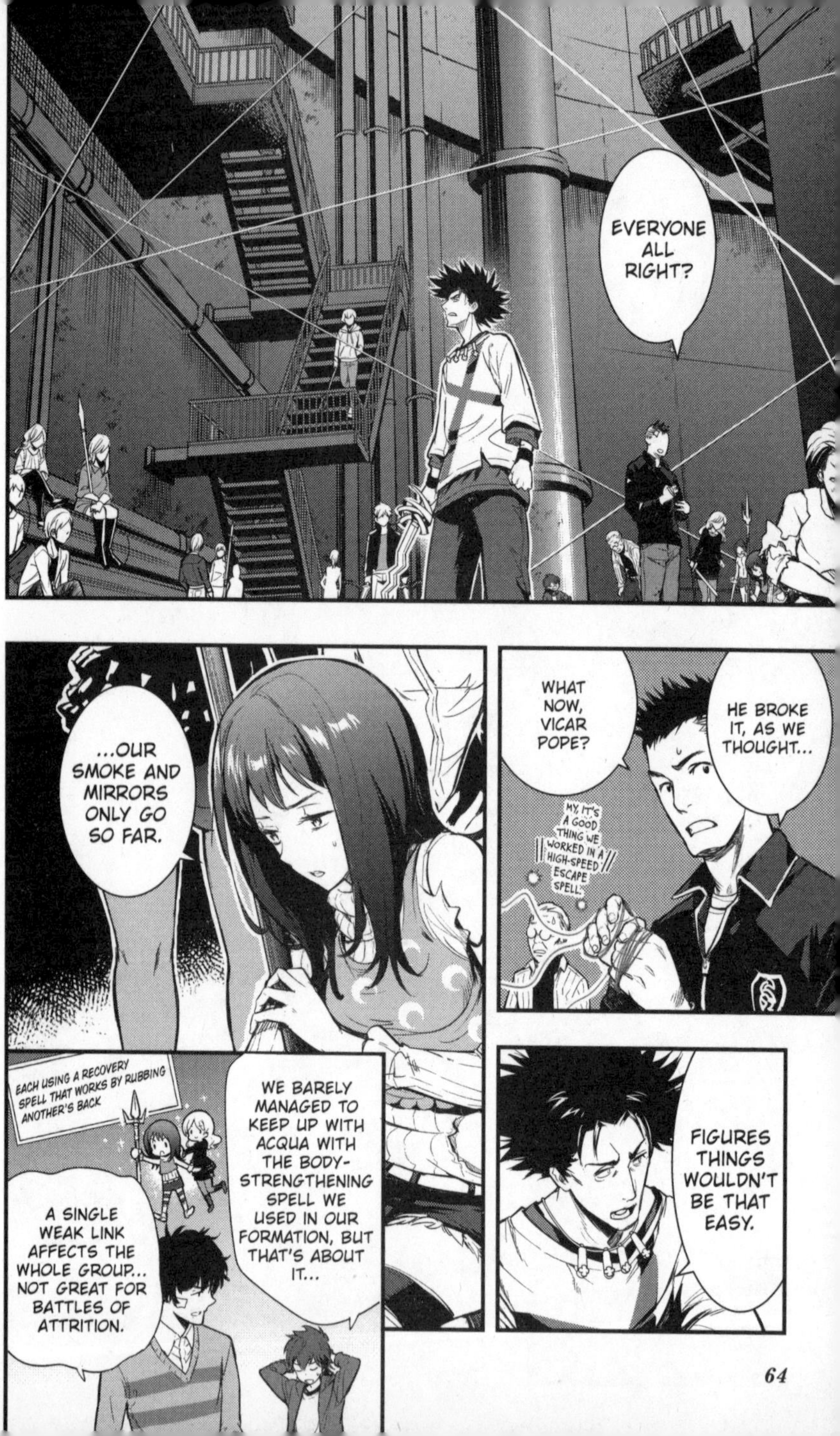
EVERYONE ALL RIGHT?
HE BROKE IT, AS WE THOUGHT...
WHAT NOW, VICAR POPE?
MY, IT'S A GOOD THING WE WORKED IN A HIGH-SPEED ESCAPE SPELL.
...OUR SMOKE AND MIRRORS ONLY GO SO FAR.
FIGURES THINGS WOULDN'T BE THAT EASY.
WE BARELY MANAGED TO KEEP UP WITH ACQUA WITH THE BODY-STRENGTHENING SPELL WE USED IN OUR FORMATION, BUT THAT'S ABOUT IT...
EACH USING A RECOVERY SPELL THAT WORKS BY RUBBING ANOTHER'S BACK
A SINGLE WEAK LINK AFFECTS THE WHOLE GROUP... NOT GREAT FOR BATTLES OF ATTRITION.

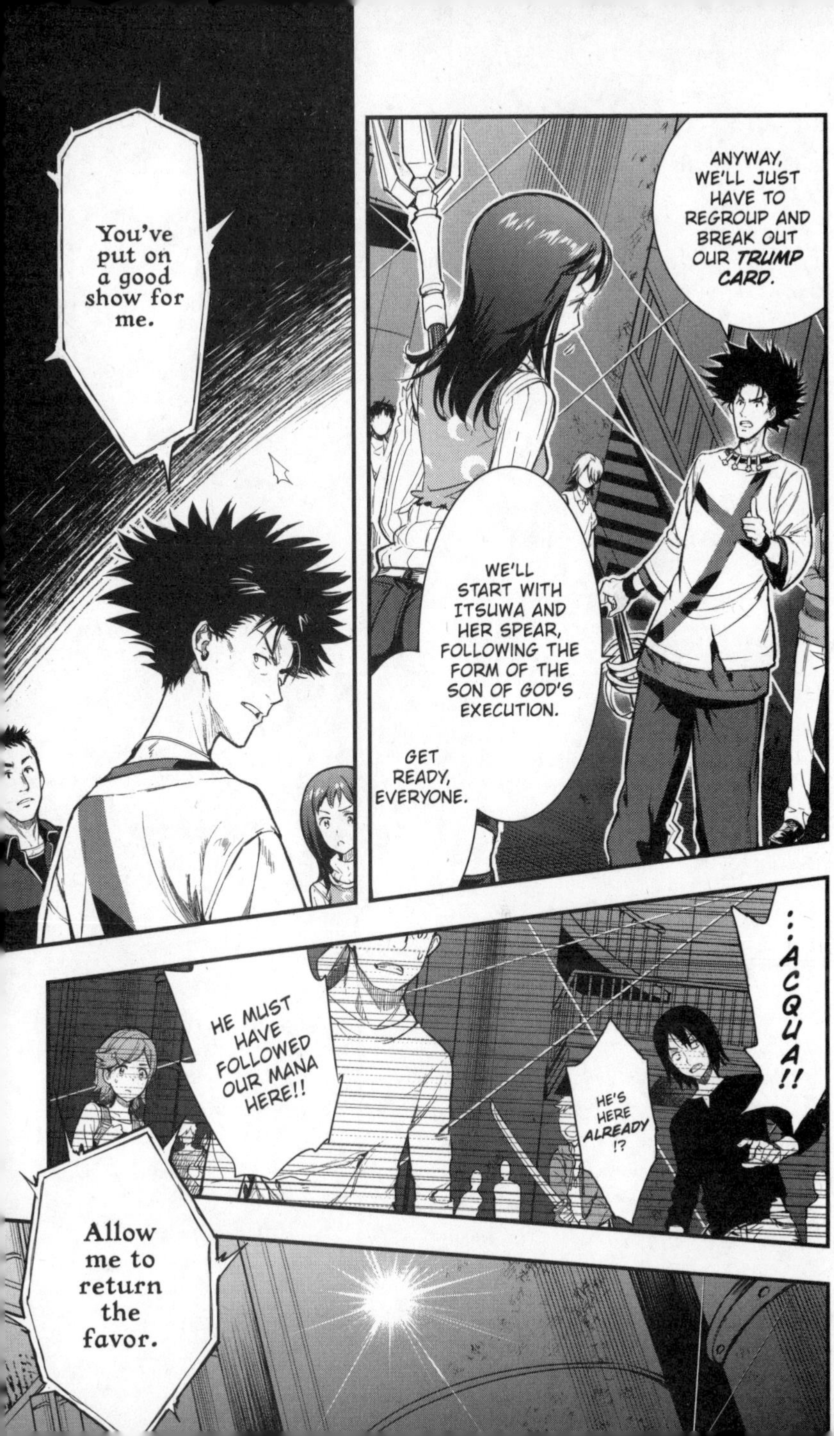
ANYWAY, WE'LL JUST HAVE TO REGROUP AND BREAK OUT OUR *TRUMP CARD*.
WE'LL START WITH ITSUWA AND HER SPEAR, FOLLOWING THE FORM OF THE SON OF GOD'S EXECUTION.
GET READY, EVERYONE.
You've put on a good show for me.
...ACQUA!!
HE'S HERE *ALREADY*!?
HE MUST HAVE FOLLOWED OUR MANA HERE!!
Allow me to return the favor.

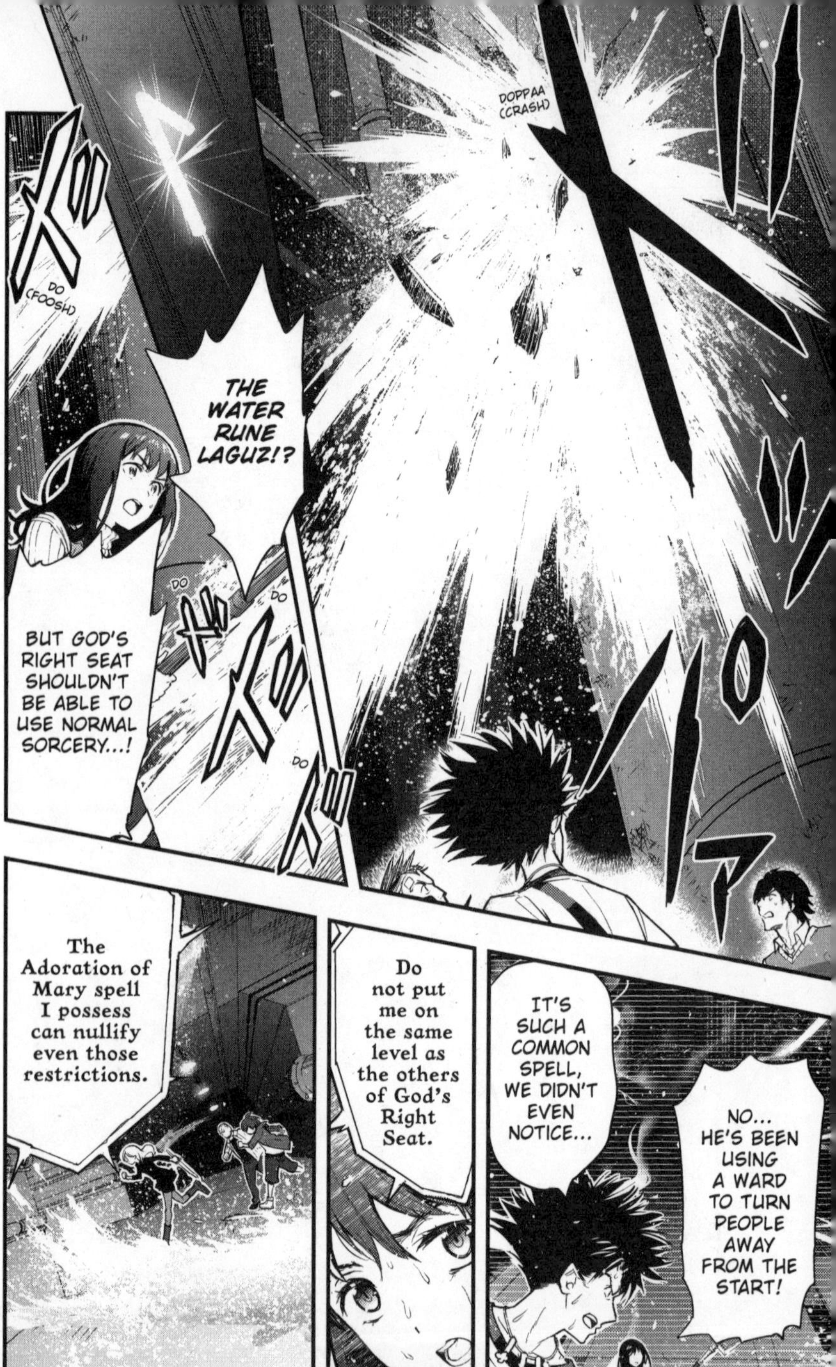
DOPPAA (CRASH)
DO (FOOSH)
THE WATER RUNE LAGUZ!?
BUT GOD'S RIGHT SEAT SHOULDN'T BE ABLE TO USE NORMAL SORCERY...!
DO
DO
DO
IT'S SUCH A COMMON SPELL, WE DIDN'T EVEN NOTICE...
NO... HE'S BEEN USING A WARD TO TURN PEOPLE AWAY FROM THE START!
Do not put me on the same level as the others of God's Right Seat.
The Adoration of Mary spell I possess can nullify even those restrictions.

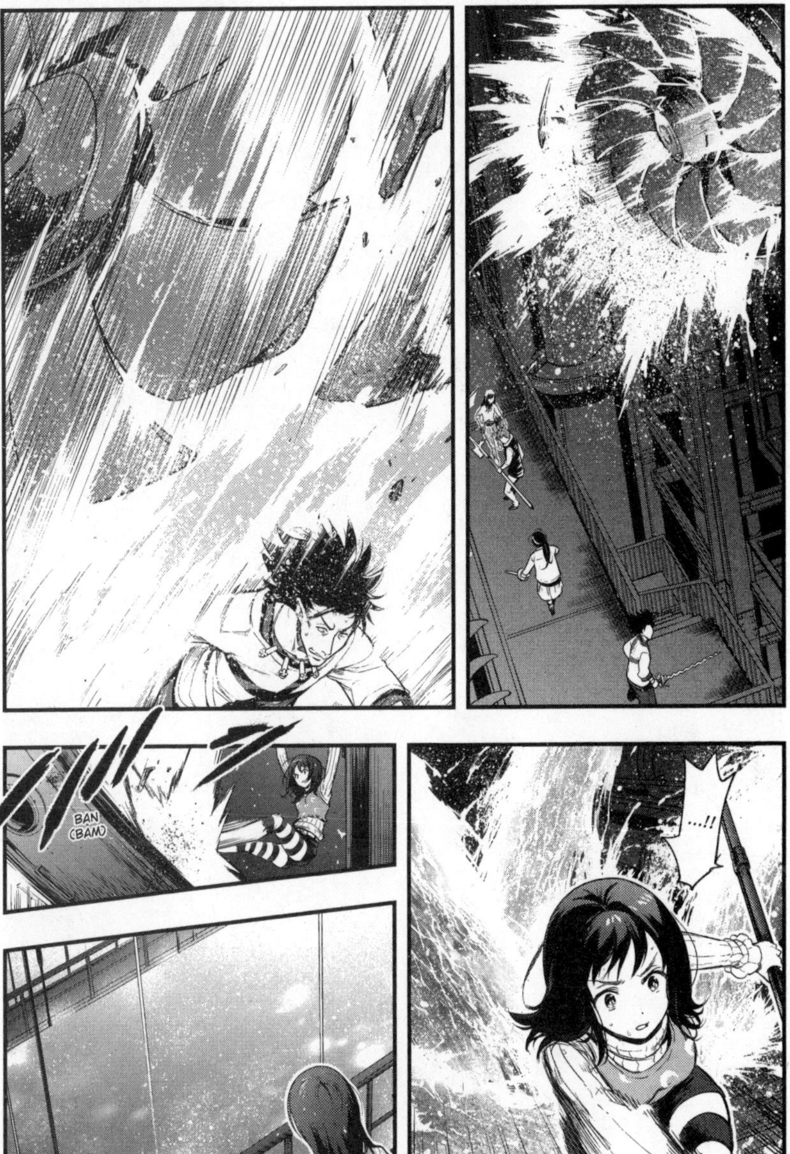
...!!
BAN
(BAM)

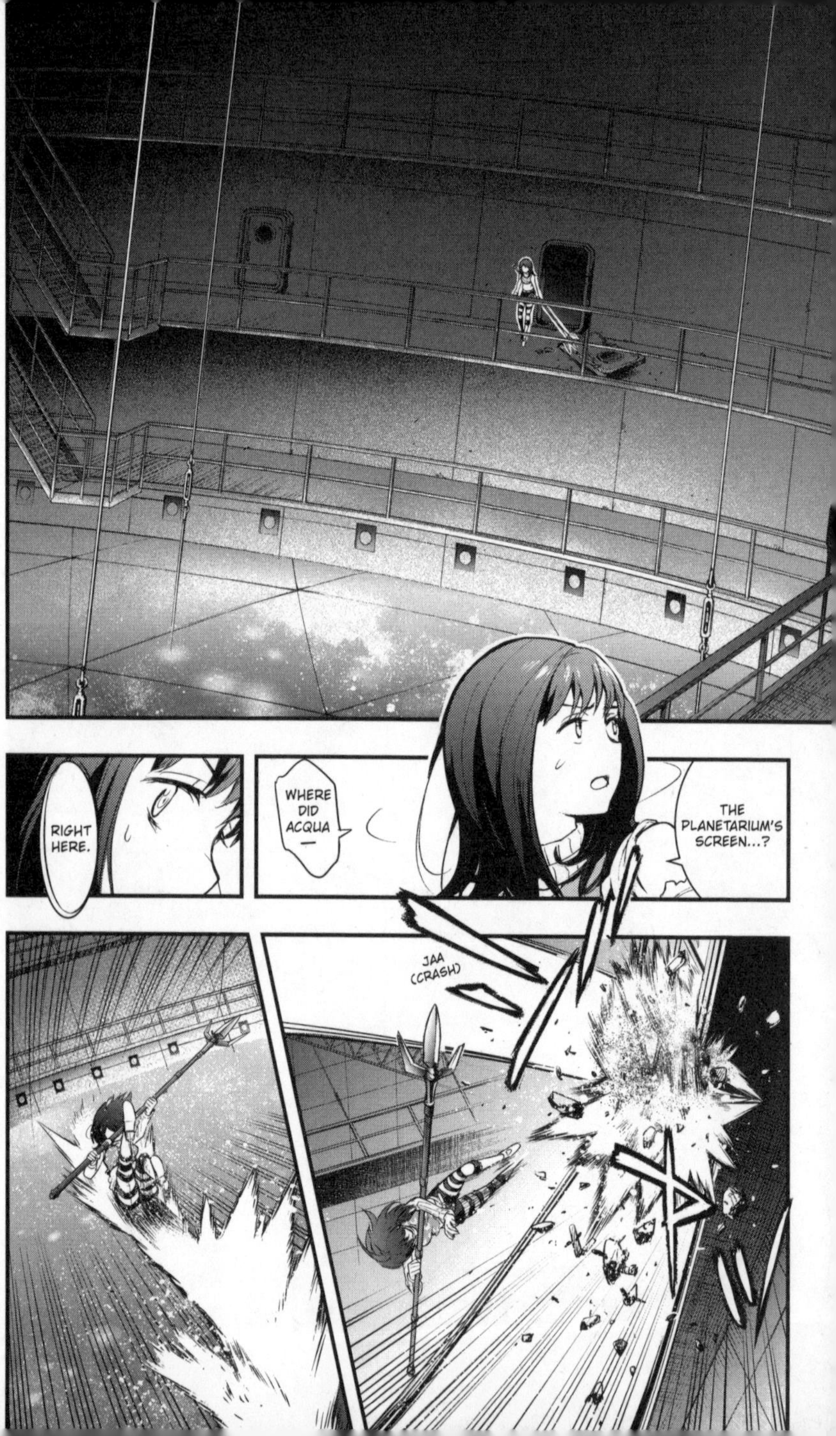
THE PLANETARIUM'S SCREEN...?
WHERE DID ACQUA —
RIGHT HERE.
JAA (CRASH)

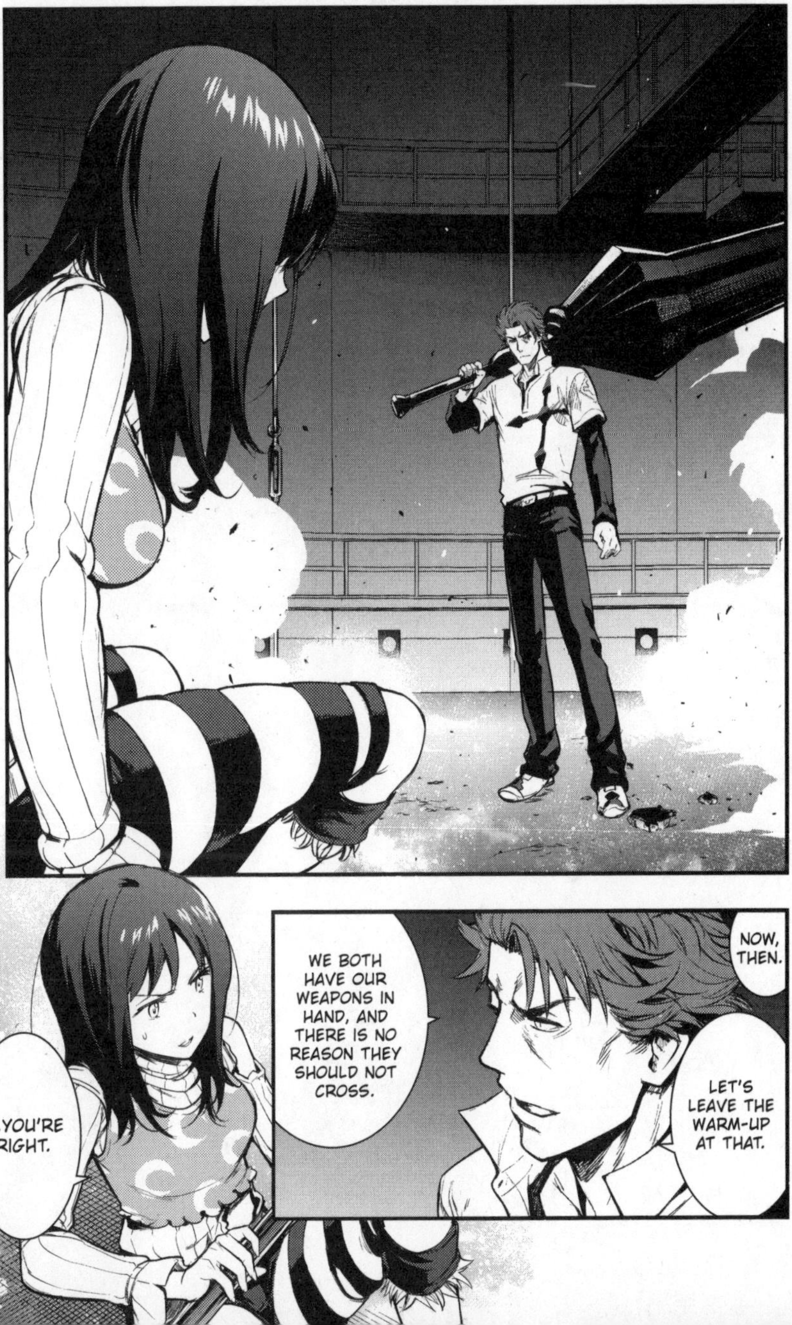
NOW, THEN.
LET'S LEAVE THE WARM-UP AT THAT.
WE BOTH HAVE OUR WEAPONS IN HAND, AND THERE IS NO REASON THEY SHOULD NOT CROSS.
...YOU'RE RIGHT.

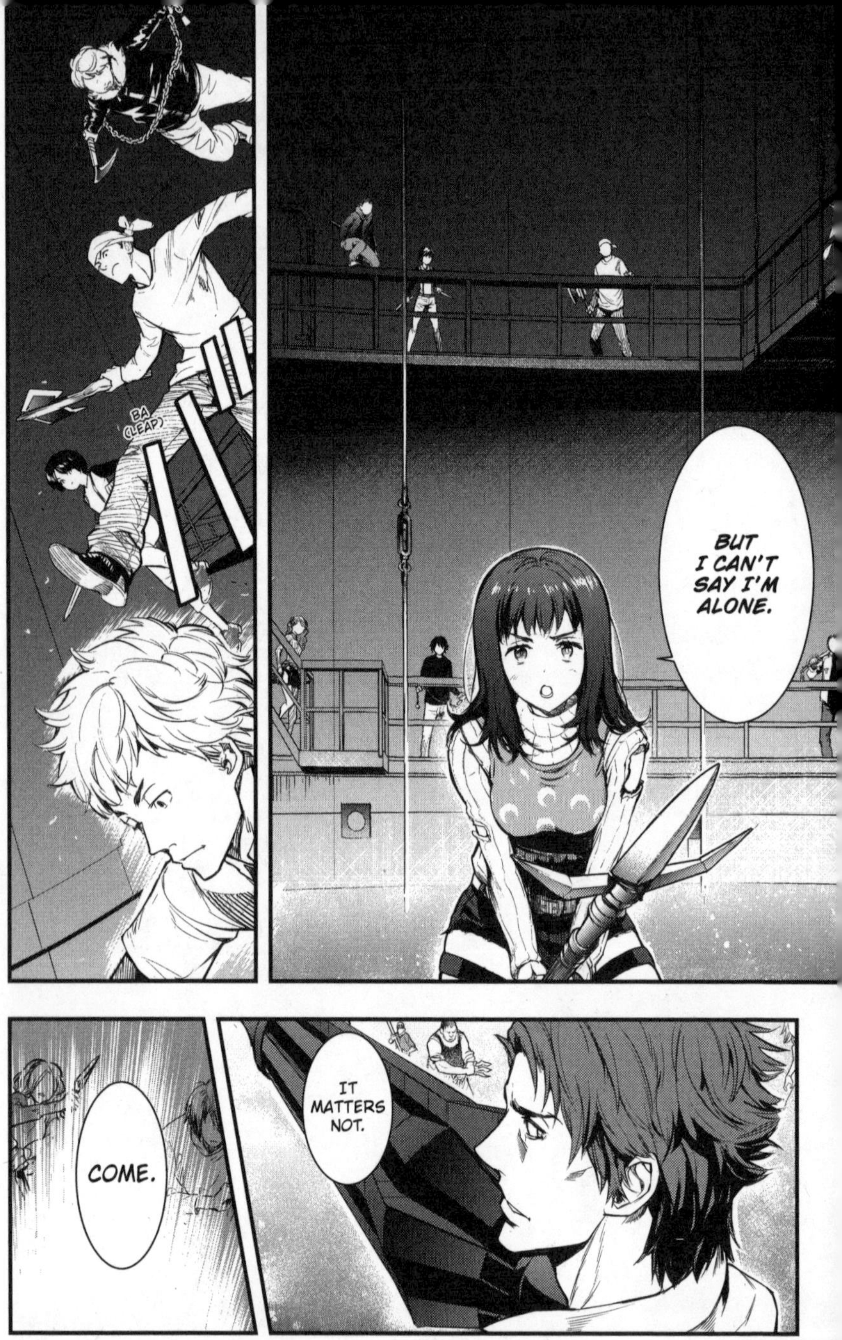
BUT I CAN'T SAY I'M ALONE.
BA (LEAP)
IT MATTERS NOT.
COME.

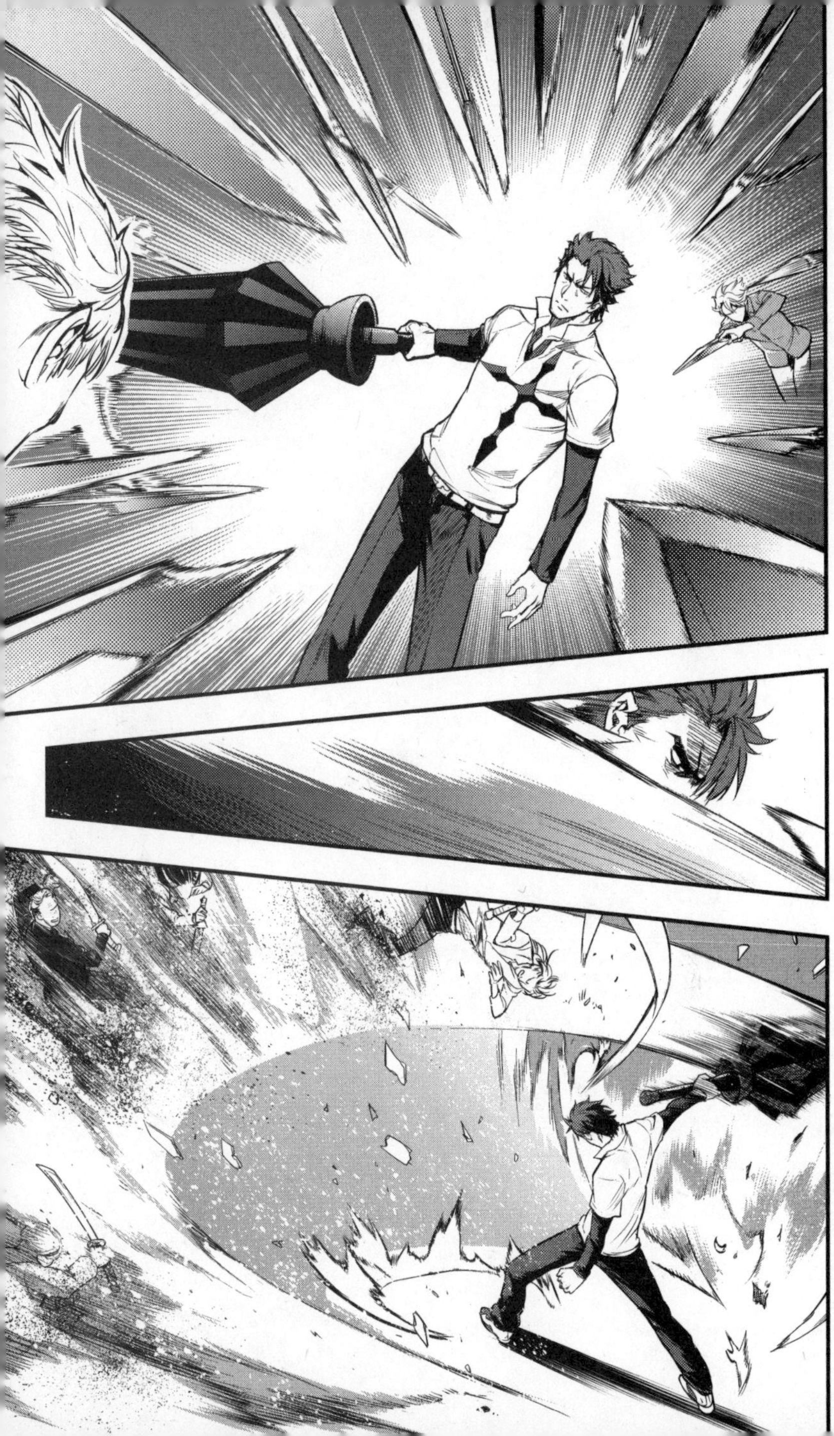

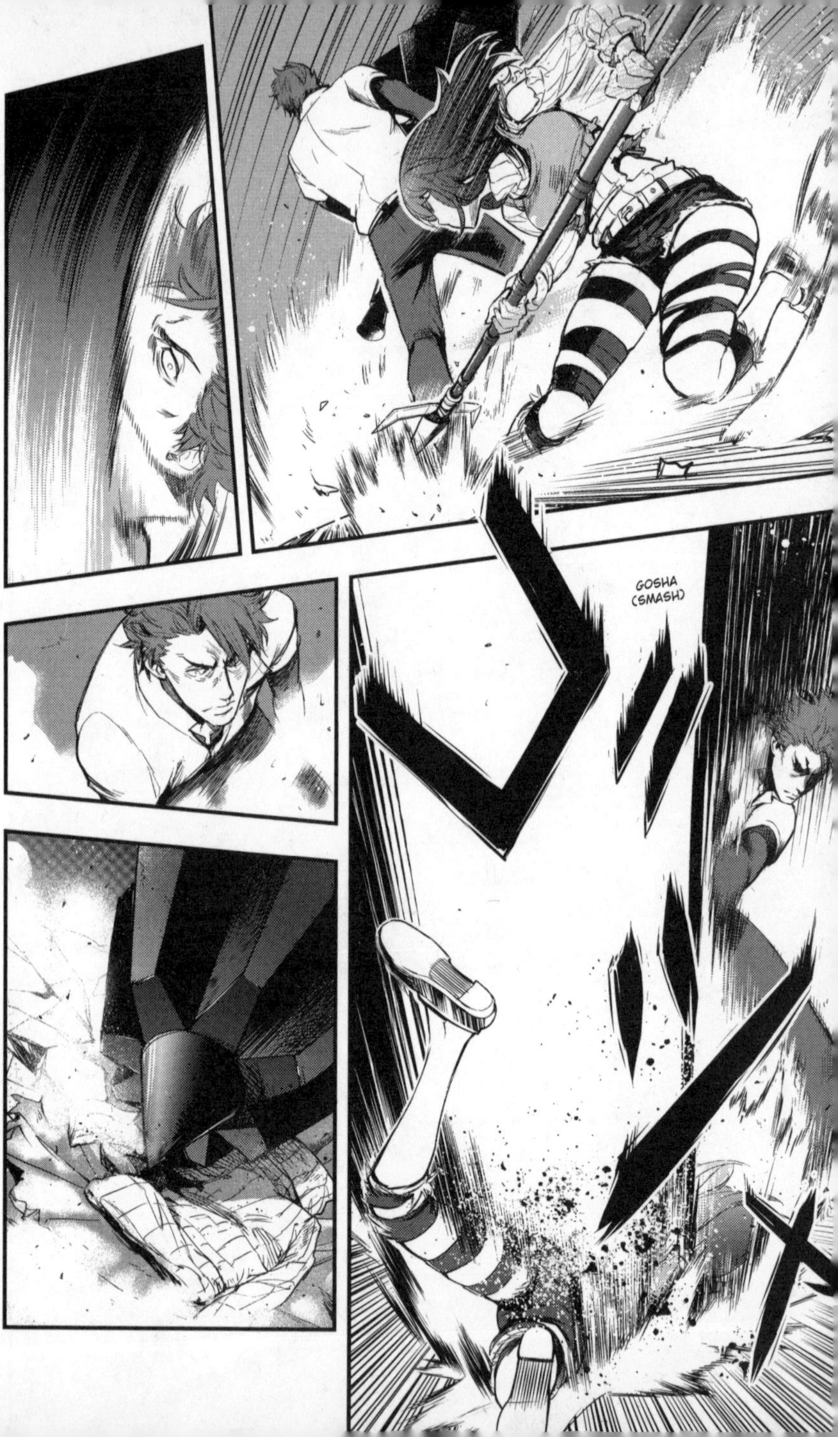
GOSHA
(SMASH)

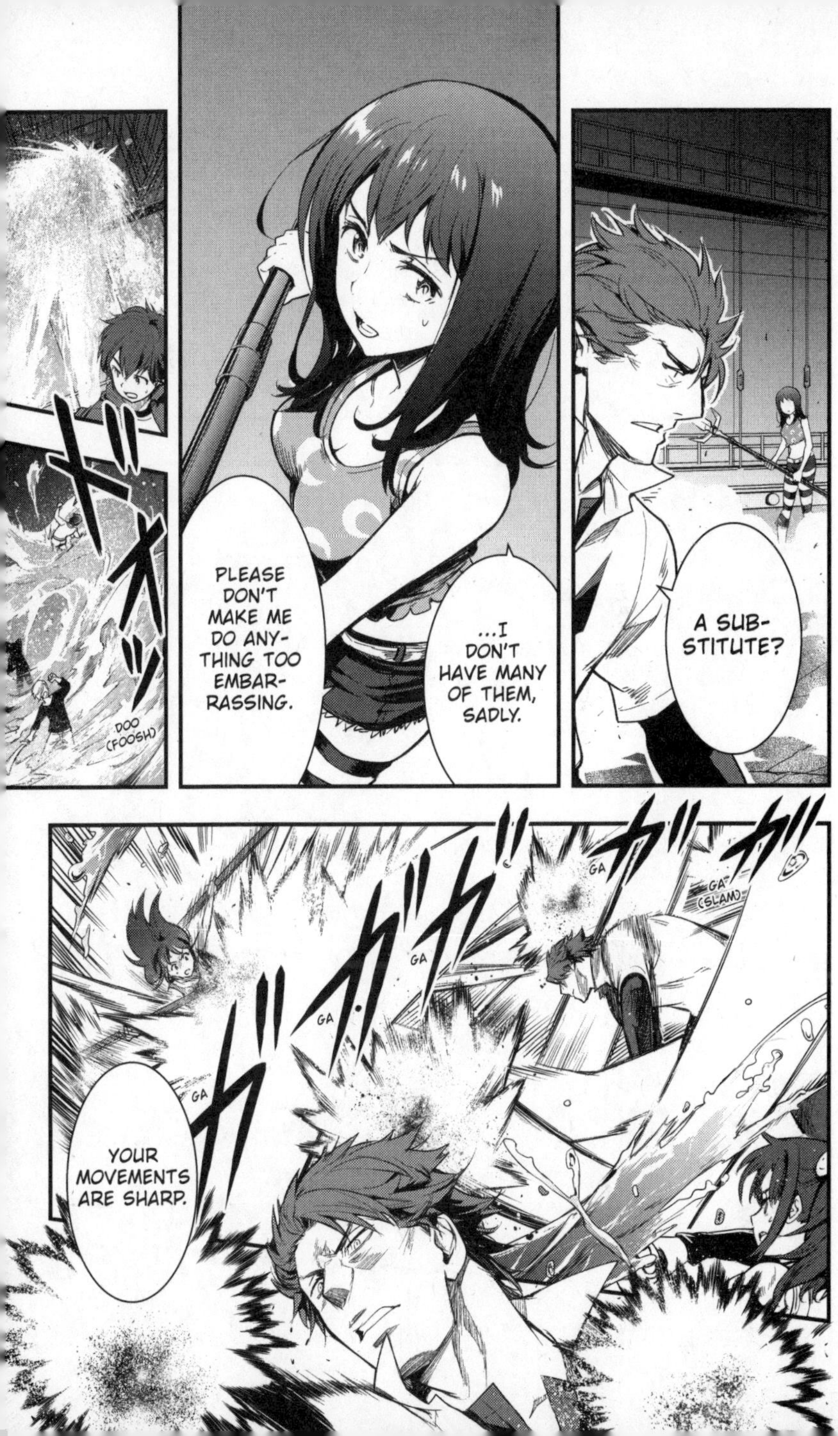
A SUB-
STITUTE?
...I
DON'T
HAVE MANY
OF THEM,
SADLY.
PLEASE
DON'T
MAKE ME
DO ANY-
THING TOO
EMBAR-
RASSING.
DOO
(FOOSH)
GA
GA
(SLAM)
GA
GA
GA
YOUR
MOVEMENTS
ARE SHARP.

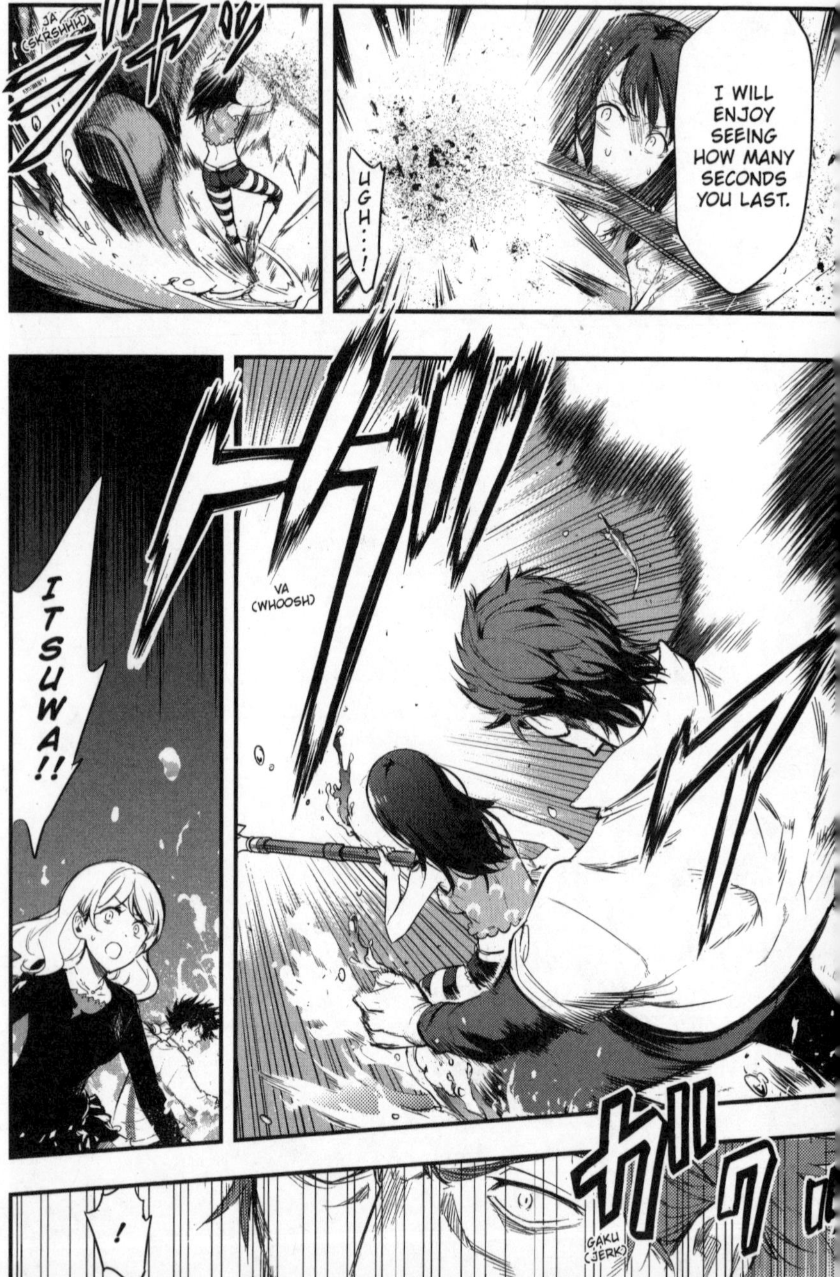
I WILL ENJOY SEEING HOW MANY SECONDS YOU LAST.
UGH...!
JA (SKRSHHH)
VA (WHOOSH)
GAKU (JERK)
ITSUWA!!
!

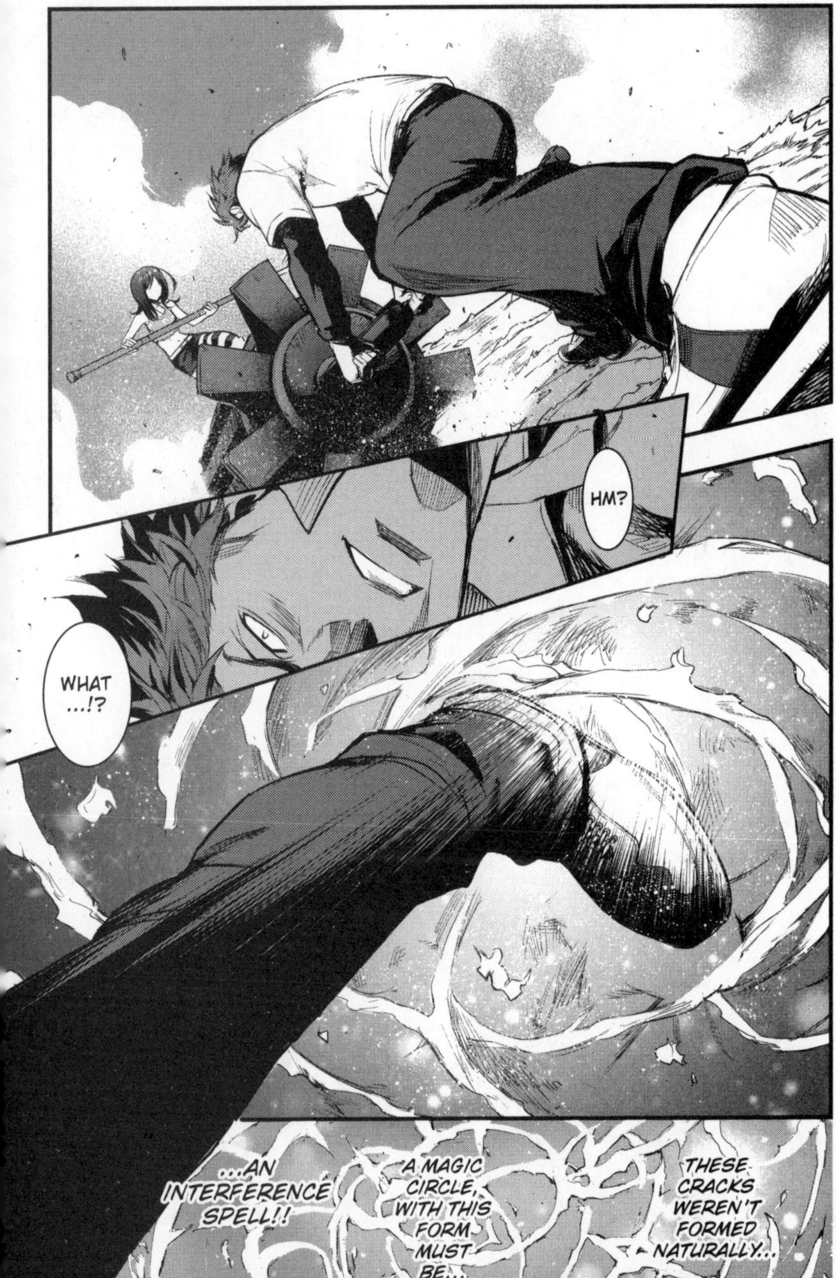
HM?
WHAT ...!?
THESE CRACKS WEREN'T FORMED NATURALLY...
A MAGIC CIRCLE, WITH THIS FORM MUST BE...
...AN INTERFERENCE SPELL!!

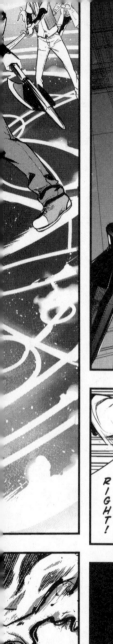

HRM!

YOUR HIGH-SPEED MOVEMENT EMPLOYING WATER MAGIC—

WE'VE SEALED IT!

TATEMIYA-SAN!!

AND EVERY-ONE ELSE TOO!

RIGHT!

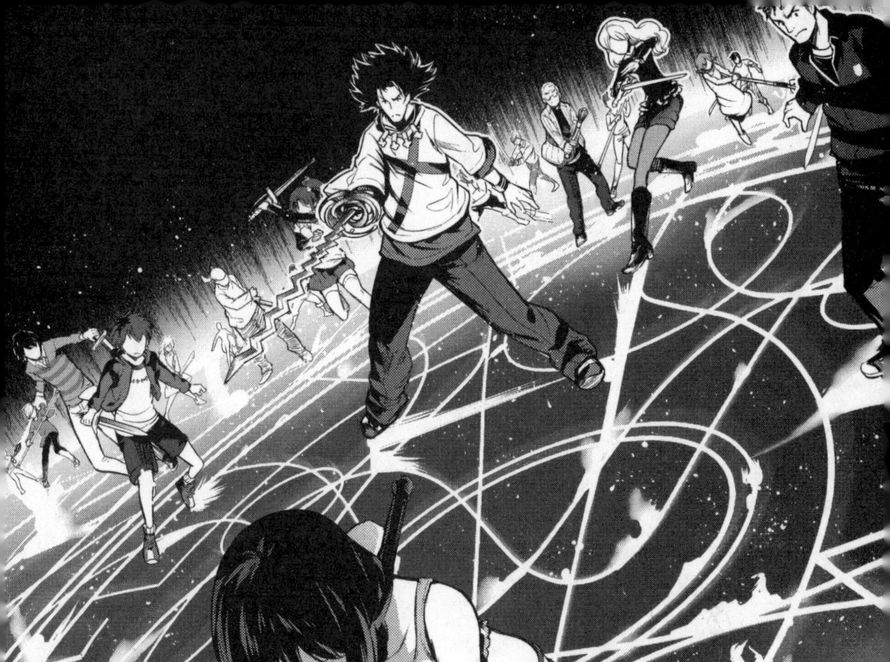

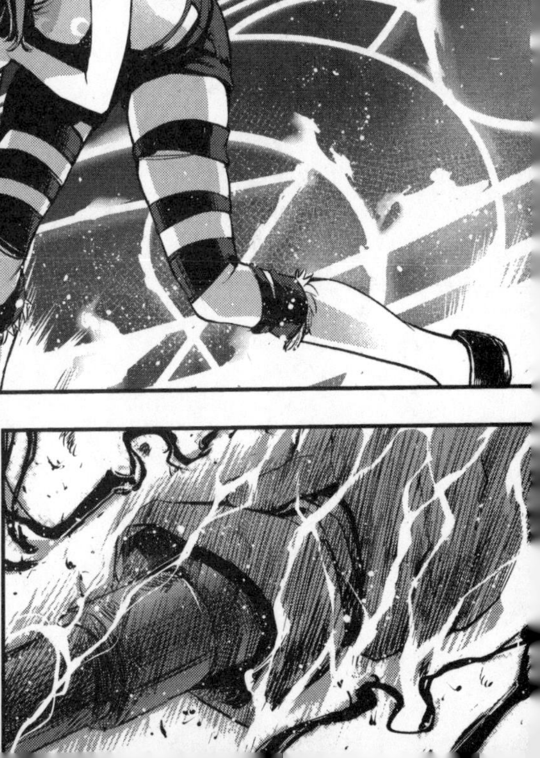

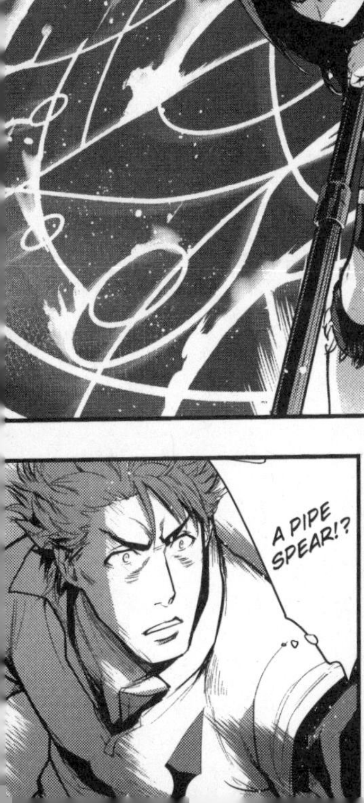
A PIPE
SPEAR!?

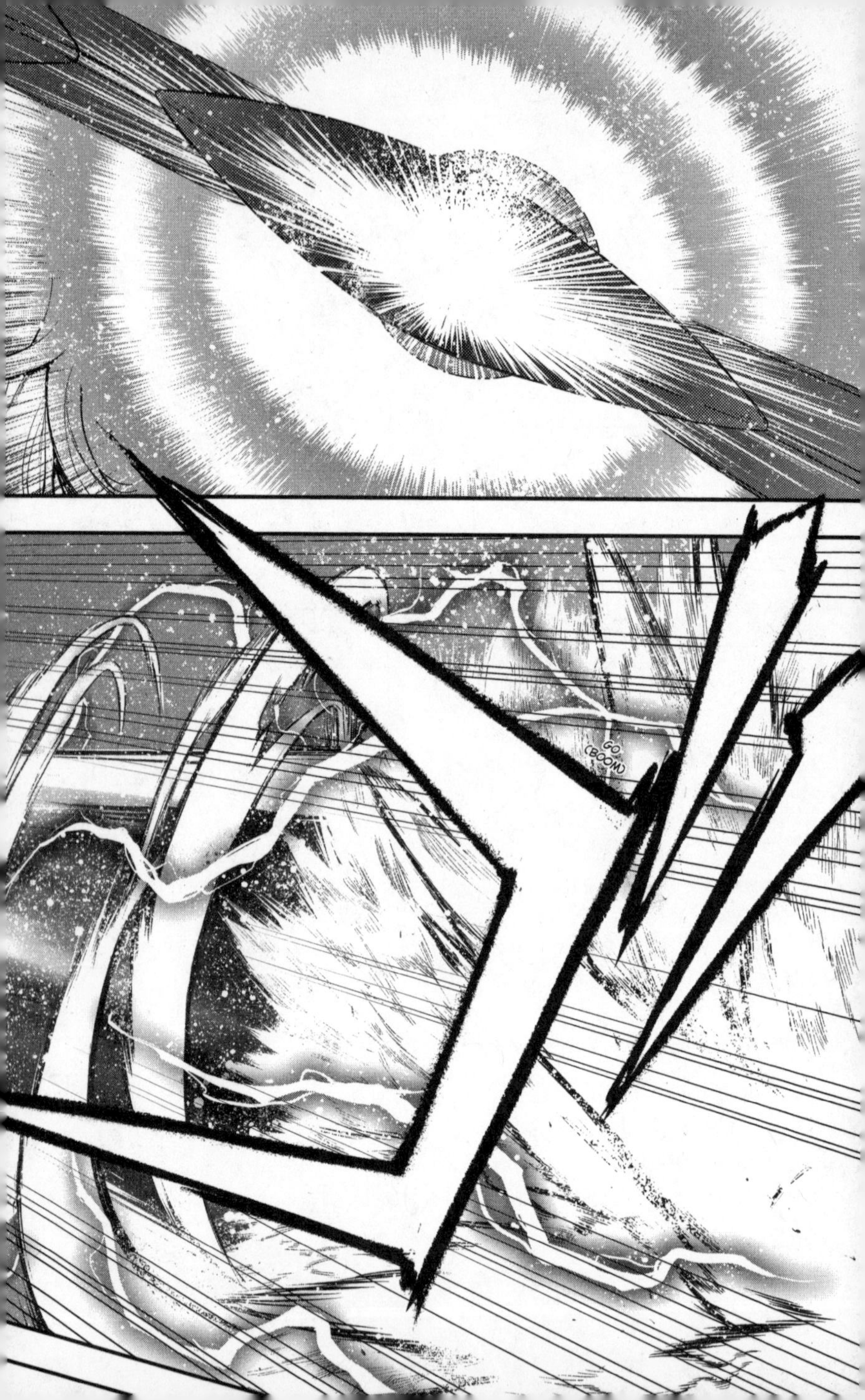
GO
(BOOM)

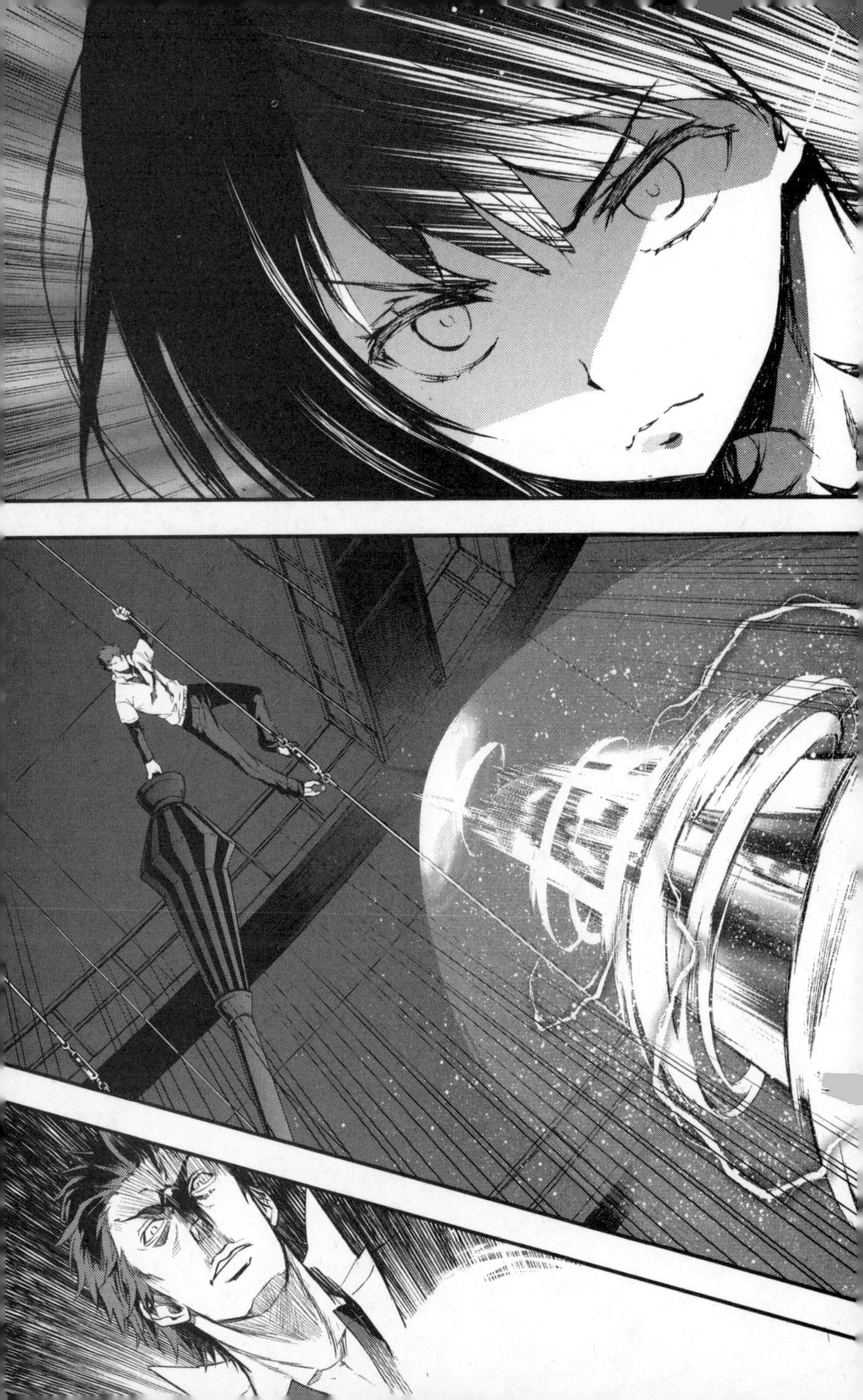

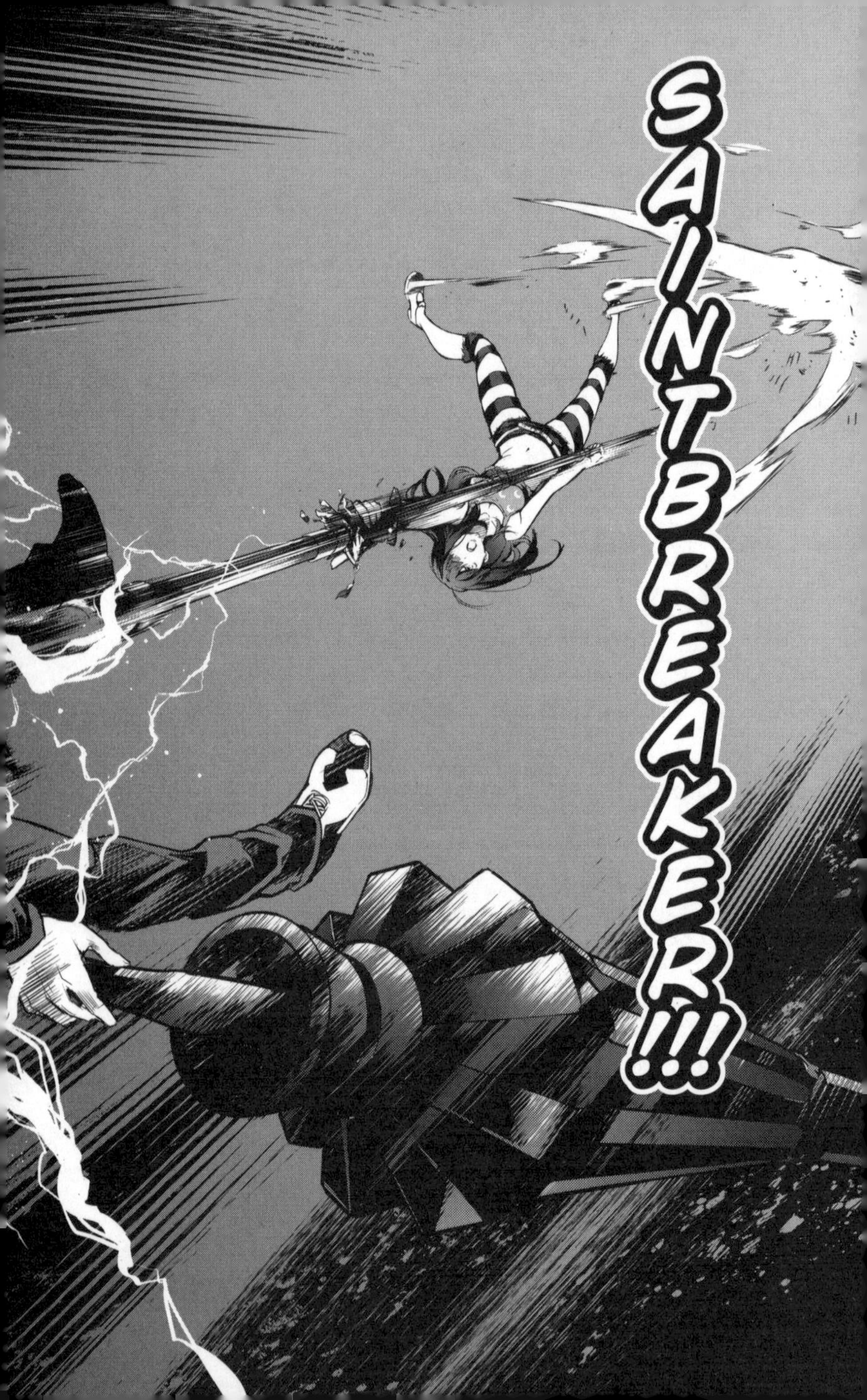
SAINTBREAKER!!!

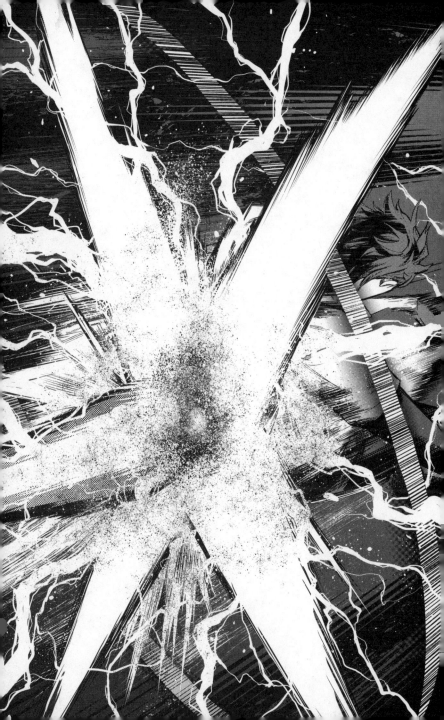

A Certain Magical Index

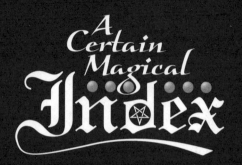

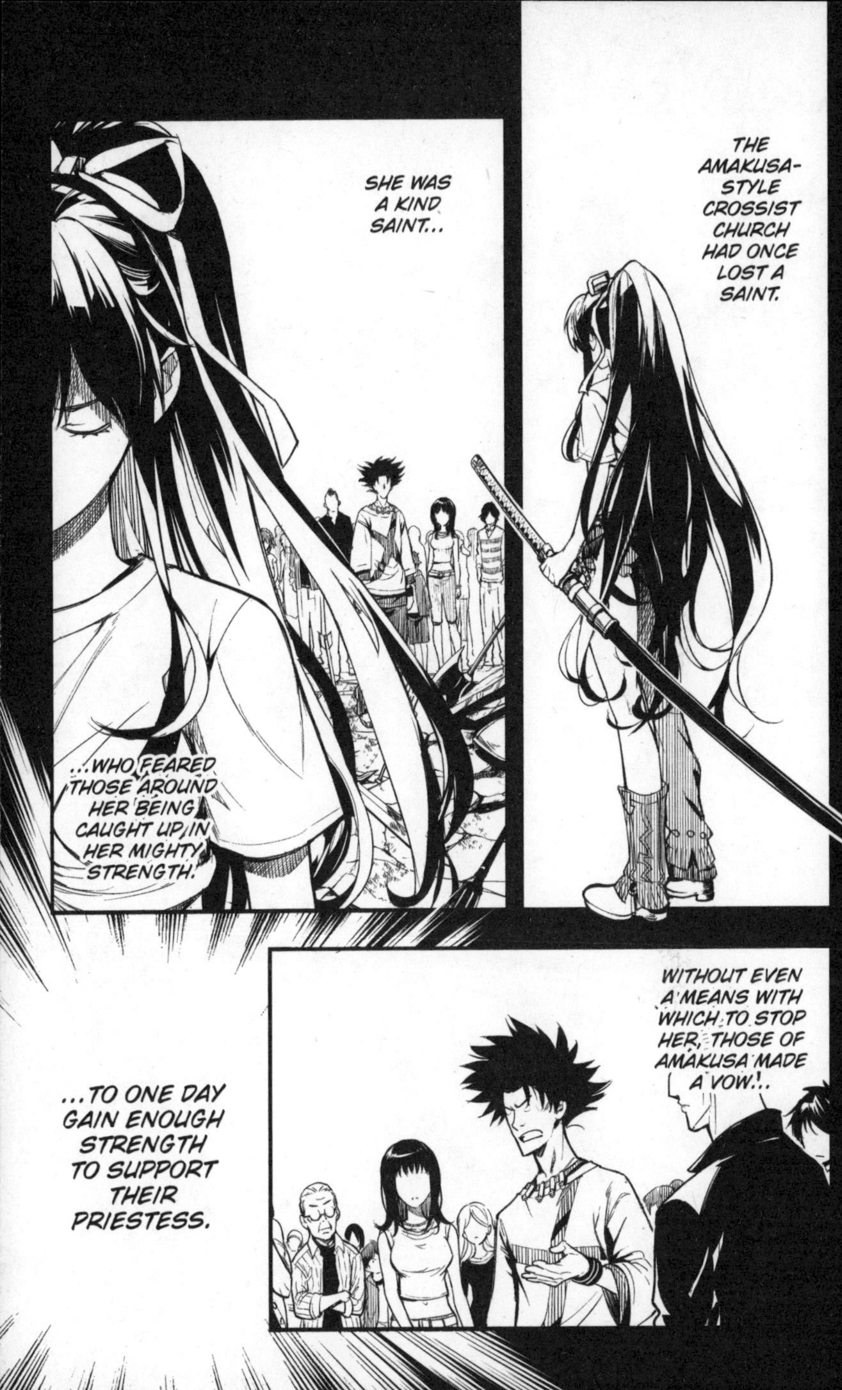
THE AMAKUSA-STYLE CROSSIST CHURCH HAD ONCE LOST A SAINT.
SHE WAS A KIND SAINT...
...WHO FEARED THOSE AROUND HER BEING CAUGHT UP IN HER MIGHTY STRENGTH.
WITHOUT EVEN A MEANS WITH WHICH TO STOP HER, THOSE OF AMAKUSA MADE A VOW...
...TO ONE DAY GAIN ENOUGH STRENGTH TO SUPPORT THEIR PRIESTESS.

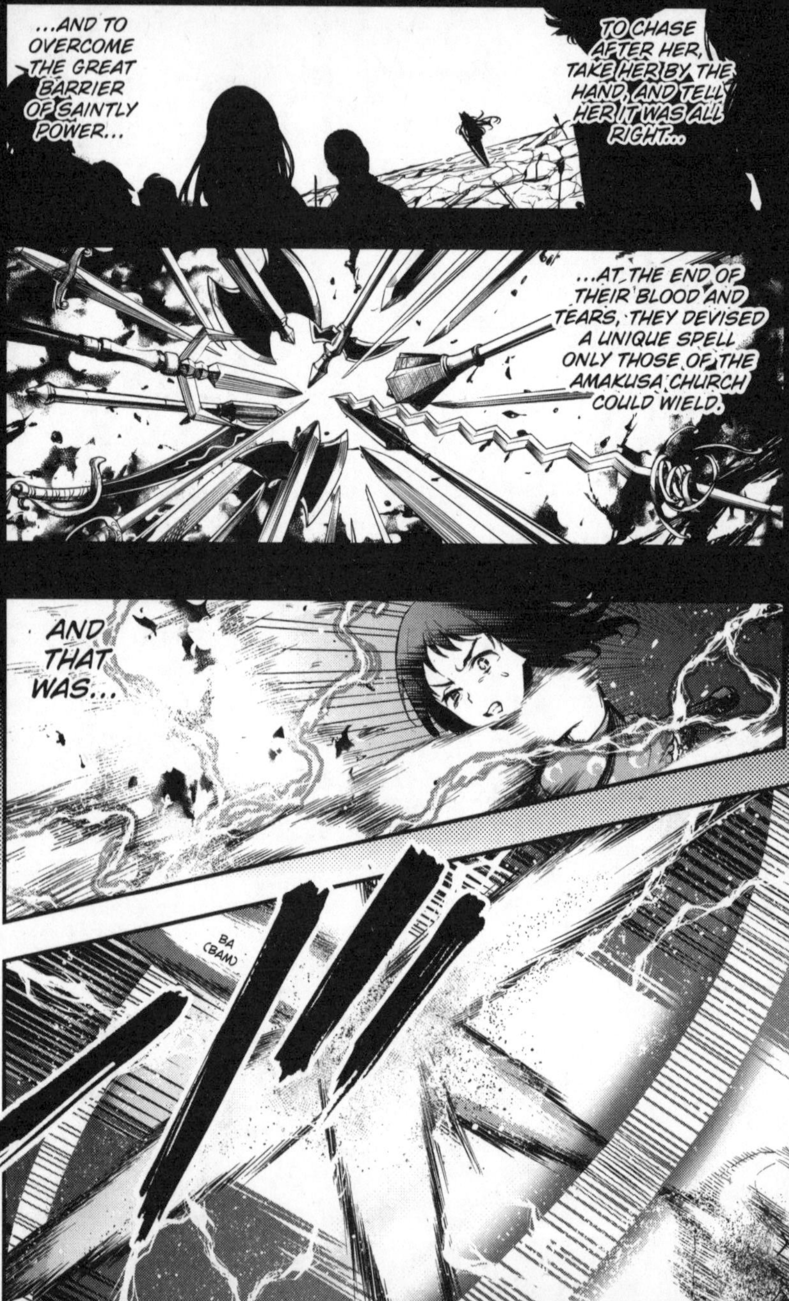
TO CHASE AFTER HER, TAKE HER BY THE HAND, AND TELL HER IT WAS ALL RIGHT...
...AND TO OVERCOME THE GREAT BARRIER OF SAINTLY POWER...
...AT THE END OF THEIR BLOOD AND TEARS, THEY DEVISED A UNIQUE SPELL ONLY THOSE OF THE AMAKUSA CHURCH COULD WIELD.
AND THAT WAS...
BA (BAM)

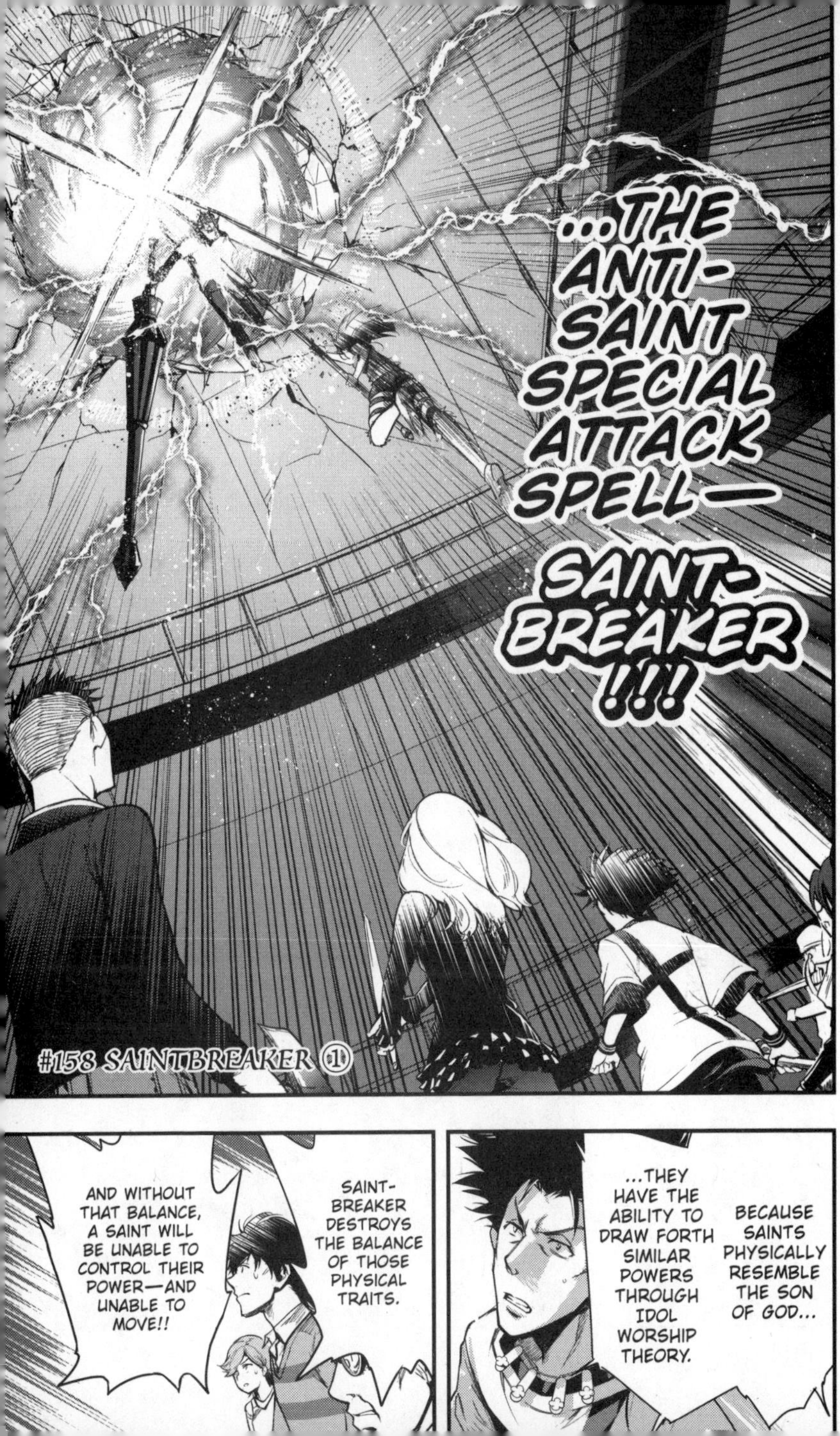
...THE ANTI-SAINT SPECIAL ATTACK SPELL—
SAINT-BREAKER!!!
#158 SAINTBREAKER ①
BECAUSE SAINTS PHYSICALLY RESEMBLE THE SON OF GOD...
...THEY HAVE THE ABILITY TO DRAW FORTH SIMILAR POWERS THROUGH IDOL WORSHIP THEORY.
SAINT-BREAKER DESTROYS THE BALANCE OF THOSE PHYSICAL TRAITS.
AND WITHOUT THAT BALANCE, A SAINT WILL BE UNABLE TO CONTROL THEIR POWER—AND UNABLE TO MOVE!!

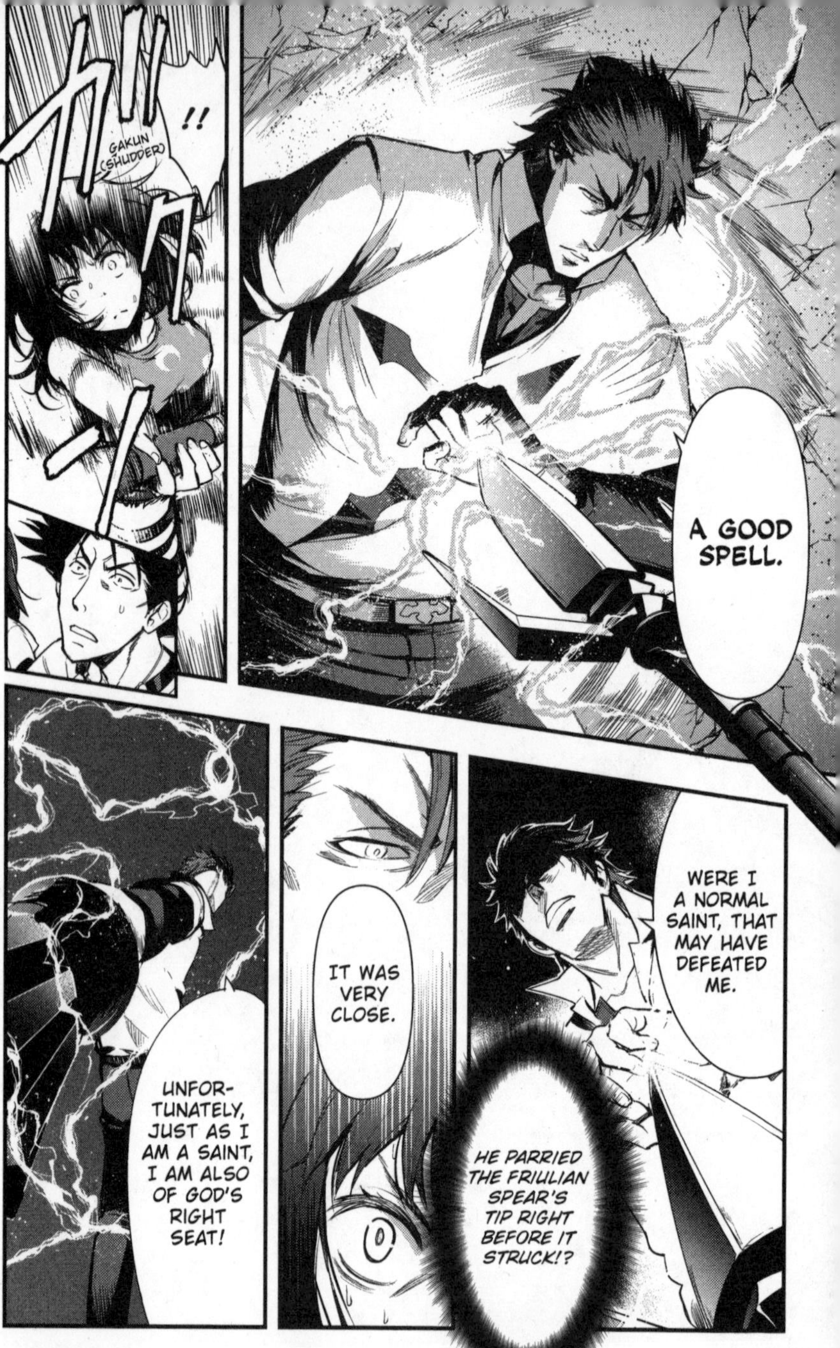
A GOOD SPELL.
GAKUN (SHUDDER)
!!
WERE I A NORMAL SAINT, THAT MAY HAVE DEFEATED ME.
IT WAS VERY CLOSE.
HE PARRIED THE FRIULIAN SPEAR'S TIP RIGHT BEFORE IT STRUCK!?
UNFOR-TUNATELY, JUST AS I AM A SAINT, I AM ALSO OF GOD'S RIGHT SEAT!

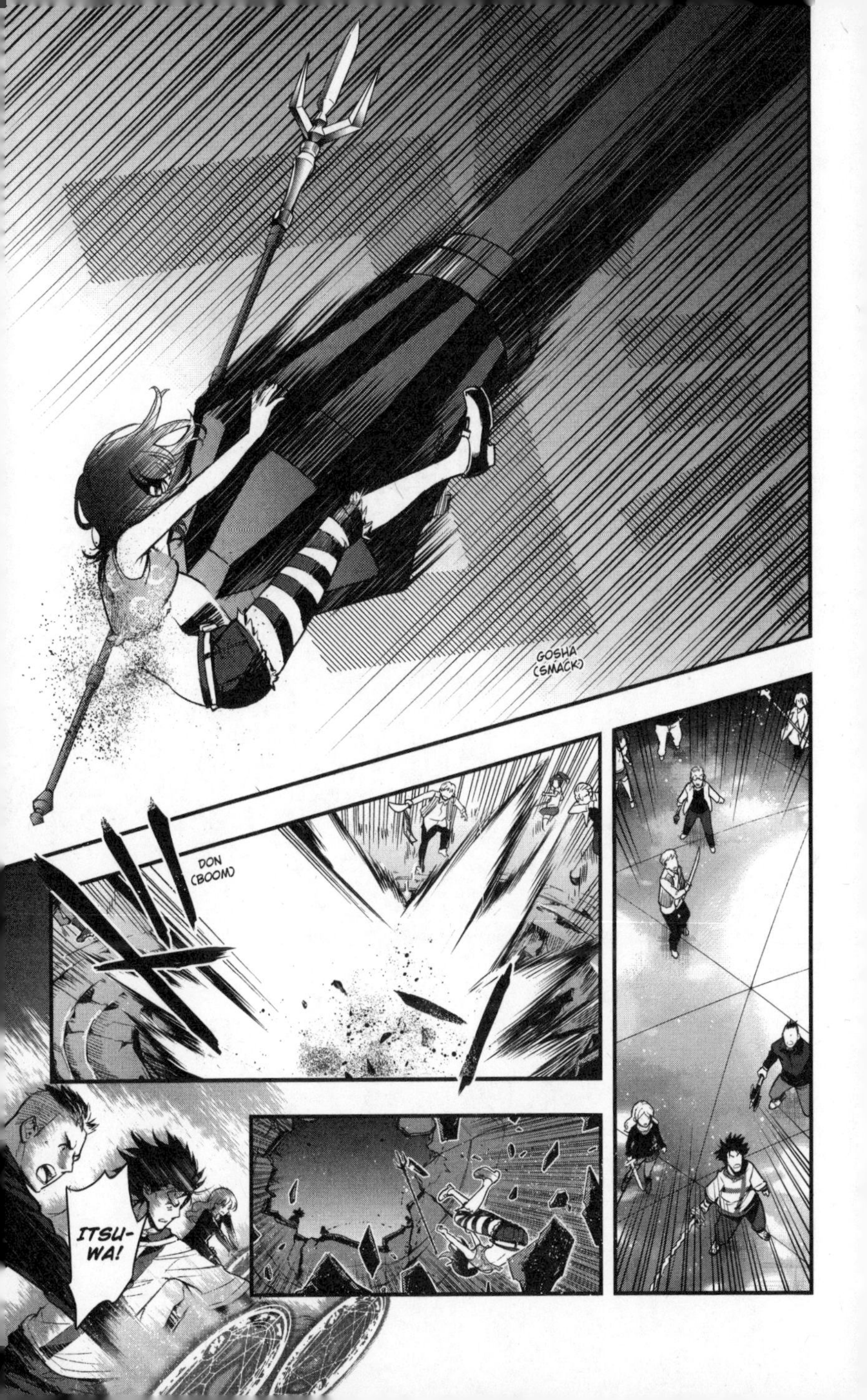
GOSHA
(SMACK)
DON
(BOOM)
ITSU-WA!

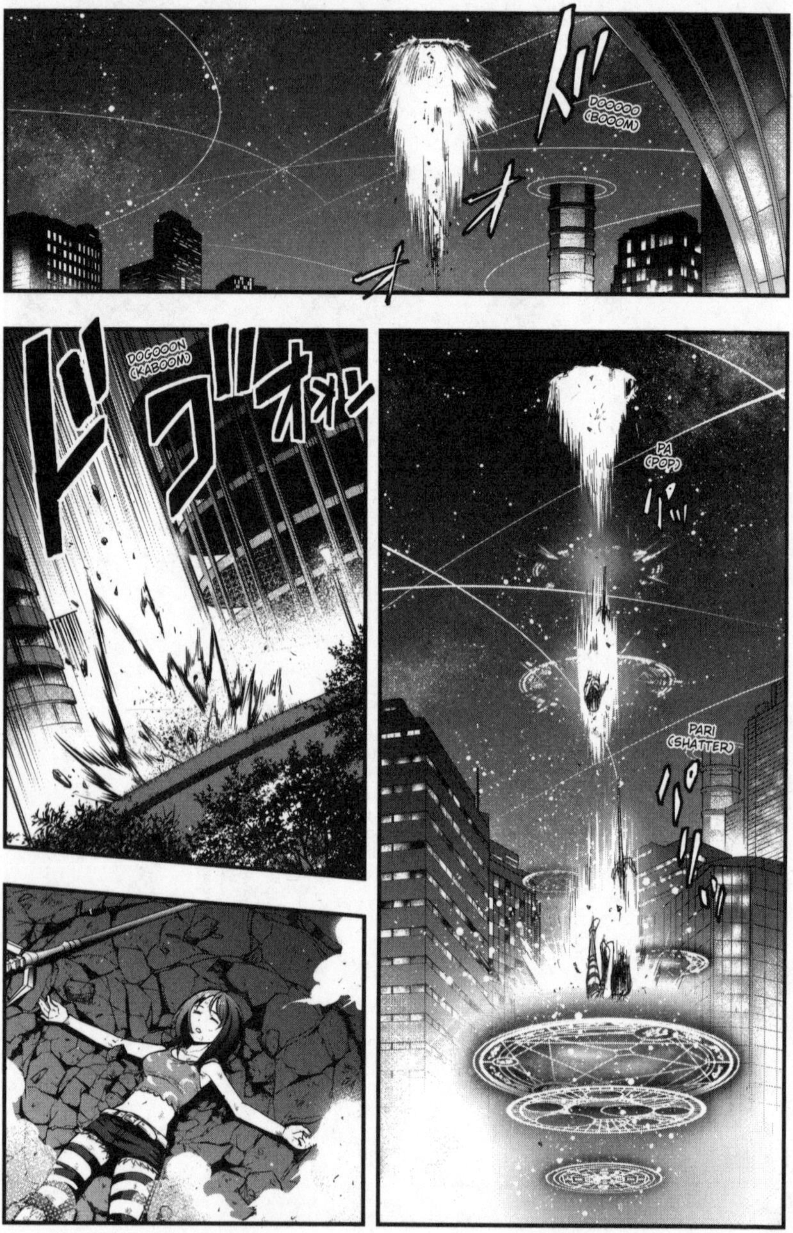
DOOOOO
(BOOOM)
PA
(POP)
PARI
(SHATTER)
DOGOOON
(KABOOM)

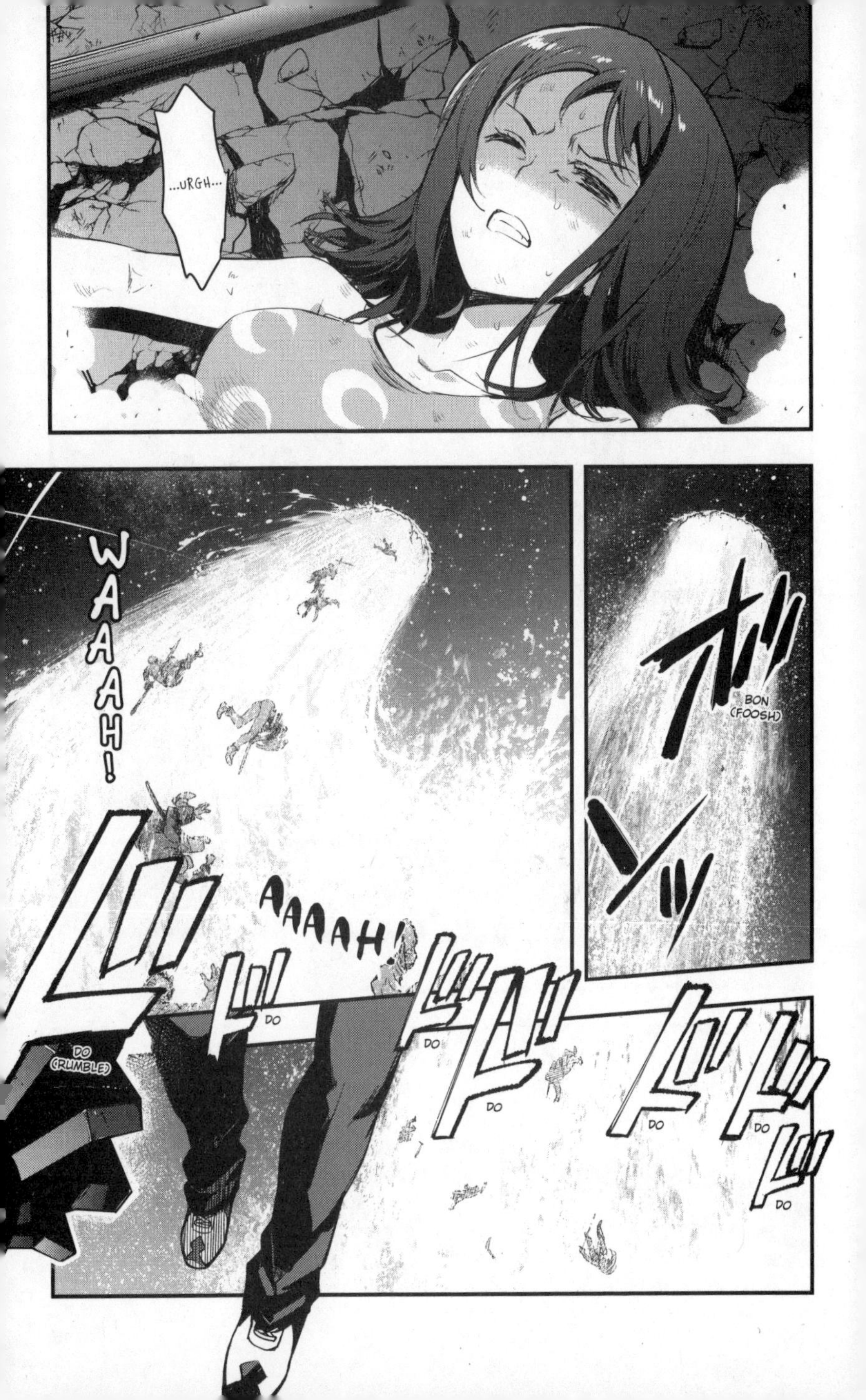

...URGH...
BON (FOOSH)
WAAAAH!
AAAAAH!
DO (RUMBLE)
DO
DO
DO
DO
DO
DO

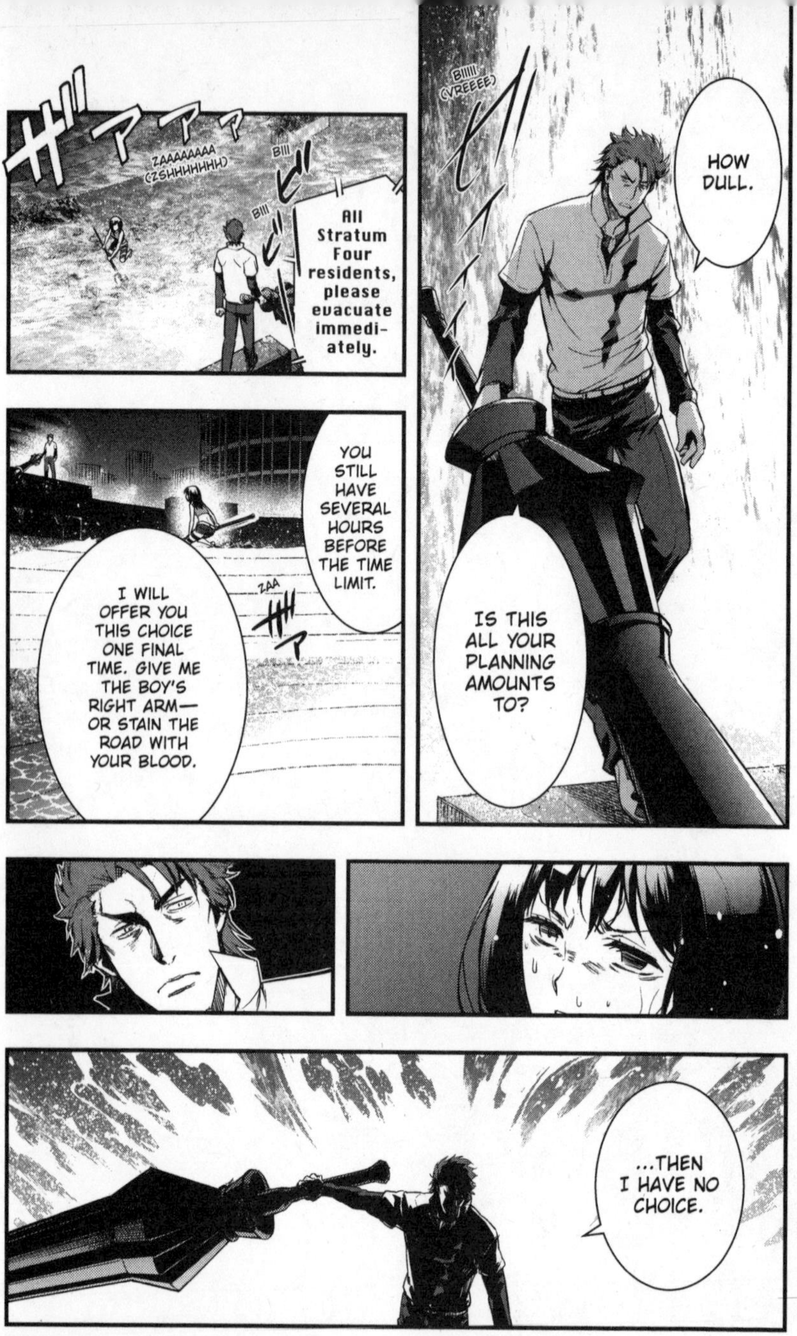
BIIIII
(VREEEE)
HOW DULL.
IS THIS ALL YOUR PLANNING AMOUNTS TO?
ZAAAAAAA
(ZSHHHHHHH)
BIII
BIII
All Stratum Four residents, please evacuate immedi-ately.
YOU STILL HAVE SEVERAL HOURS BEFORE THE TIME LIMIT.
I WILL OFFER YOU THIS CHOICE ONE FINAL TIME. GIVE ME THE BOY'S RIGHT ARM—OR STAIN THE ROAD WITH YOUR BLOOD.
ZAA
...THEN I HAVE NO CHOICE.

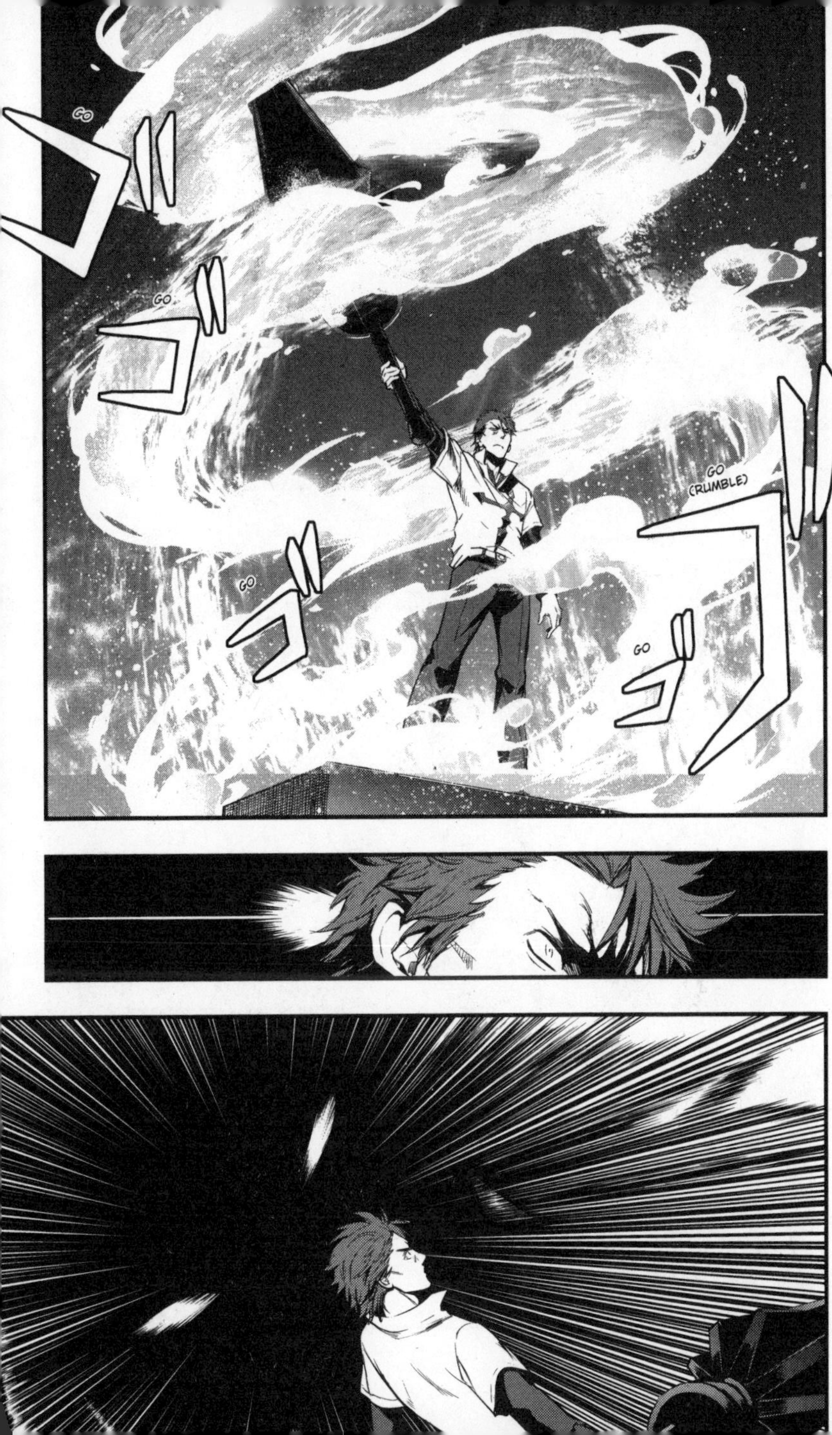
GO
GO
GO
(RUMBLE)
GO
GO

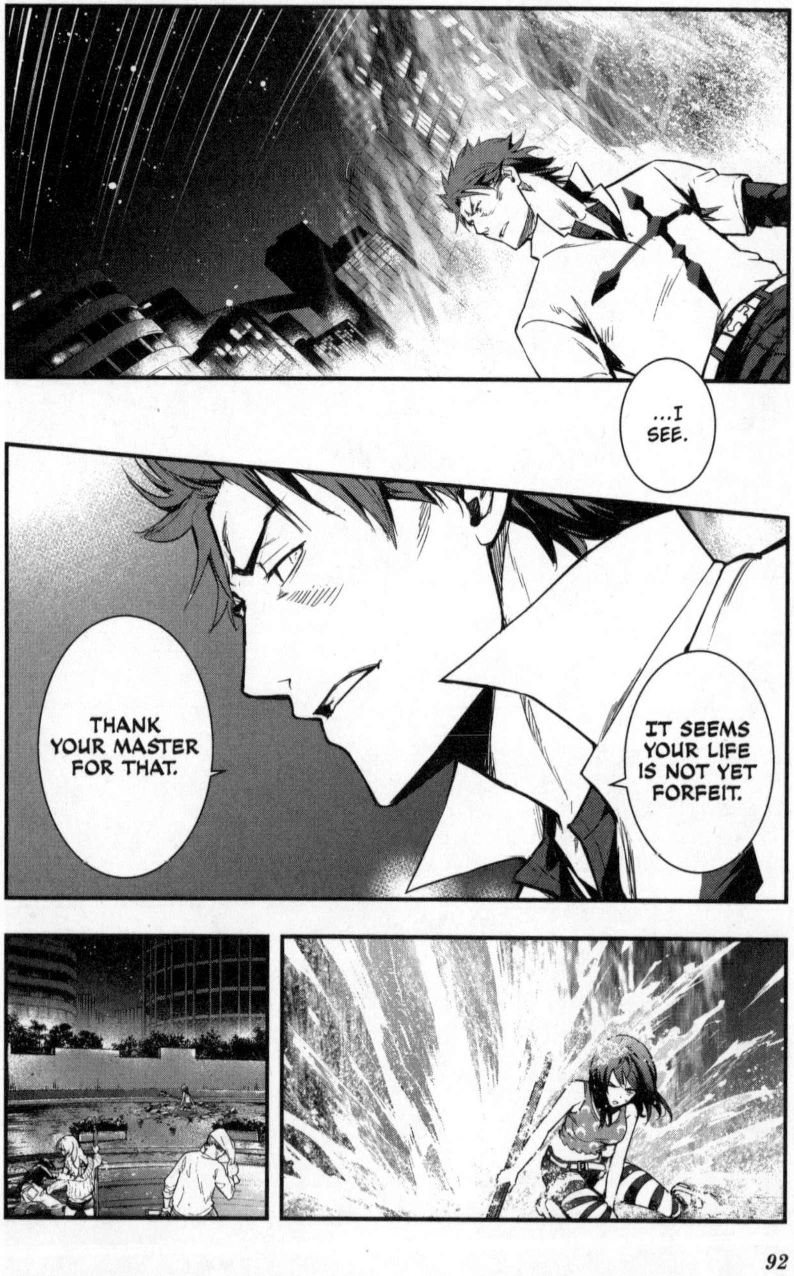
...I SEE.
IT SEEMS YOUR LIFE IS NOT YET FORFEIT.
THANK YOUR MASTER FOR THAT.

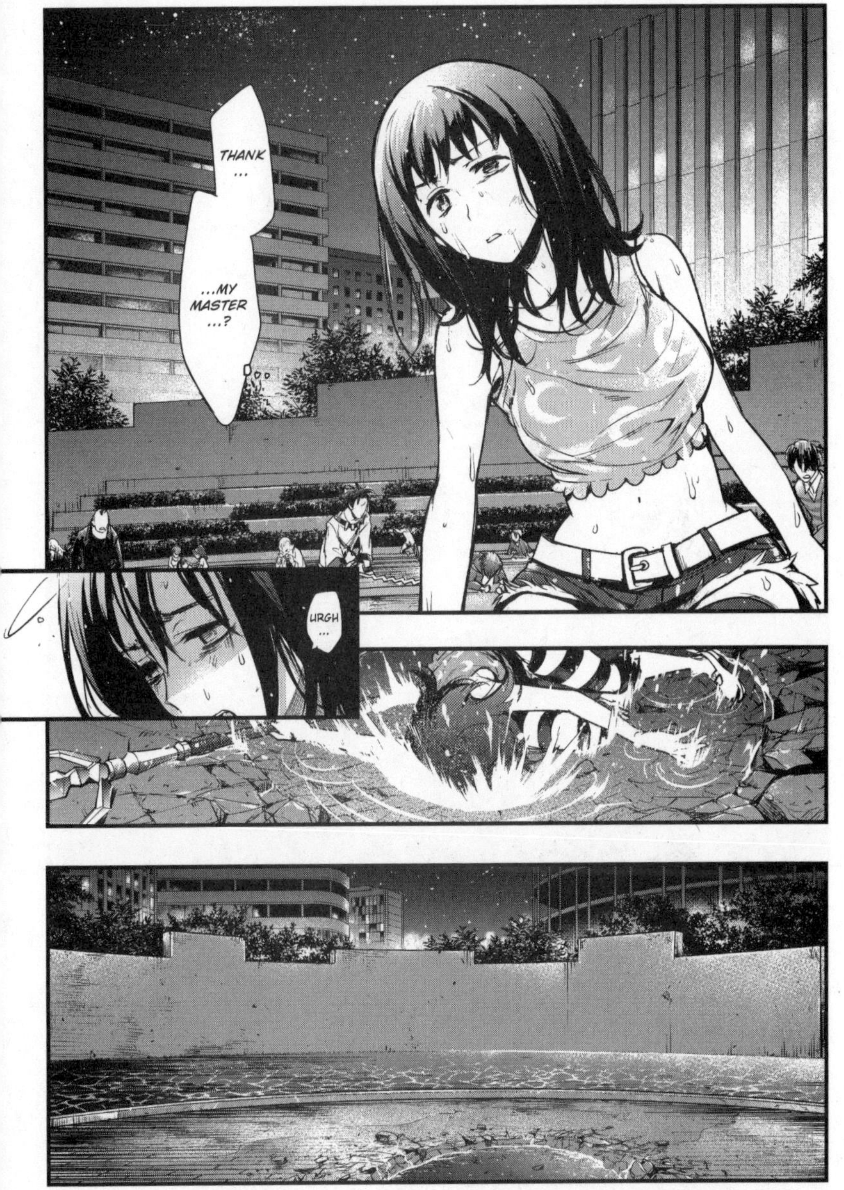
THANK...
...MY MASTER...?
URGH...

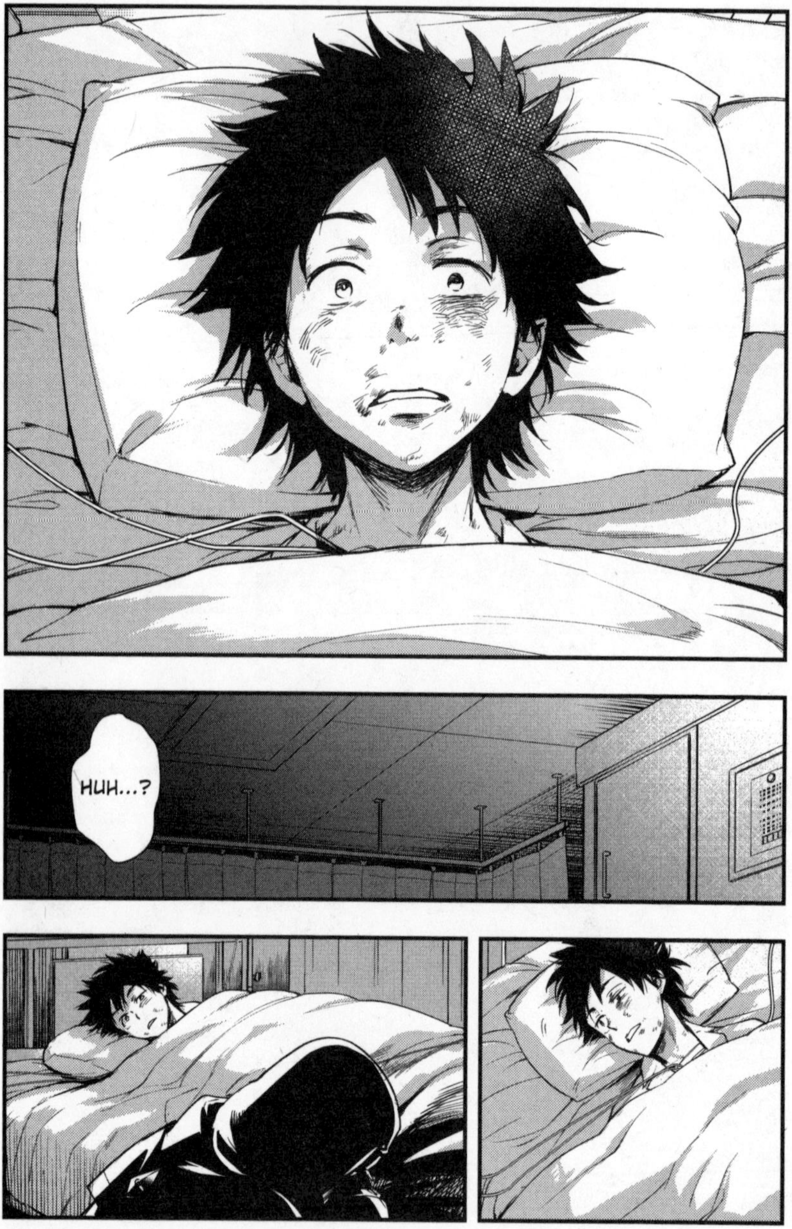
HUH...?

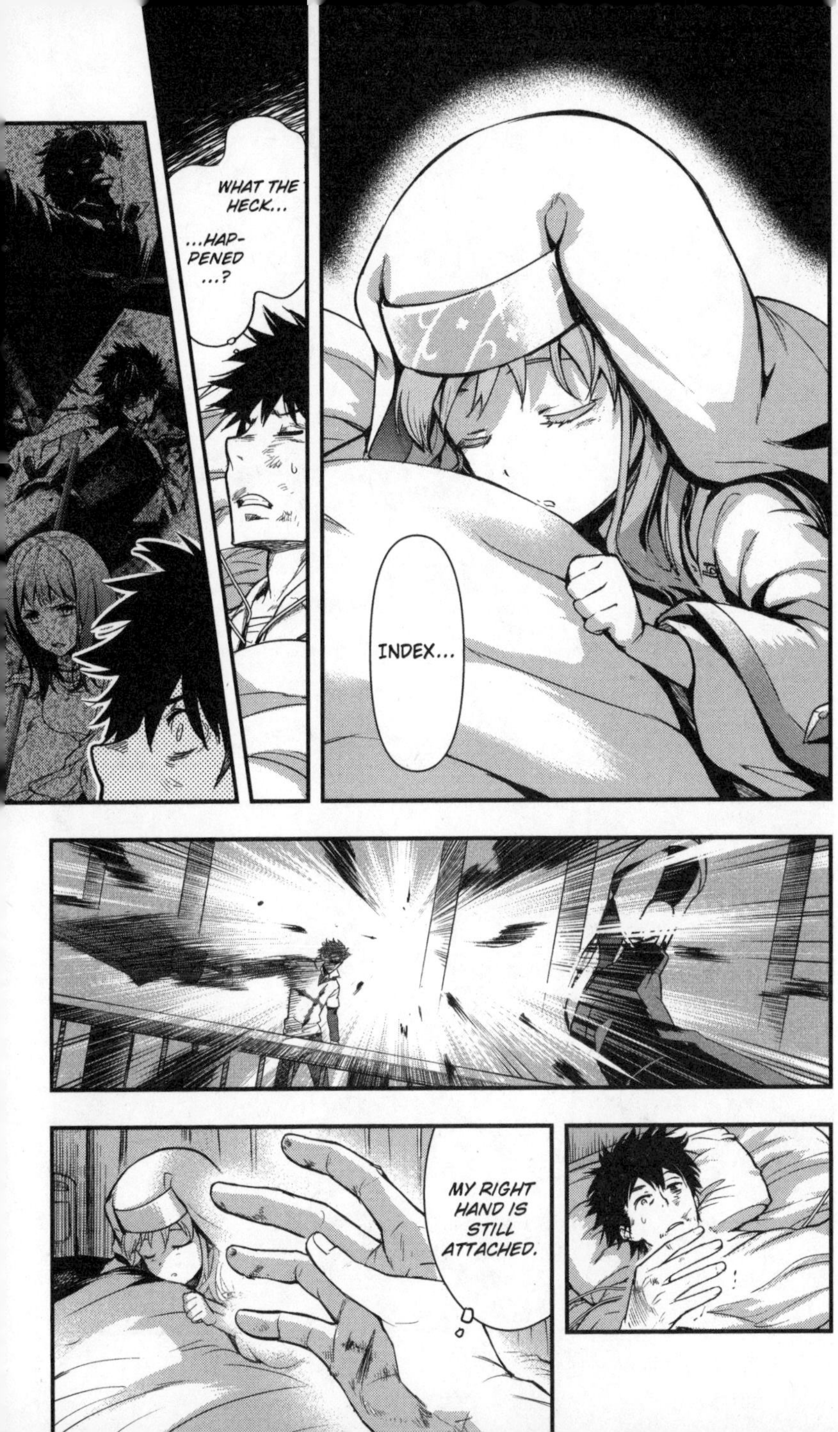
INDEX...
WHAT THE HECK...
...HAP-PENED ...?
MY RIGHT HAND IS STILL ATTACHED.

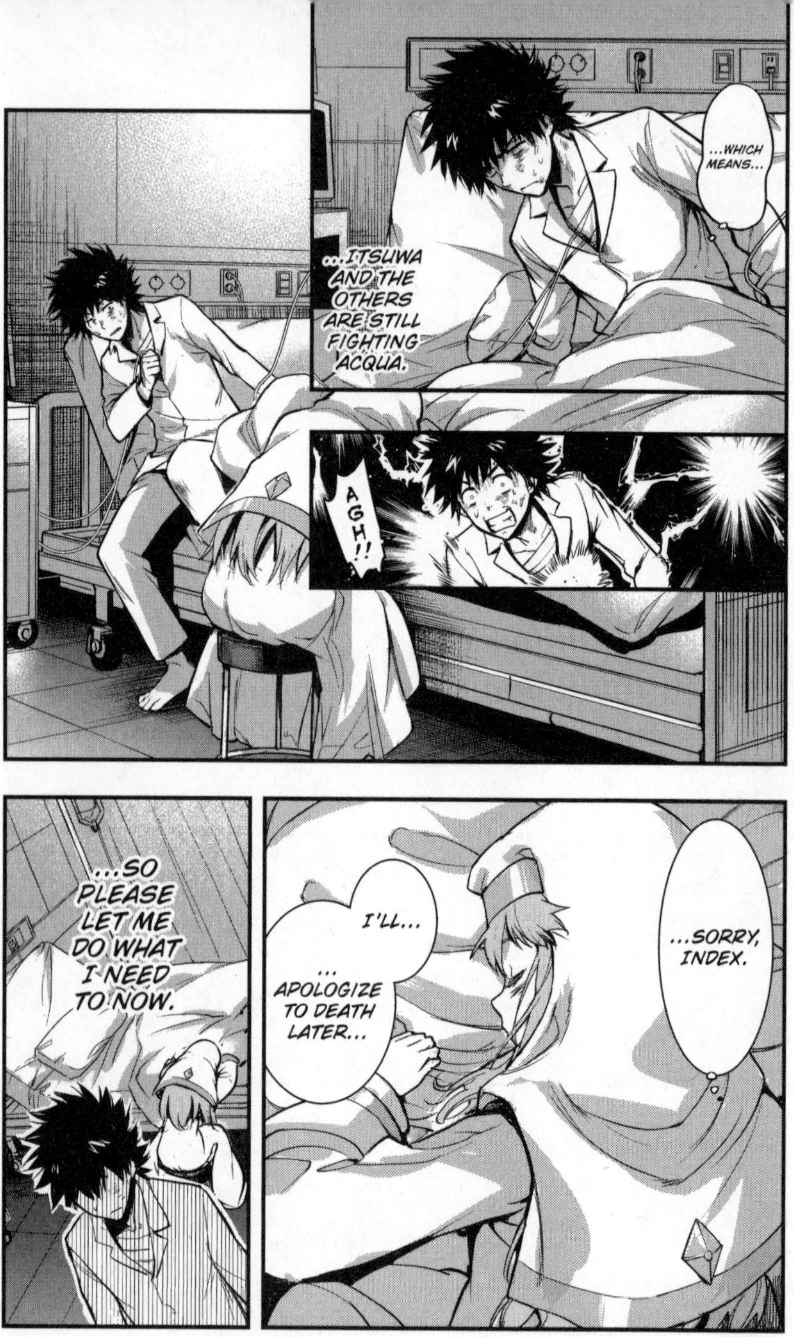
...WHICH MEANS...
...ITSUWA AND THE OTHERS ARE STILL FIGHTING ACQUA.
AGH!!
...SORRY, INDEX.
I'LL...
...APOLOGIZE TO DEATH LATER...
...SO PLEASE LET ME DO WHAT I NEED TO NOW.

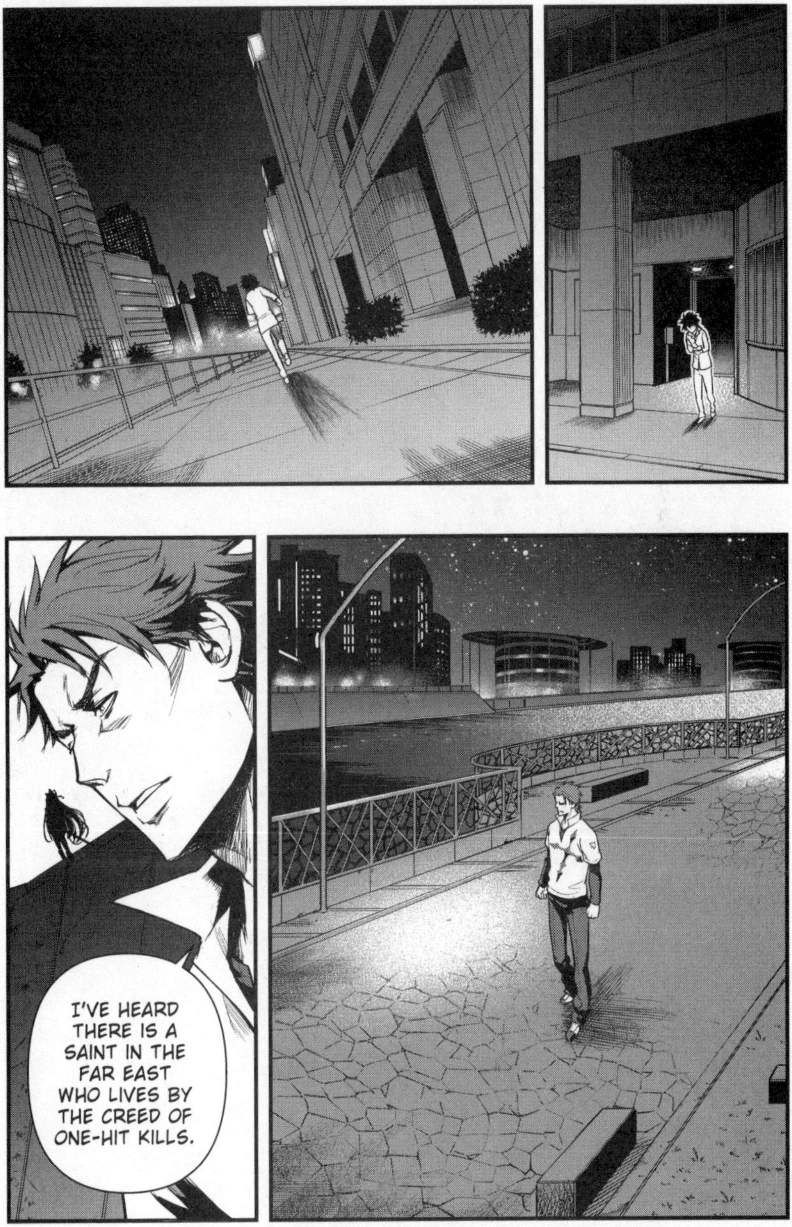
I'VE HEARD THERE IS A SAINT IN THE FAR EAST WHO LIVES BY THE CREED OF ONE-HIT KILLS.

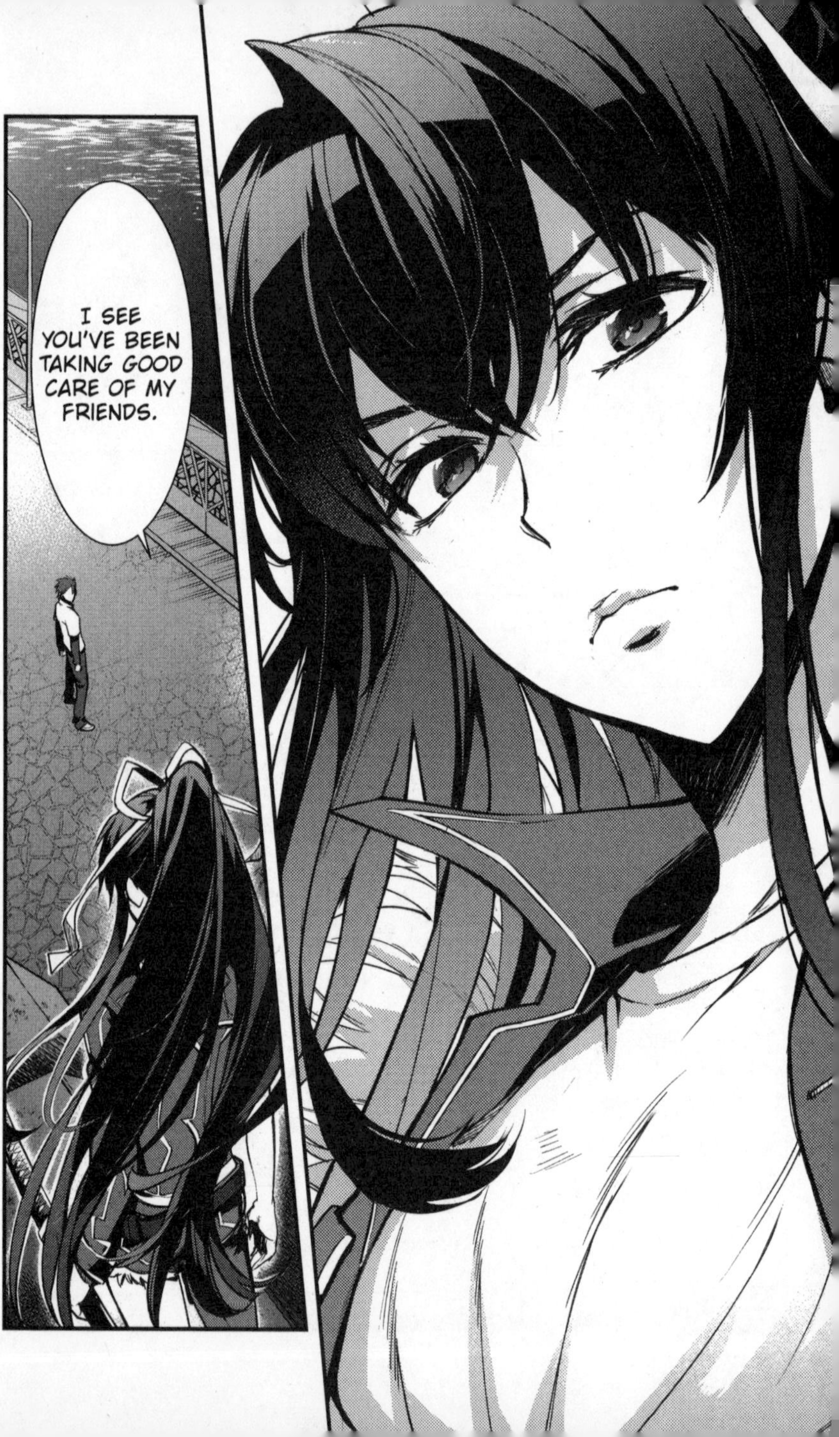
I SEE YOU'VE BEEN TAKING GOOD CARE OF MY FRIENDS.

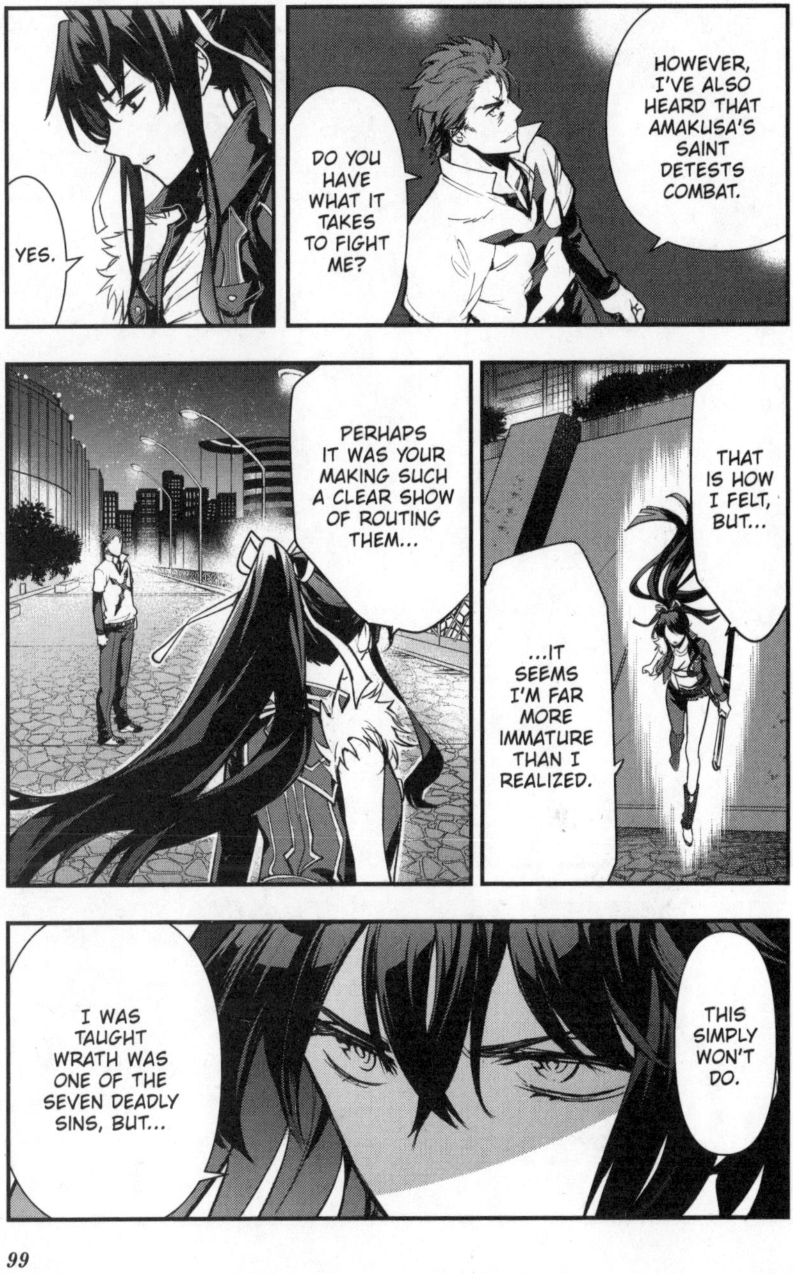
HOWEVER, I'VE ALSO HEARD THAT AMAKUSA'S SAINT DETESTS COMBAT.
DO YOU HAVE WHAT IT TAKES TO FIGHT ME?
YES.
THAT IS HOW I FELT, BUT...
...IT SEEMS I'M FAR MORE IMMATURE THAN I REALIZED.
PERHAPS IT WAS YOUR MAKING SUCH A CLEAR SHOW OF ROUTING THEM...
THIS SIMPLY WON'T DO.
I WAS TAUGHT WRATH WAS ONE OF THE SEVEN DEADLY SINS, BUT...

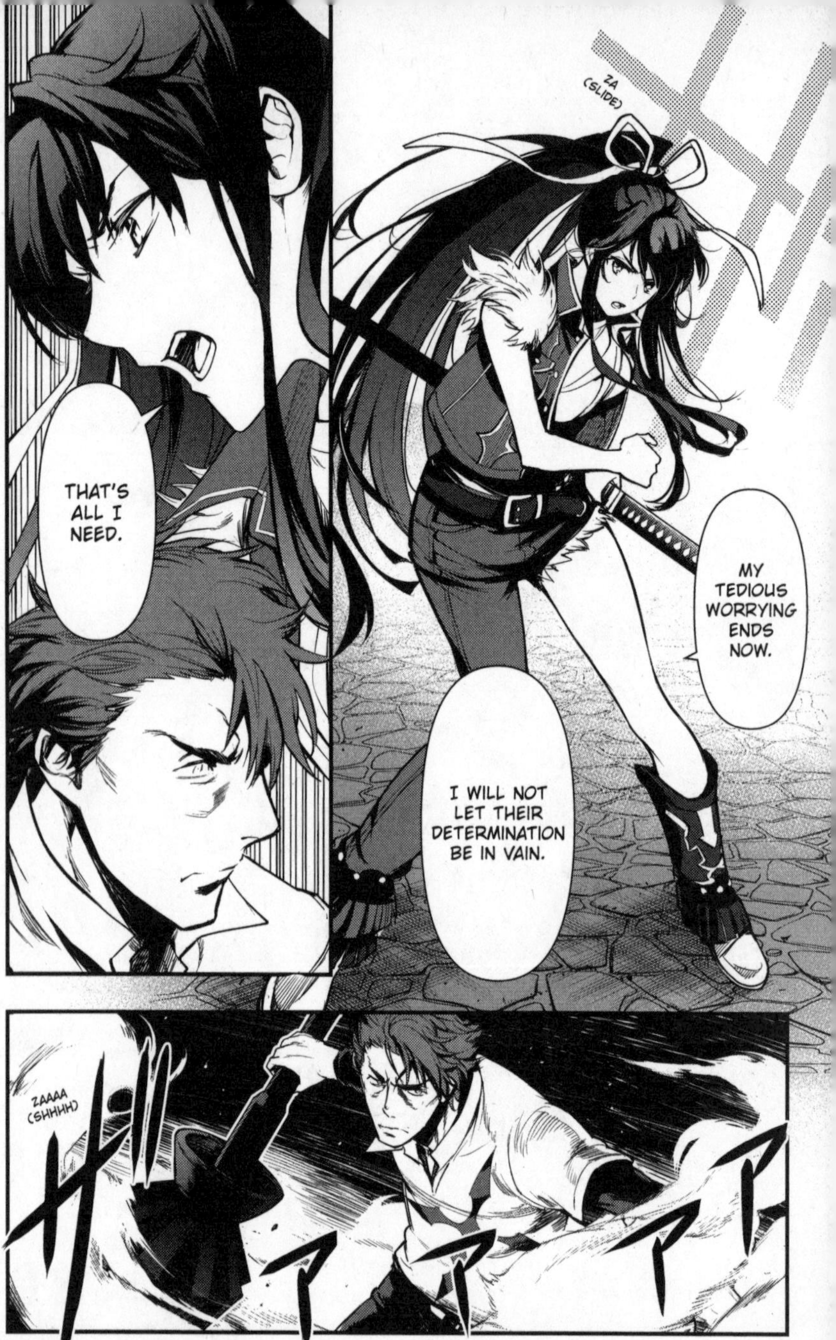
ZA (SLIDE)
MY TEDIOUS WORRYING ENDS NOW.
I WILL NOT LET THEIR DETERMINATION BE IN VAIN.
THAT'S ALL I NEED.
ZAAAA (SHHHH)

A Certain Magical Index

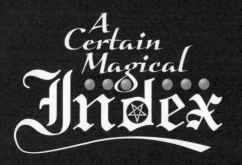

A Certain Magical Index

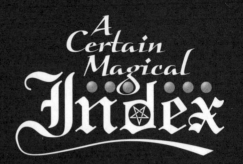

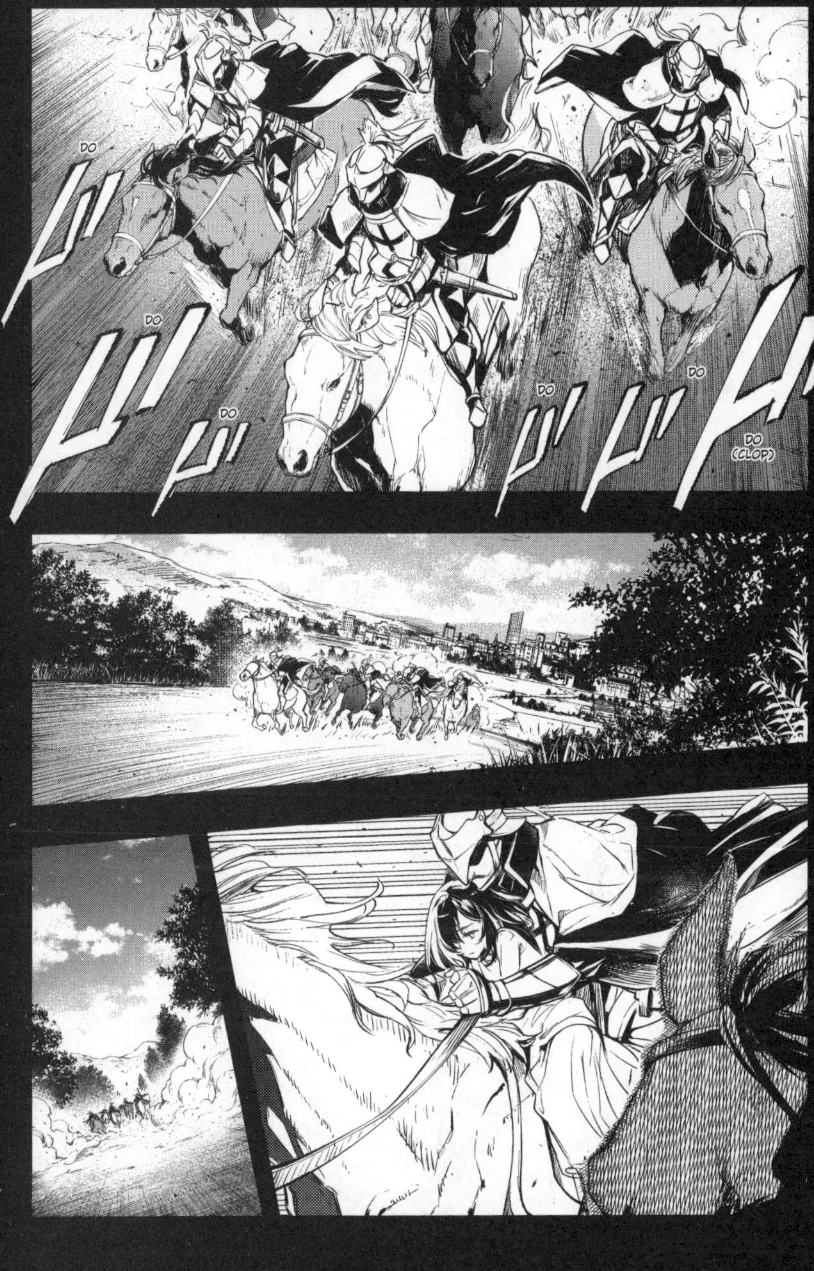
DO
(CLOP)
DO
DO
DO
DO
DO

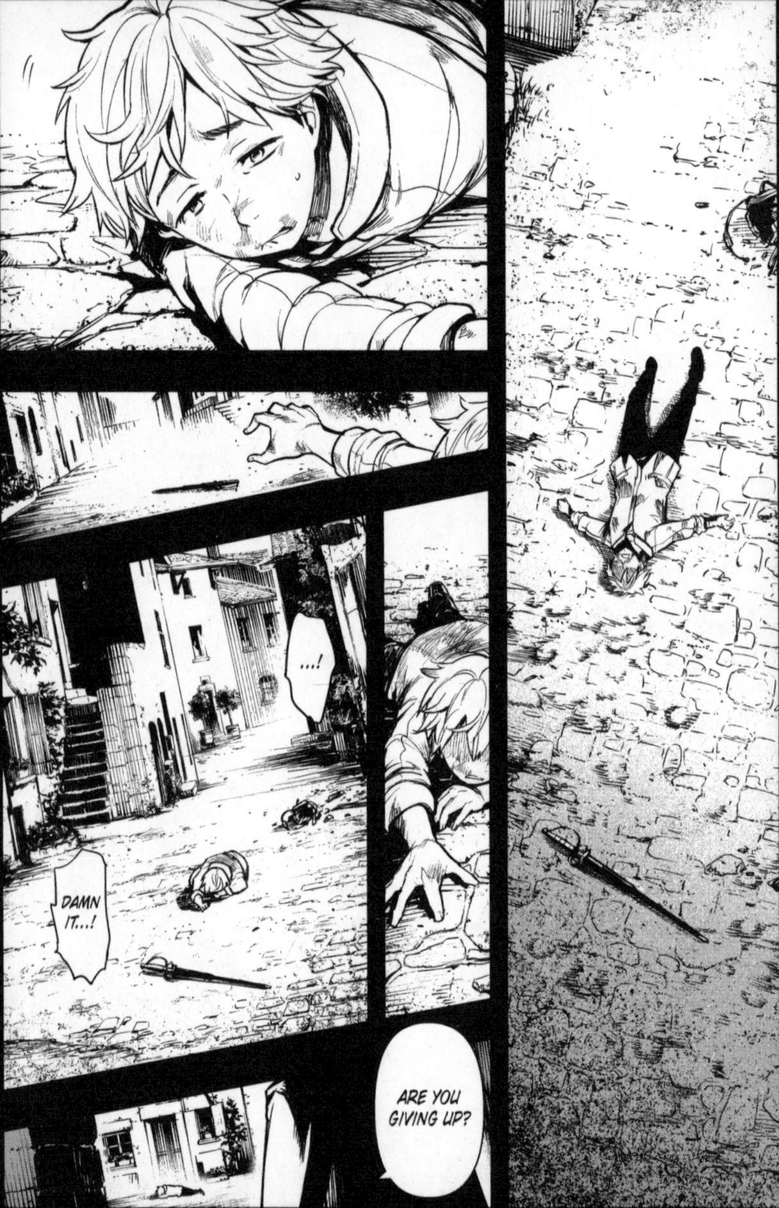
...!
DAMN IT...!
ARE YOU GIVING UP?

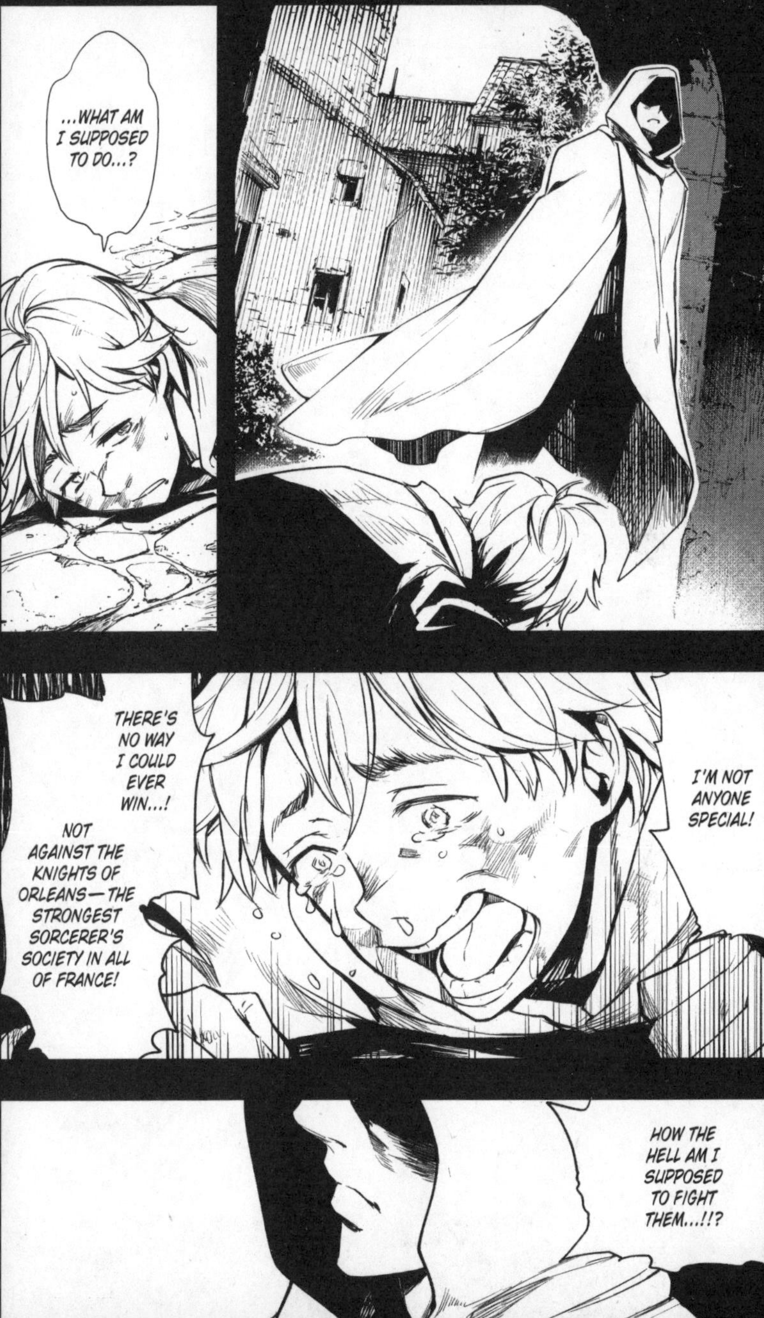
...WHAT AM I SUPPOSED TO DO...?
I'M NOT ANYONE SPECIAL!
THERE'S NO WAY I COULD EVER WIN...!
NOT AGAINST THE KNIGHTS OF ORLEANS—THE STRONGEST SORCERER'S SOCIETY IN ALL OF FRANCE!
HOW THE HELL AM I SUPPOSED TO FIGHT THEM...!!?

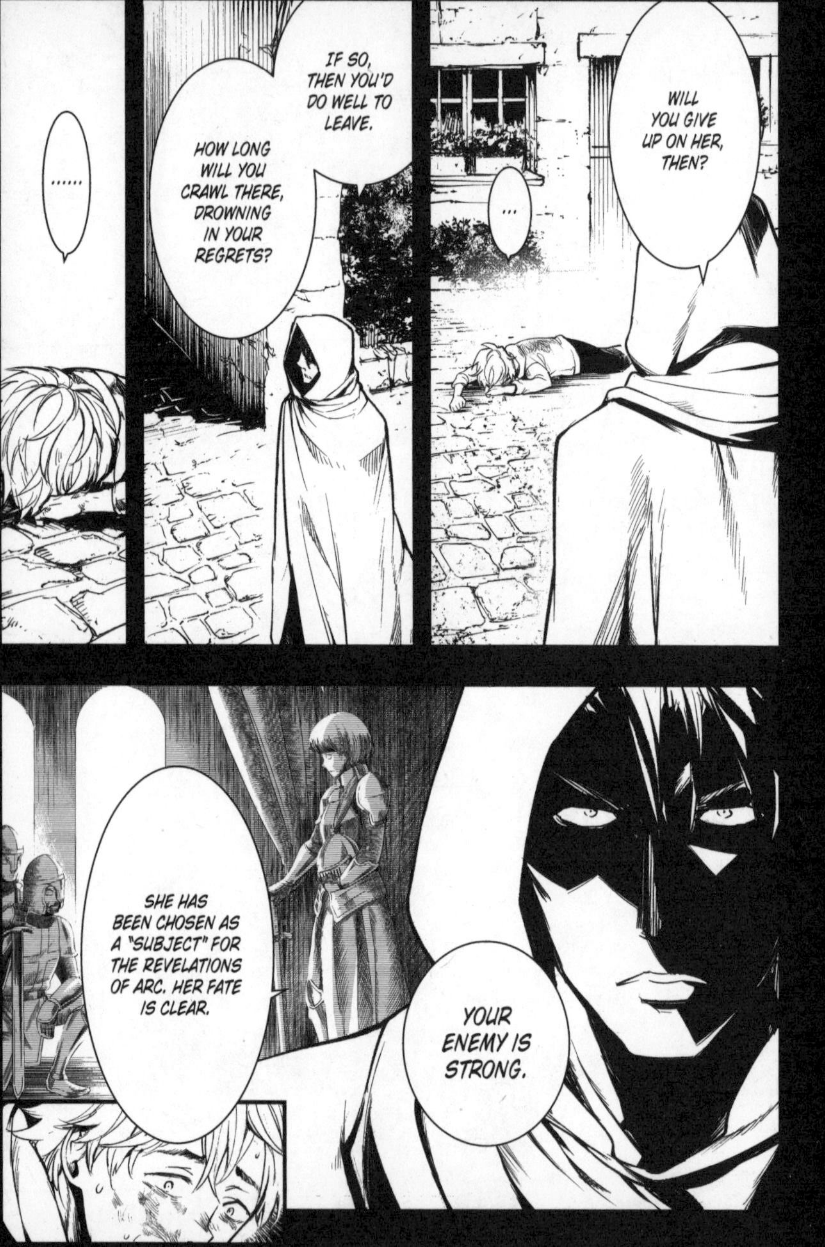
WILL YOU GIVE UP ON HER, THEN?
...
IF SO, THEN YOU'D DO WELL TO LEAVE.
HOW LONG WILL YOU CRAWL THERE, DROWNING IN YOUR REGRETS?
......
YOUR ENEMY IS STRONG.
SHE HAS BEEN CHOSEN AS A "SUBJECT" FOR THE REVELATIONS OF ARC. HER FATE IS CLEAR.

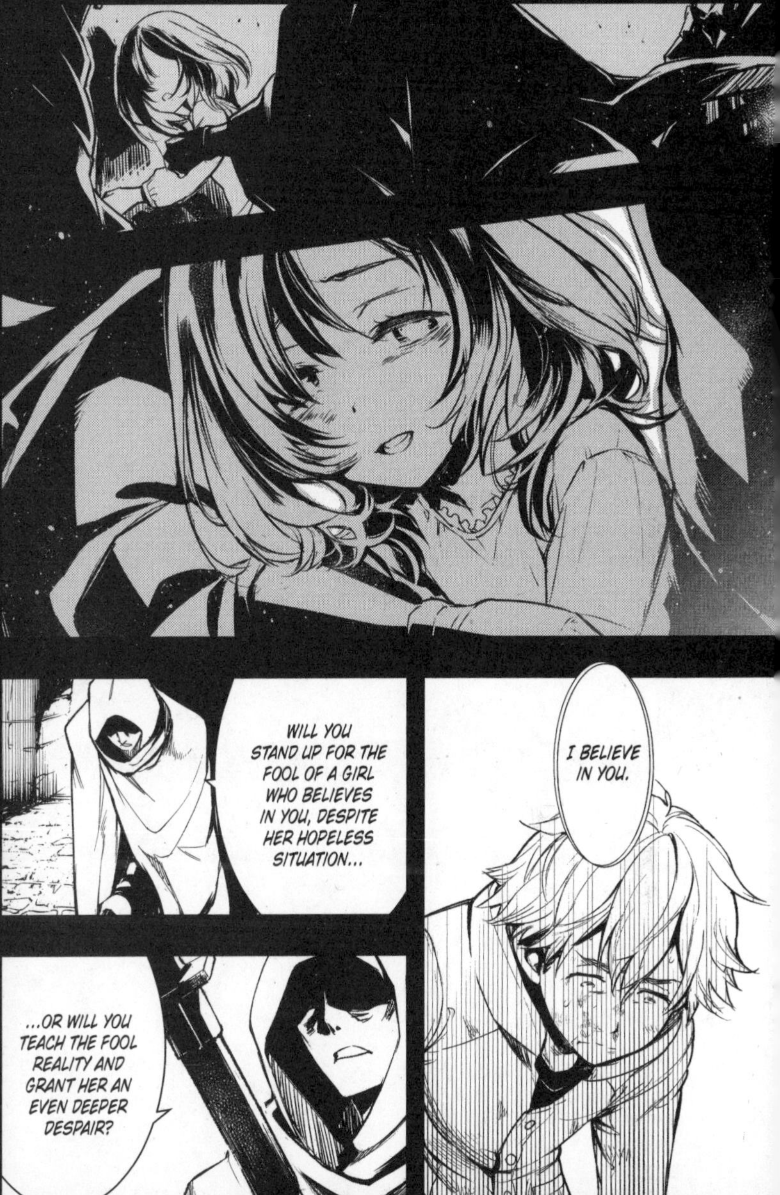
I BELIEVE IN YOU.
WILL YOU STAND UP FOR THE FOOL OF A GIRL WHO BELIEVES IN YOU, DESPITE HER HOPELESS SITUATION...
...OR WILL YOU TEACH THE FOOL REALITY AND GRANT HER AN EVEN DEEPER DESPAIR?

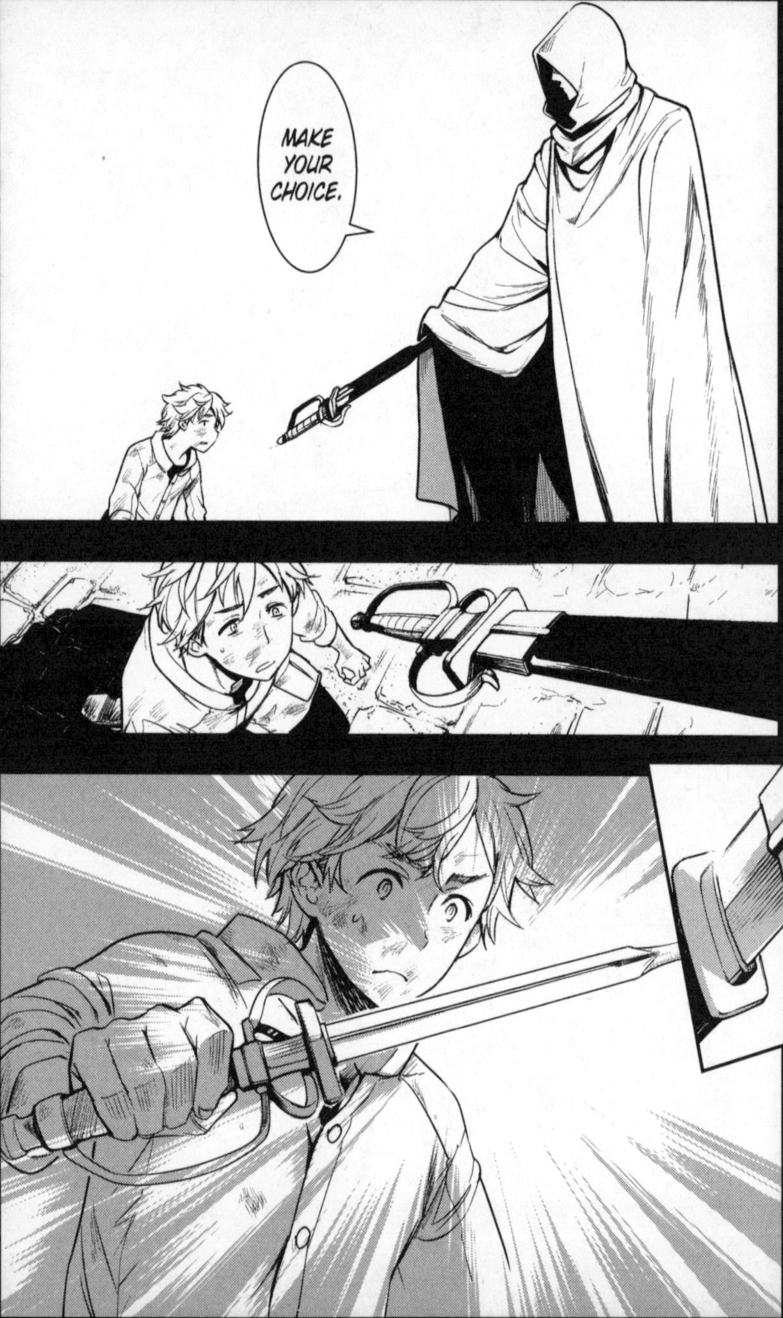
MAKE YOUR CHOICE.

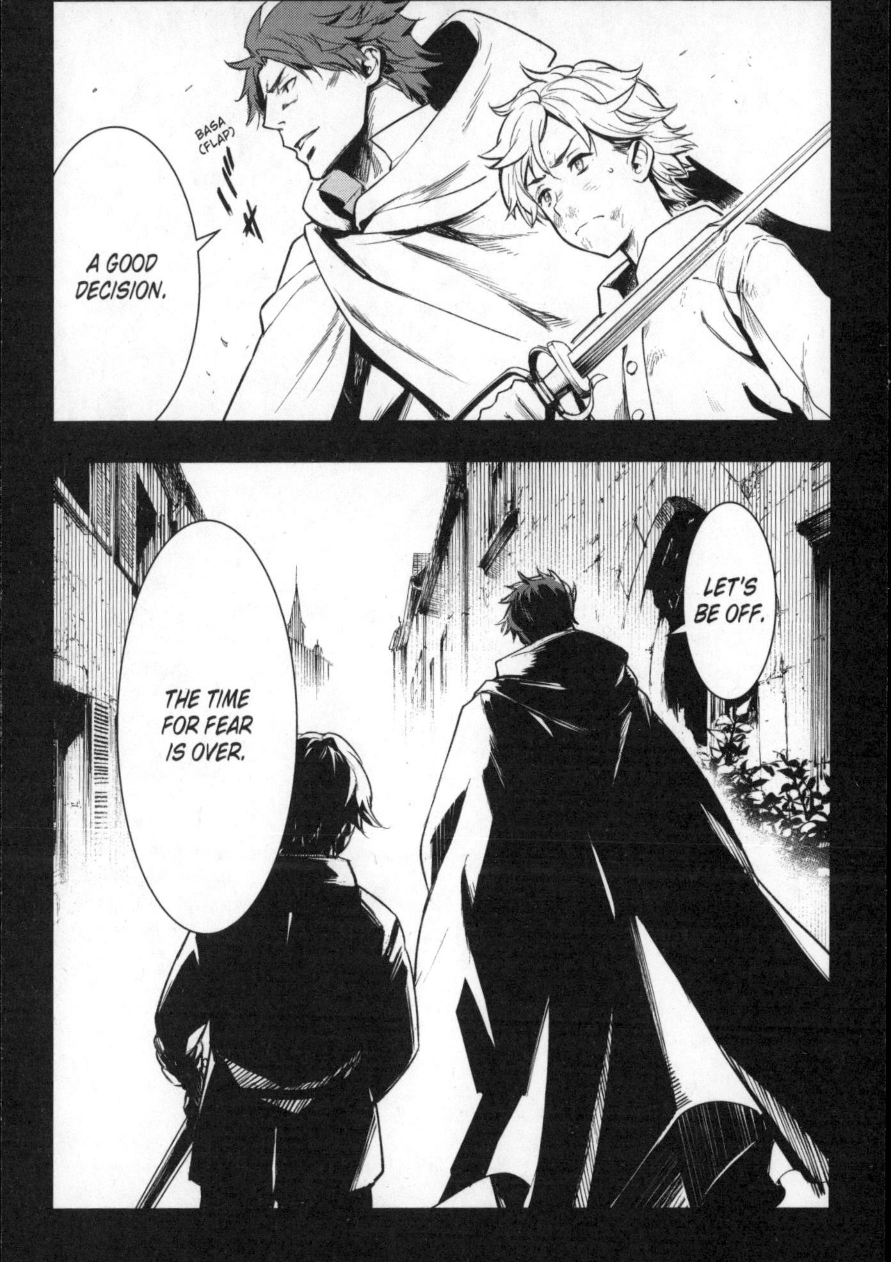
BASA (FLAP)
A GOOD DECISION.
LET'S BE OFF.
THE TIME FOR FEAR IS OVER.

#159 SAINTBREAKER ②

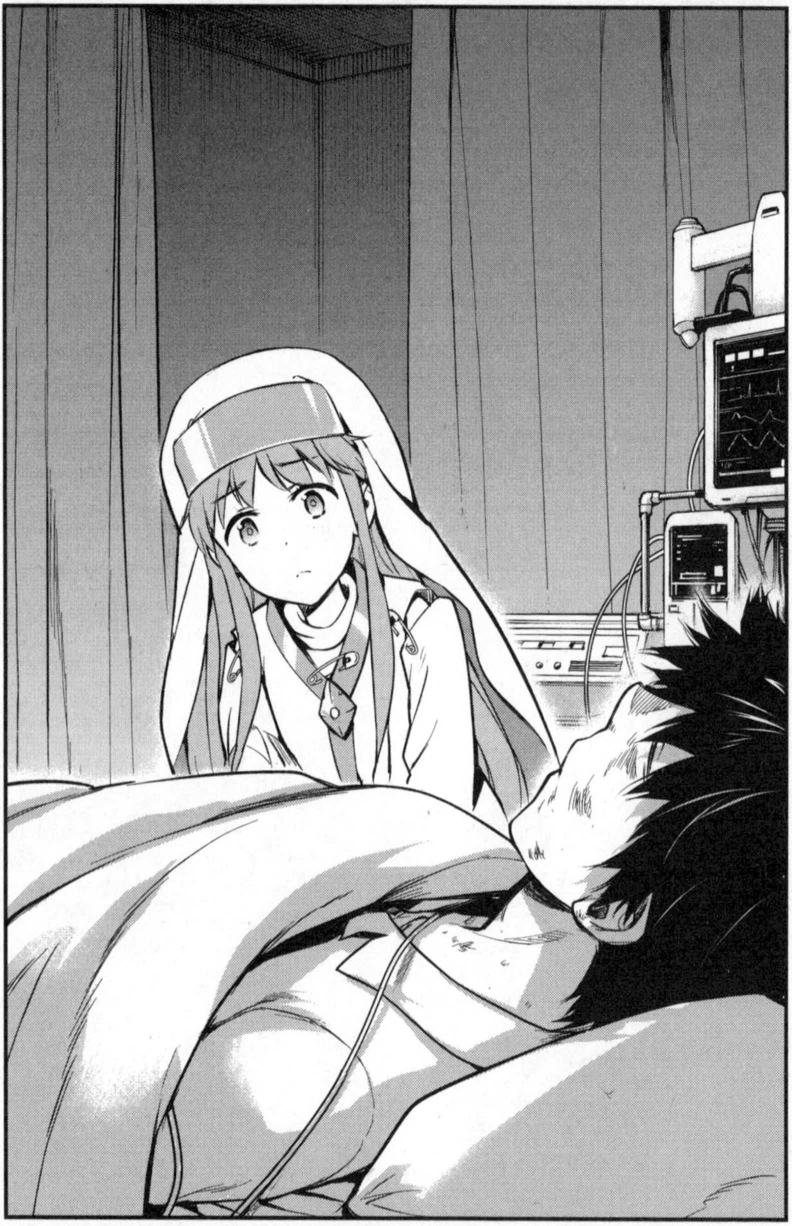

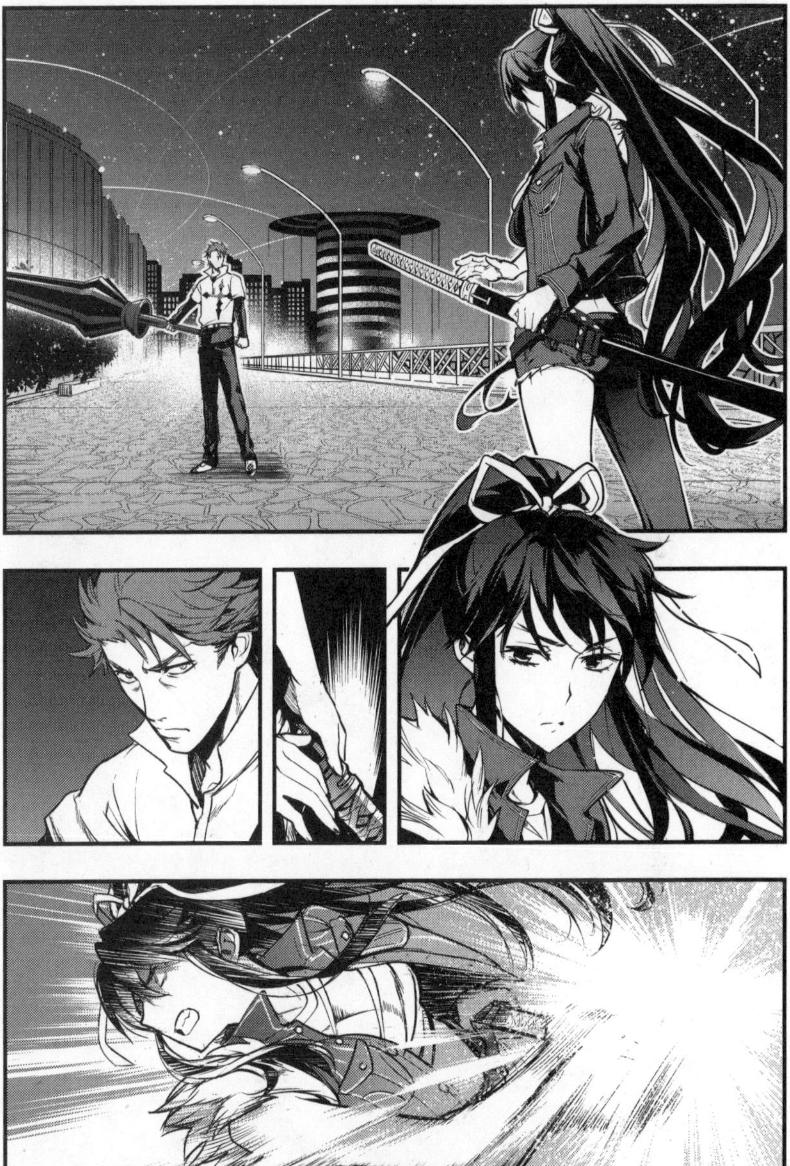

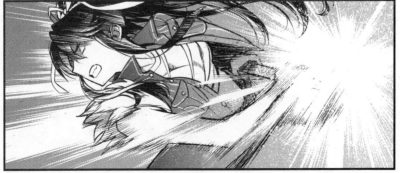

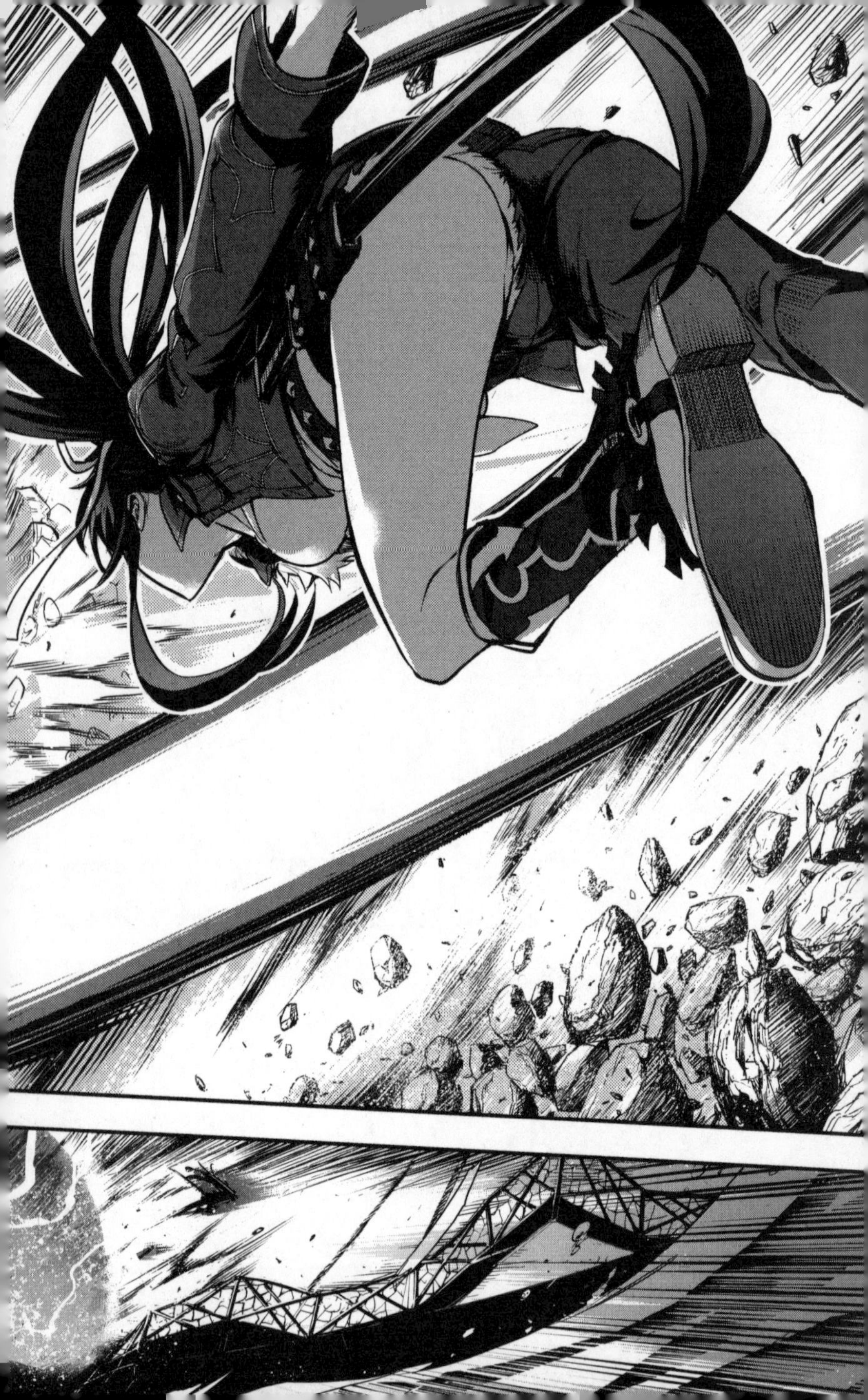

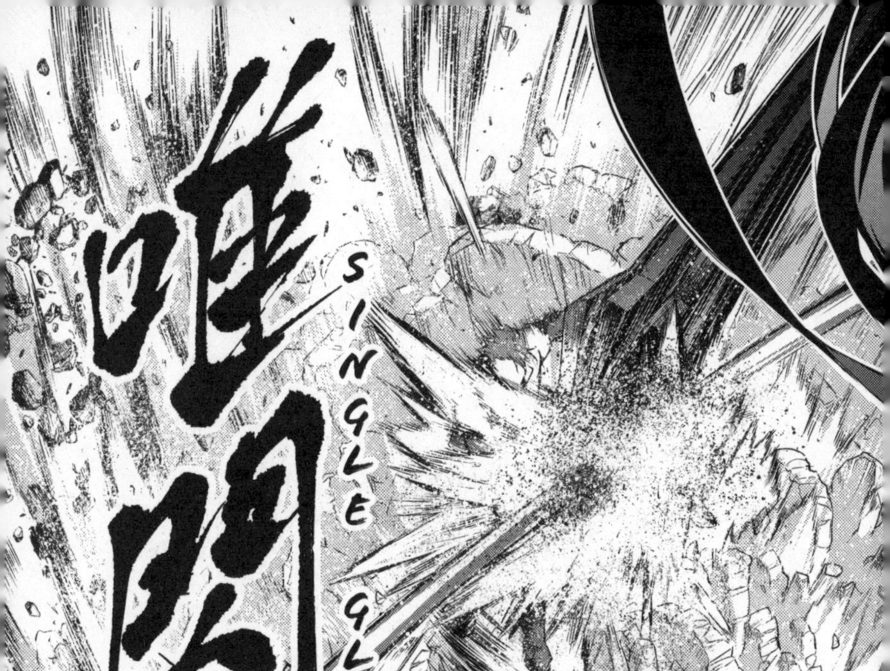
唯閃!!!
SINGLE GLINT!!!
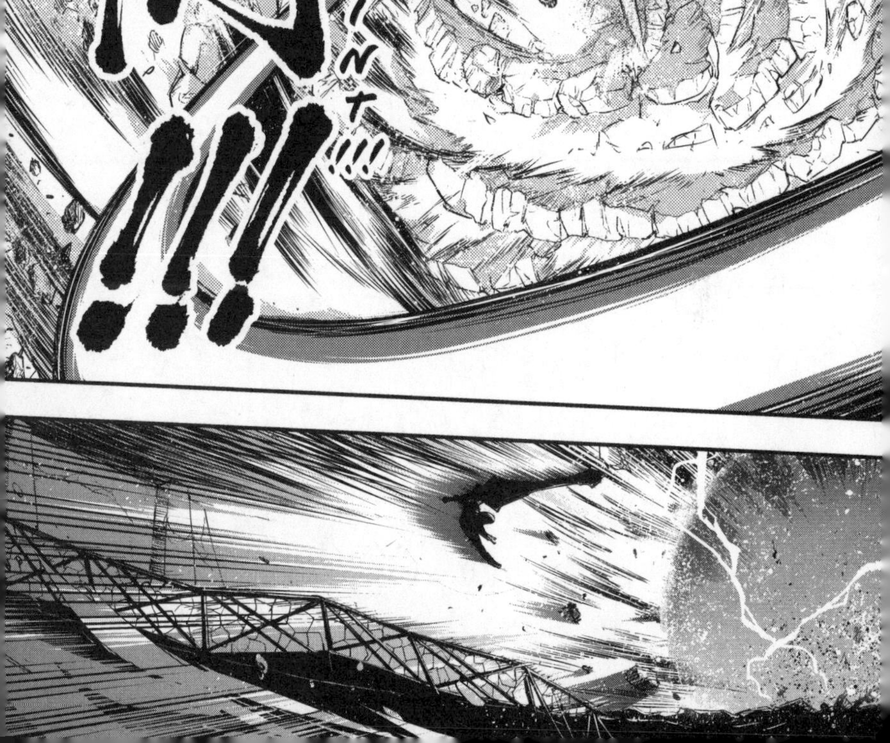

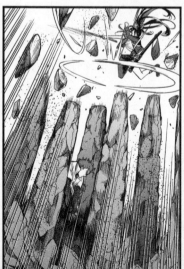

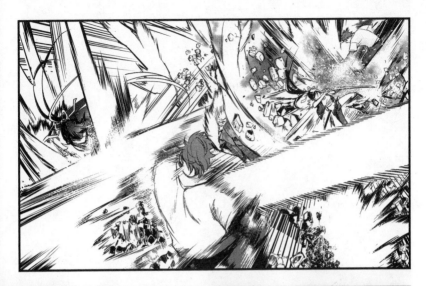

HOW-
EVER...

A GOD-SPEED SLASH—IF THE CROSSIST SPELL IS BLOCKED, IT TURNS INTO A BUDDHIST SPELL. IF THAT IS DEALT WITH, IT SWITCHES TO A SHINTO ONE...

WITH THIS, YOU COULD LIKELY CLEAVE THROUGH EVEN THE ANGELS OF MONO-THEISTIC RELIGIONS.

FOR SUCH STRENGTH TO GATHER FOR THE SAKE OF A SINGLE PERSON—

THAT BOY IS QUITE POPULAR.

WONDER-FUL.

GI
(CREAK)

JIGI
(CREAK)

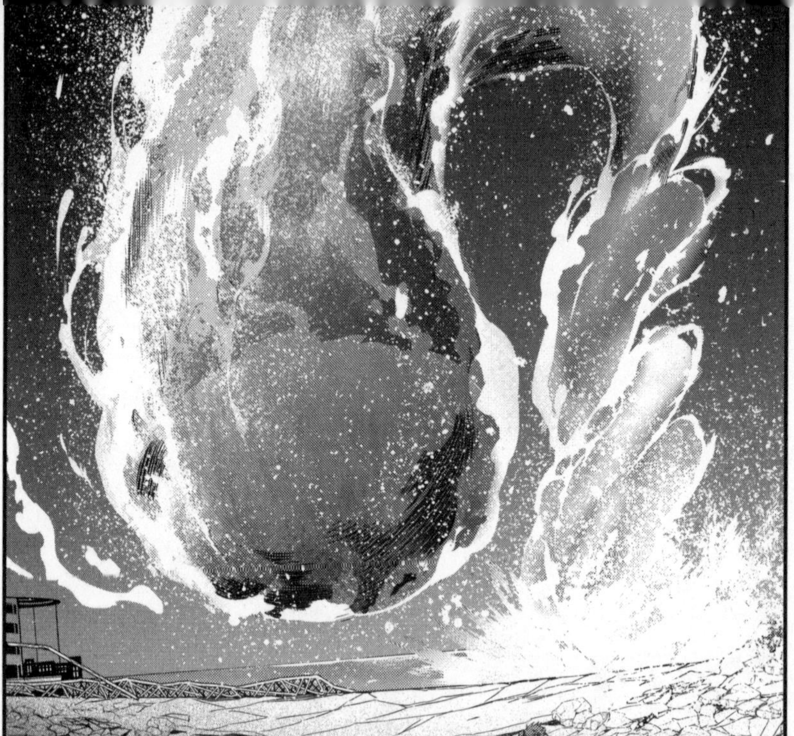
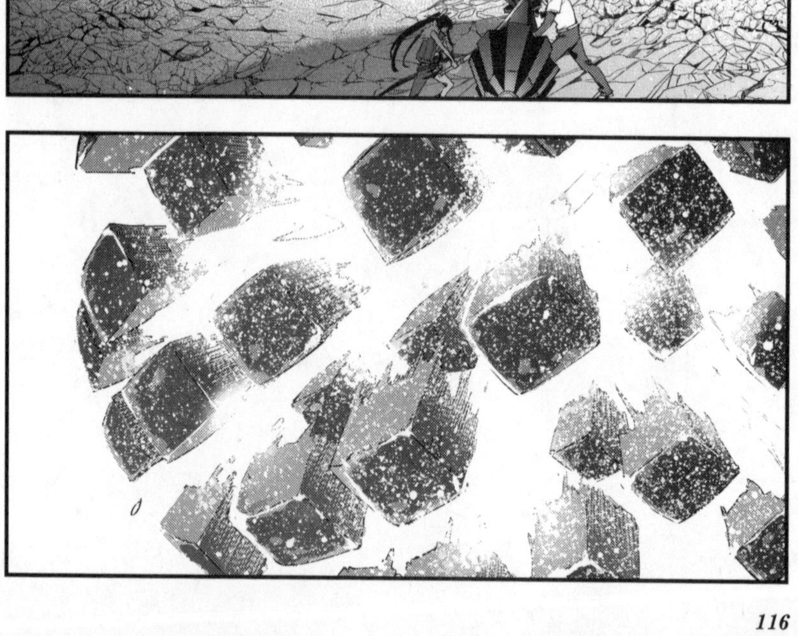

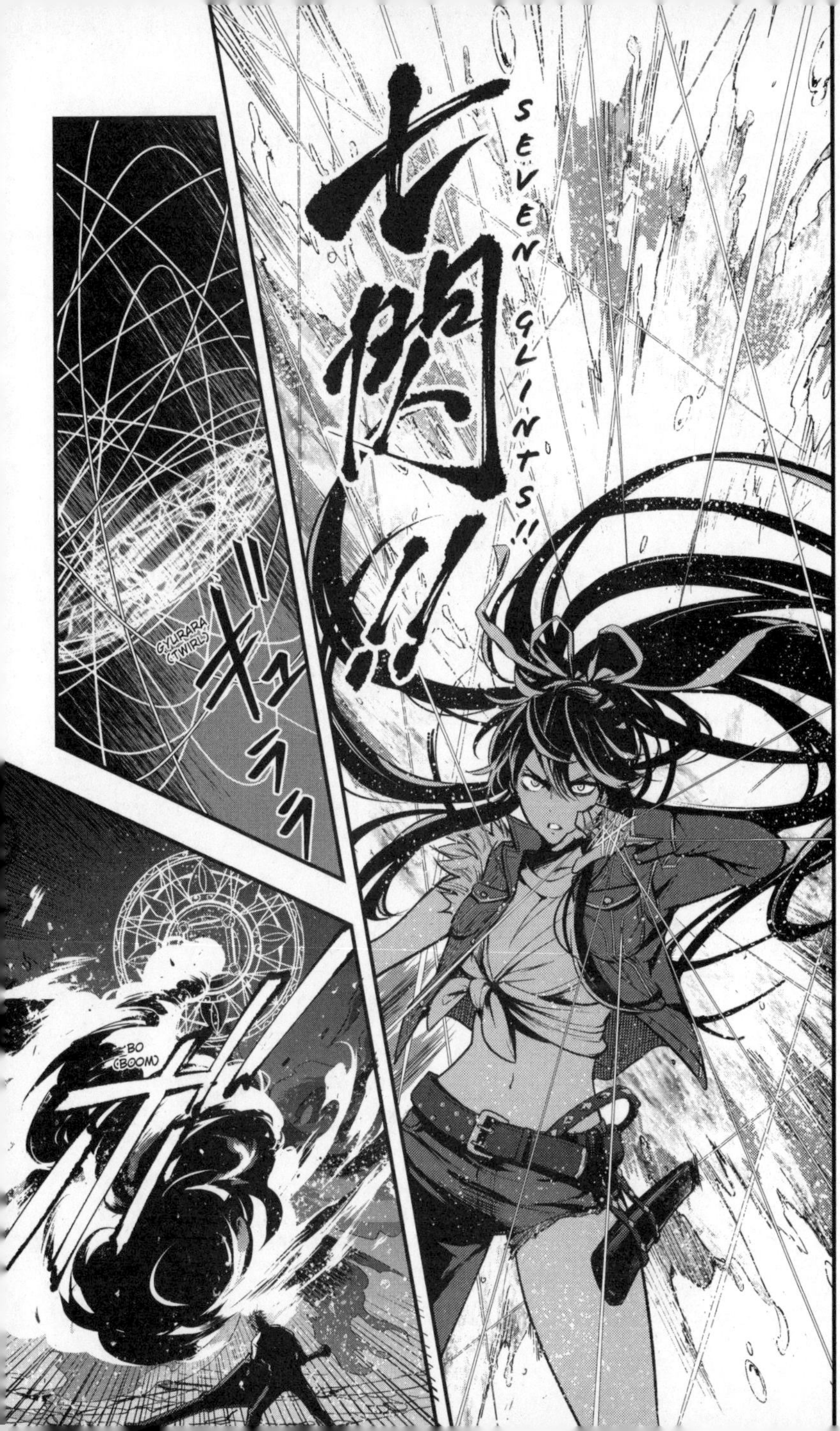
SEVEN GLINTS!!
GYURARA (TWIRL)
BO (BOOM)

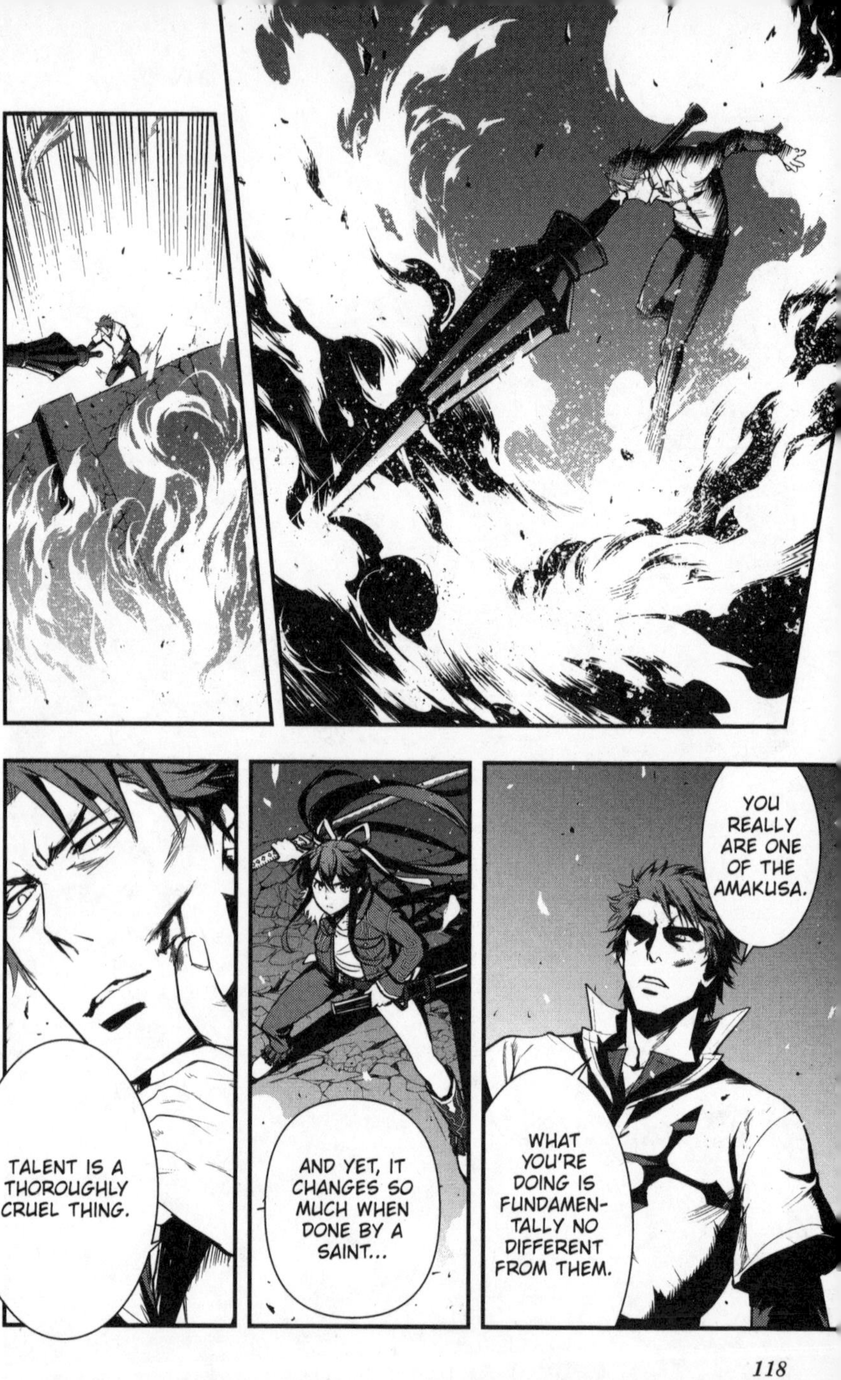
YOU REALLY ARE ONE OF THE AMAKUSA.
WHAT YOU'RE DOING IS FUNDAMEN-TALLY NO DIFFERENT FROM THEM.
AND YET, IT CHANGES SO MUCH WHEN DONE BY A SAINT...
TALENT IS A THOROUGHLY CRUEL THING.

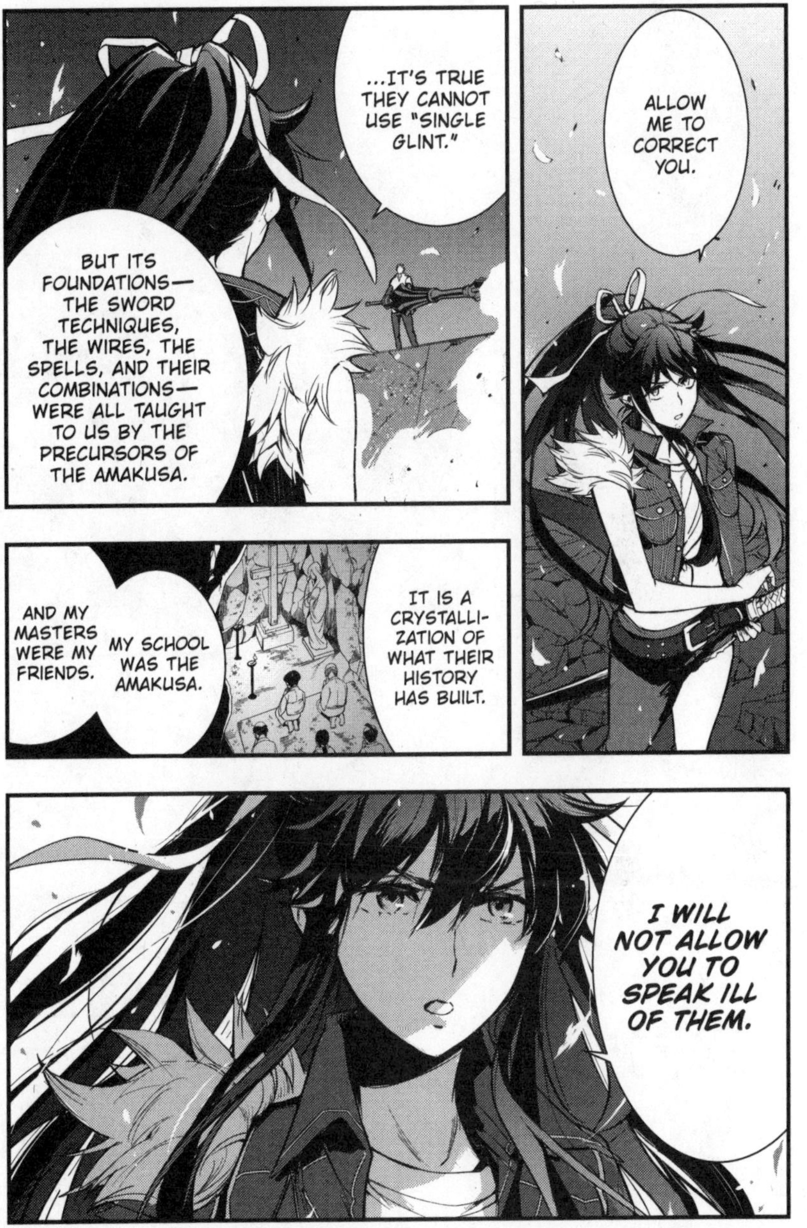
ALLOW ME TO CORRECT YOU.
...IT'S TRUE THEY CANNOT USE "SINGLE GLINT."
BUT ITS FOUNDATIONS—THE SWORD TECHNIQUES, THE WIRES, THE SPELLS, AND THEIR COMBINATIONS—WERE ALL TAUGHT TO US BY THE PRECURSORS OF THE AMAKUSA.
IT IS A CRYSTALLIZATION OF WHAT THEIR HISTORY HAS BUILT.
MY SCHOOL WAS THE AMAKUSA.
AND MY MASTERS WERE MY FRIENDS.
I WILL NOT ALLOW YOU TO SPEAK ILL OF THEM.

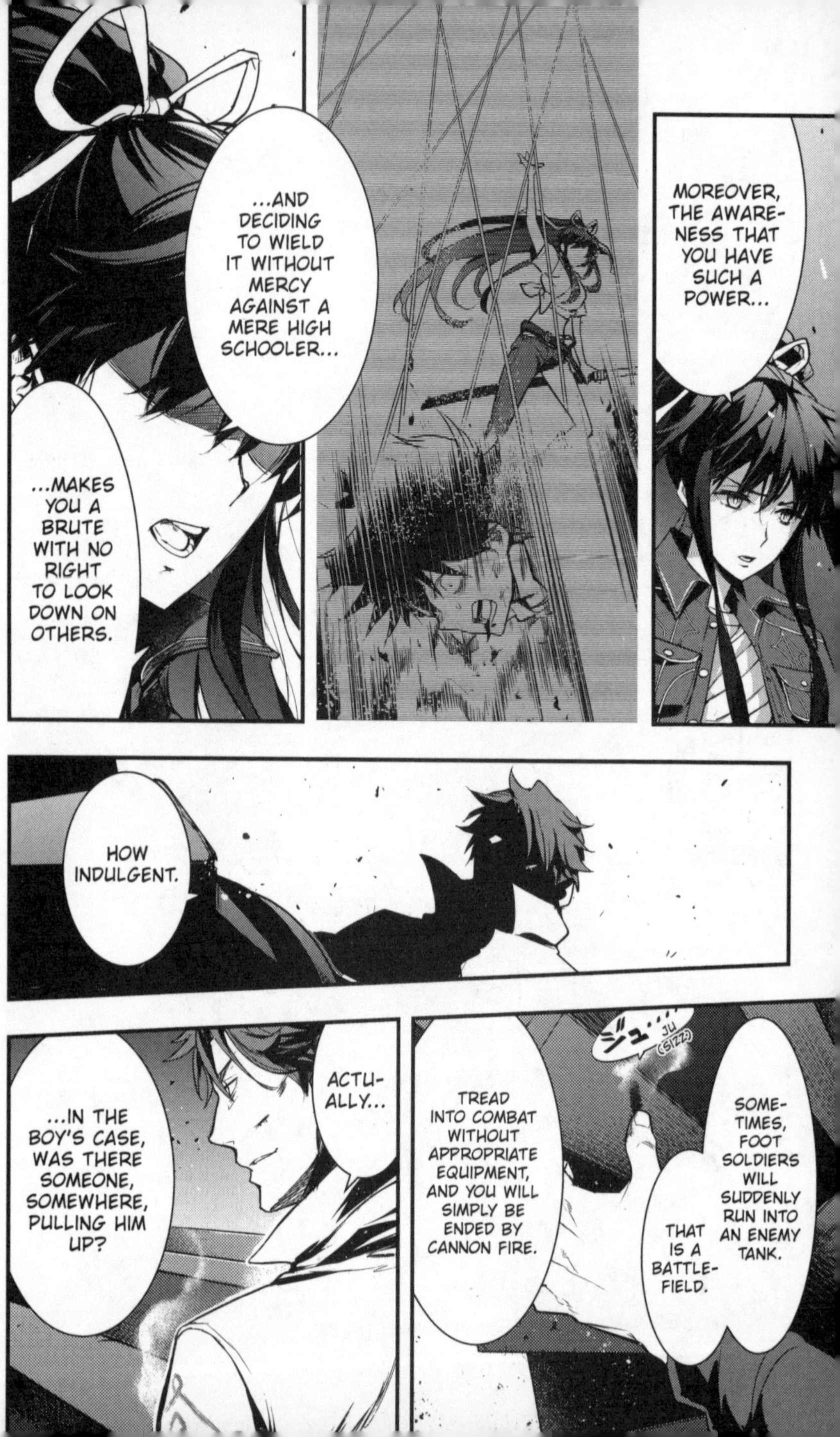
MOREOVER, THE AWARENESS THAT YOU HAVE SUCH A POWER...
...AND DECIDING TO WIELD IT WITHOUT MERCY AGAINST A MERE HIGH SCHOOLER...
...MAKES YOU A BRUTE WITH NO RIGHT TO LOOK DOWN ON OTHERS.
HOW INDULGENT.
ジュ…
JU (SIZZ)
SOMETIMES, FOOT SOLDIERS WILL SUDDENLY RUN INTO AN ENEMY TANK.
THAT IS A BATTLEFIELD.
TREAD INTO COMBAT WITHOUT APPROPRIATE EQUIPMENT, AND YOU WILL SIMPLY BE ENDED BY CANNON FIRE.
ACTUALLY...
...IN THE BOY'S CASE, WAS THERE SOMEONE, SOMEWHERE, PULLING HIM UP?

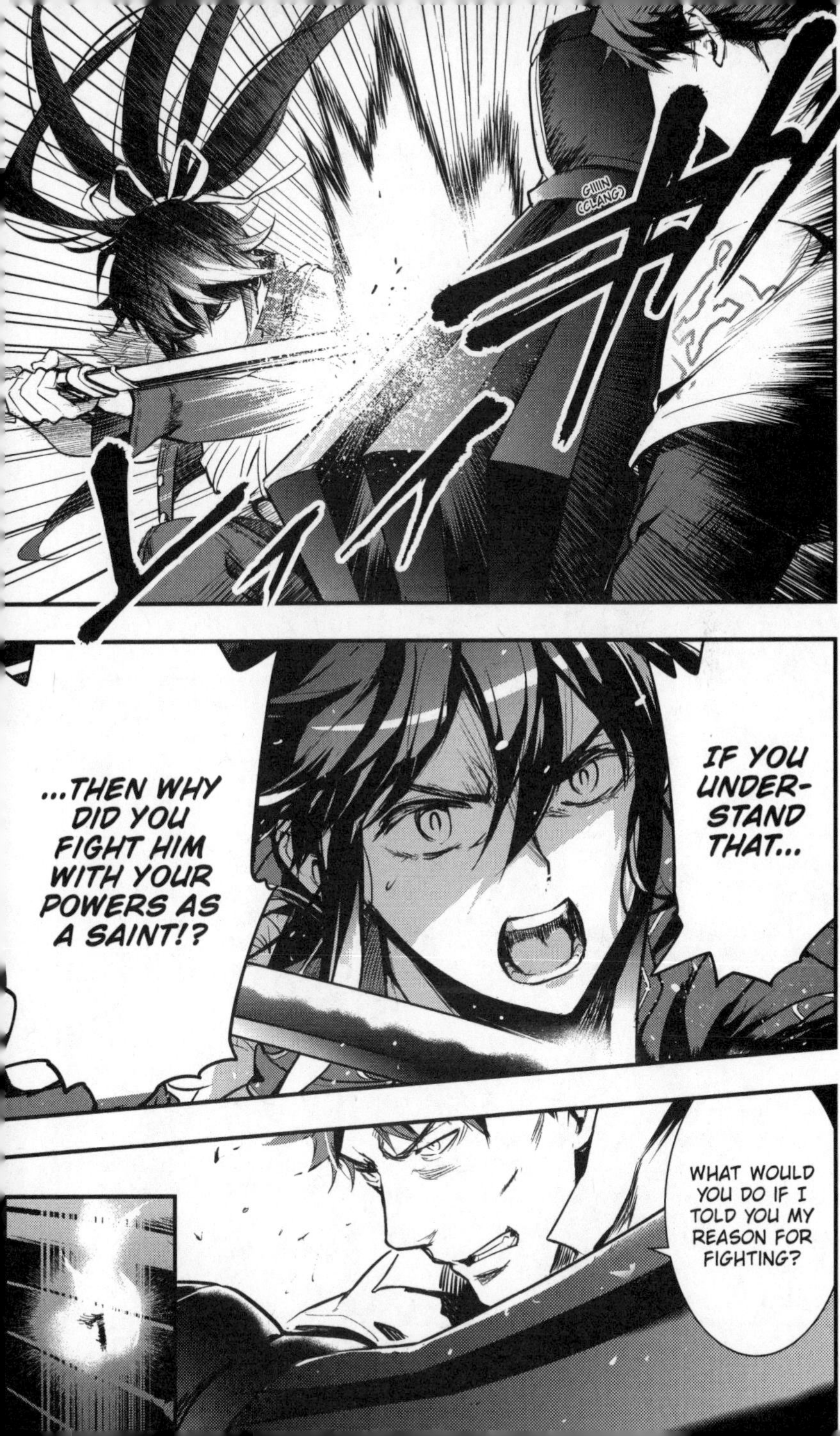
GIIIN (CLANG)
IF YOU UNDER-STAND THAT...
...THEN WHY DID YOU FIGHT HIM WITH YOUR POWERS AS A SAINT!?
WHAT WOULD YOU DO IF I TOLD YOU MY REASON FOR FIGHTING?

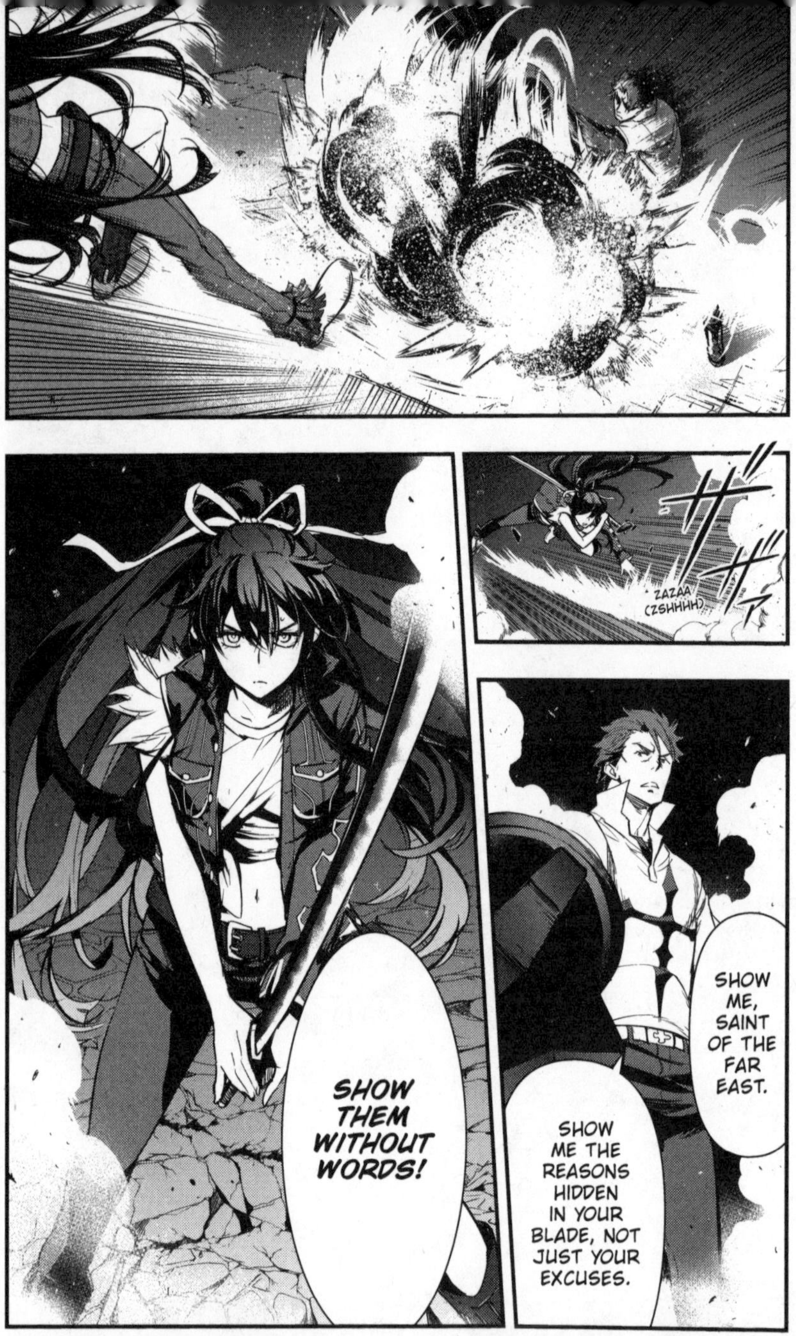
ザザァ
ZAZAA (ZSHHHH)
SHOW ME, SAINT OF THE FAR EAST.
SHOW ME THE REASONS HIDDEN IN YOUR BLADE, NOT JUST YOUR EXCUSES.
SHOW THEM WITHOUT WORDS!

A
Certain
Magical
Index

A Certain Magical Index

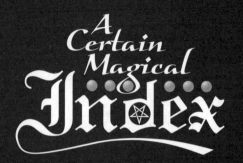

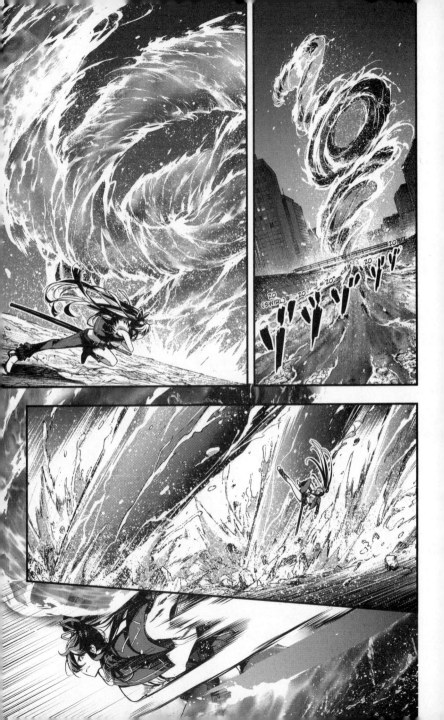

ZO
ZO
ZO
ZO
ZO
(SWIRL)

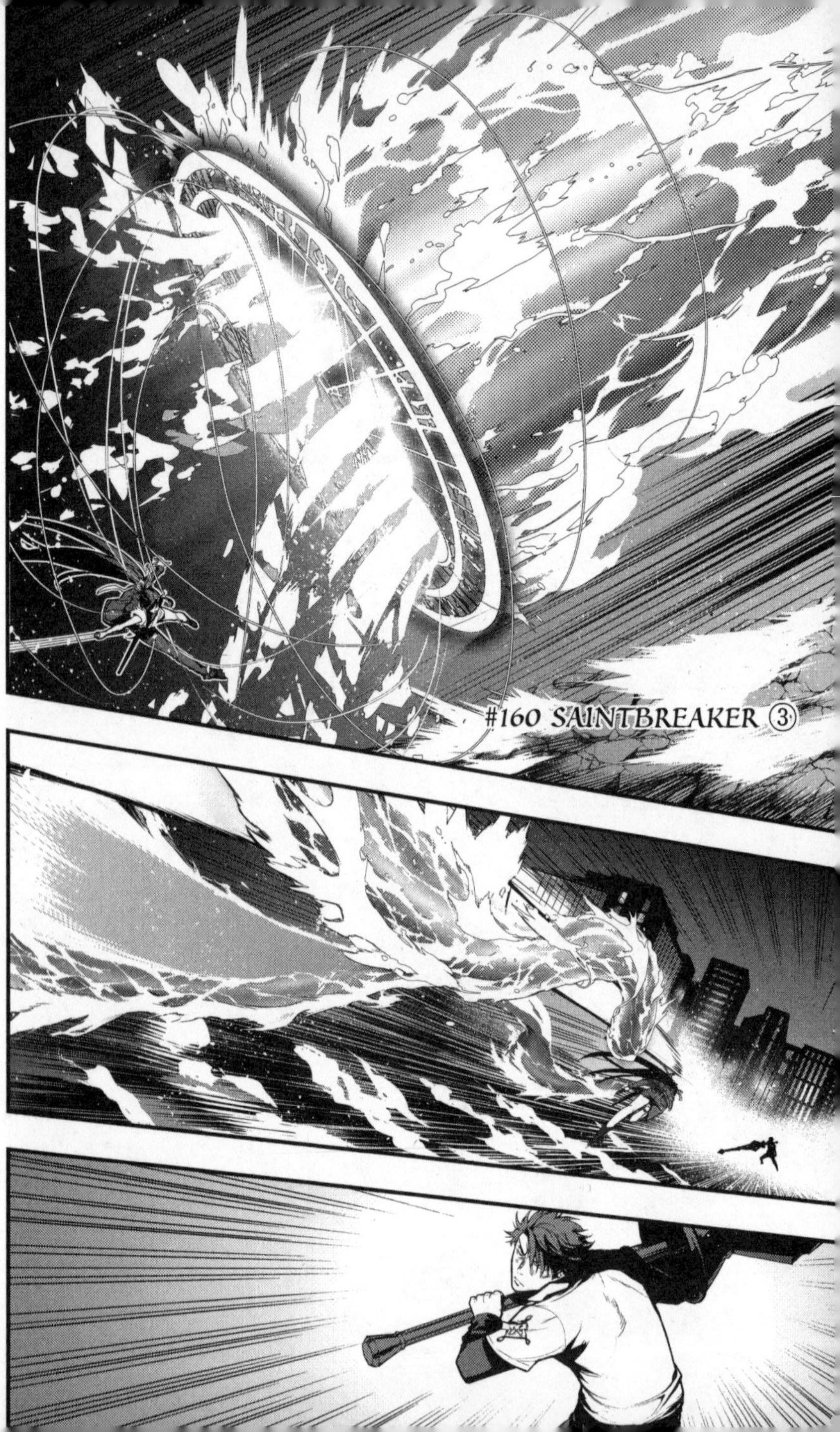
#160 SAINTBREAKER ③

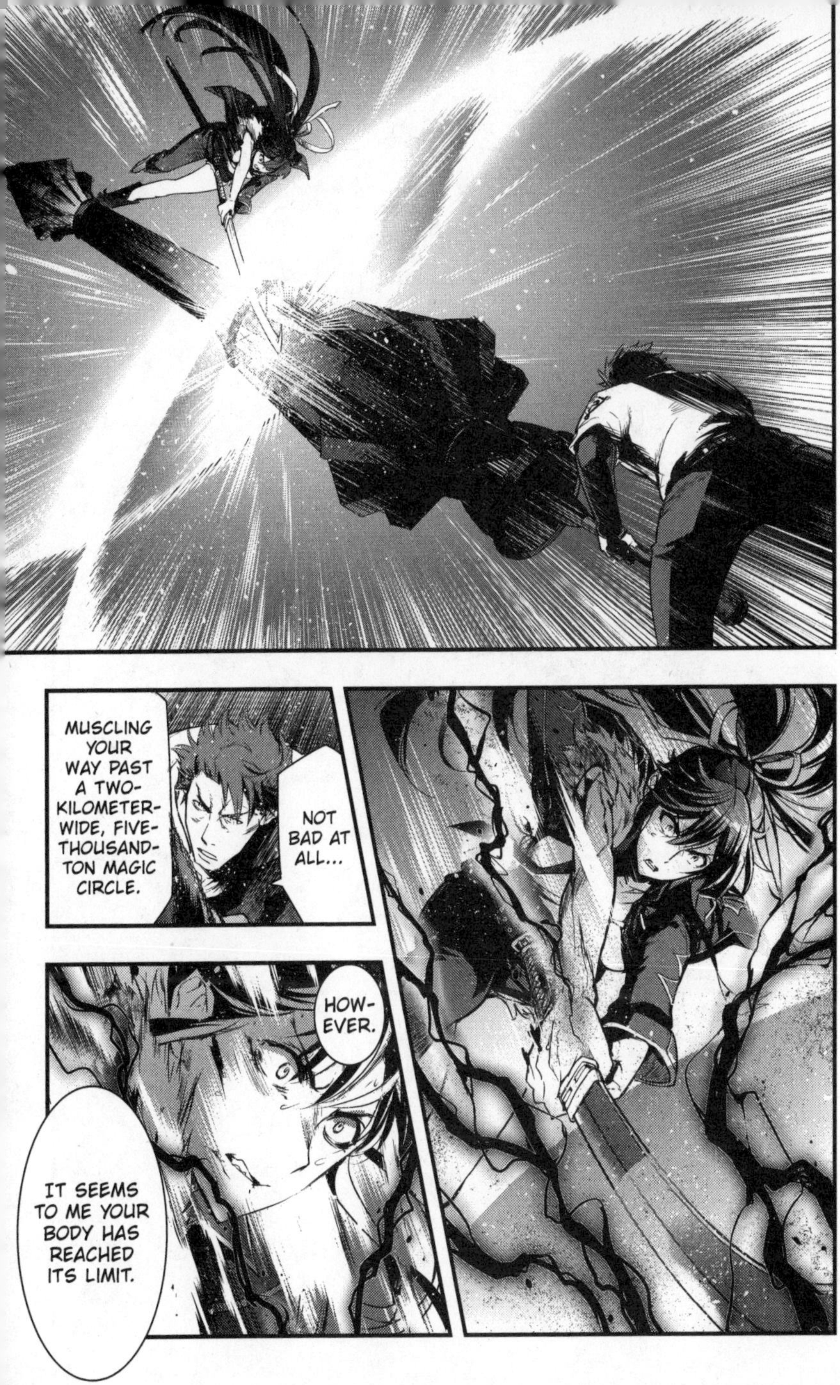
MUSCLING YOUR WAY PAST A TWO-KILOMETER-WIDE, FIVE-THOUSAND-TON MAGIC CIRCLE.
NOT BAD AT ALL...
HOW-EVER.
IT SEEMS TO ME YOUR BODY HAS REACHED ITS LIMIT.

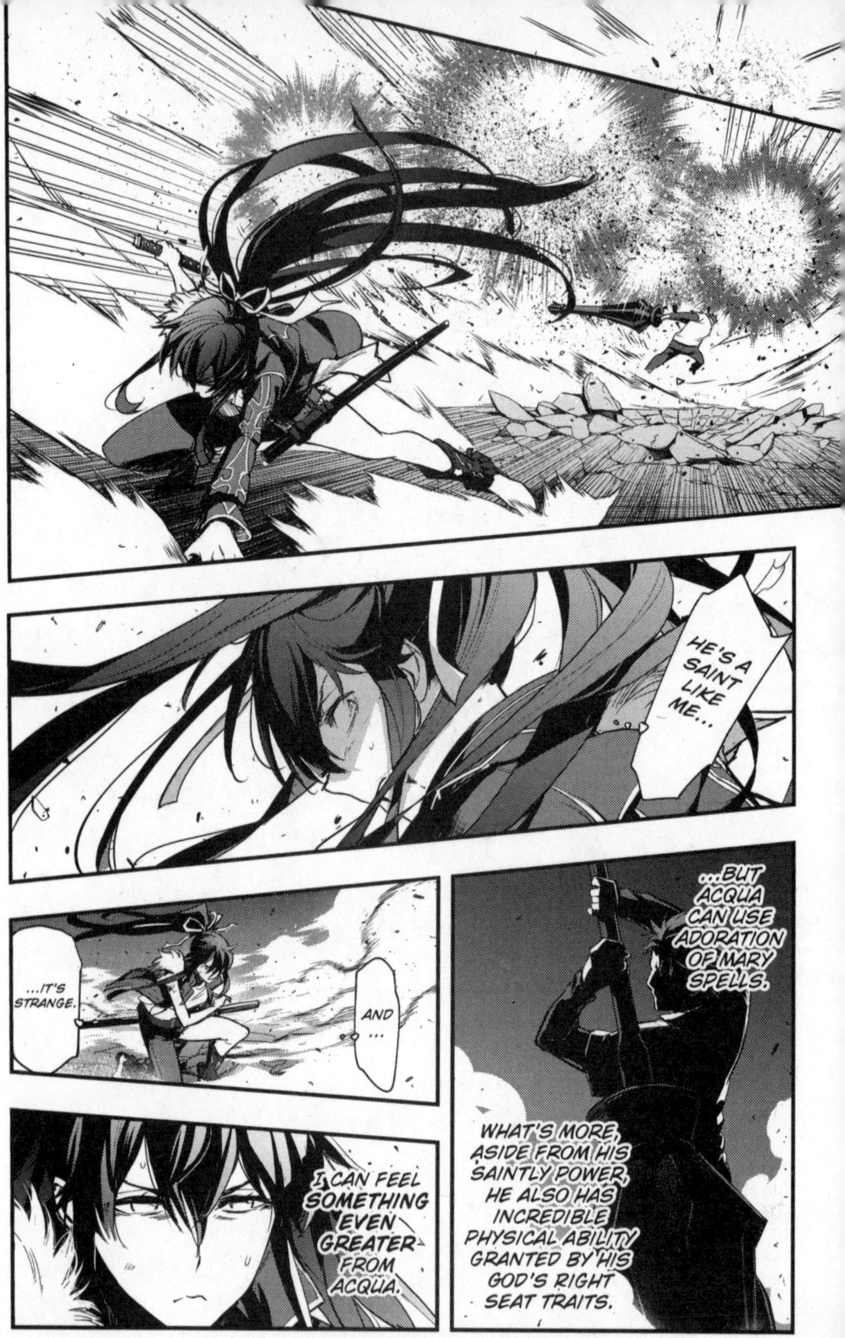
HE'S A SAINT LIKE ME...
...BUT ACQUA CAN USE ADORATION OF MARY SPELLS.
WHAT'S MORE, ASIDE FROM HIS SAINTLY POWER, HE ALSO HAS INCREDIBLE PHYSICAL ABILITY GRANTED BY HIS GOD'S RIGHT SEAT TRAITS.
...IT'S STRANGE.
AND...
I CAN FEEL SOMETHING EVEN GREATER FROM ACQUA.

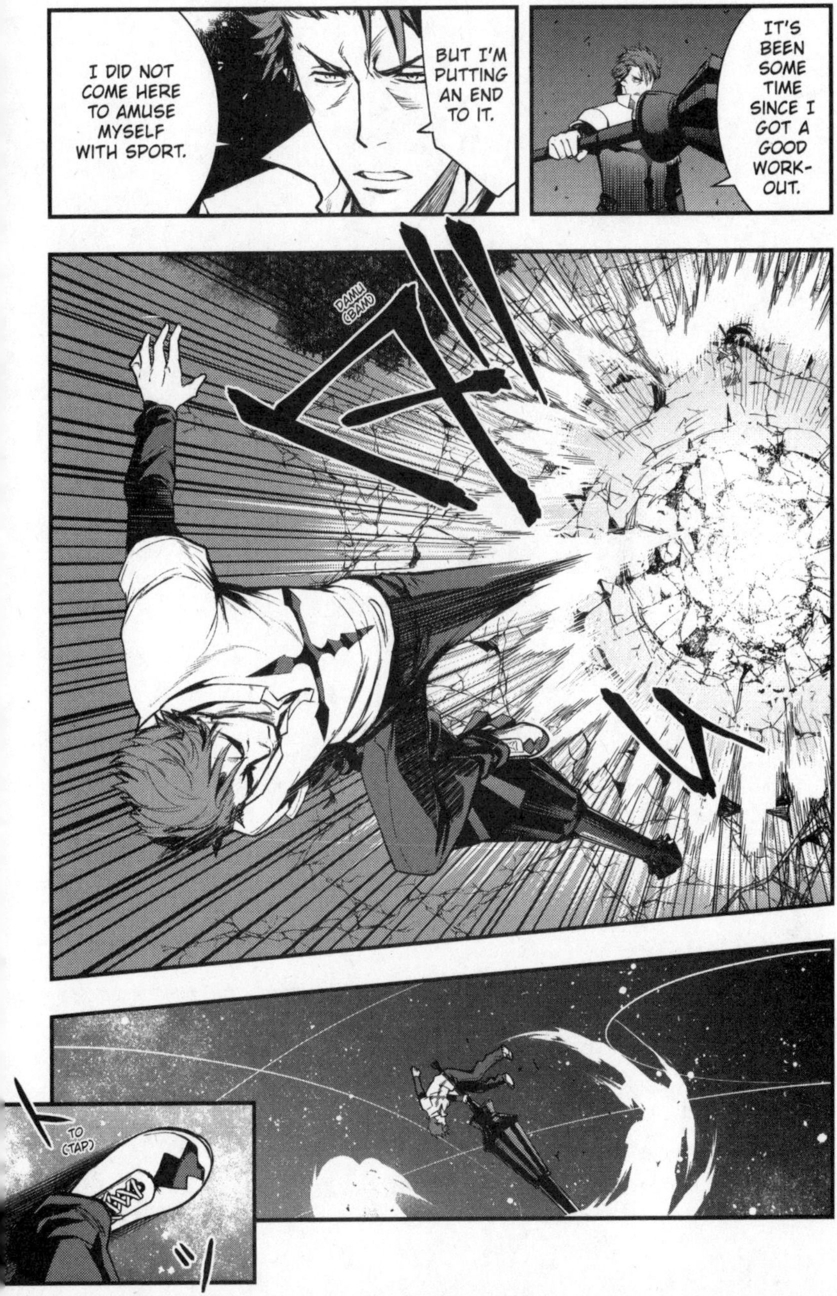
IT'S BEEN SOME TIME SINCE I GOT A GOOD WORK-OUT.
BUT I'M PUTTING AN END TO IT.
I DID NOT COME HERE TO AMUSE MYSELF WITH SPORT.
DAMU (BAM)
TO (TAP)

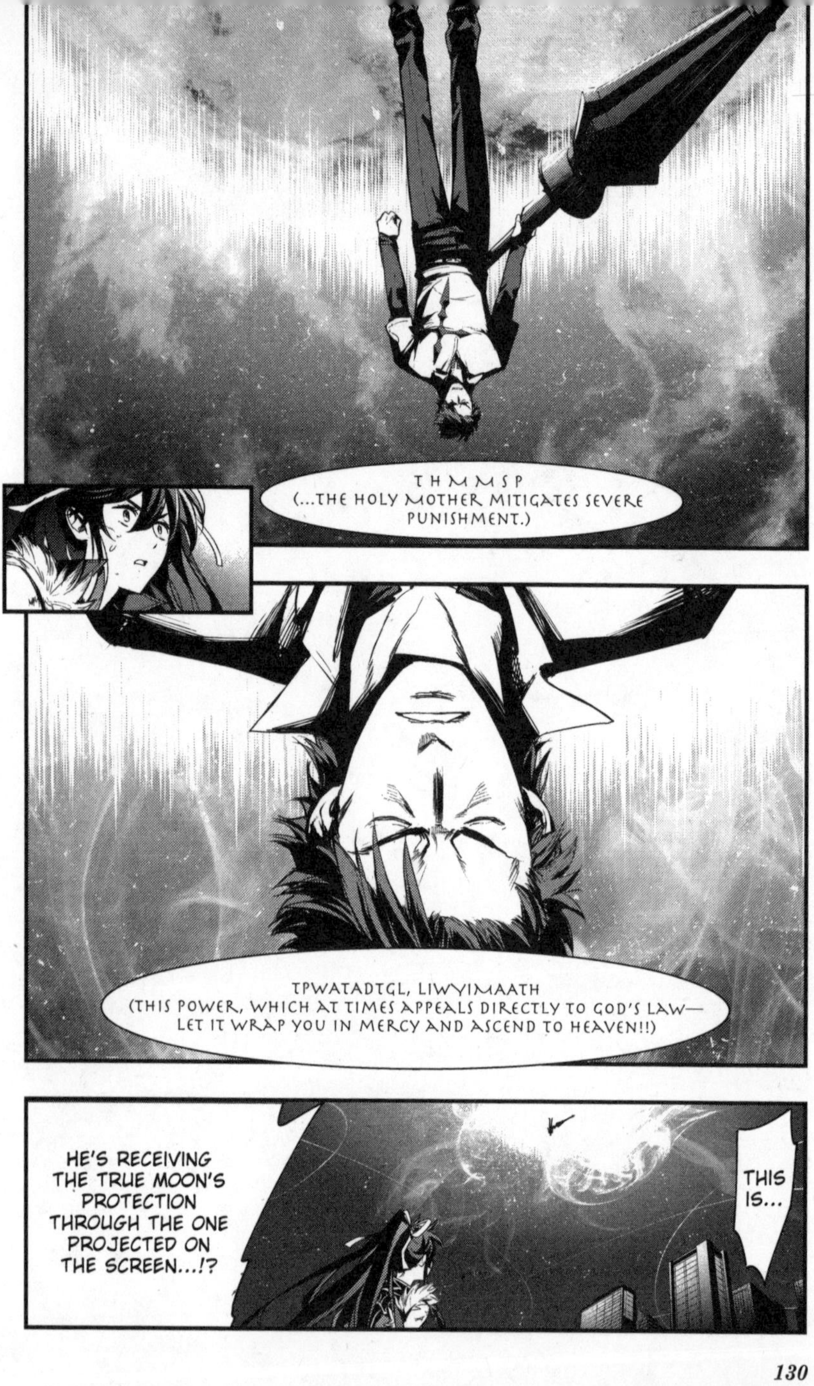
THMMSP
(...THE HOLY MOTHER MITIGATES SEVERE PUNISHMENT.)
TPWATADTGL, LIWYIMAATH
(THIS POWER, WHICH AT TIMES APPEALS DIRECTLY TO GOD'S LAW—LET IT WRAP YOU IN MERCY AND ASCEND TO HEAVEN!!)
THIS IS...
HE'S RECEIVING THE TRUE MOON'S PROTECTION THROUGH THE ONE PROJECTED ON THE SCREEN...!?

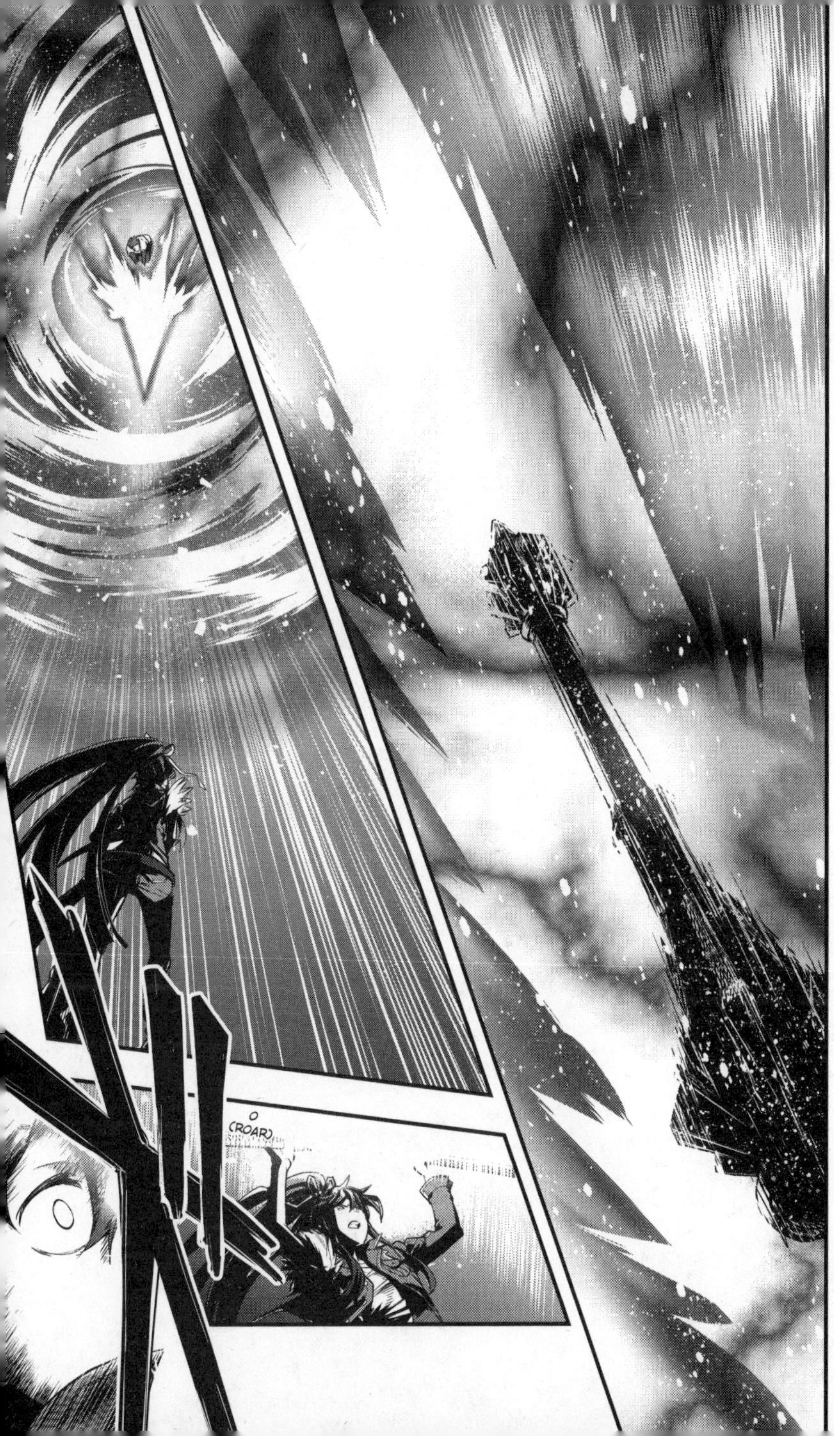
O
(ROAR)

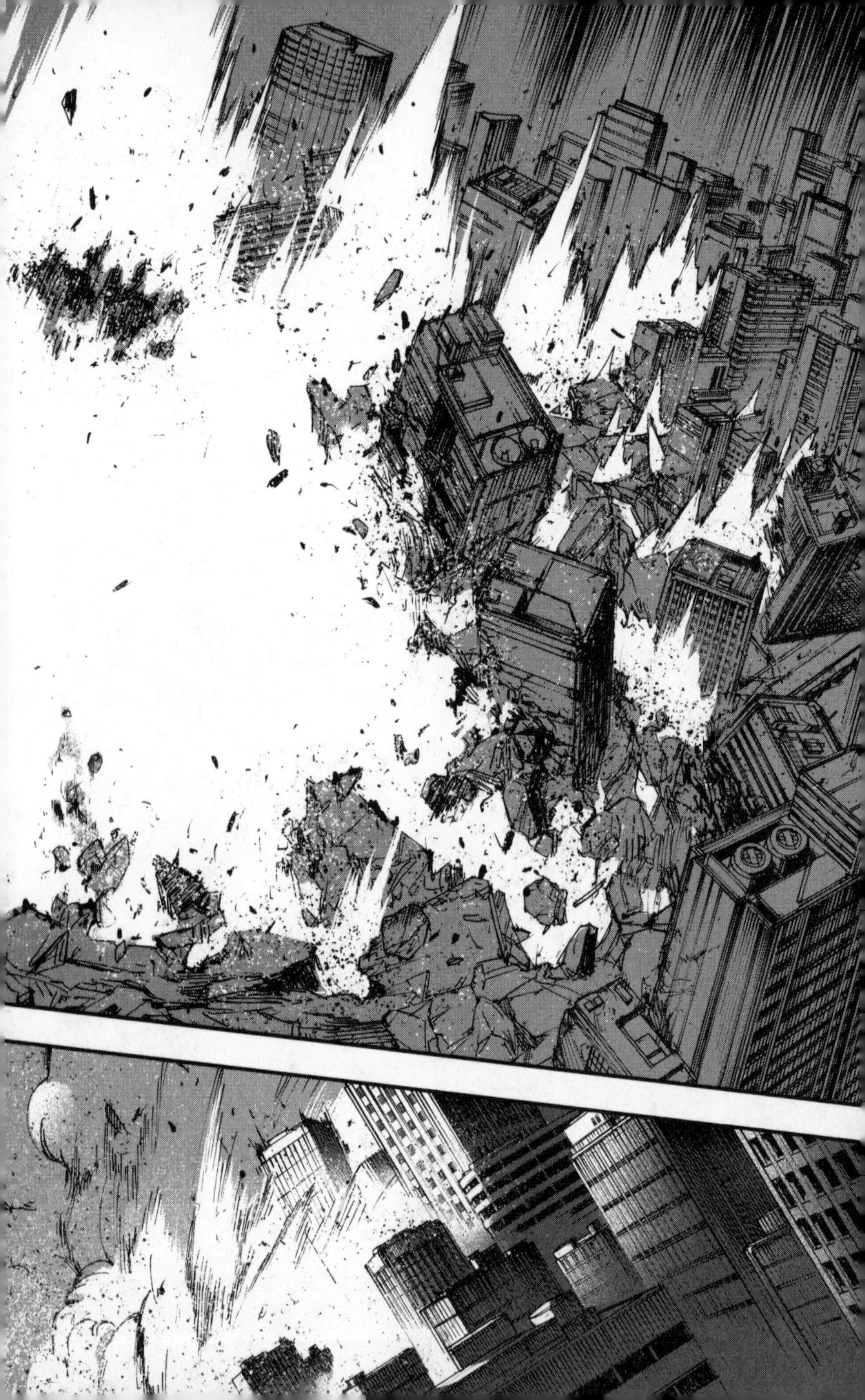

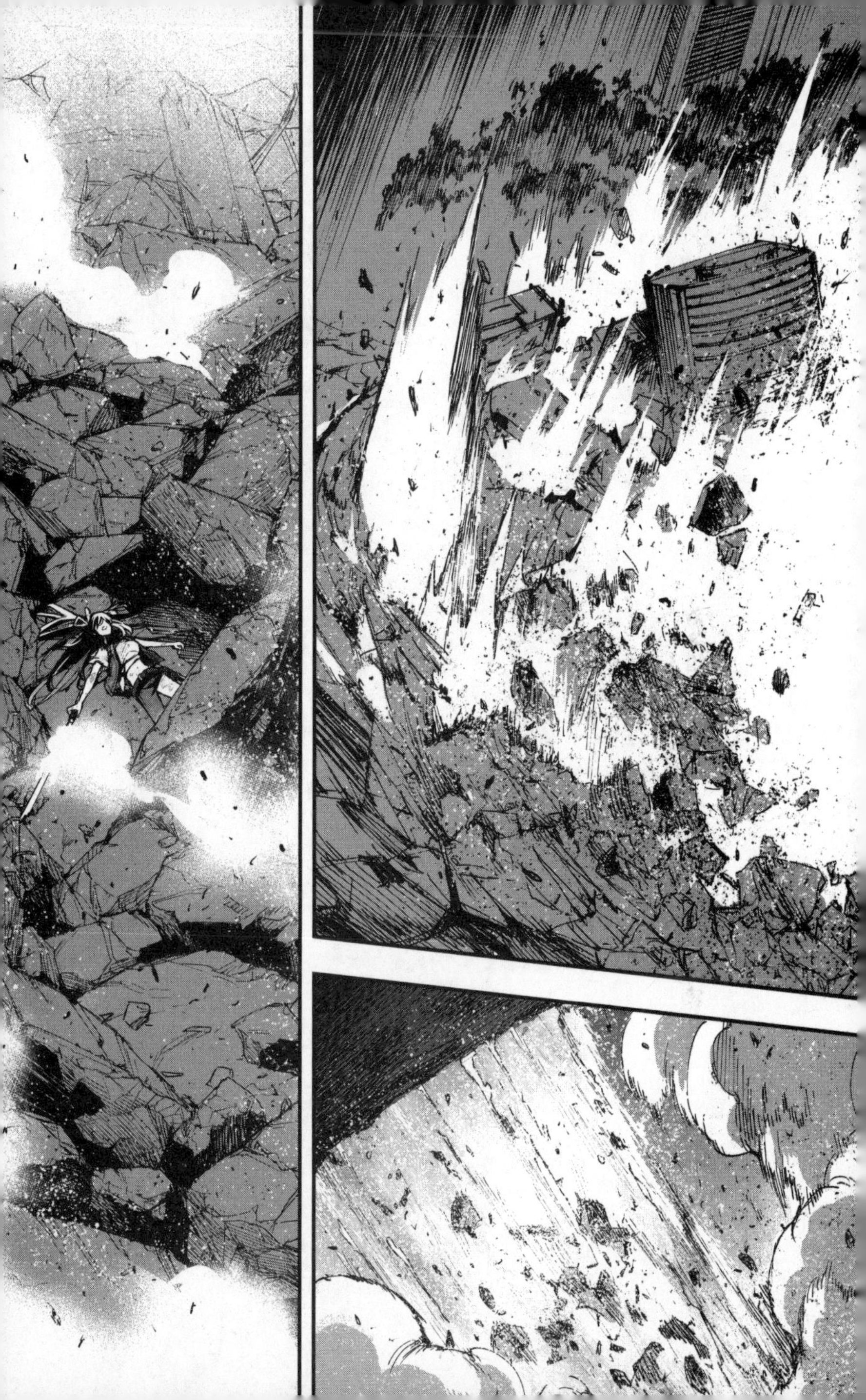

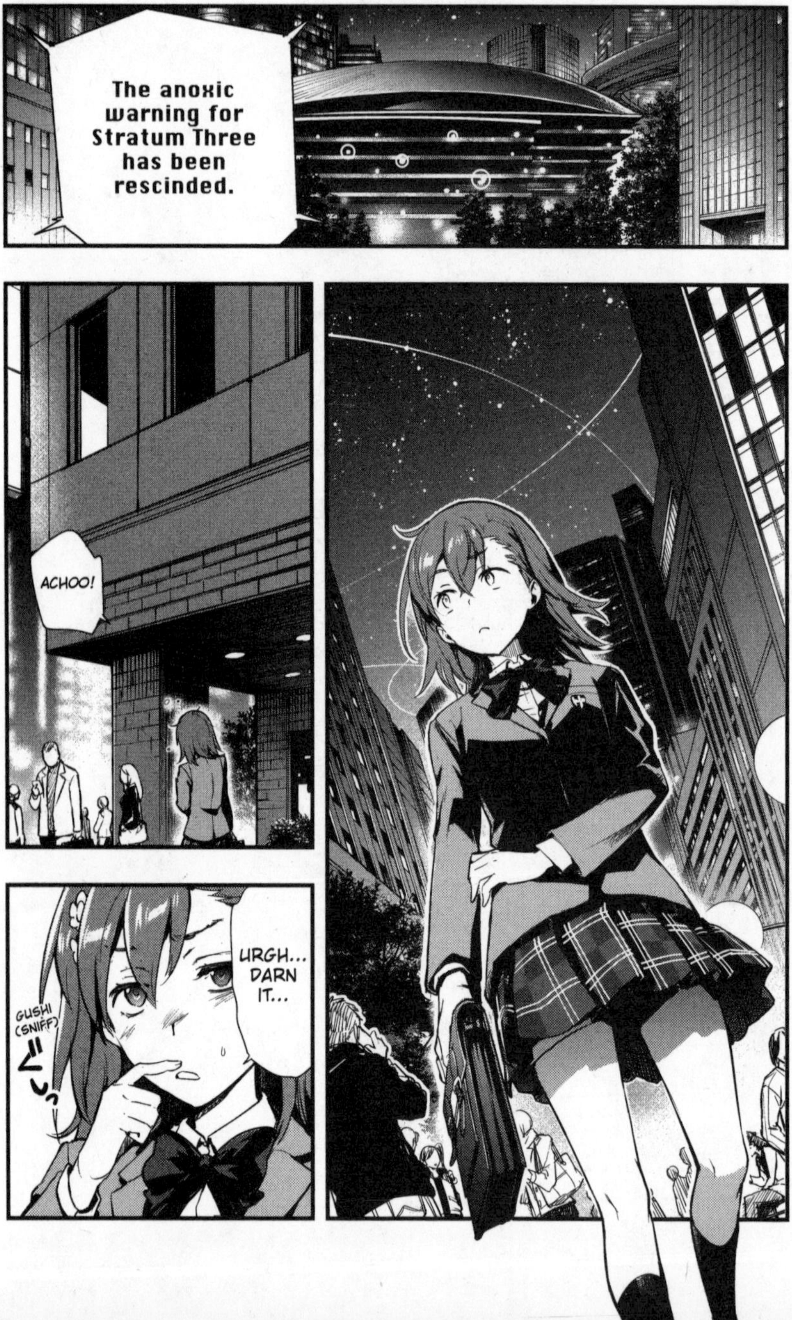
The anoxic warning for Stratum Three has been rescinded.
ACHOO!
URGH... DARN IT...
GUSHI (SNIFF)

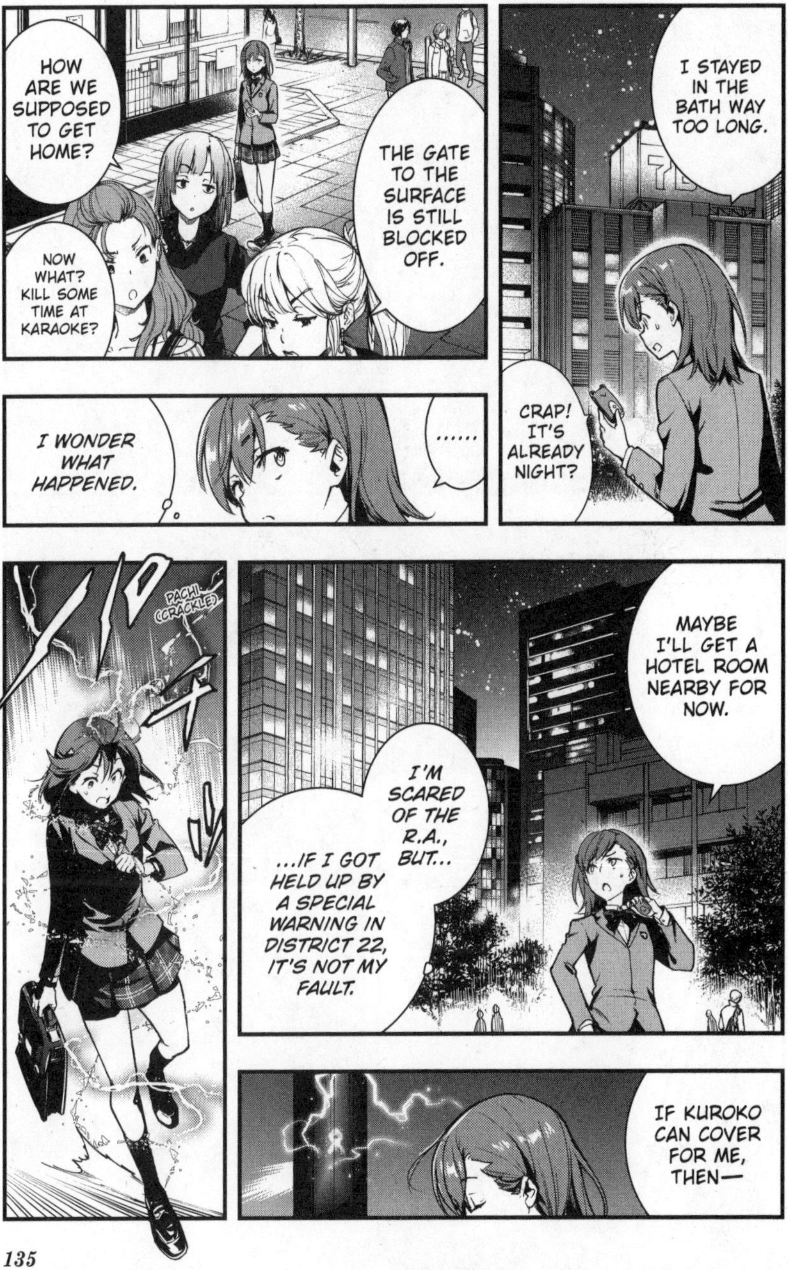
I STAYED IN THE BATH WAY TOO LONG.
CRAP! IT'S ALREADY NIGHT?
THE GATE TO THE SURFACE IS STILL BLOCKED OFF.
HOW ARE WE SUPPOSED TO GET HOME?
NOW WHAT? KILL SOME TIME AT KARAOKE?
......
I WONDER WHAT HAPPENED.
MAYBE I'LL GET A HOTEL ROOM NEARBY FOR NOW.
I'M SCARED OF THE R.A., BUT...
...IF I GOT HELD UP BY A SPECIAL WARNING IN DISTRICT 22, IT'S NOT MY FAULT.
IF KUROKO CAN COVER FOR ME, THEN—
PACHI (CRACKLE)

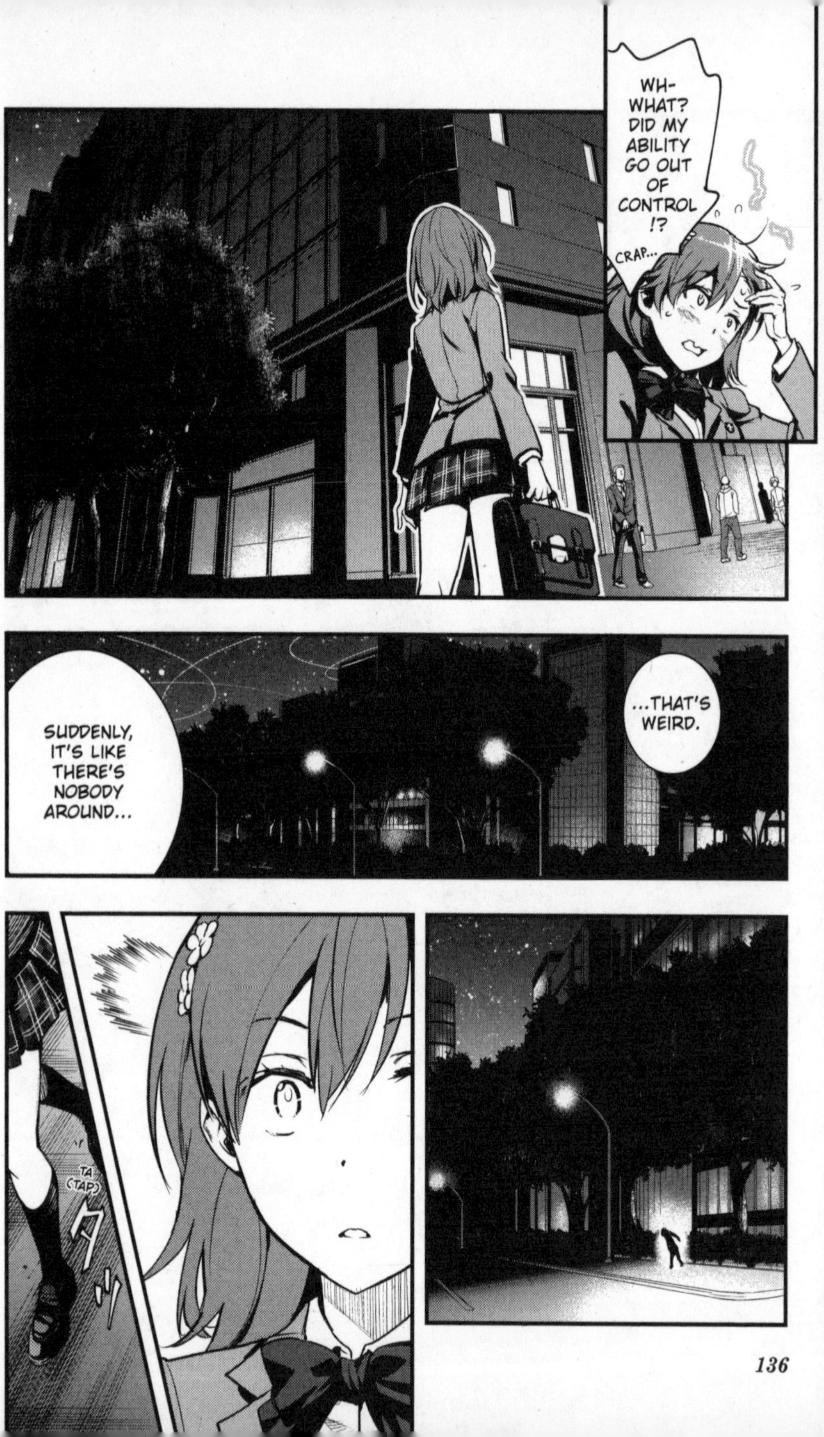
WH- WHAT? DID MY ABILITY GO OUT OF CONTROL !?
CRAP...
...THAT'S WEIRD.
SUDDENLY, IT'S LIKE THERE'S NOBODY AROUND...
TA (TAP)

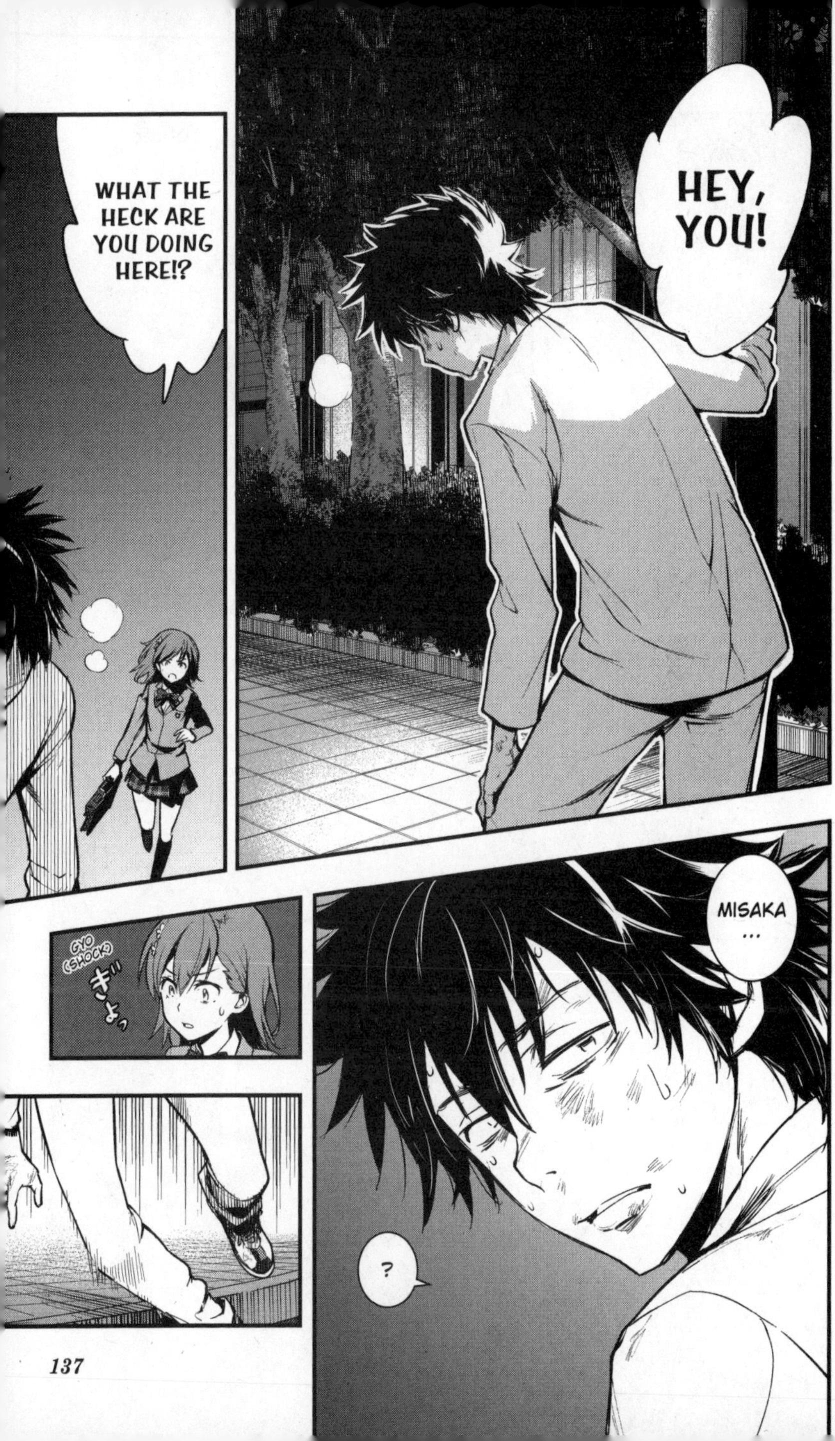
HEY, YOU!
WHAT THE HECK ARE YOU DOING HERE!?
MISAKA ...
GYO (SHOCK)
?

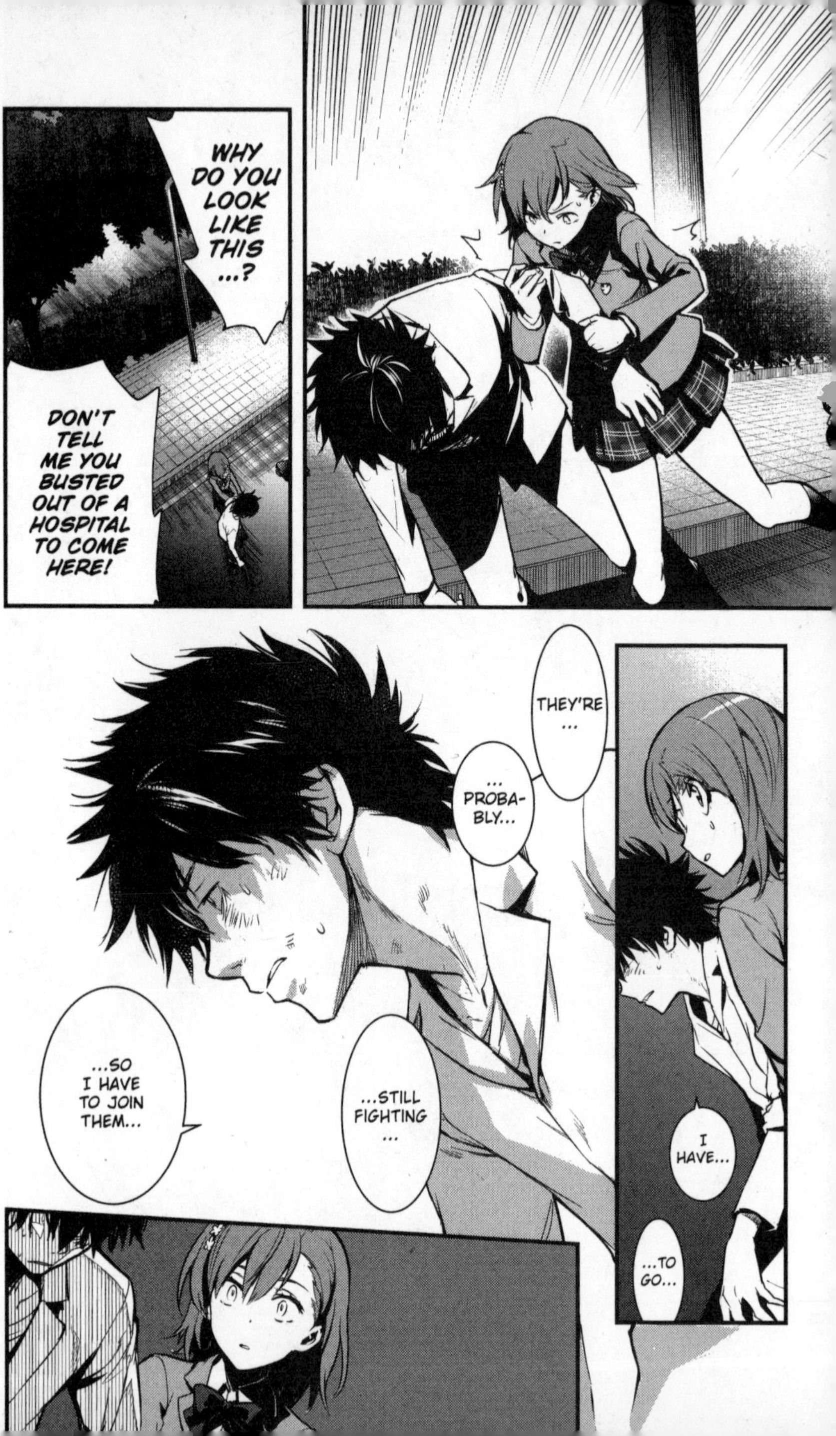
WHY DO YOU LOOK LIKE THIS ...?
DON'T TELL ME YOU BUSTED OUT OF A HOSPITAL TO COME HERE!
THEY'RE ...
... PROBA-BLY...
...STILL FIGHTING ...
...SO I HAVE TO JOIN THEM...
I HAVE...
...TO GO...

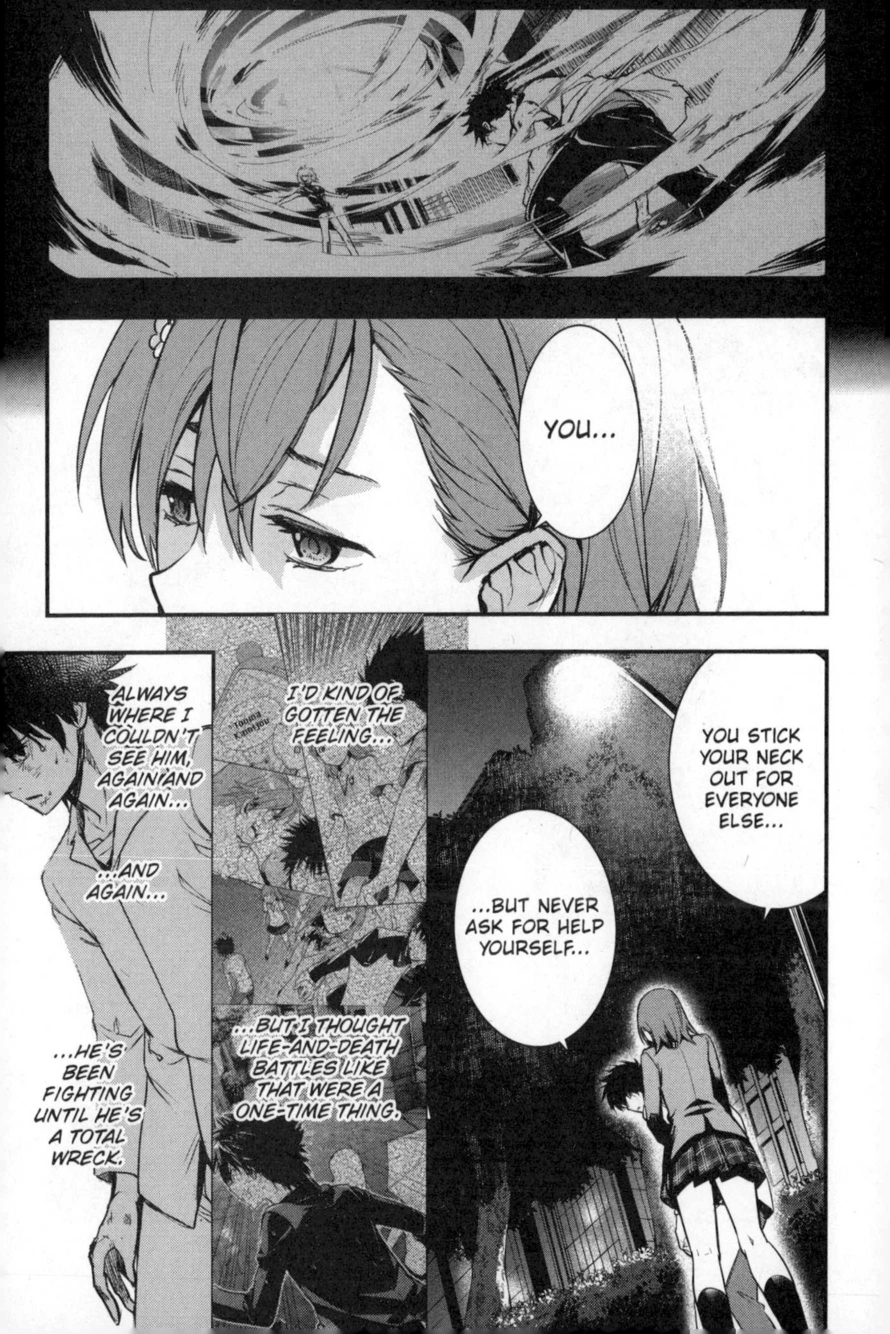
YOU...
YOU STICK YOUR NECK OUT FOR EVERYONE ELSE...
...BUT NEVER ASK FOR HELP YOURSELF...
I'D KIND OF GOTTEN THE FEELING...
...BUT I THOUGHT LIFE-AND-DEATH BATTLES LIKE THAT WERE A ONE-TIME THING.
ALWAYS WHERE I COULDN'T SEE HIM, AGAIN AND AGAIN...
...AND AGAIN...
...HE'S BEEN FIGHTING UNTIL HE'S A TOTAL WRECK.

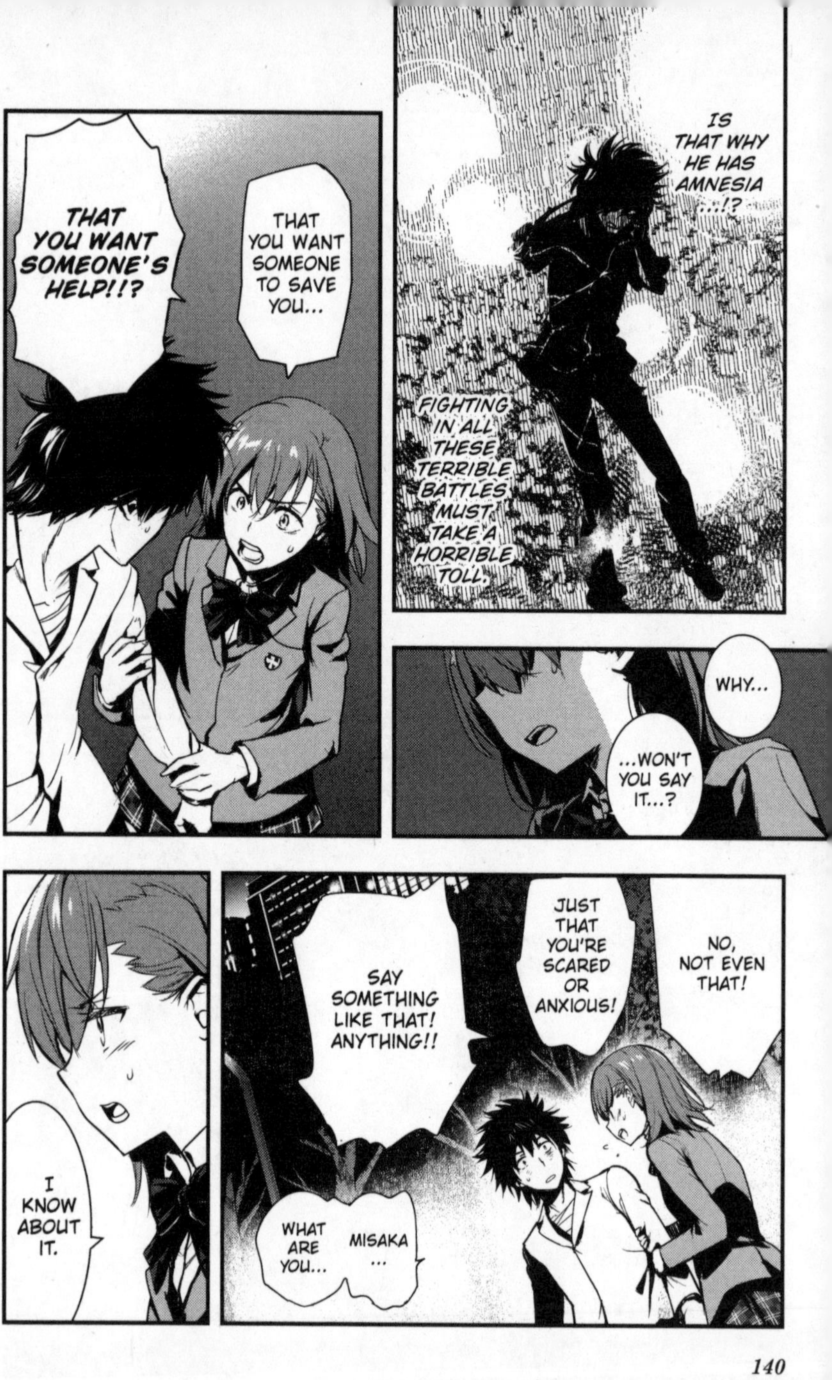
IS THAT WHY HE HAS AMNESIA ...!?
FIGHTING IN ALL THESE TERRIBLE BATTLES MUST TAKE A HORRIBLE TOLL.
WHY...
...WON'T YOU SAY IT...?
THAT YOU WANT SOMEONE TO SAVE YOU...
THAT YOU WANT SOMEONE'S HELP!!?
NO, NOT EVEN THAT!
JUST THAT YOU'RE SCARED OR ANXIOUS!
SAY SOMETHING LIKE THAT! ANYTHING!!
MISAKA ...
WHAT ARE YOU...
I KNOW ABOUT IT.

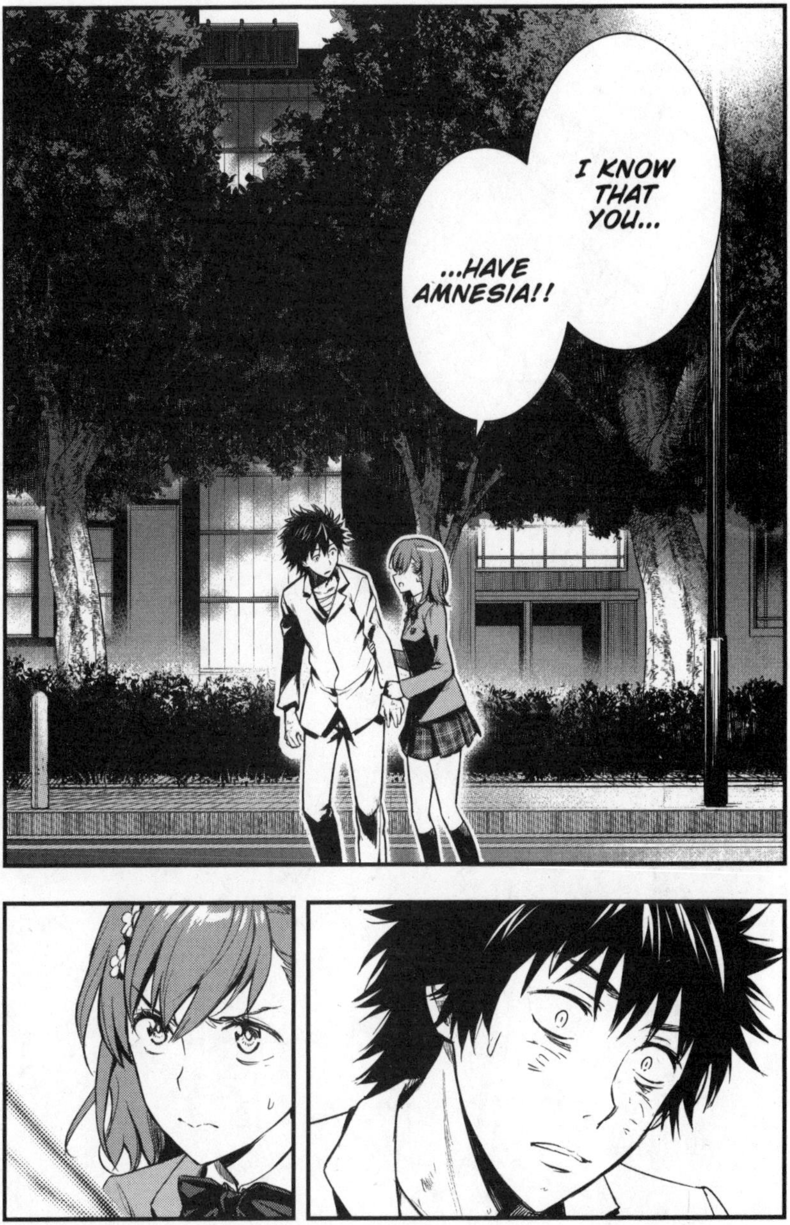
I KNOW THAT YOU...
...HAVE AMNESIA!!

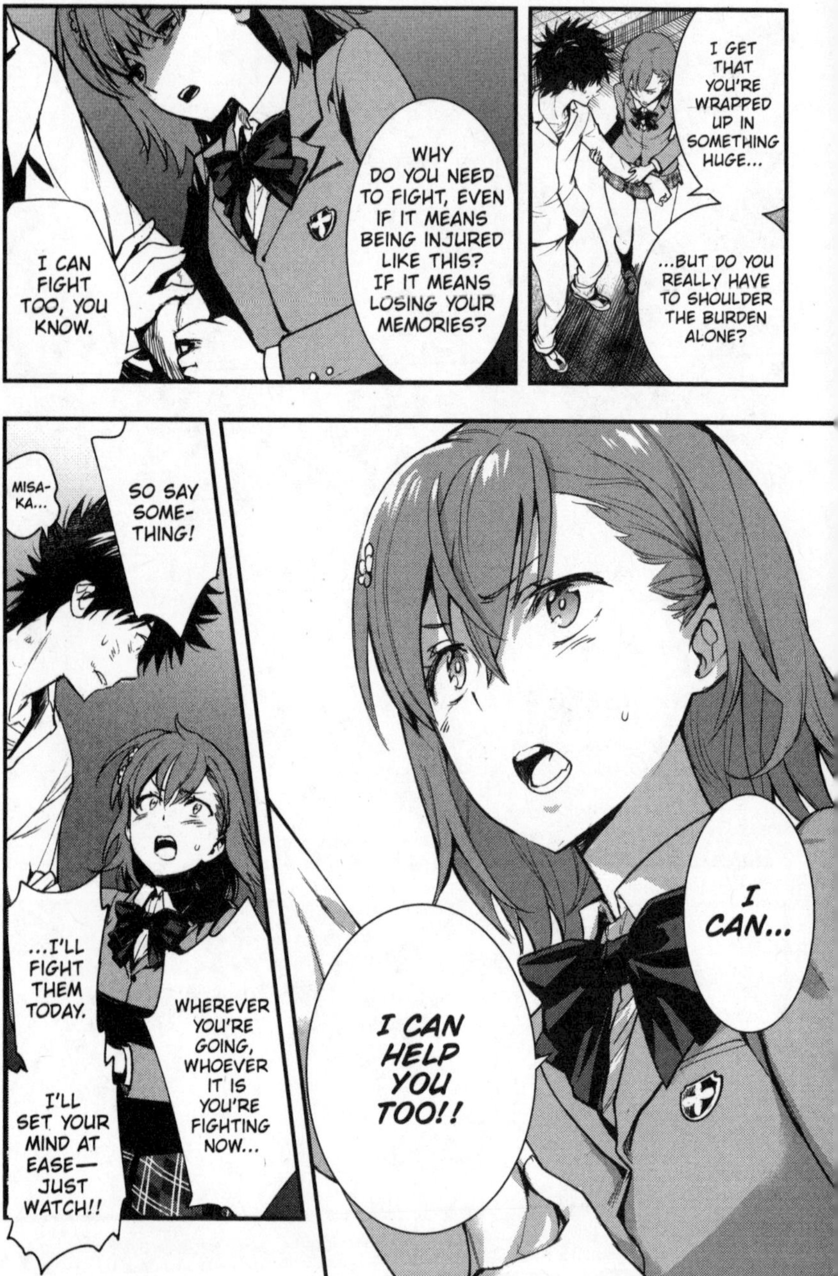
I GET THAT YOU'RE WRAPPED UP IN SOMETHING HUGE...
...BUT DO YOU REALLY HAVE TO SHOULDER THE BURDEN ALONE?
WHY DO YOU NEED TO FIGHT, EVEN IF IT MEANS BEING INJURED LIKE THIS? IF IT MEANS LOSING YOUR MEMORIES?
I CAN FIGHT TOO, YOU KNOW.
I CAN...
I CAN HELP YOU TOO!!
SO SAY SOME-THING!
MISA-KA...
WHEREVER YOU'RE GOING, WHOEVER IT IS YOU'RE FIGHTING NOW...
...I'LL FIGHT THEM TODAY.
I'LL SET YOUR MIND AT EASE—JUST WATCH!!

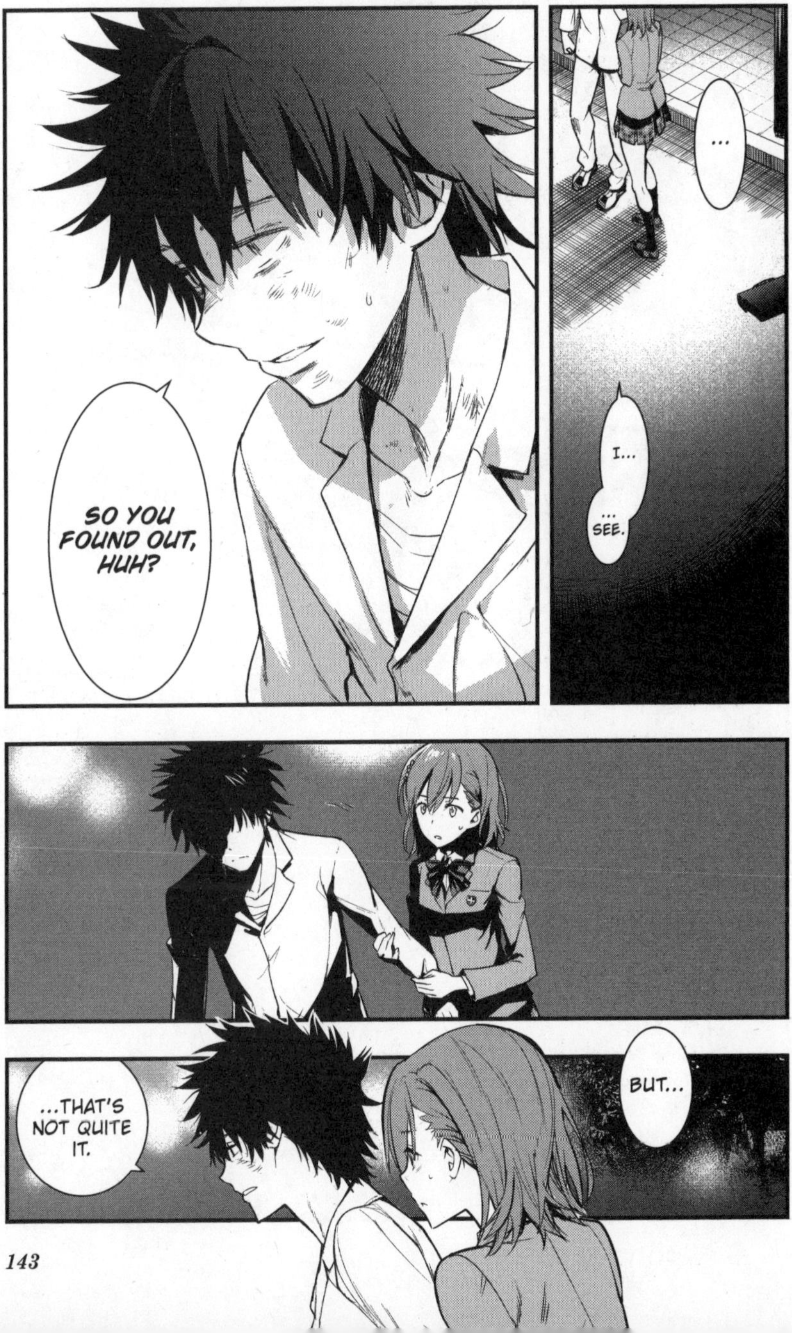
...
I...
...SEE.
SO YOU FOUND OUT, HUH?
BUT...
...THAT'S NOT QUITE IT.

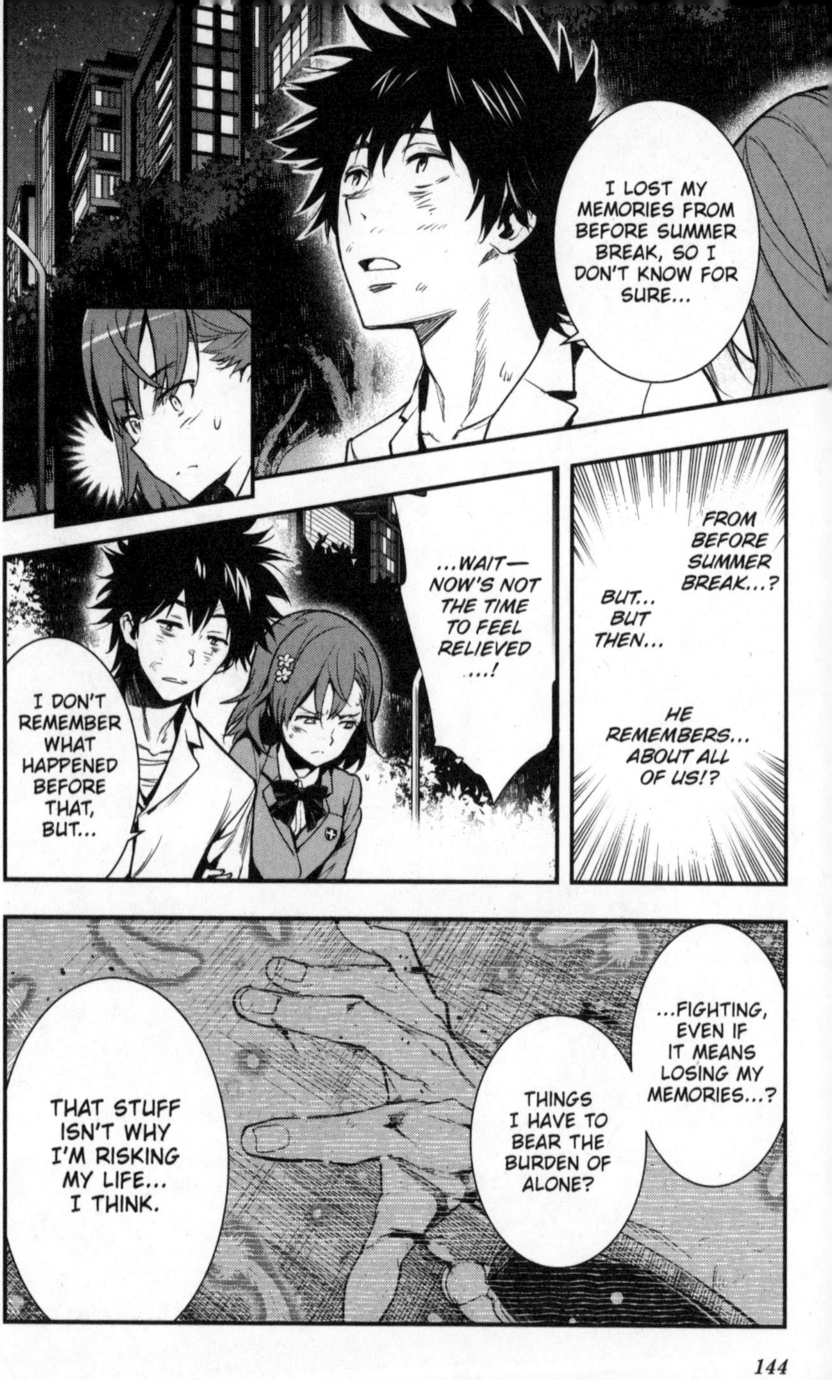
I LOST MY MEMORIES FROM BEFORE SUMMER BREAK, SO I DON'T KNOW FOR SURE...
FROM BEFORE SUMMER BREAK...?
BUT... BUT THEN...
HE REMEMBERS... ABOUT ALL OF US!?
...WAIT— NOW'S NOT THE TIME TO FEEL RELIEVED ...!
I DON'T REMEMBER WHAT HAPPENED BEFORE THAT, BUT...
...FIGHTING, EVEN IF IT MEANS LOSING MY MEMORIES...?
THINGS I HAVE TO BEAR THE BURDEN OF ALONE?
THAT STUFF ISN'T WHY I'M RISKING MY LIFE... I THINK.

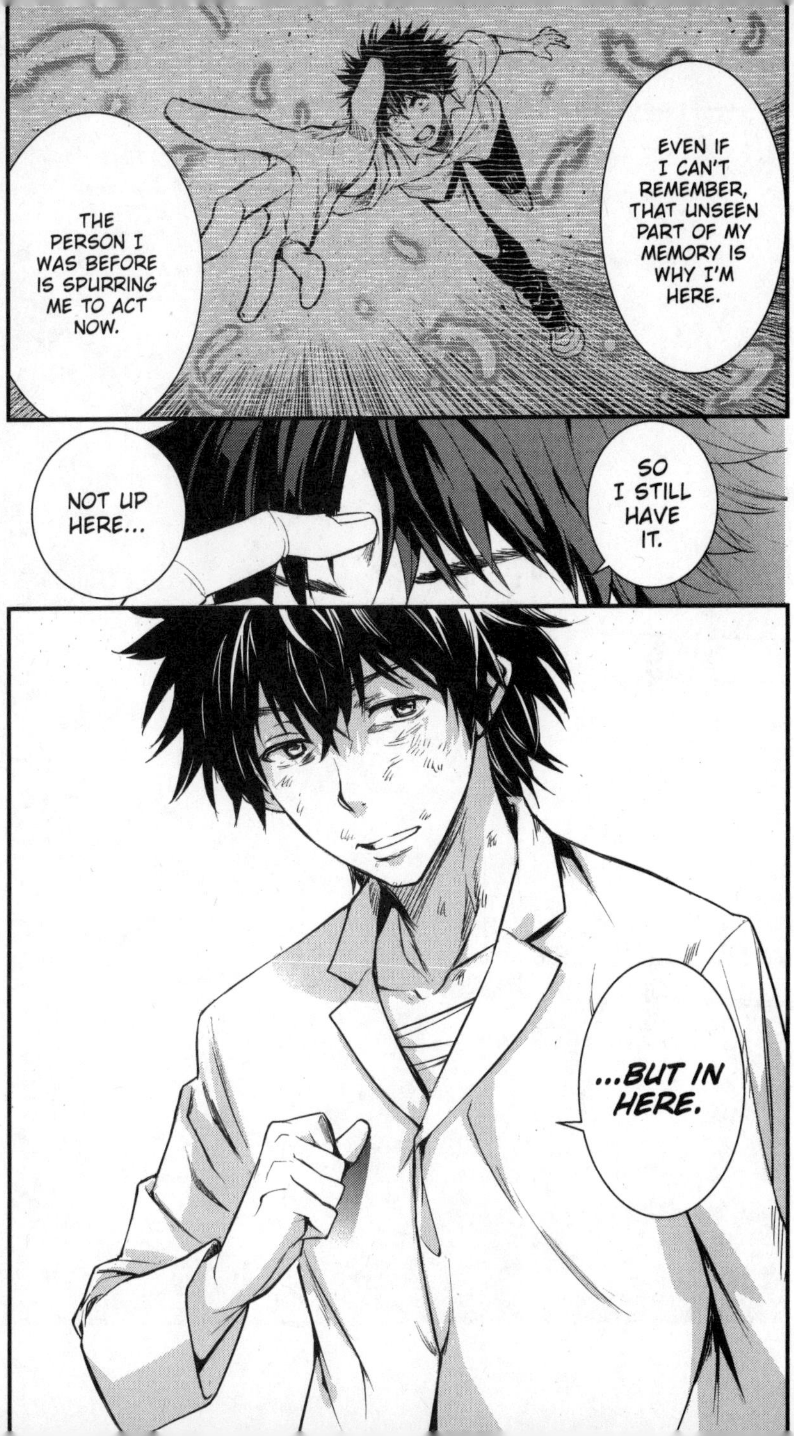
EVEN IF I CAN'T REMEMBER, THAT UNSEEN PART OF MY MEMORY IS WHY I'M HERE.
THE PERSON I WAS BEFORE IS SPURRING ME TO ACT NOW.
SO I STILL HAVE IT.
NOT UP HERE...
...BUT IN HERE.

MISAKA...

I'M SORRY.

YOU SHOULD GO BACK HOME.

THAT'S HOW I KNOW EXACTLY WHAT I WAS TRYING TO DO...

...AND EXACTLY WHAT I NEED TO DO NOW.

THIS ISN'T SOMETHING I CAN LEAVE TO SOMEONE ELSE. THERE'S NOTHING FORCING ME TO DO IT, BUT...

WHETHER I HAVE MY MEMORIES OR NOT, TOUMA KAMIJOU JUST HAS TO DO THE SAME THING HE'S ALWAYS DONE.

IN THE END, NOTHING'S CHANGED.

...I'M STILL GOING.

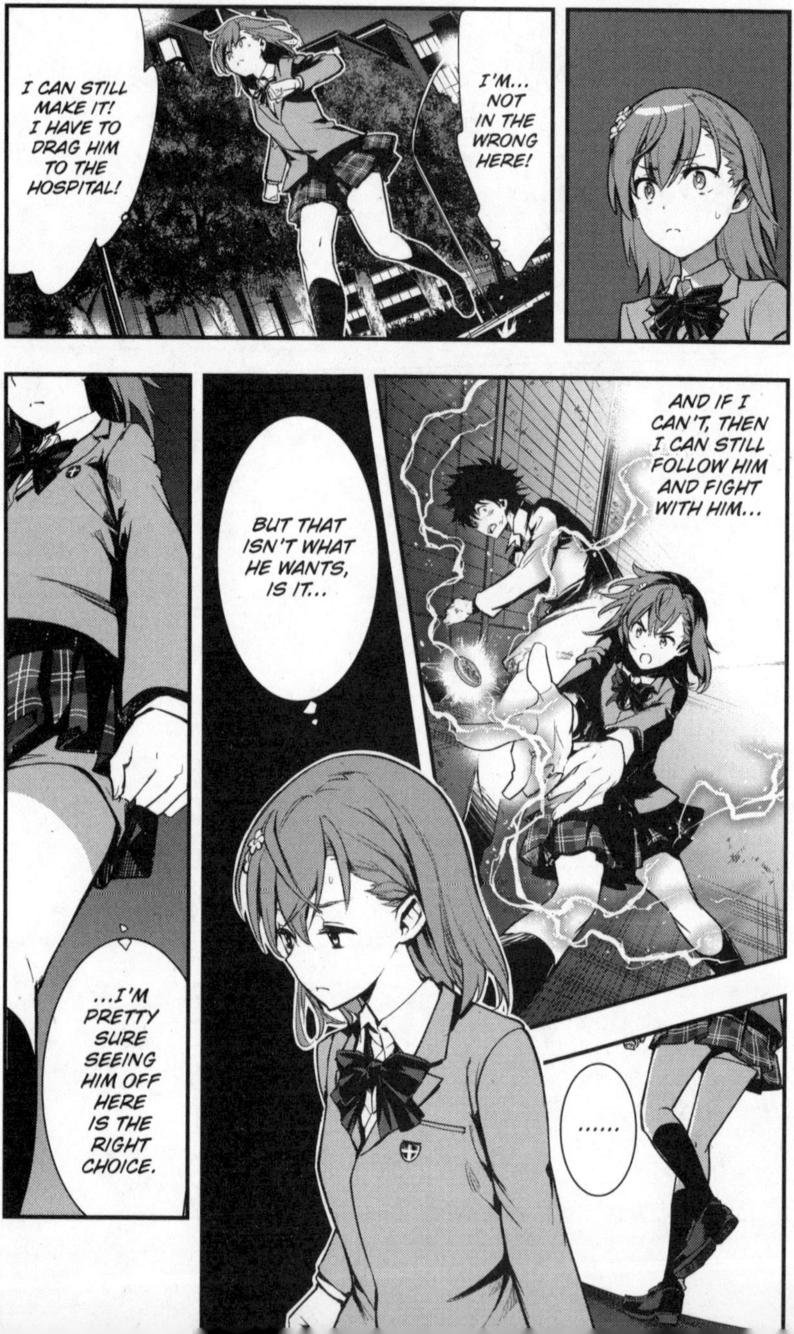
I'M... NOT IN THE WRONG HERE!
I CAN STILL MAKE IT! I HAVE TO DRAG HIM TO THE HOSPITAL!
AND IF I CAN'T, THEN I CAN STILL FOLLOW HIM AND FIGHT WITH HIM...
BUT THAT ISN'T WHAT HE WANTS, IS IT...
......
...I'M PRETTY SURE SEEING HIM OFF HERE IS THE RIGHT CHOICE.

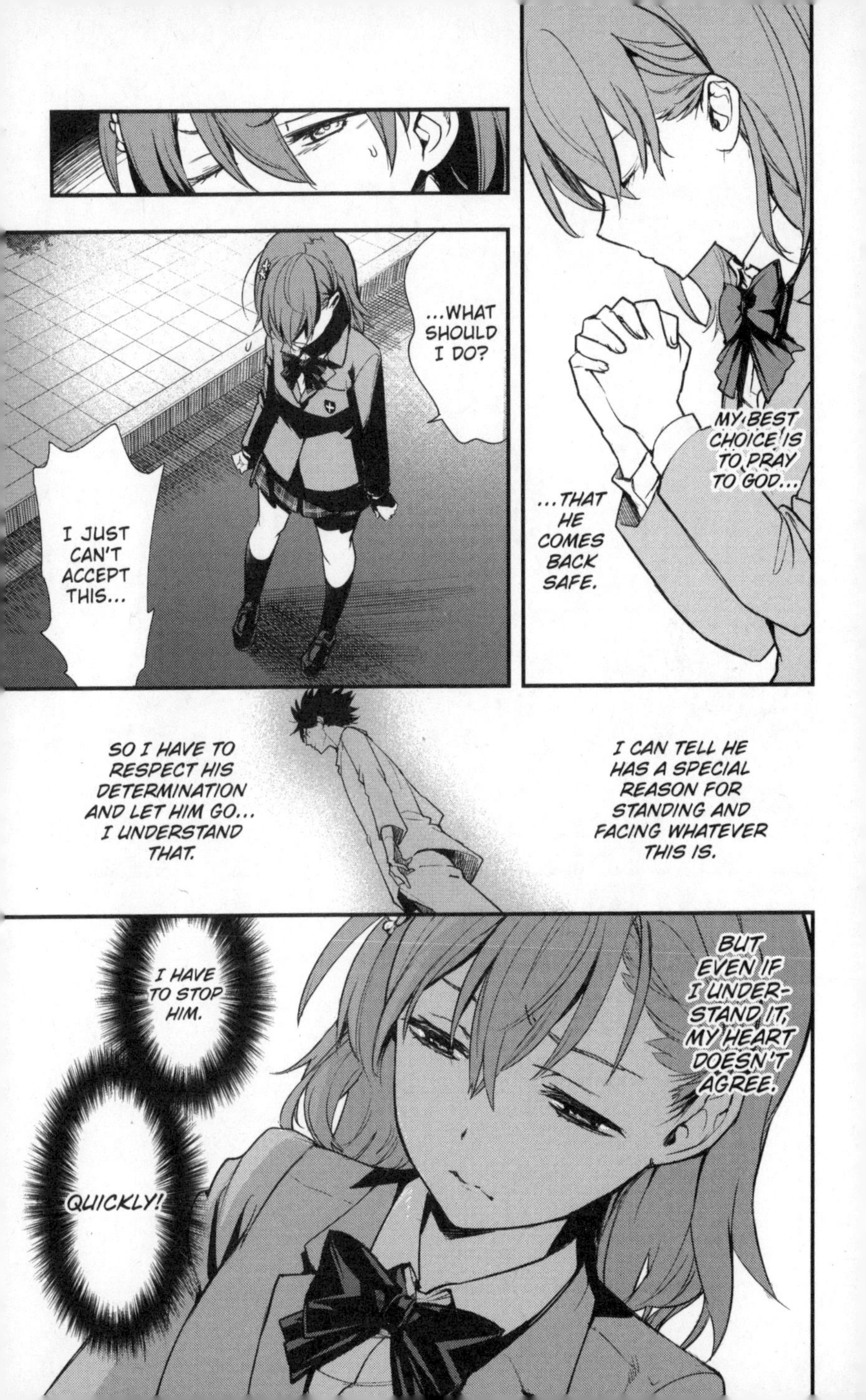
MY BEST CHOICE IS TO PRAY TO GOD...
...THAT HE COMES BACK SAFE.
...WHAT SHOULD I DO?
I JUST CAN'T ACCEPT THIS...
I CAN TELL HE HAS A SPECIAL REASON FOR STANDING AND FACING WHATEVER THIS IS.
SO I HAVE TO RESPECT HIS DETERMINATION AND LET HIM GO... I UNDERSTAND THAT.
BUT EVEN IF I UNDER-STAND IT, MY HEART DOESN'T AGREE.
I HAVE TO STOP HIM.
QUICKLY!

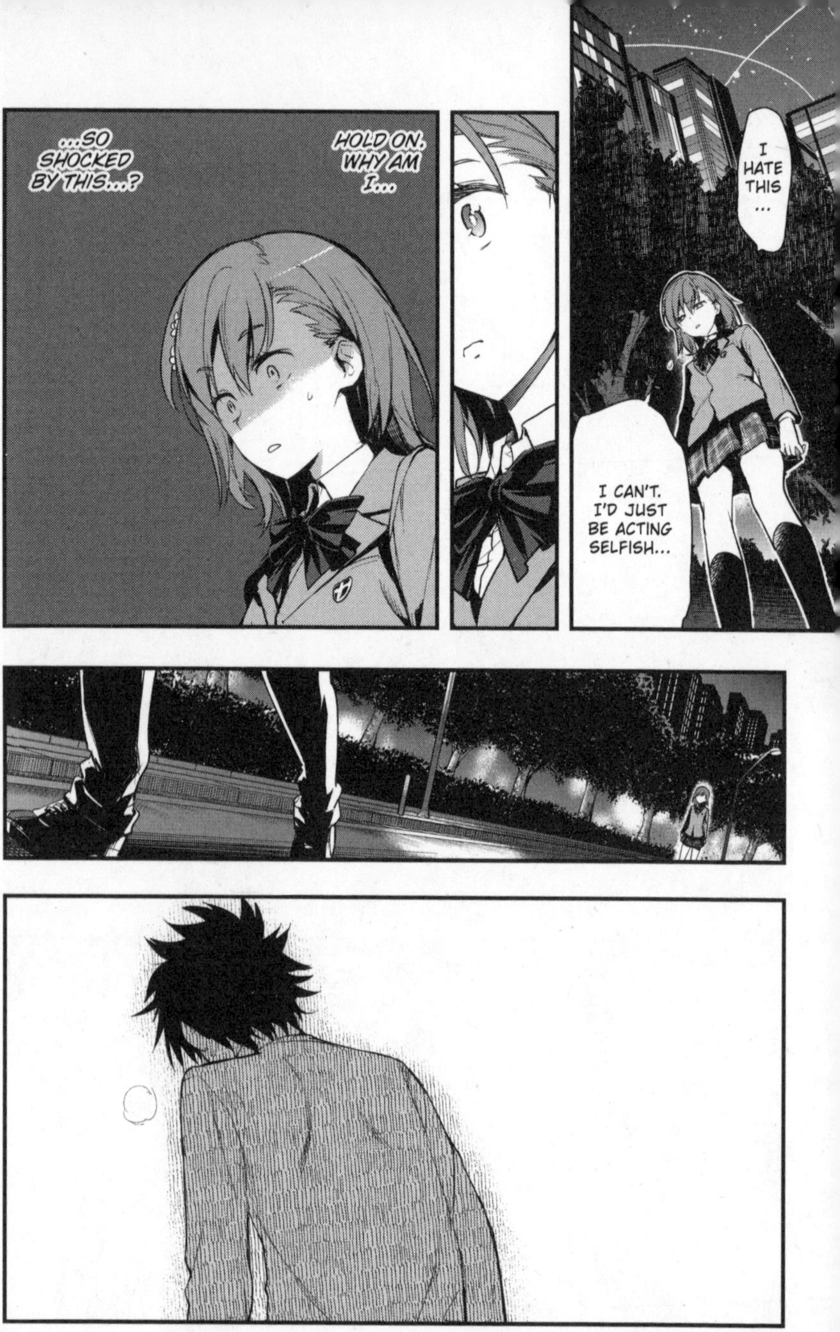
I HATE THIS ...
I CAN'T. I'D JUST BE ACTING SELFISH...
HOLD ON. WHY AM I...
...SO SHOCKED BY THIS...?

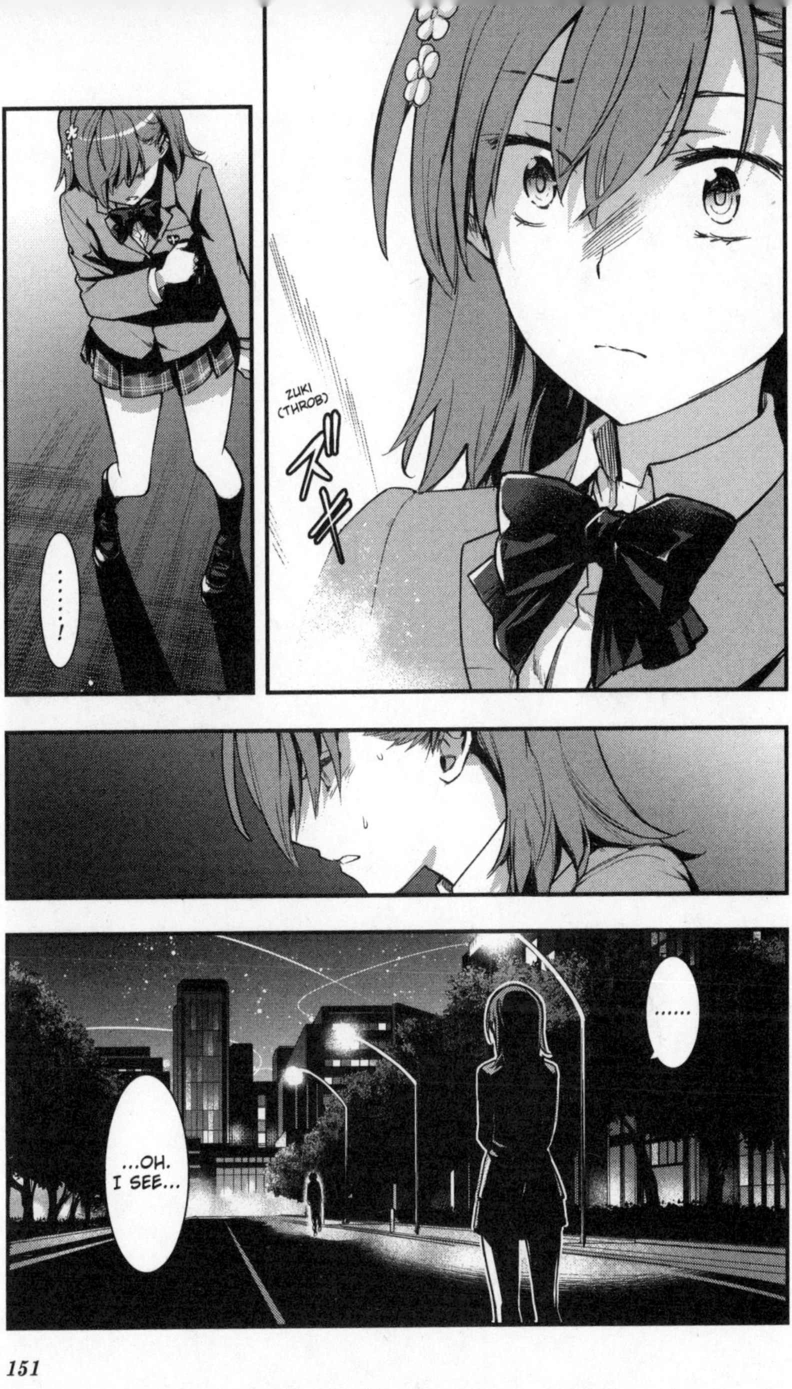
ZUKI (THROB)
......!
......
...OH. I SEE...

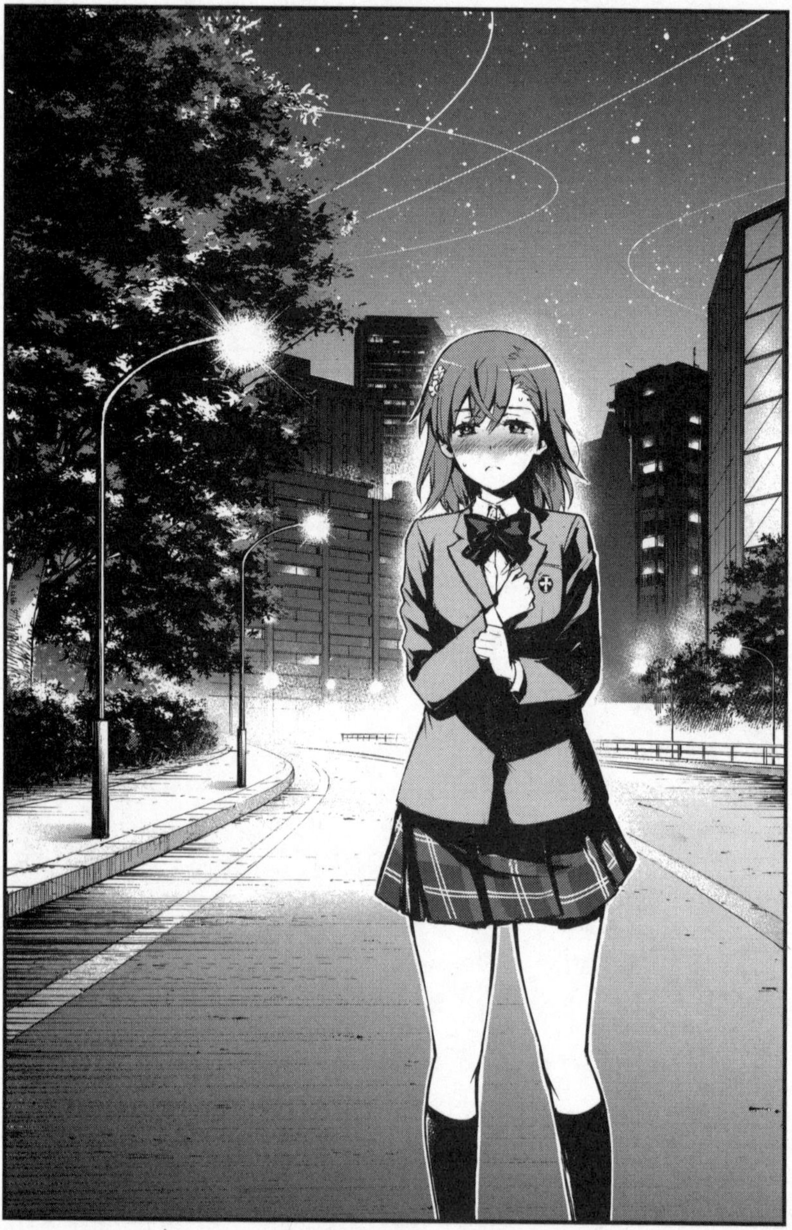

A Certain Magical Index

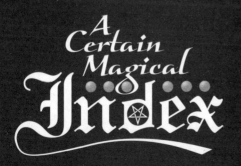

A Certain Magical Index

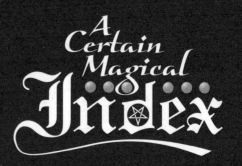

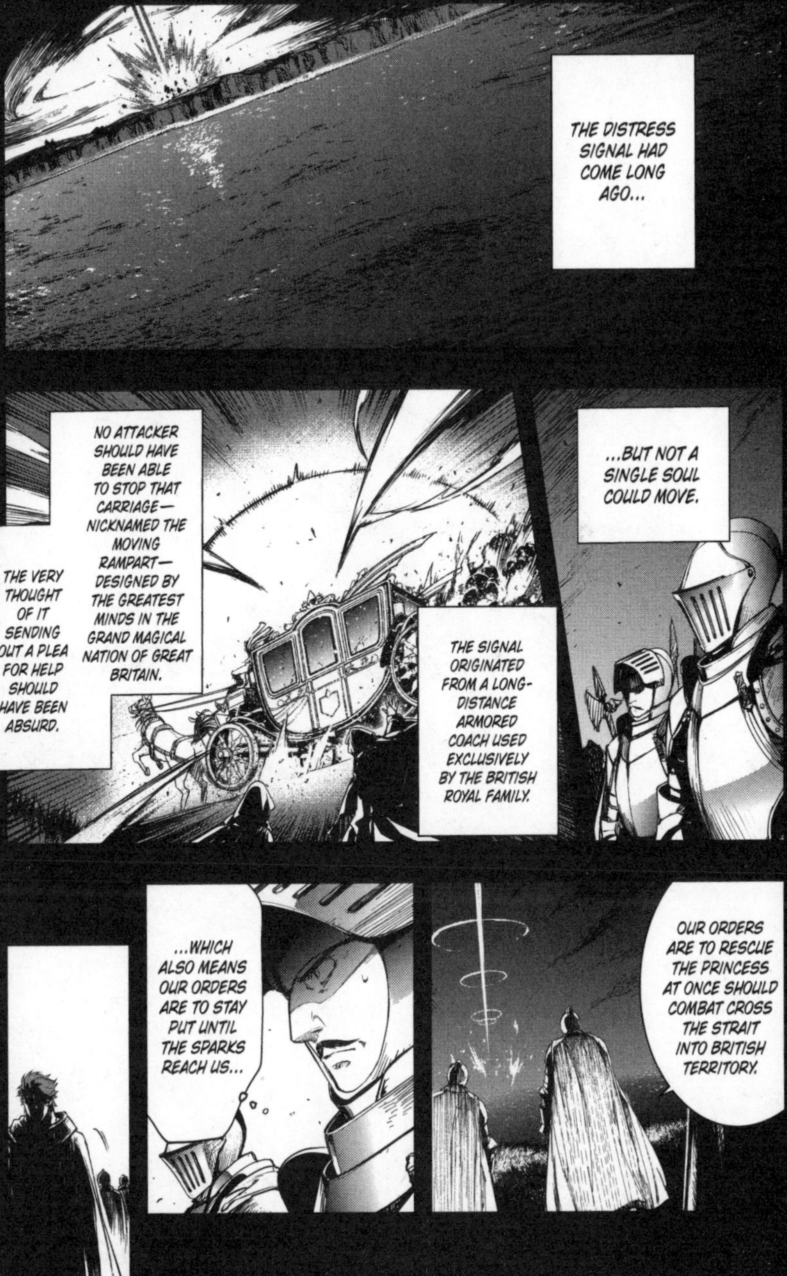
THE DISTRESS SIGNAL HAD COME LONG AGO...
...BUT NOT A SINGLE SOUL COULD MOVE.
THE SIGNAL ORIGINATED FROM A LONG-DISTANCE ARMORED COACH USED EXCLUSIVELY BY THE BRITISH ROYAL FAMILY.
NO ATTACKER SHOULD HAVE BEEN ABLE TO STOP THAT CARRIAGE—NICKNAMED THE MOVING RAMPART—DESIGNED BY THE GREATEST MINDS IN THE GRAND MAGICAL NATION OF GREAT BRITAIN.
THE VERY THOUGHT OF IT SENDING OUT A PLEA FOR HELP SHOULD HAVE BEEN ABSURD.
OUR ORDERS ARE TO RESCUE THE PRINCESS AT ONCE SHOULD COMBAT CROSS THE STRAIT INTO BRITISH TERRITORY.
...WHICH ALSO MEANS OUR ORDERS ARE TO STAY PUT UNTIL THE SPARKS REACH US...

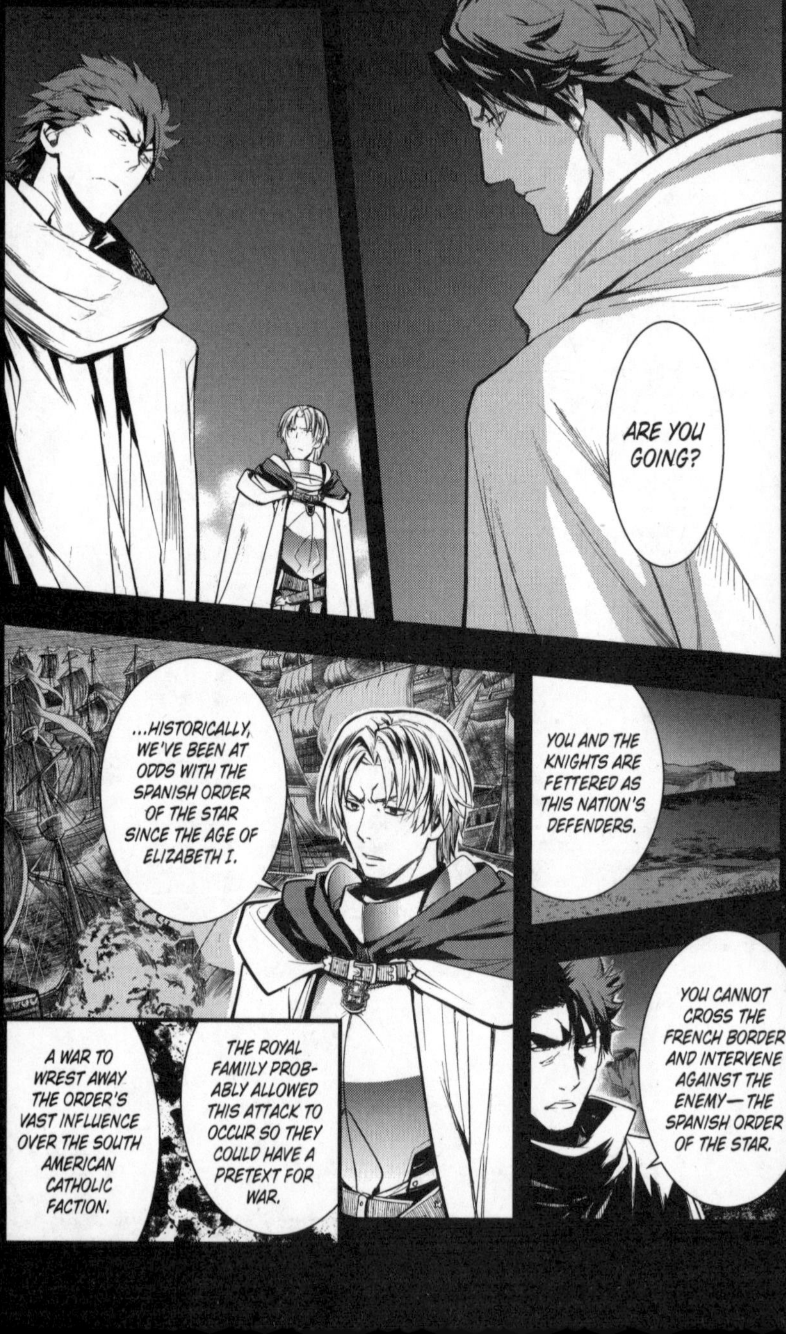
ARE YOU GOING?
YOU AND THE KNIGHTS ARE FETTERED AS THIS NATION'S DEFENDERS.
YOU CANNOT CROSS THE FRENCH BORDER AND INTERVENE AGAINST THE ENEMY—THE SPANISH ORDER OF THE STAR.
...HISTORICALLY, WE'VE BEEN AT ODDS WITH THE SPANISH ORDER OF THE STAR SINCE THE AGE OF ELIZABETH I.
THE ROYAL FAMIILY PROB-ABLY ALLOWED THIS ATTACK TO OCCUR SO THEY COULD HAVE A PRETEXT FOR WAR.
A WAR TO WREST AWAY THE ORDER'S VAST INFLUENCE OVER THE SOUTH AMERICAN CATHOLIC FACTION.

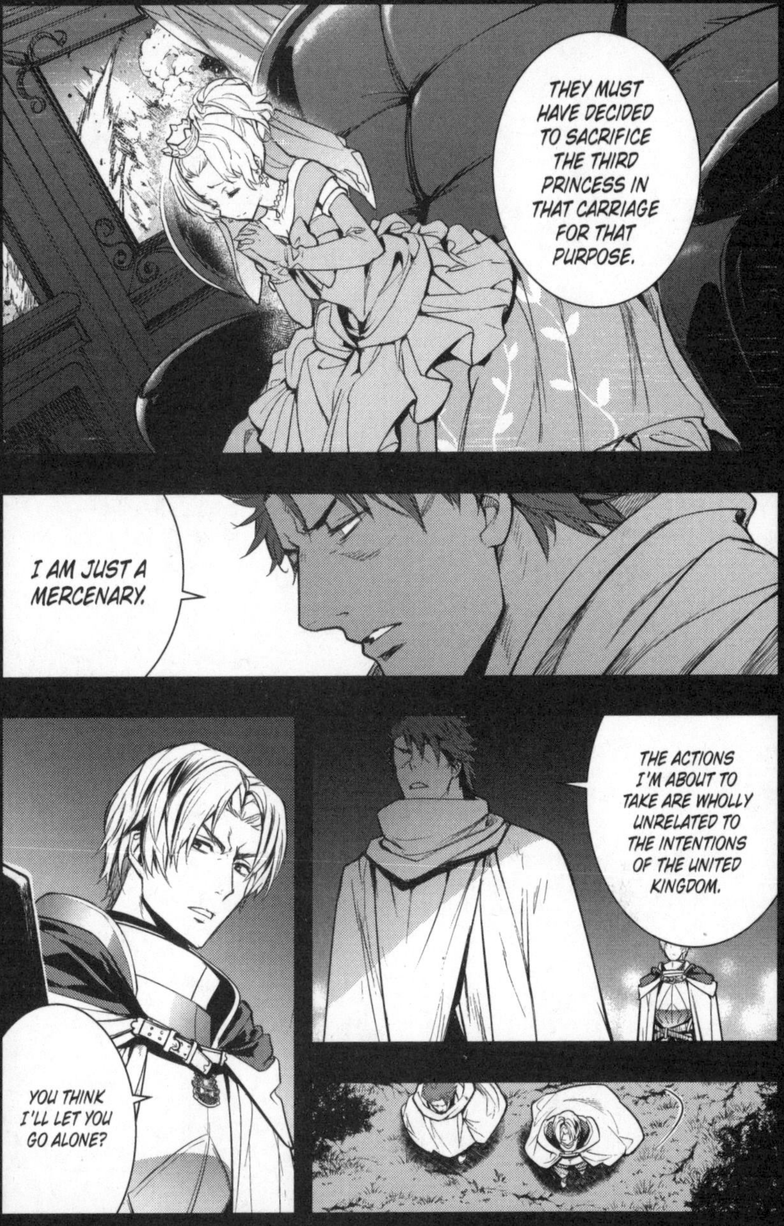
THEY MUST HAVE DECIDED TO SACRIFICE THE THIRD PRINCESS IN THAT CARRIAGE FOR THAT PURPOSE.
I AM JUST A MERCENARY.
THE ACTIONS I'M ABOUT TO TAKE ARE WHOLLY UNRELATED TO THE INTENTIONS OF THE UNITED KINGDOM.
YOU THINK I'LL LET YOU GO ALONE?

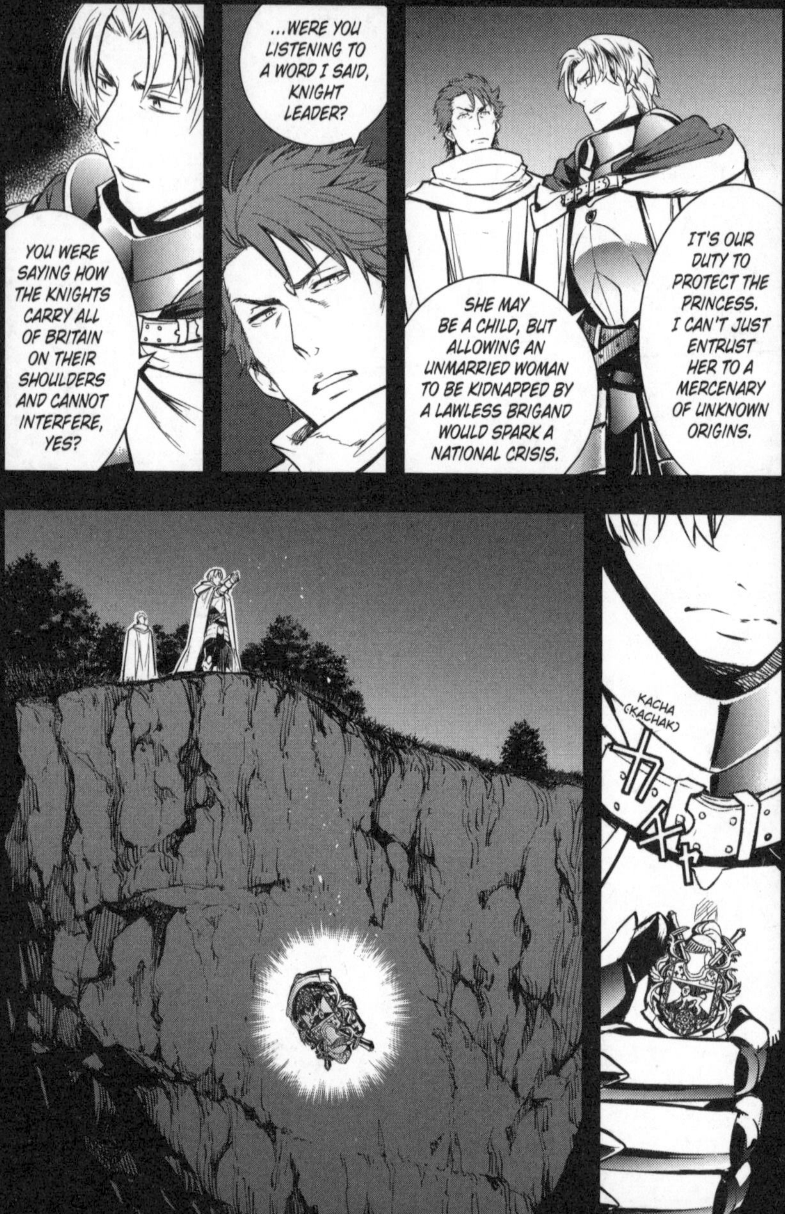
IT'S OUR DUTY TO PROTECT THE PRINCESS. I CAN'T JUST ENTRUST HER TO A MERCENARY OF UNKNOWN ORIGINS.
SHE MAY BE A CHILD, BUT ALLOWING AN UNMARRIED WOMAN TO BE KIDNAPPED BY A LAWLESS BRIGAND WOULD SPARK A NATIONAL CRISIS.
...WERE YOU LISTENING TO A WORD I SAID, KNIGHT LEADER?
YOU WERE SAYING HOW THE KNIGHTS CARRY ALL OF BRITAIN ON THEIR SHOULDERS AND CANNOT INTERFERE, YES?
KACHA (KACHAK)

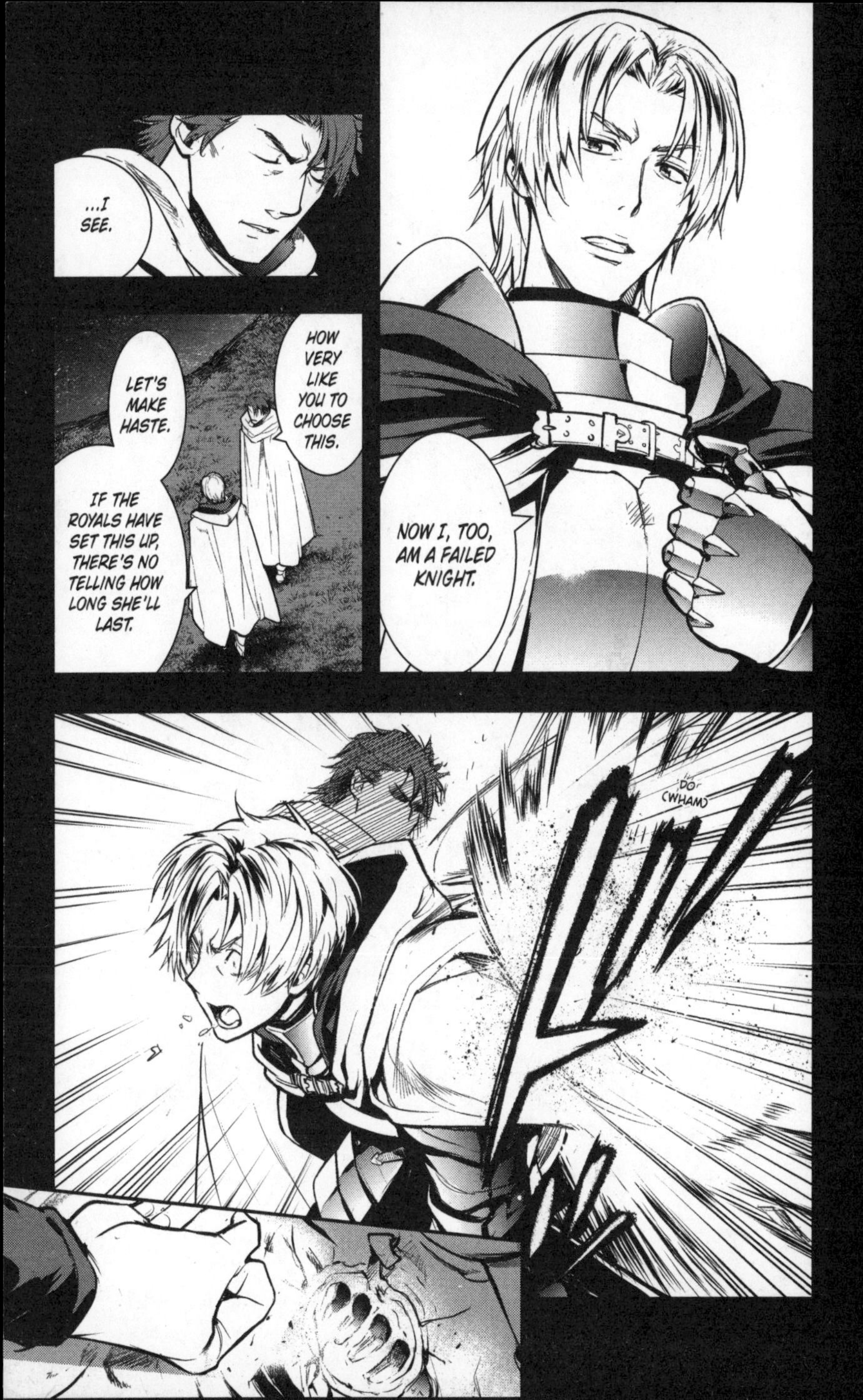
NOW I, TOO, AM A FAILED KNIGHT.
...I SEE.
HOW VERY LIKE YOU TO CHOOSE THIS.
LET'S MAKE HASTE.
IF THE ROYALS HAVE SET THIS UP, THERE'S NO TELLING HOW LONG SHE'LL LAST.
DO
(WHAM)

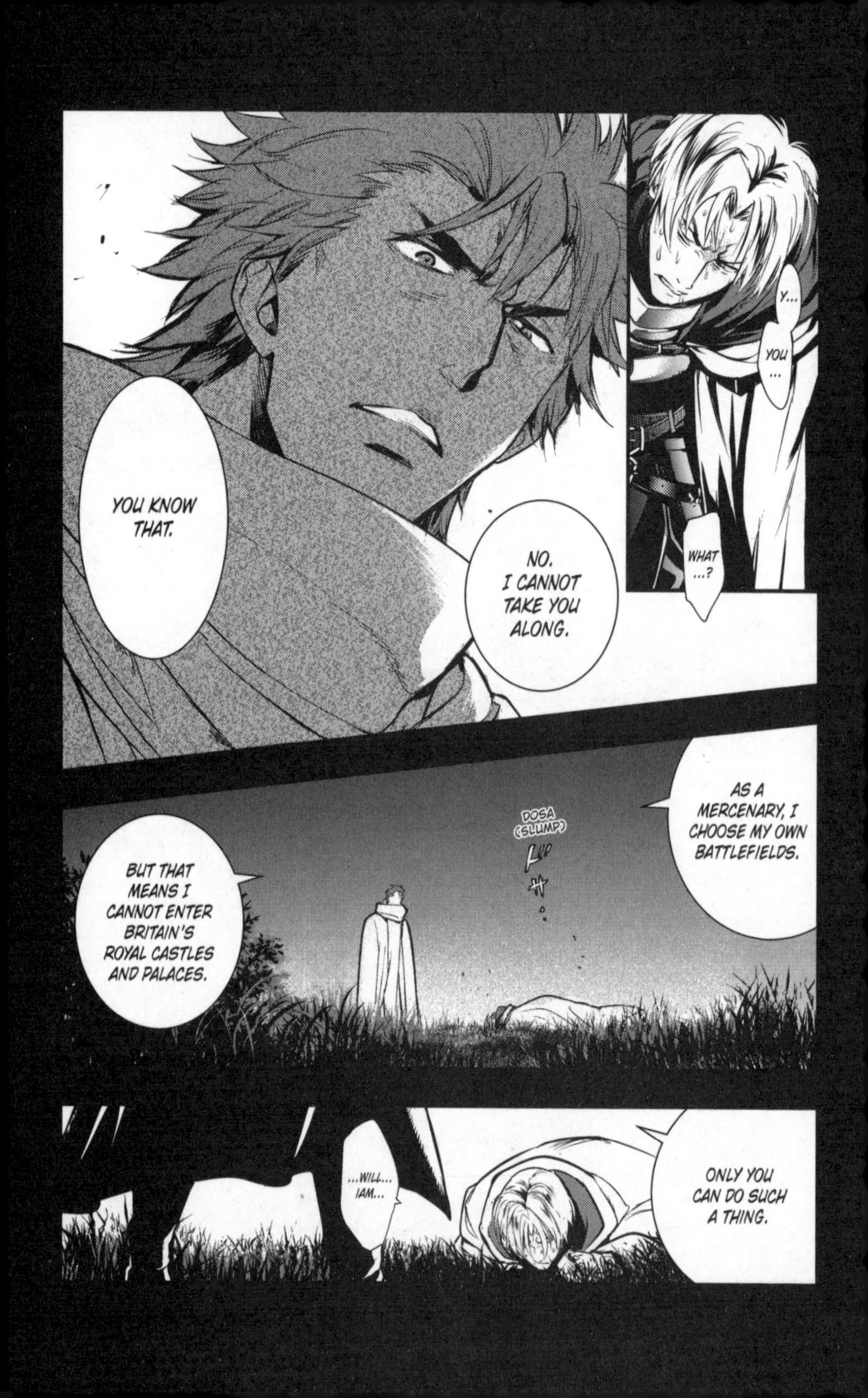
Y... YOU...
WHAT ...?
NO. I CANNOT TAKE YOU ALONG.
YOU KNOW THAT.
AS A MERCENARY, I CHOOSE MY OWN BATTLEFIELDS.
DOSA (SLUMP)
BUT THAT MEANS I CANNOT ENTER BRITAIN'S ROYAL CASTLES AND PALACES.
ONLY YOU CAN DO SUCH A THING.
...WILL... IAM...

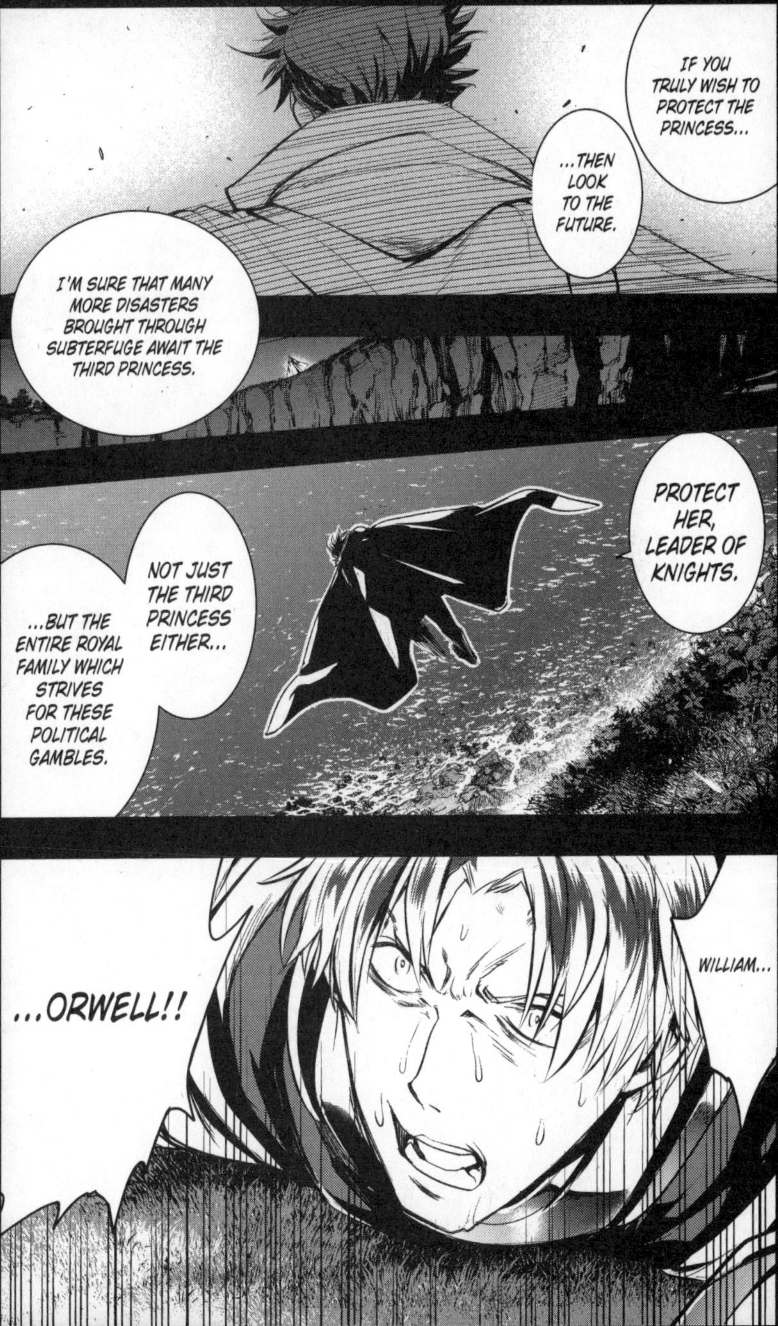
IF YOU TRULY WISH TO PROTECT THE PRINCESS...
...THEN LOOK TO THE FUTURE.
I'M SURE THAT MANY MORE DISASTERS BROUGHT THROUGH SUBTERFUGE AWAIT THE THIRD PRINCESS.
PROTECT HER, LEADER OF KNIGHTS.
NOT JUST THE THIRD PRINCESS EITHER...
...BUT THE ENTIRE ROYAL FAMILY WHICH STRIVES FOR THESE POLITICAL GAMBLES.
WILLIAM...
...ORWELL!!

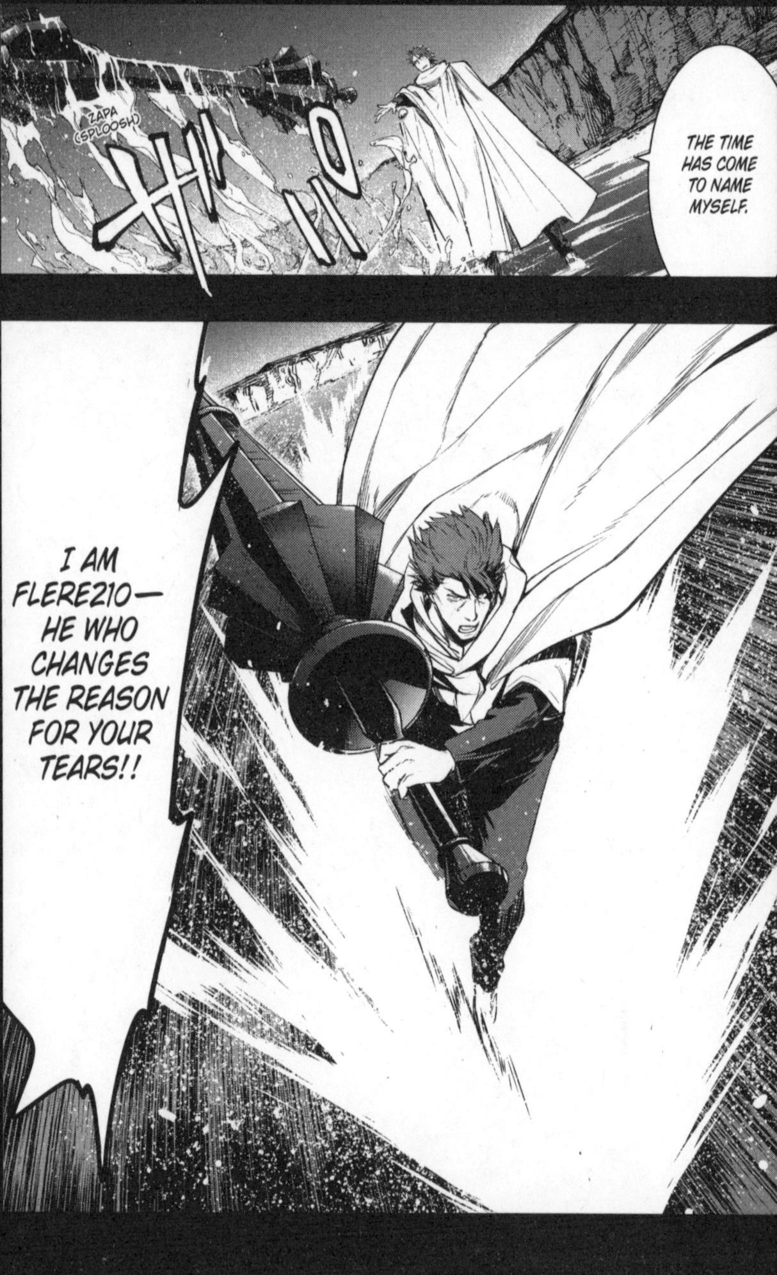
THE TIME HAS COME TO NAME MYSELF.
ZAPA (SPLOOSH)
I AM FLEREZIO—HE WHO CHANGES THE REASON FOR YOUR TEARS!!

#161 SAINTBREAKER ④

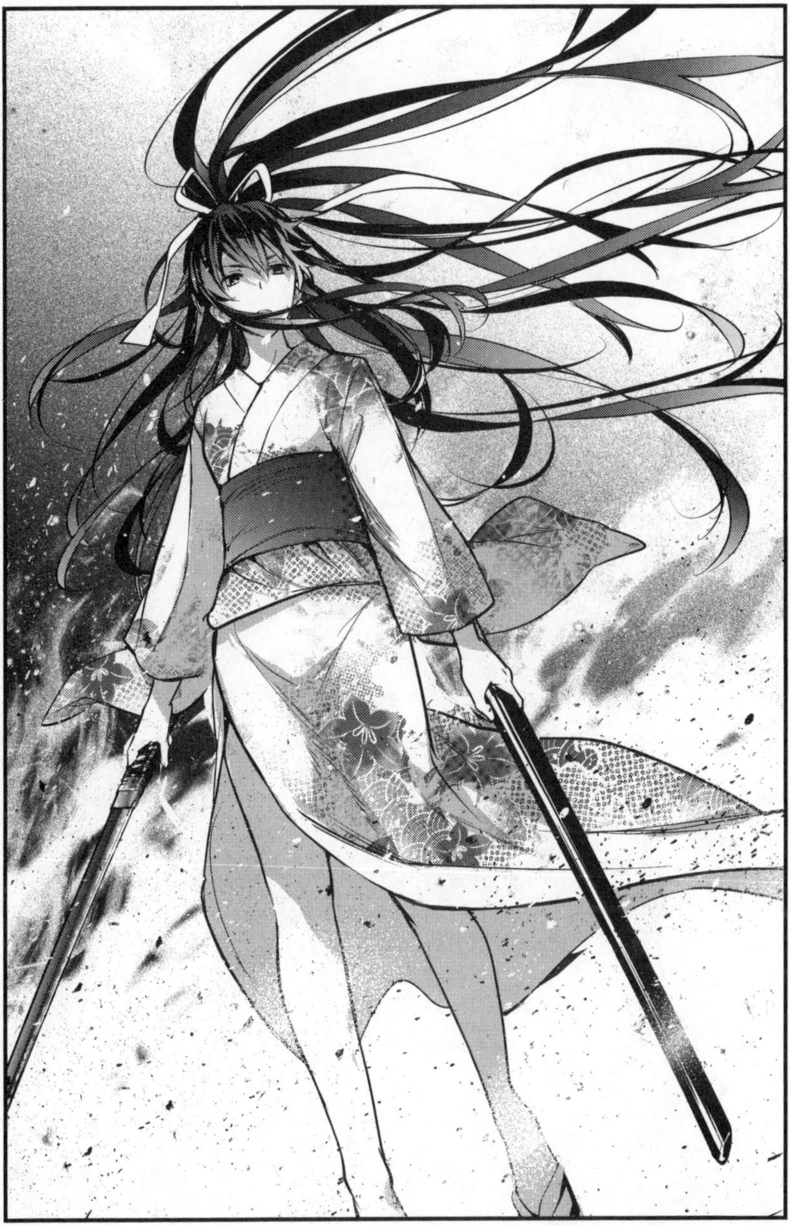

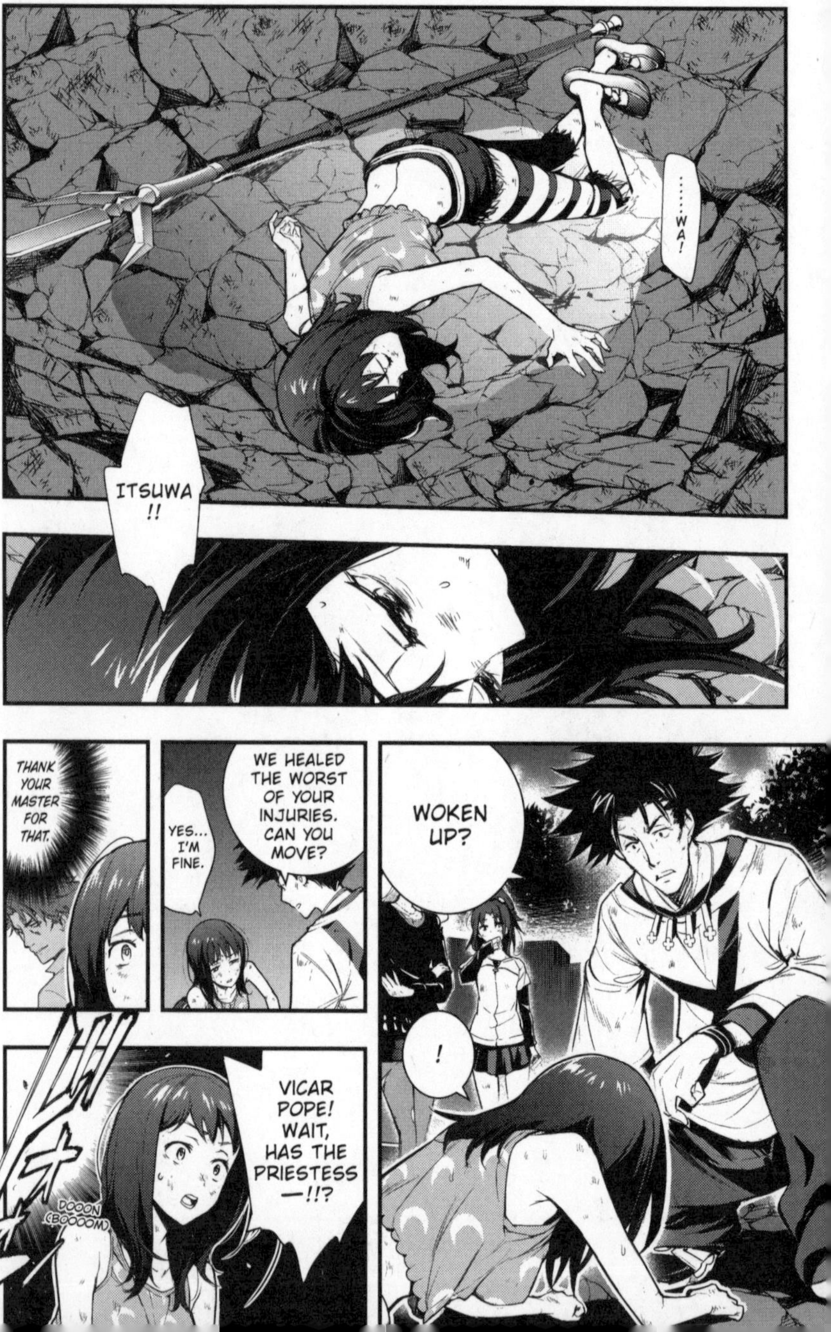

......WA!
ITSUWA !!
WOKEN UP?
!
WE HEALED THE WORST OF YOUR INJURIES. CAN YOU MOVE?
YES... I'M FINE.
THANK YOUR MASTER FOR THAT.
VICAR POPE! WAIT, HAS THE PRIESTESS—!!?
DOOON (BOOOOM)

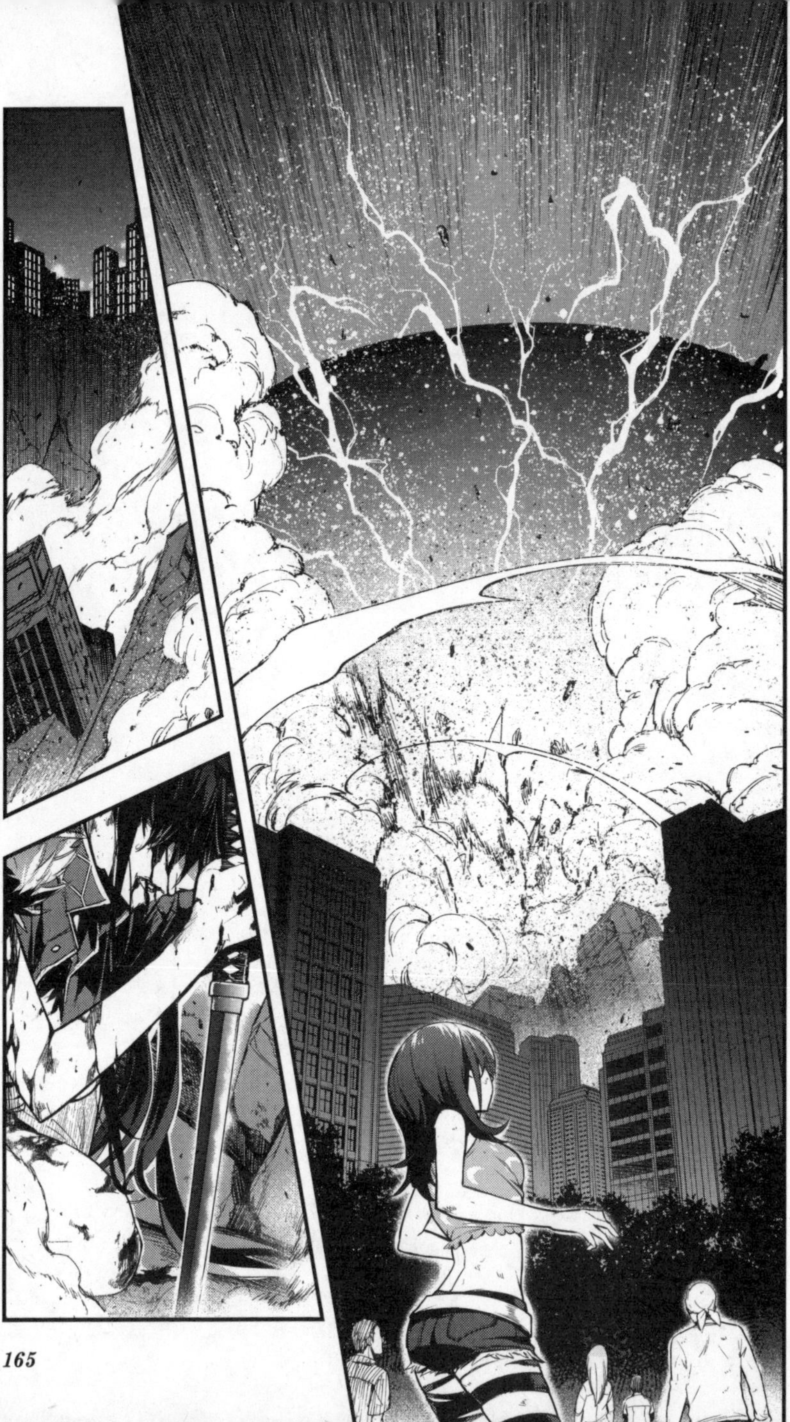

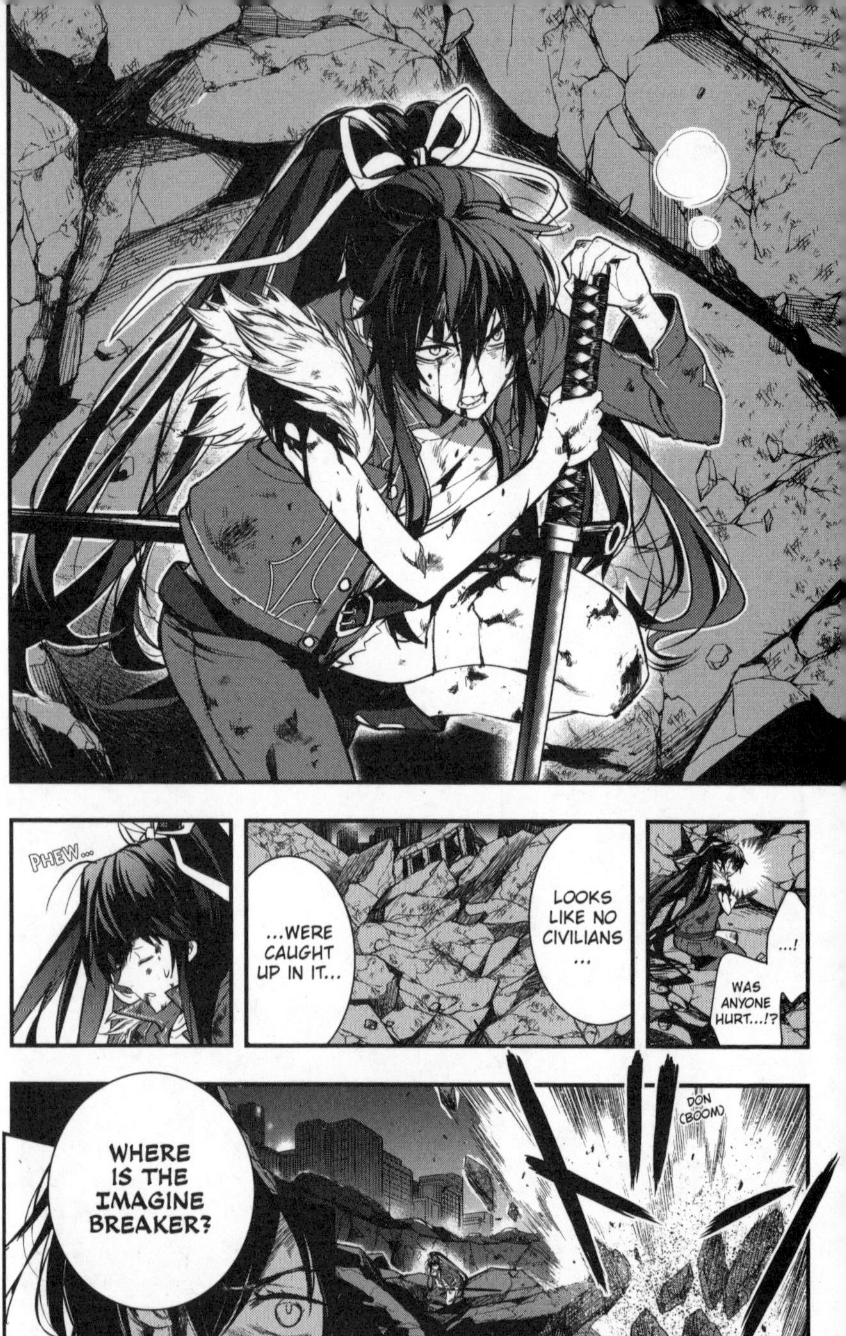
...!
WAS ANYONE HURT...!?
LOOKS LIKE NO CIVILIANS ...
...WERE CAUGHT UP IN IT...
PHEW...
DON (BOOM)
WHERE IS THE IMAGINE BREAKER?

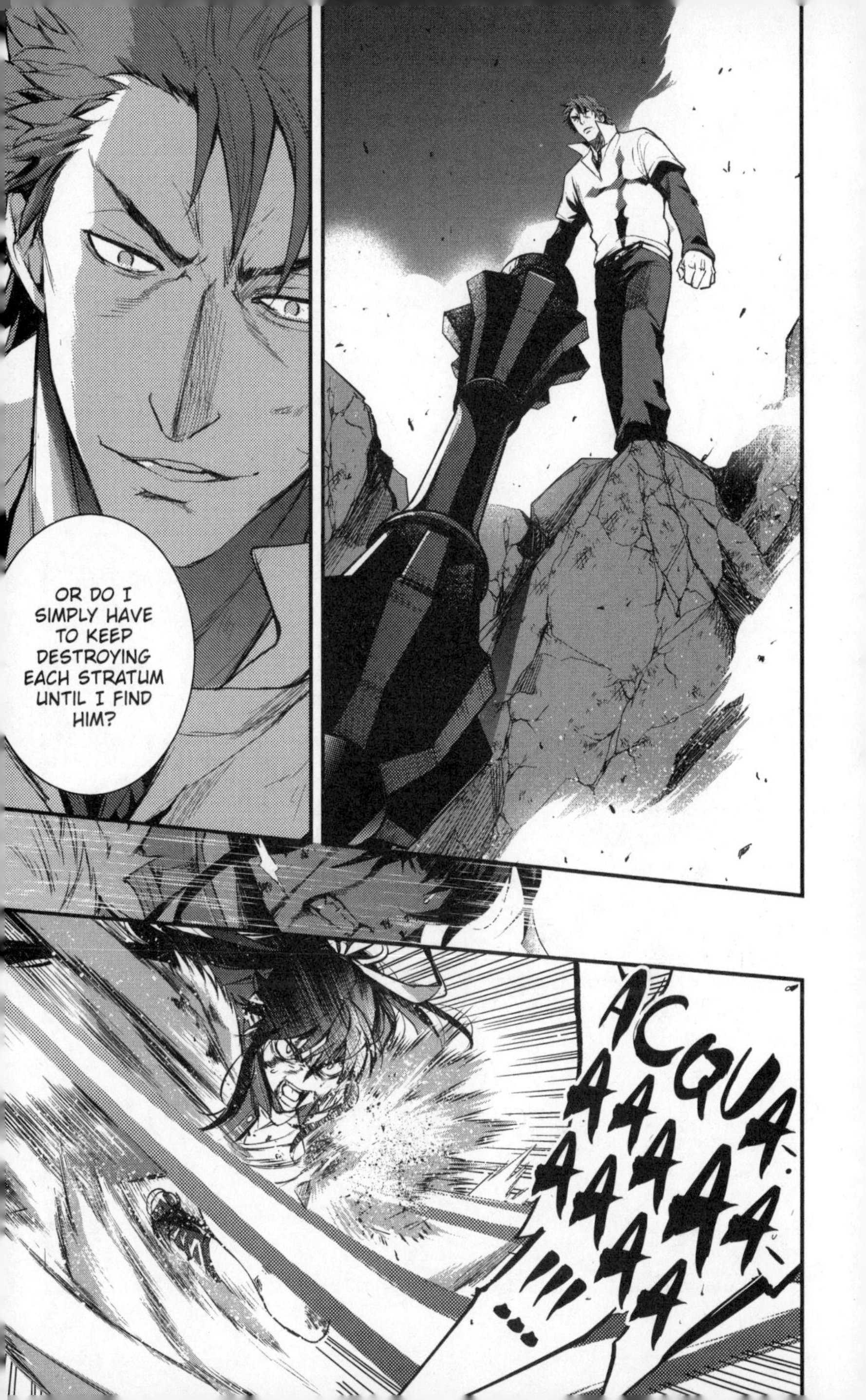
OR DO I SIMPLY HAVE TO KEEP DESTROYING EACH STRATUM UNTIL I FIND HIM?
ACQUAAAAAAAAAAAA...!!!

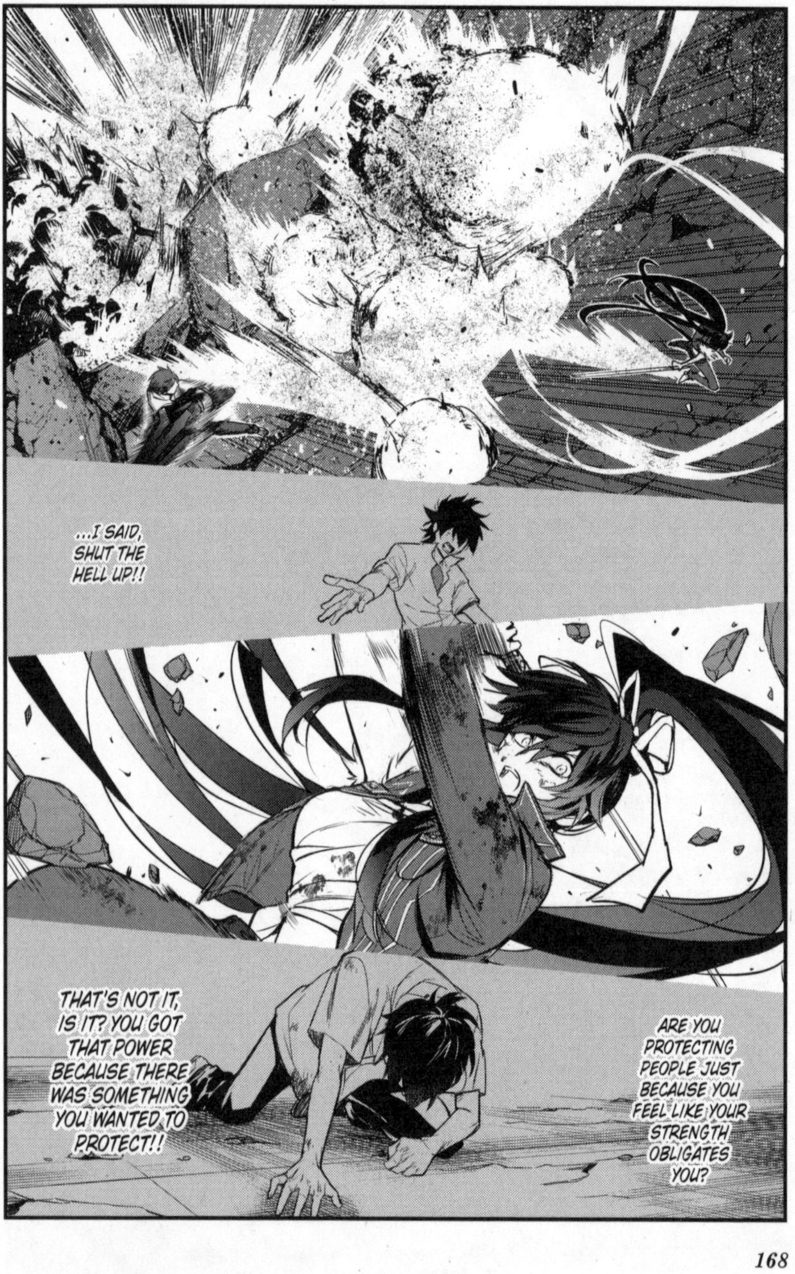
...I SAID, SHUT THE HELL UP!!
ARE YOU PROTECTING PEOPLE JUST BECAUSE YOU FEEL LIKE YOUR STRENGTH OBLIGATES YOU?
THAT'S NOT IT, IS IT? YOU GOT THAT POWER BECAUSE THERE WAS SOMETHING YOU WANTED TO PROTECT!!

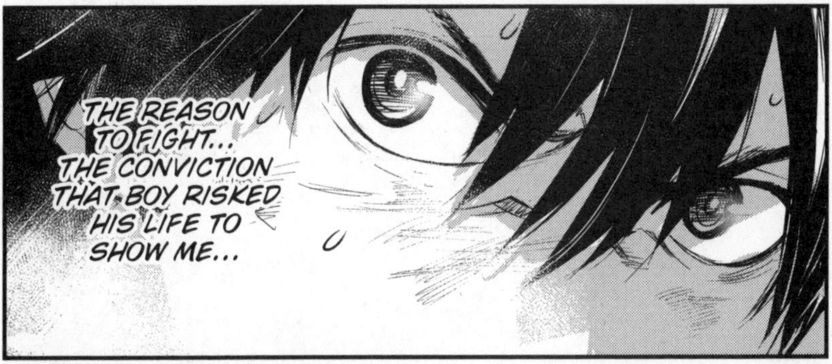
THE REASON TO FIGHT... THE CONVICTION THAT BOY RISKED HIS LIFE TO SHOW ME...
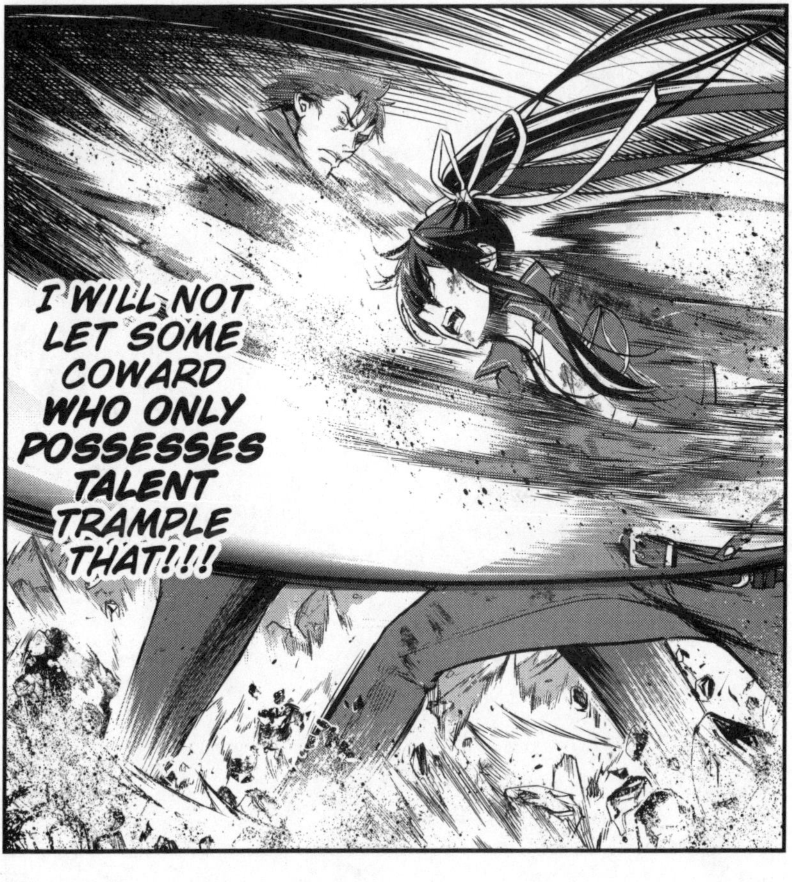
I WILL NOT LET SOME COWARD WHO ONLY POSSESSES TALENT TRAMPLE THAT!!!

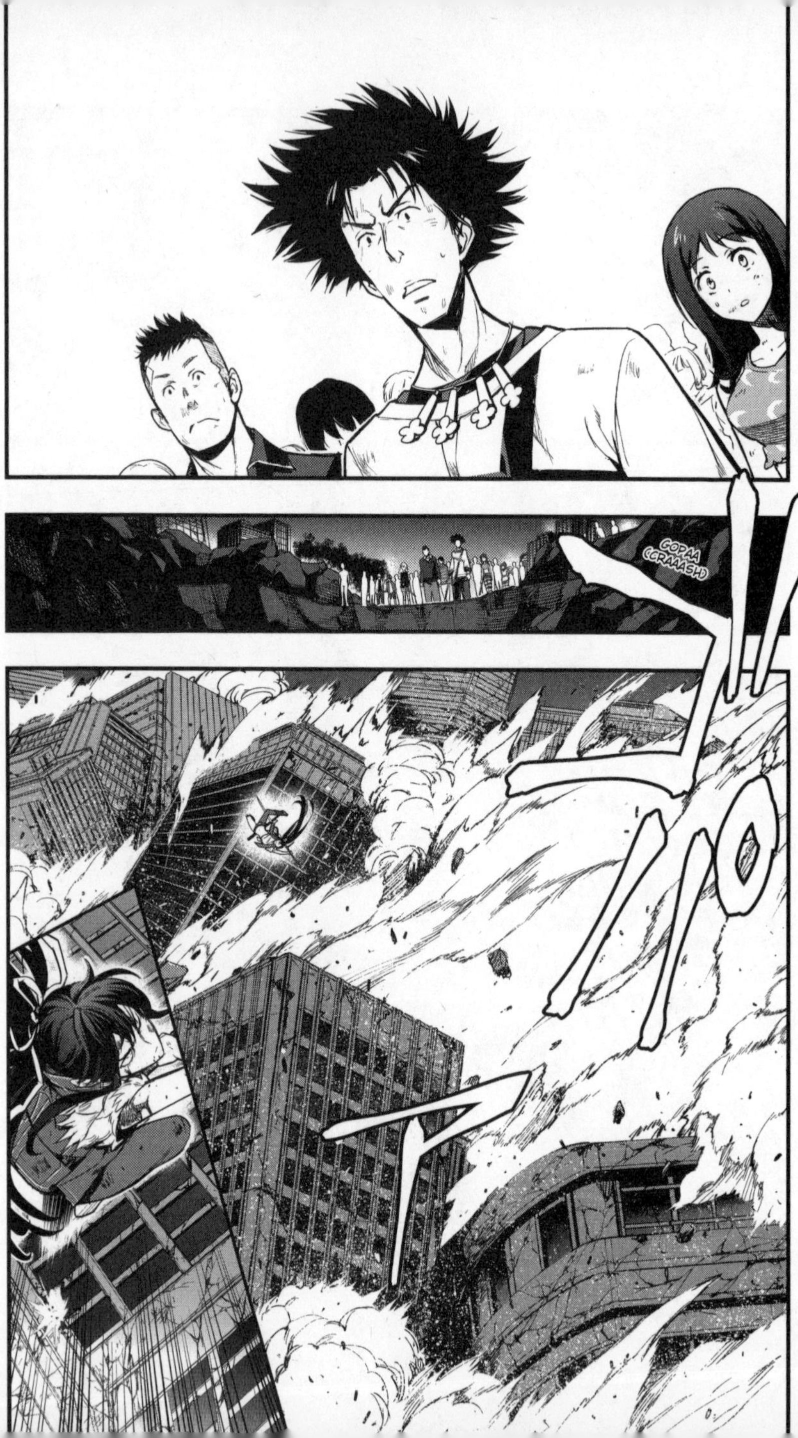
GOPAA
(CRAAASH)

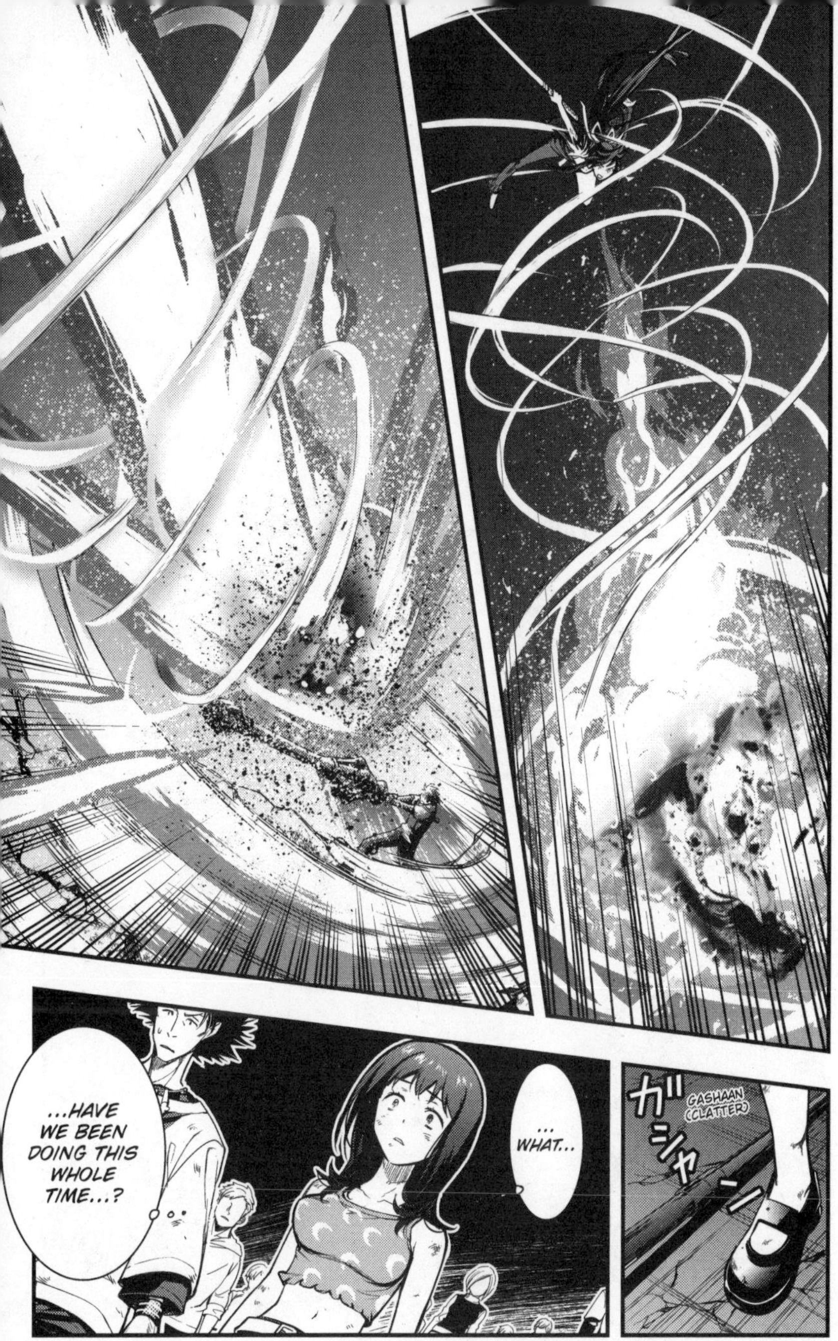
ガシャーン
GASHAAN (CLATTER)
... WHAT...
...HAVE WE BEEN DOING THIS WHOLE TIME...?

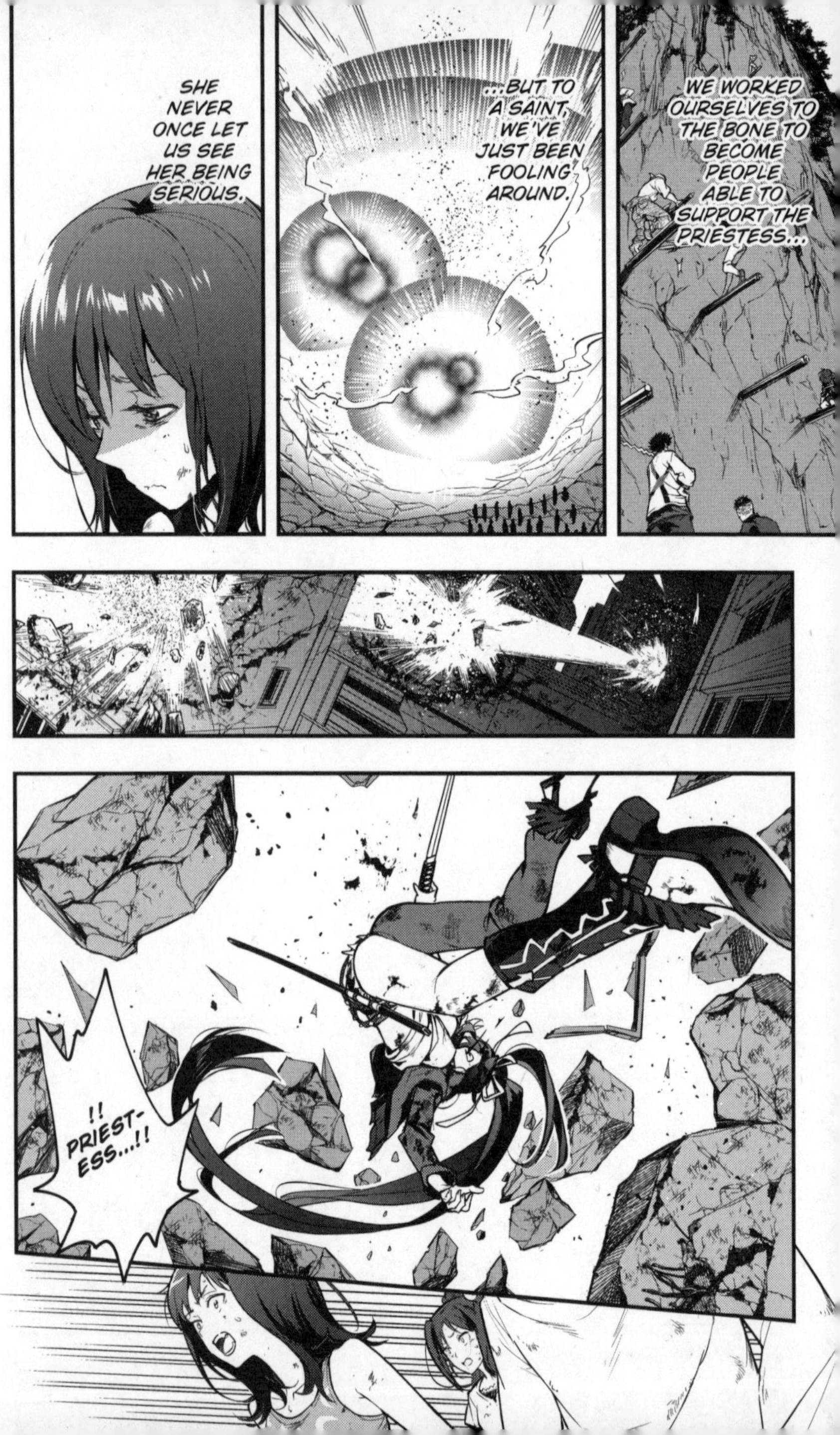
WE WORKED OURSELVES TO THE BONE TO BECOME PEOPLE ABLE TO SUPPORT THE PRIESTESS...
...BUT TO A SAINT, WE'VE JUST BEEN FOOLING AROUND.
SHE NEVER ONCE LET US SEE HER BEING SERIOUS.
!! PRIEST-ESS...!!

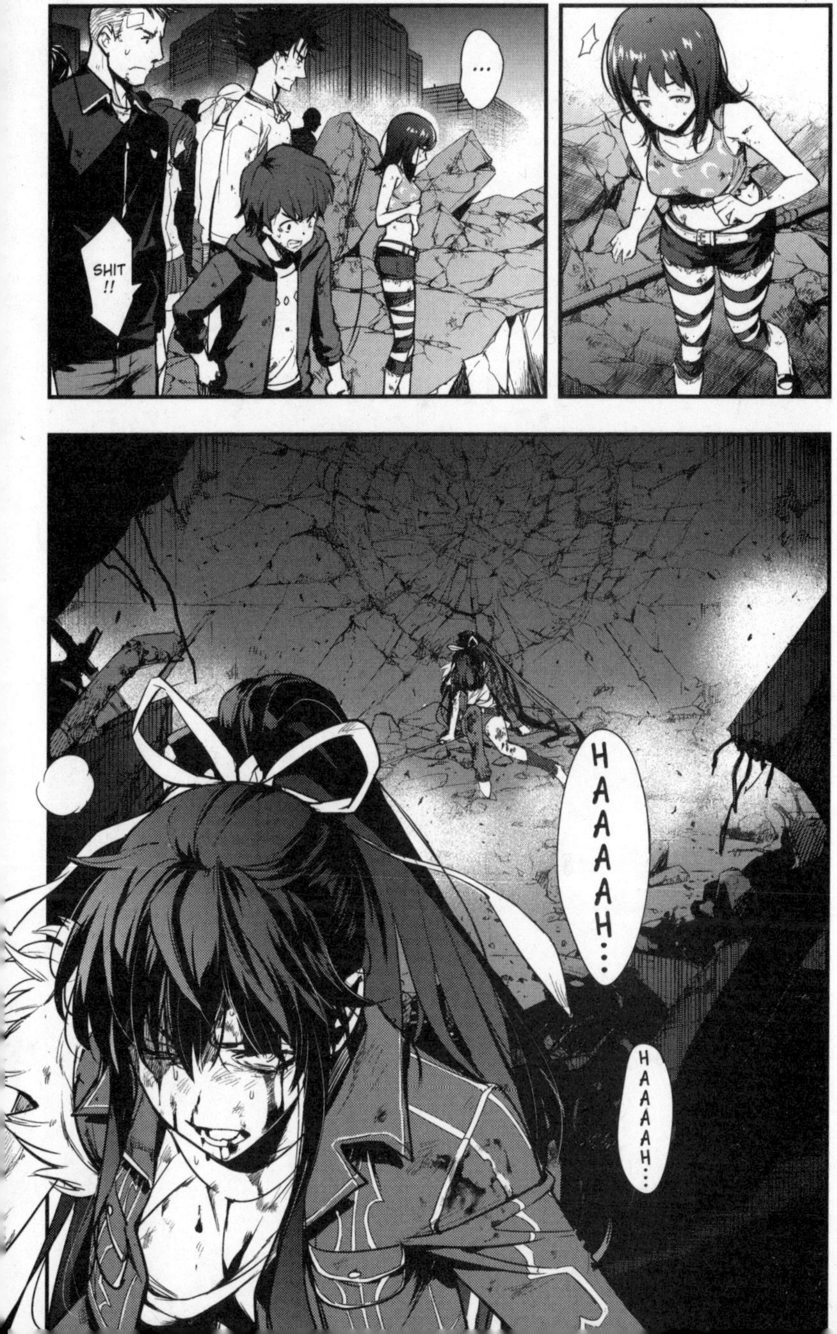
...
SHIT !!
HAAAAAH...
HAAAAAH...

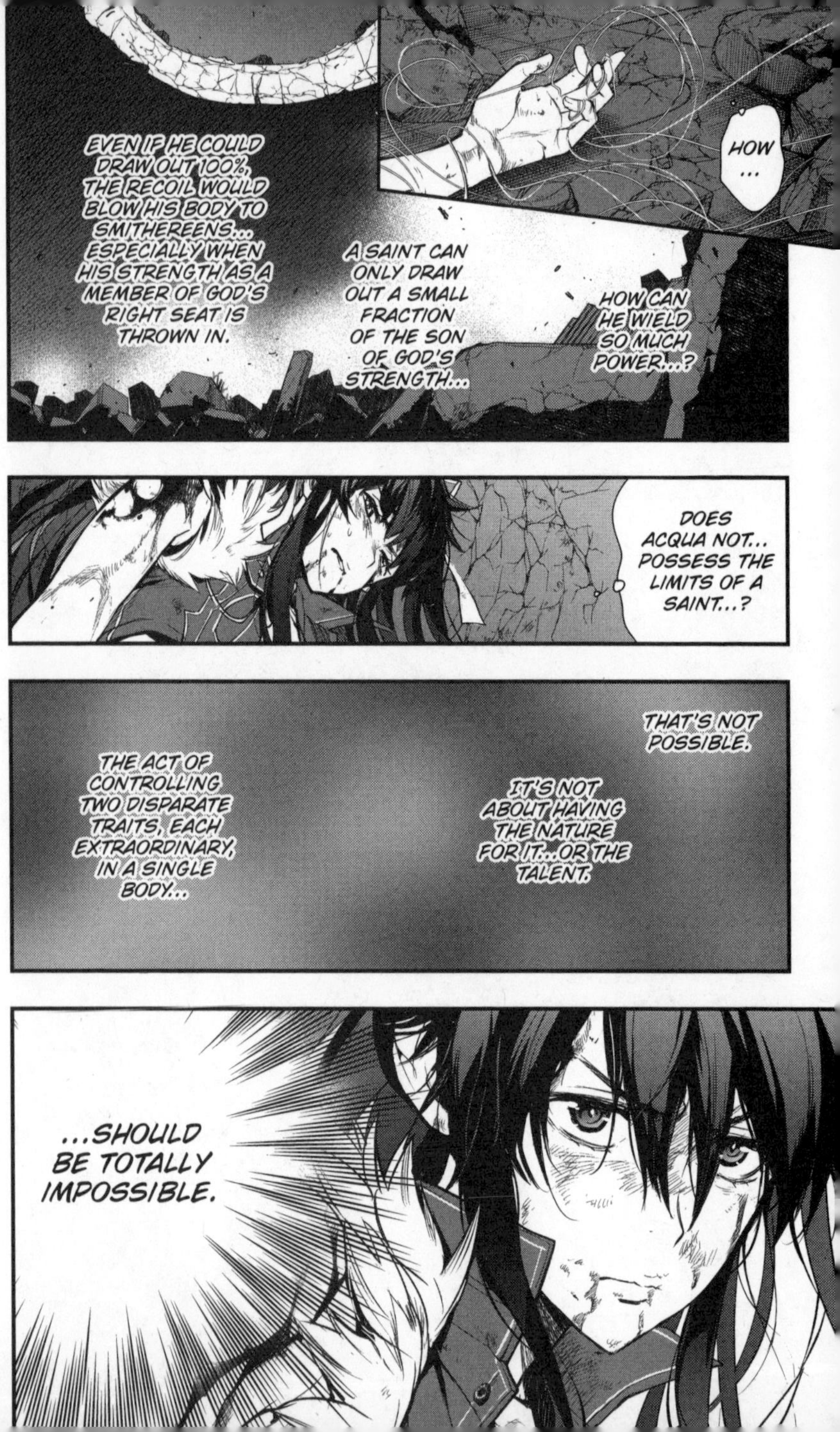
HOW ...
HOW CAN HE WIELD SO MUCH POWER...?
A SAINT CAN ONLY DRAW OUT A SMALL FRACTION OF THE SON OF GOD'S STRENGTH...
EVEN IF HE COULD DRAW OUT 100%, THE RECOIL WOULD BLOW HIS BODY TO SMITHEREENS... ESPECIALLY WHEN HIS STRENGTH AS A MEMBER OF GOD'S RIGHT SEAT IS THROWN IN.
DOES ACQUA NOT... POSSESS THE LIMITS OF A SAINT...?
THAT'S NOT POSSIBLE.
IT'S NOT ABOUT HAVING THE NATURE FOR IT...OR THE TALENT.
THE ACT OF CONTROLLING TWO DISPARATE TRAITS, EACH EXTRAORDINARY, IN A SINGLE BODY...
...SHOULD BE TOTALLY IMPOSSIBLE.

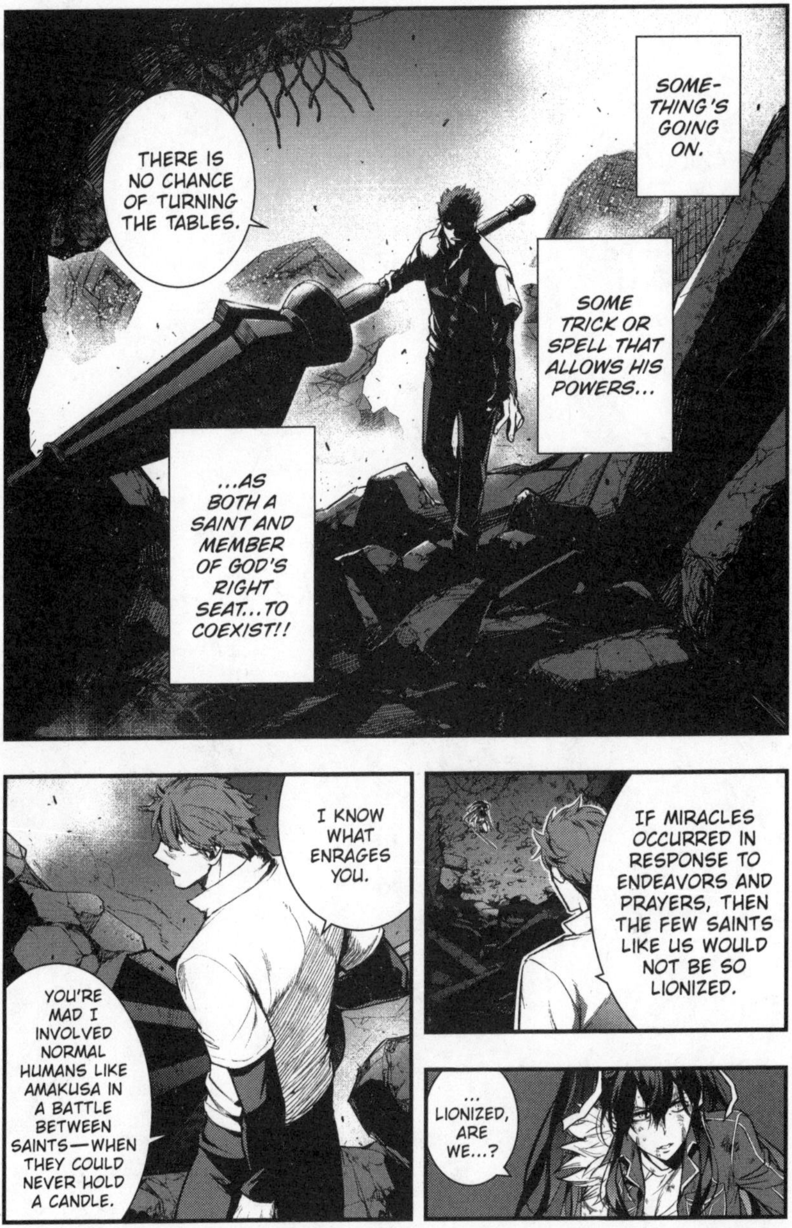
SOME-THING'S GOING ON.
THERE IS NO CHANCE OF TURNING THE TABLES.
SOME TRICK OR SPELL THAT ALLOWS HIS POWERS...
...AS BOTH A SAINT AND MEMBER OF GOD'S RIGHT SEAT...TO COEXIST!!
IF MIRACLES OCCURRED IN RESPONSE TO ENDEAVORS AND PRAYERS, THEN THE FEW SAINTS LIKE US WOULD NOT BE SO LIONIZED.
...LIONIZED, ARE WE...?
I KNOW WHAT ENRAGES YOU.
YOU'RE MAD I INVOLVED NORMAL HUMANS LIKE AMAKUSA IN A BATTLE BETWEEN SAINTS—WHEN THEY COULD NEVER HOLD A CANDLE.

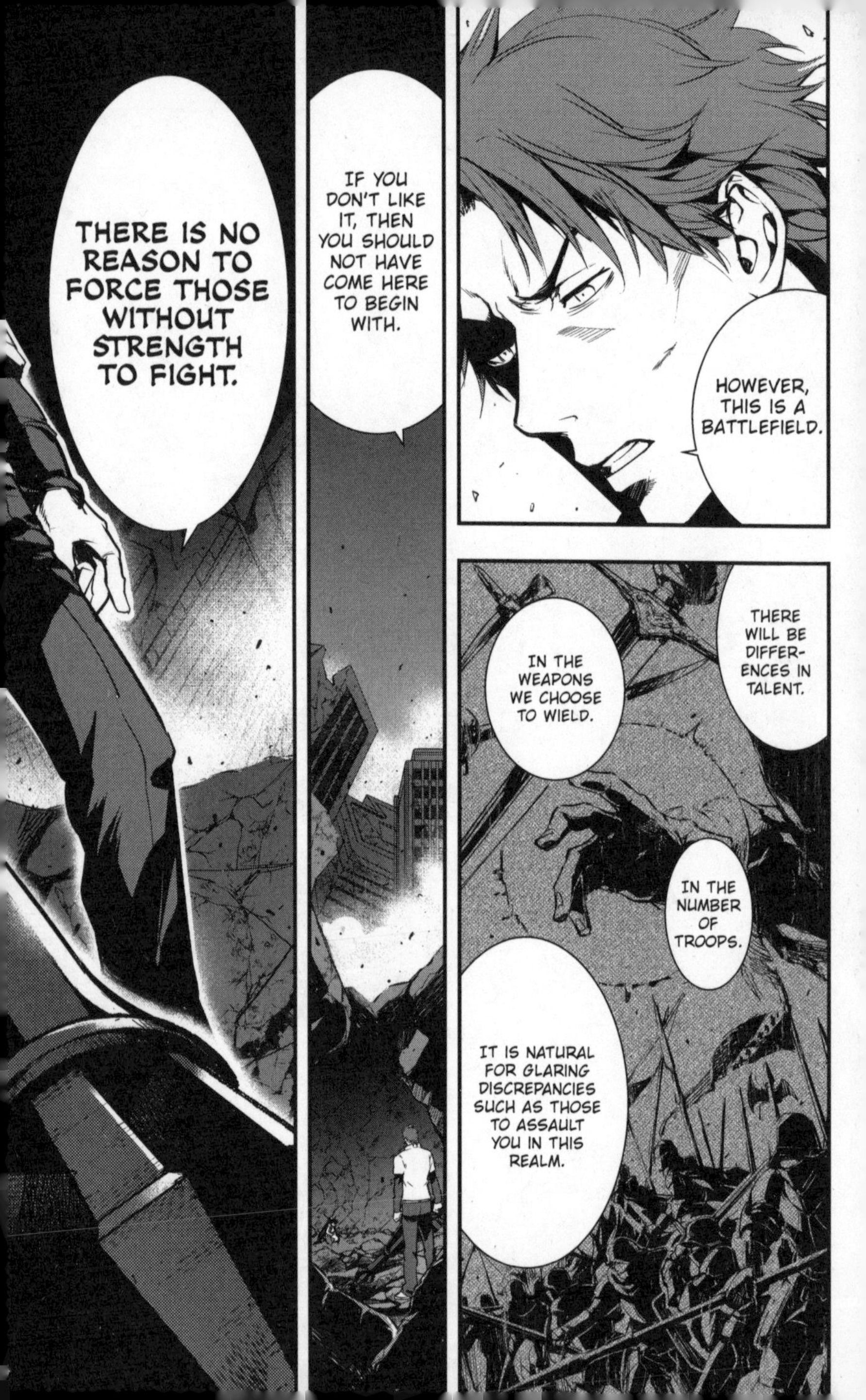
HOWEVER, THIS IS A BATTLEFIELD.
THERE WILL BE DIFFER-ENCES IN TALENT.
IN THE WEAPONS WE CHOOSE TO WIELD.
IN THE NUMBER OF TROOPS.
IT IS NATURAL FOR GLARING DISCREPANCIES SUCH AS THOSE TO ASSAULT YOU IN THIS REALM.
IF YOU DON'T LIKE IT, THEN YOU SHOULD NOT HAVE COME HERE TO BEGIN WITH.
THERE IS NO REASON TO FORCE THOSE WITHOUT STRENGTH TO FIGHT.

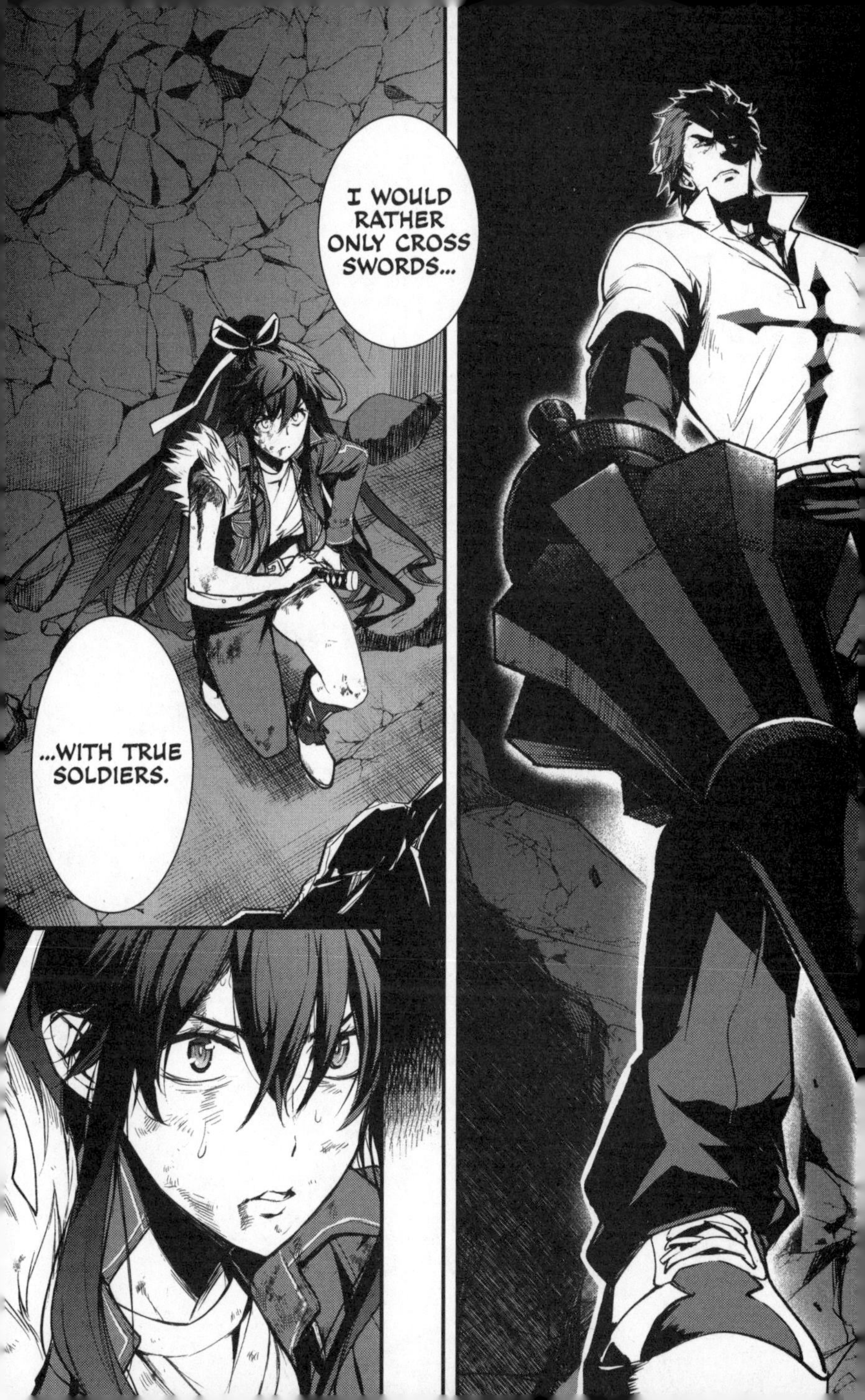
I WOULD RATHER ONLY CROSS SWORDS...
...WITH TRUE SOLDIERS.

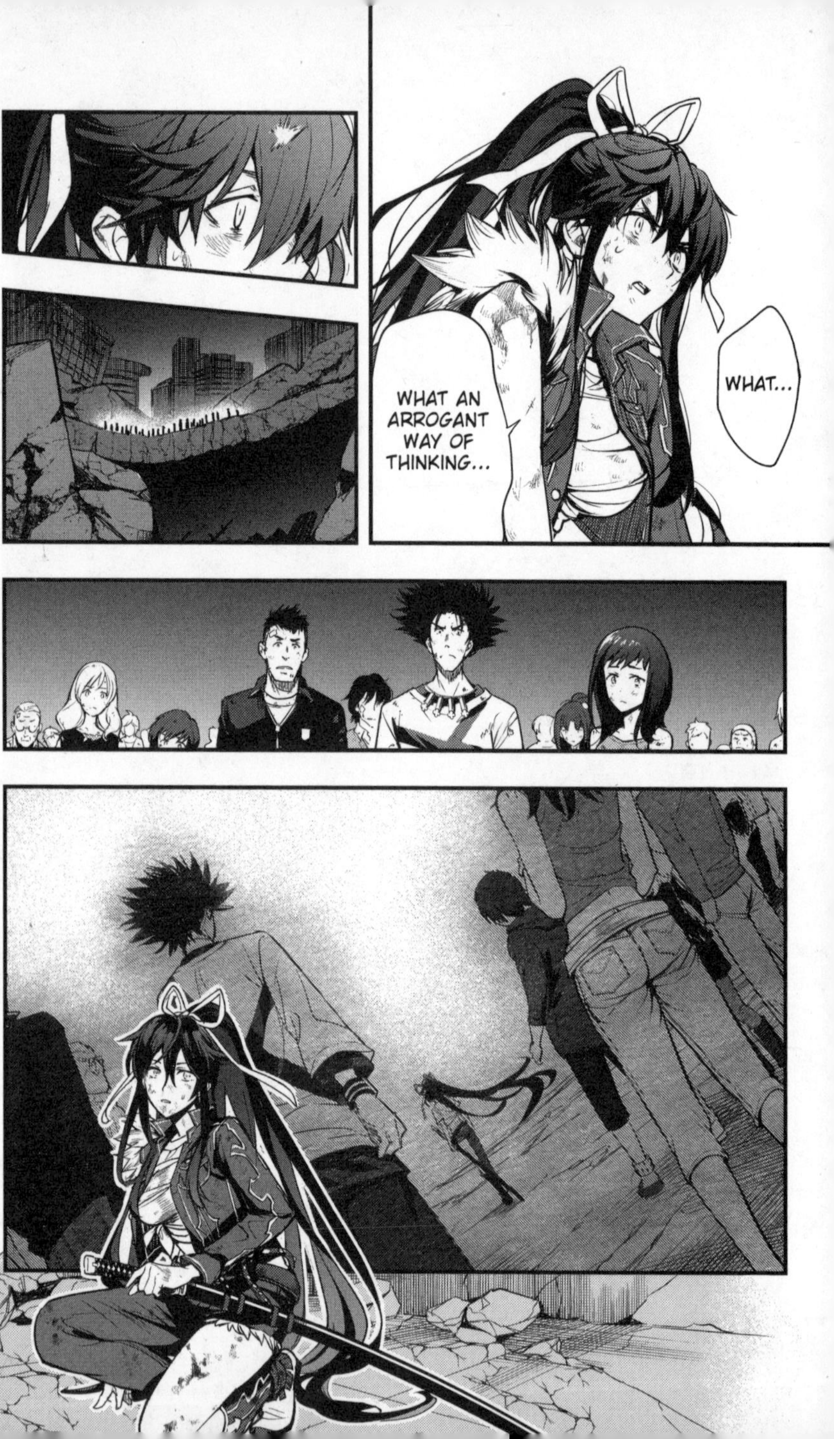
WHAT...
WHAT AN ARROGANT WAY OF THINKING...

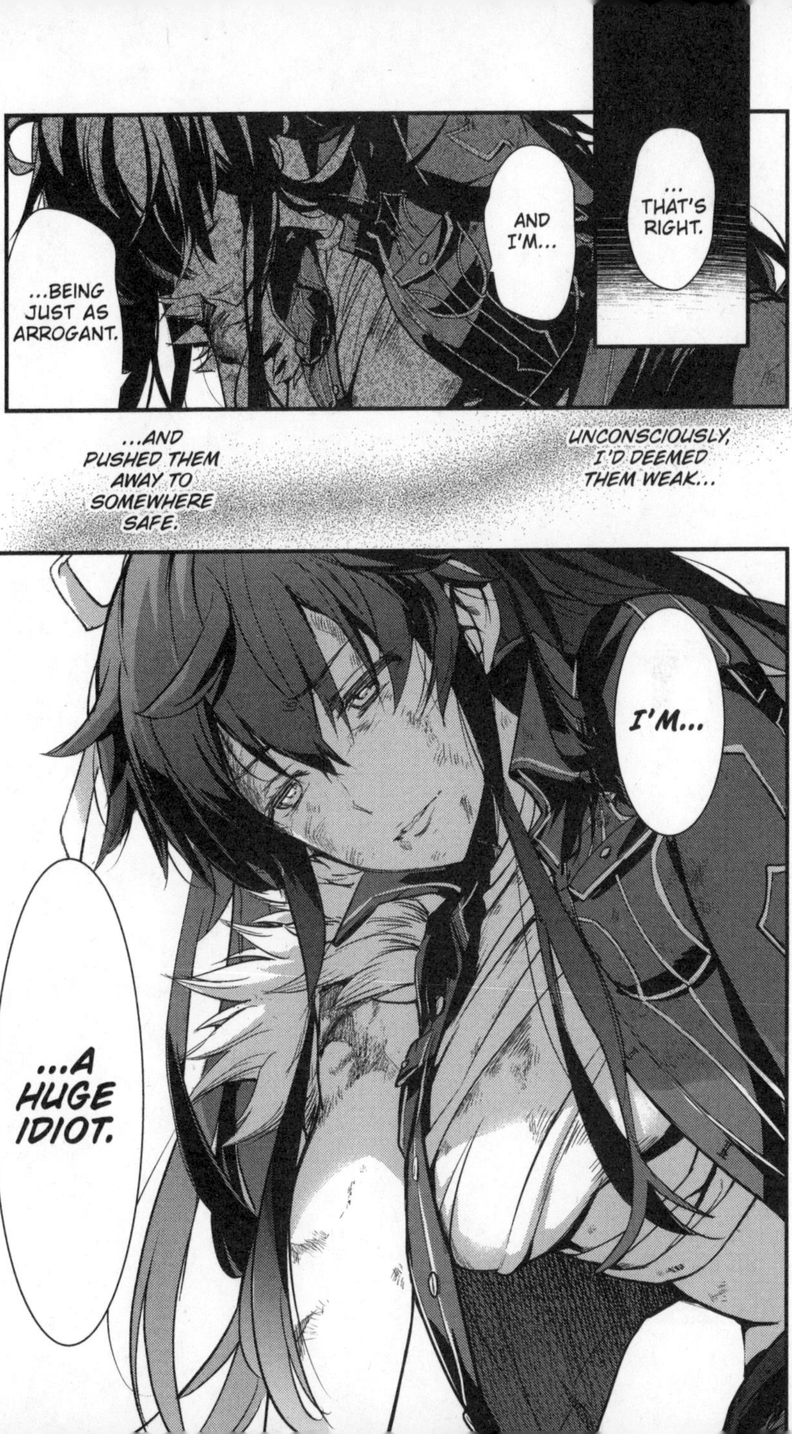
...THAT'S RIGHT.
AND I'M...
...BEING JUST AS ARROGANT.
UNCONSCIOUSLY, I'D DEEMED THEM WEAK...
...AND PUSHED THEM AWAY TO SOMEWHERE SAFE.
I'M...
...A HUGE IDIOT.

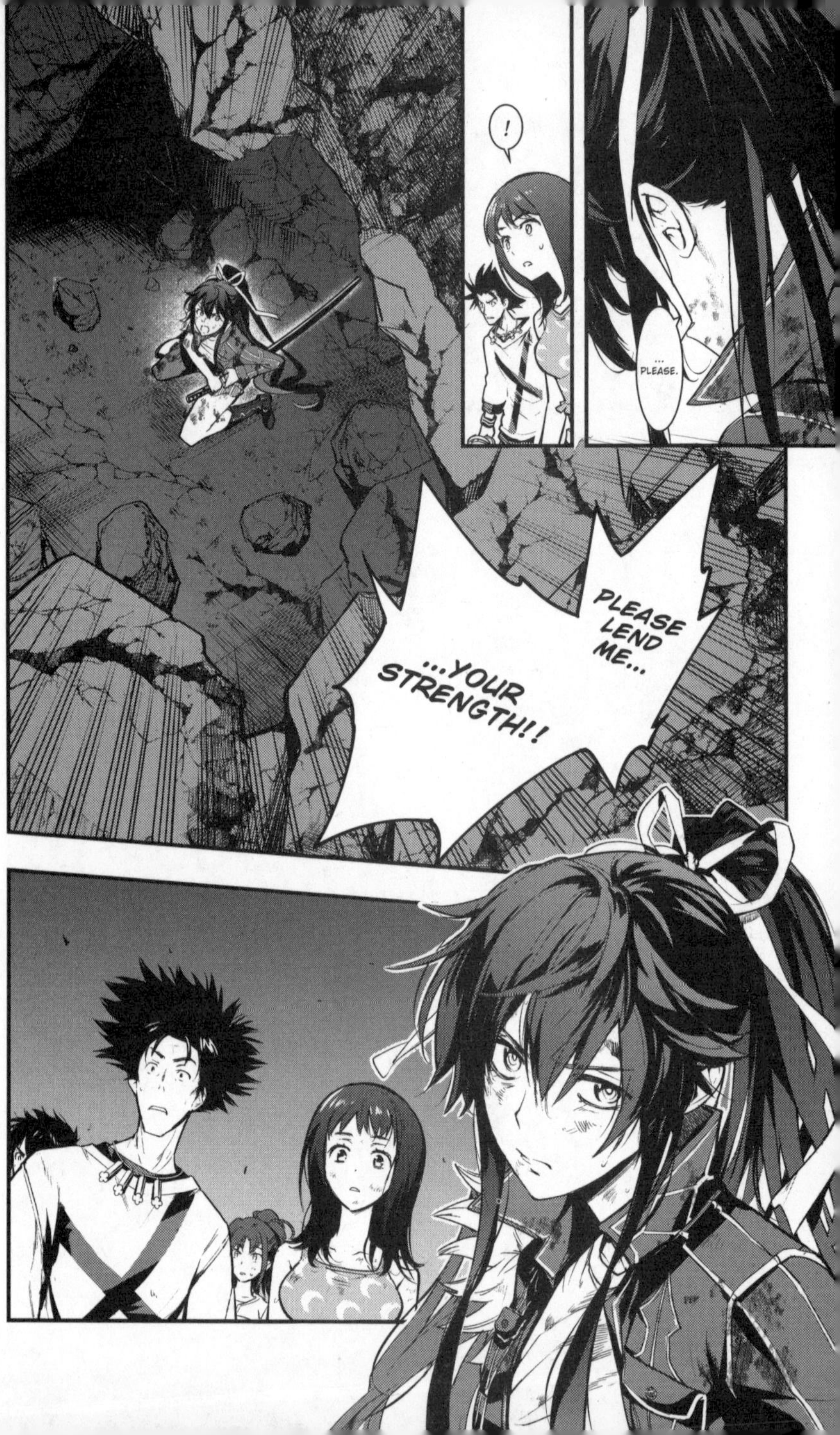
...PLEASE.
!
PLEASE LEND ME...
...YOUR STRENGTH!!

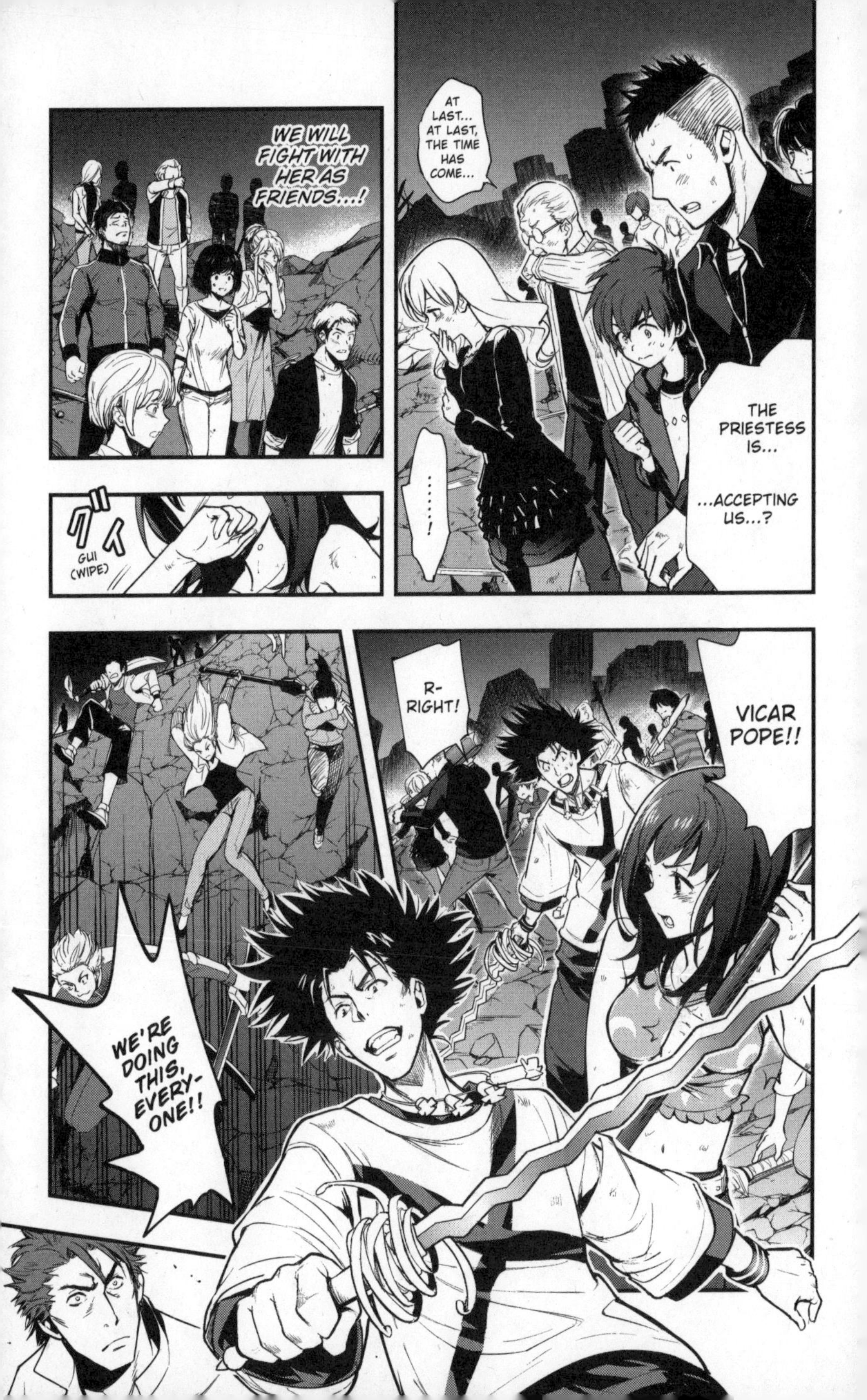
AT LAST... AT LAST, THE TIME HAS COME...
THE PRIESTESS IS...
...ACCEPTING US...?
......!
WE WILL FIGHT WITH HER AS FRIENDS...!
GUI (WIPE)
VICAR POPE!!
R-RIGHT!
WE'RE DOING THIS, EVERYONE!!

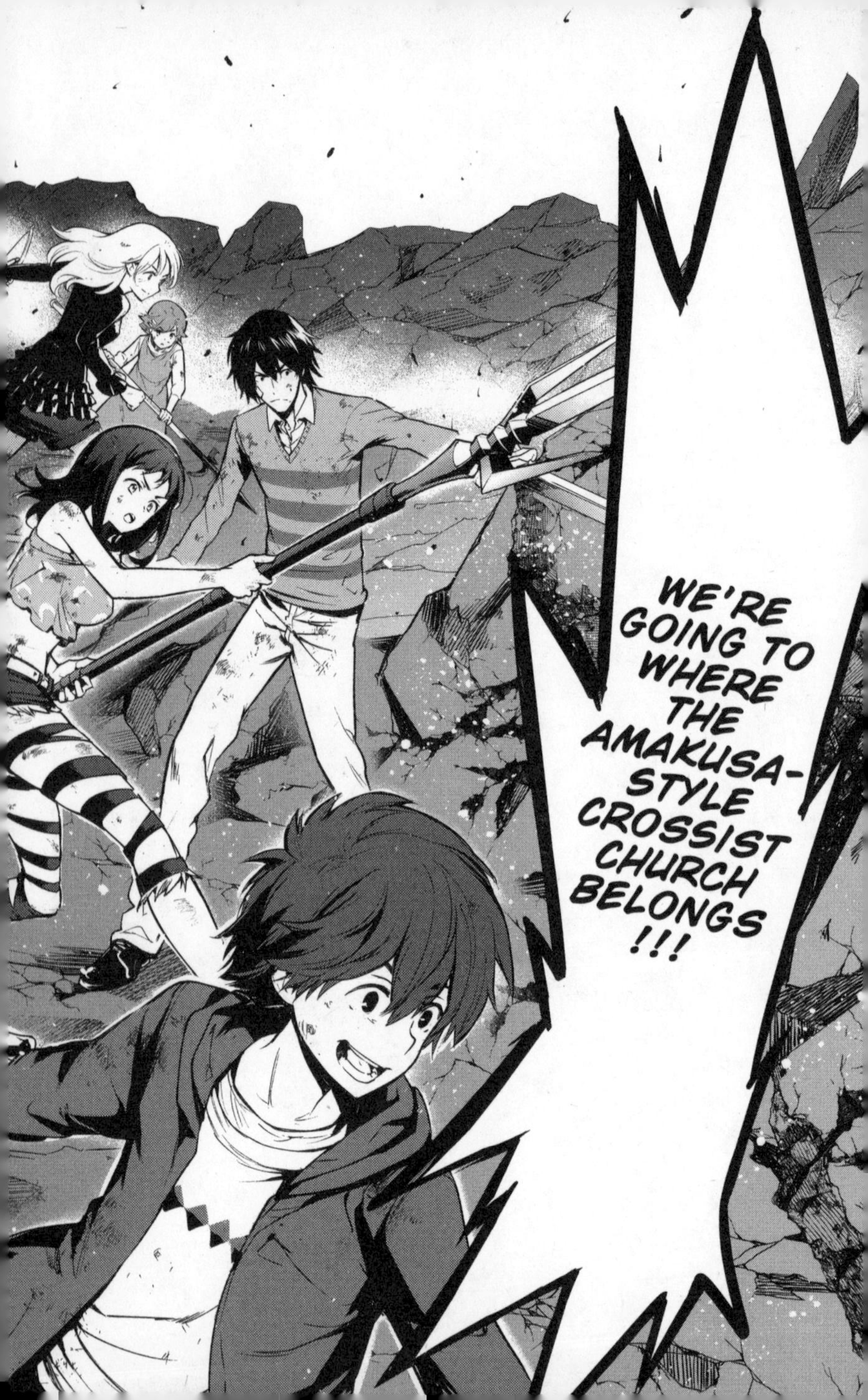
WE'RE GOING TO WHERE THE AMAKUSA-STYLE CROSSIST CHURCH BELONGS!!!

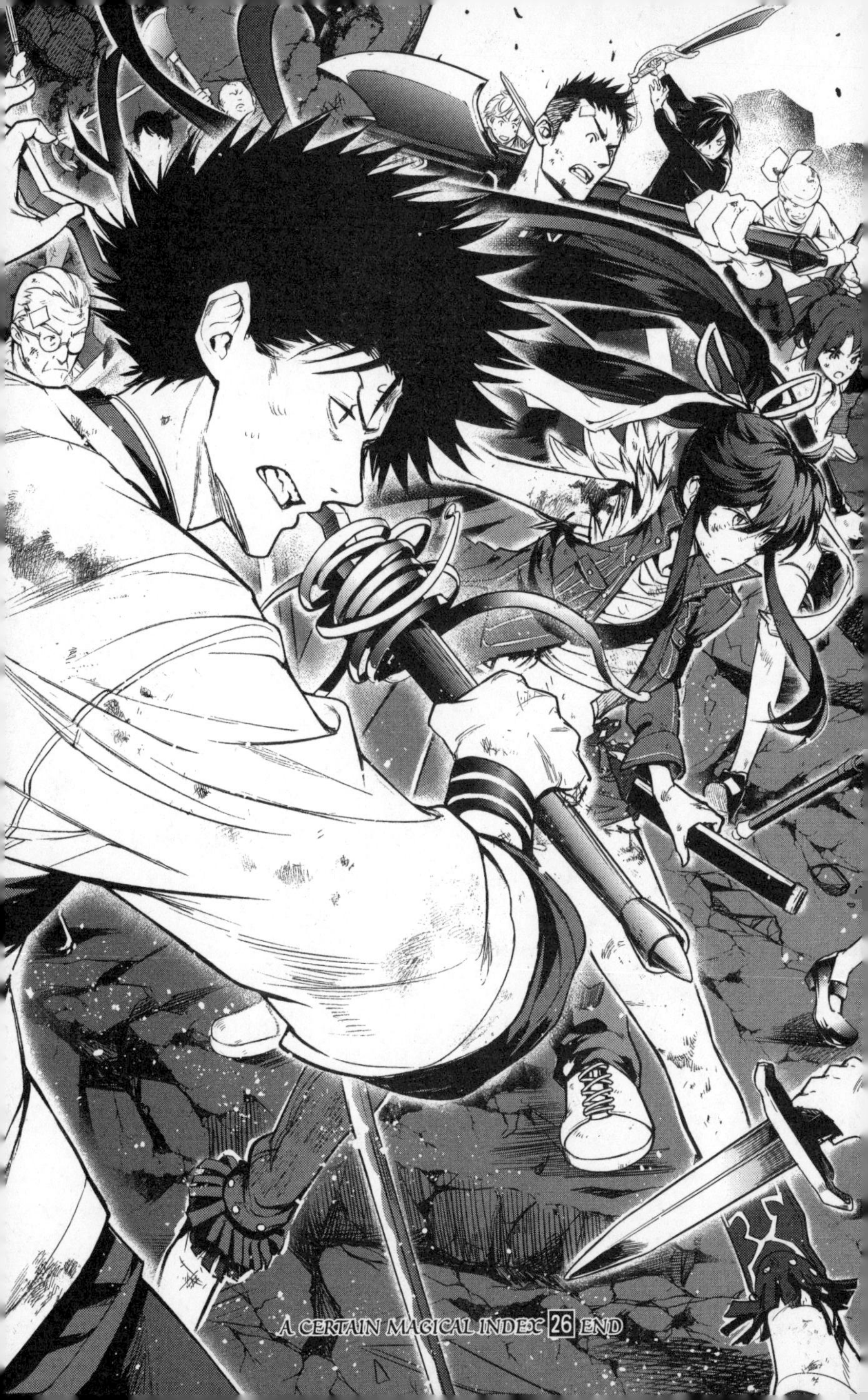
A CERTAIN MAGICAL INDEX 26 END

A Certain Magical Index

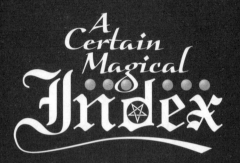

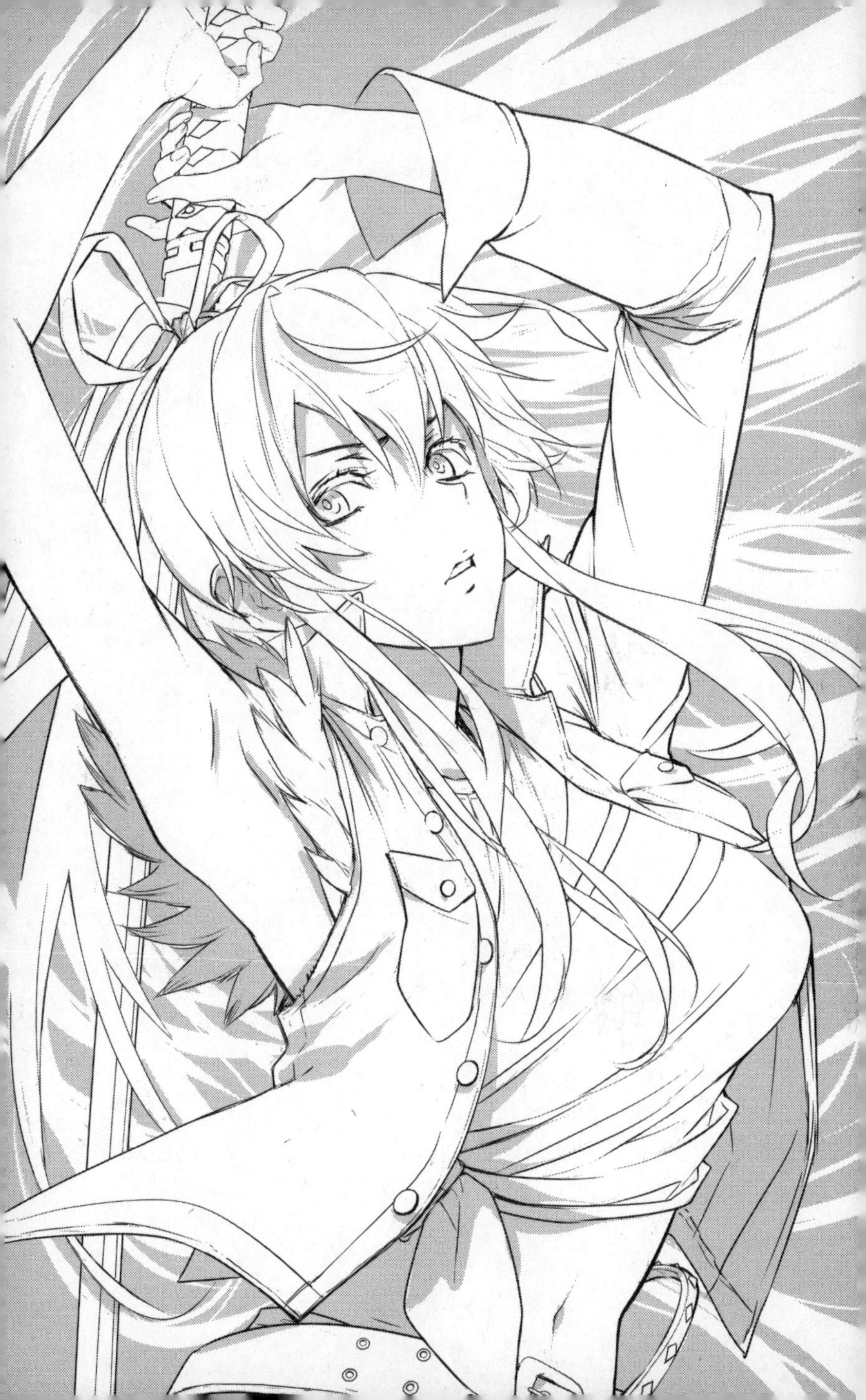

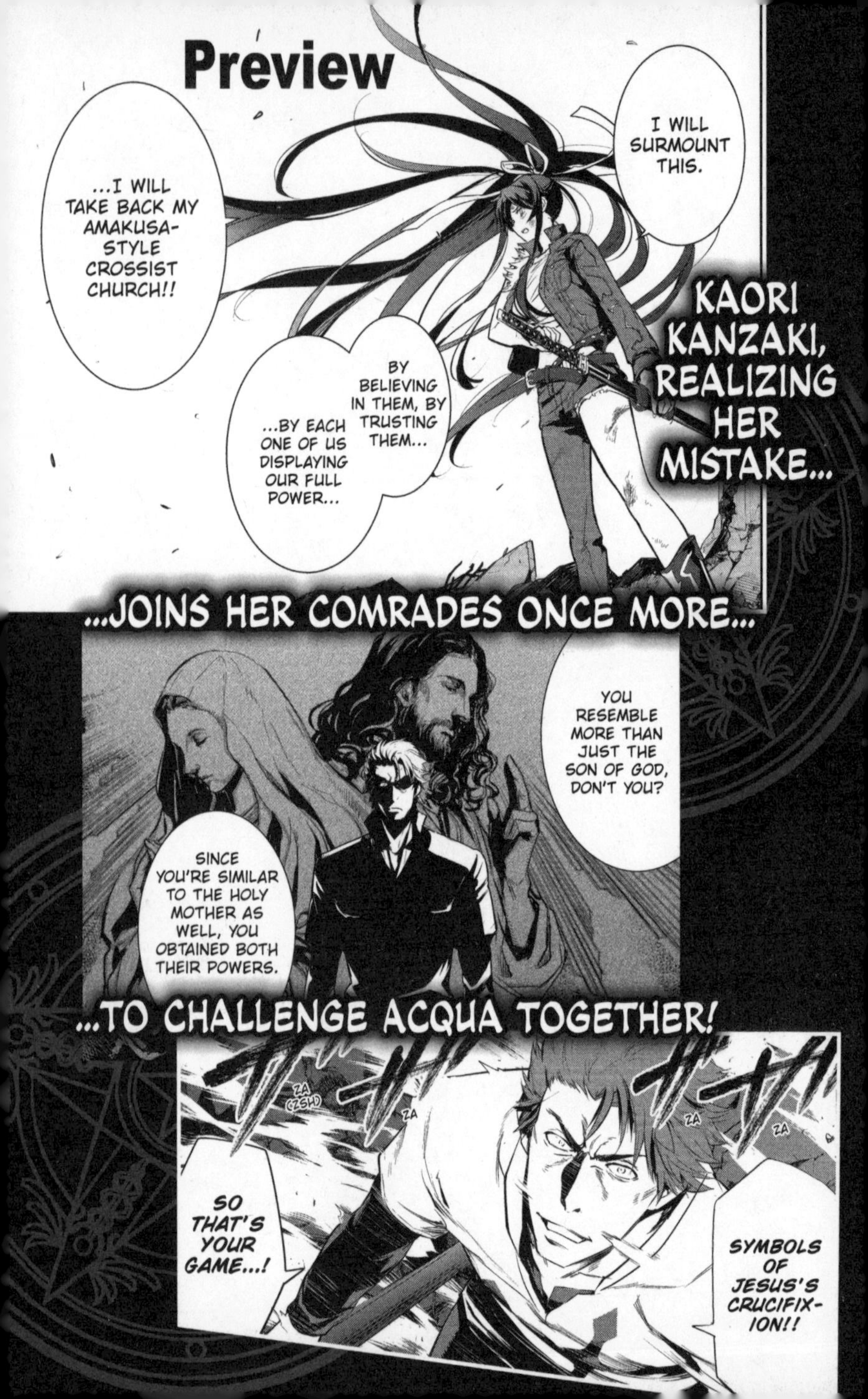
Preview
I WILL SURMOUNT THIS.
KAORI KANZAKI, REALIZING HER MISTAKE...
BY BELIEVING IN THEM, BY TRUSTING THEM...
...BY EACH ONE OF US DISPLAYING OUR FULL POWER...
...I WILL TAKE BACK MY AMAKUSA-STYLE CROSSIST CHURCH!!
...JOINS HER COMRADES ONCE MORE...
YOU RESEMBLE MORE THAN JUST THE SON OF GOD, DON'T YOU?
SINCE YOU'RE SIMILAR TO THE HOLY MOTHER AS WELL, YOU OBTAINED BOTH THEIR POWERS.
...TO CHALLENGE ACQUA TOGETHER!
ZA
ZA
ZA
ZA (ZSH)
SYMBOLS OF JESUS'S CRUCIFIXION!!
SO THAT'S YOUR GAME...!

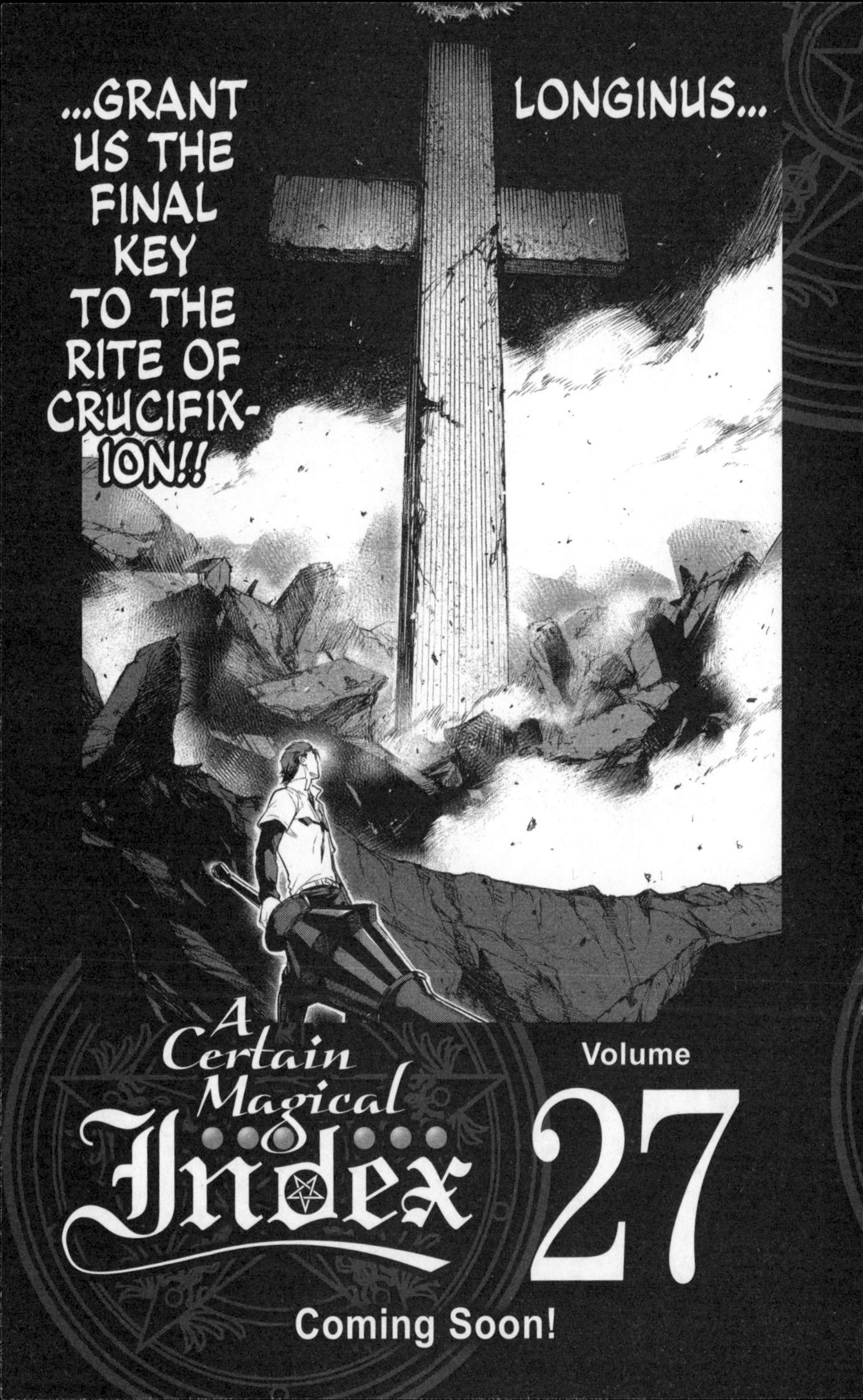
LONGINUS...
...GRANT US THE FINAL KEY TO THE RITE OF CRUCIFIX-ION!!
A Certain Magical Index
Volume
27
Coming Soon!

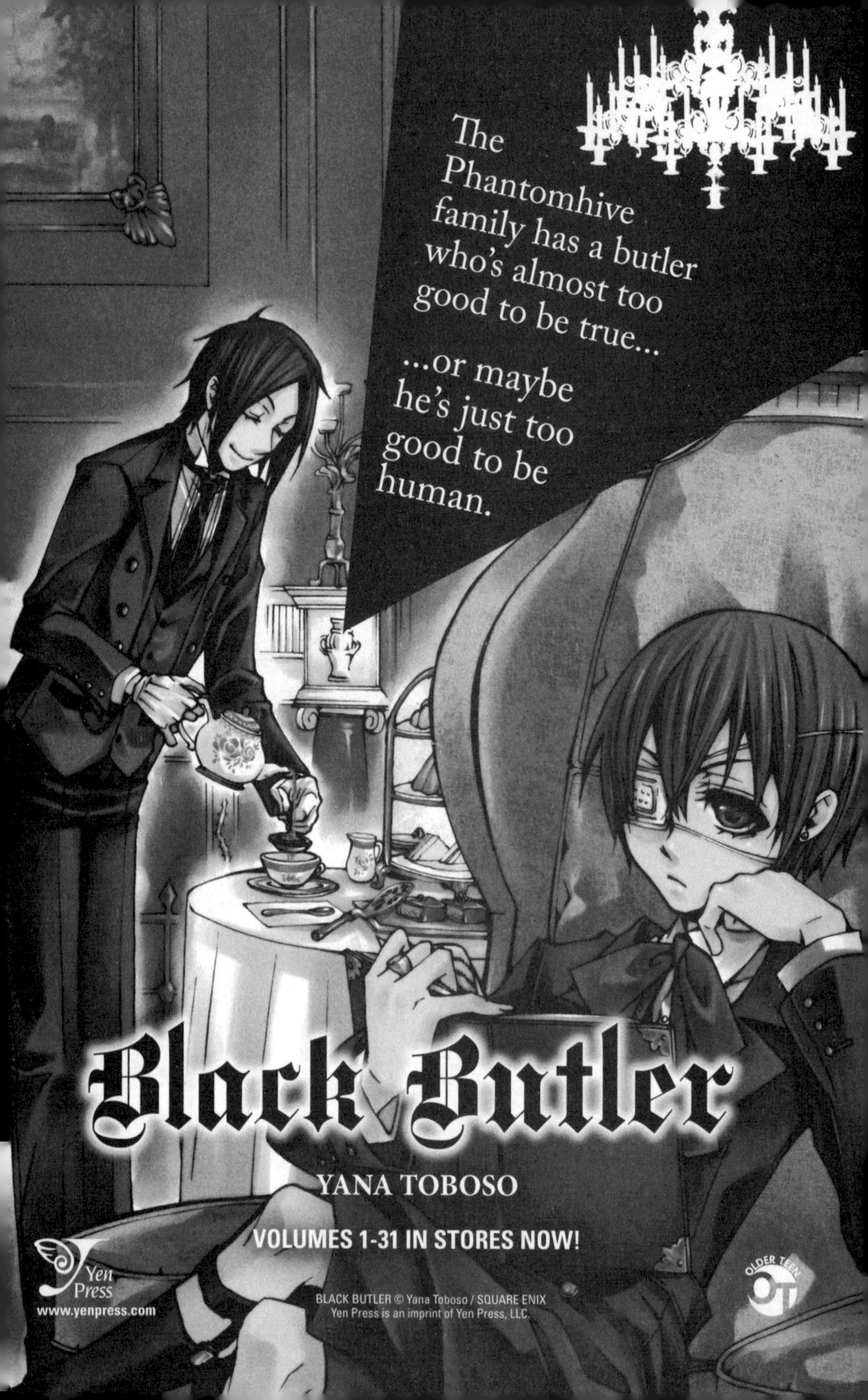
The Phantomhive family has a butler who's almost too good to be true...
...or maybe he's just too good to be human.
Black Butler
YANA TOBOSO
VOLUMES 1-31 IN STORES NOW!
Yen Press
www.yenpress.com
BLACK BUTLER © Yana Toboso / SQUARE ENIX
Yen Press is an imprint of Yen Press, LLC.
OLDER TEEN
OT

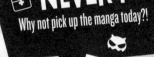

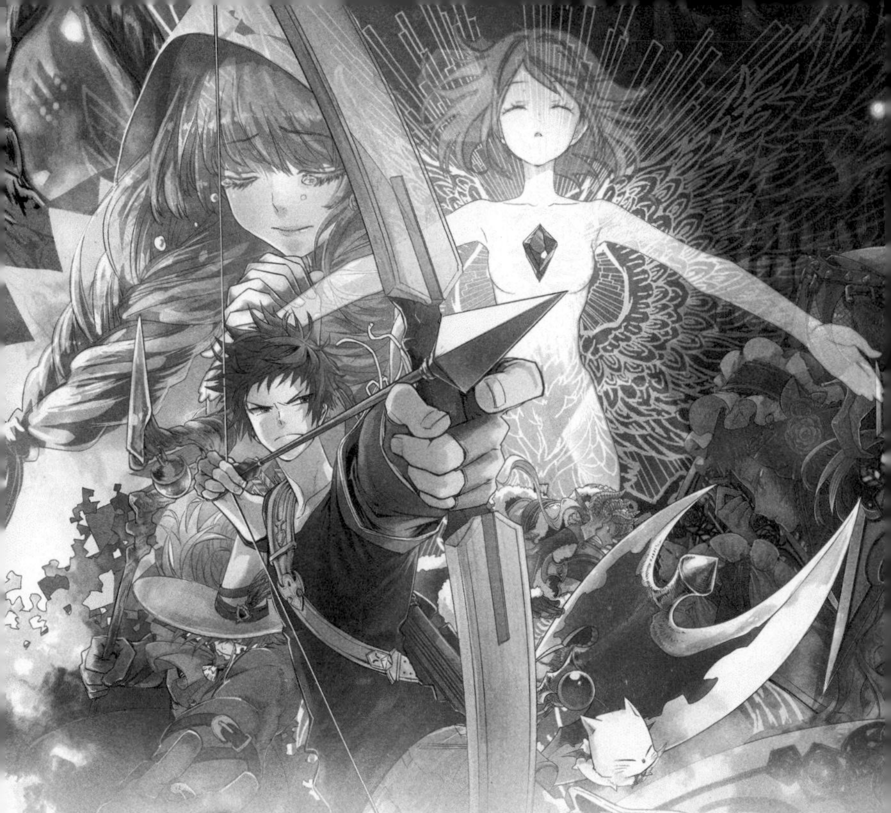

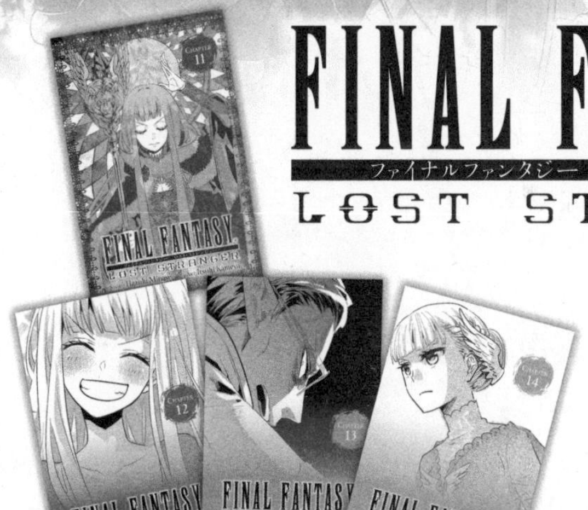

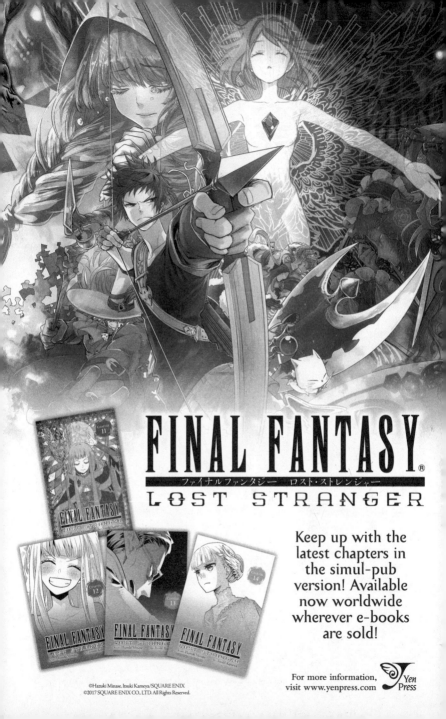

INDEX ㉖

...ma Kamachi
...ka Haimura
...uya Kogino

Translation: Alice Prowse

Lettering: Phil Christie

TOARU MAJYUTSU NO INDEX Vol. 26
© 2021 Kazuma Kamachi
© 2021 Chuya Kogino / SQUARE ENIX CO., LTD.
Licensed by KADOKAWA CORPORATION ASCII MEDIA WORKS
First published in Japan in 2021 by SQUARE ENIX CO., LTD.
English translation rights arranged with SQUARE ENIX CO., LTD.
and Yen Press, LLC through Tuttle-Mori Agency, Inc.

English translation © 2022 by SQUARE ENIX CO., LTD.

Yen Press
150 West 30th Street, 19th Floor
New York, NY 10001

Visit us at yenpress.com
facebook.com/yenpress
twitter.com/yenpress
yenpress.tumblr.com
instagram.com/yenpress

First Yen Press Edition: November 2022
Edited by Yen Press Editorial: Thomas McAlister
Designed by Yen Press Design: Liz Parlett

Yen Press is an imprint of Yen Press, LLC.
The Yen Press name and logo are trademarks of Yen Press, LLC.

Library of Congress Control Number: 2015373809

ISBN: 978-1-9753-4745-1 (paperback)

10 9 8 7 6 5 4 3 2 1

WOR

Printed in the United States of America